Recent Algorithms and Applications in Swarm Intelligence Research

Yuhui Shi
Xi'an Jiaotong–Liverpool University, China

Managing Director:	Lindsay Johnston
Editorial Director:	Joel Gamon
Book Production Manager:	Jennifer Romanchak
Publishing Systems Analyst:	Adrienne Freeland
Assistant Acquisitions Editor:	Kayla Wolfe
Typesetter:	Alyson Zerbe
Cover Design:	Nick Newcomer

Published in the United States of America by
Information Science Reference (an imprint of IGI Global)
701 E. Chocolate Avenue
Hershey PA 17033
Tel: 717-533-8845
Fax: 717-533-8661
E-mail: cust@igi-global.com
Web site: http://www.igi-global.com

Library of Congress Cataloging-in-Publication Data

Recent algorithms and applications in swarm intelligence research / Yuhui Shi, editor.
    pages cm
 Summary: "This book highlights the current research on swarm intelligence algorithms and their applications, including research, survey and application chapters"-- Provided by publisher.
 Includes bibliographical references and index.
 ISBN 978-1-4666-2479-5 (hardcover) -- ISBN (invalid) 978-1-4666-2480-1 (ebook) -- ISBN (invalid) 978-1-4666-2481-8 (print & perpetual access) 1. Swarm intelligence. I. Shi, Yuhui, editor of compilation.
 Q337.3.R43 2013
 006.3--dc23
                        2012023345

British Cataloguing in Publication Data
A Cataloguing in Publication record for this book is available from the British Library.

The views expressed in this book are those of the authors, but not necessarily of the publisher.

Mahamed G. H. Omran, *Gulf University for Science & Technology, Kuwait*
Kevin M. Passino, *Ohio State University, USA*
William Spears, *University of Wyoming, USA*
Ke Tang, *University of Science and Technology of China, China*
Lei Wang, *Tongji University, China*
Yanqing Zhang, *Georgia State University, USA*

Table of Contents

Section 1
Swarm Intelligence Algorithms

Rafael Martí, Universidad de Valencia, Spain
Juan-José Pantrigo, Universidad Rey Juan Carlos, Spain
Abraham Duarte, Universidad Rey Juan Carlos, Spain
Vicente Campos, Universidad de Valencia, Spain
Fred Glover, OptTek Systems, Inc., USA

Peng-Yeng Yin, National Chi Nan University, Taiwan
Fred Glover, OptTek Systems, Inc., USA
Manuel Laguna, University of Colorado, USA
Jia-Xian Zhu, National Chi Nan University, Taiwan

Volodymyr P. Shylo, Institute of Cybernetics NAS of Ukraine, Ukraine
Oleg V. Shylo, University of Pittsburgh, USA

Tabitha James, Virginia Tech, USA
Cesar Rego, University of Mississippi, USA

Detailed Table of Contents

Section 1
Swarm Intelligence Algorithms

Chapter 1

Rafael Martí, Universidad de Valencia, Spain
Juan-José Pantrigo, Universidad Rey Juan Carlos, Spain
Abraham Duarte, Universidad Rey Juan Carlos, Spain
Vicente Campos, Universidad de Valencia, Spain
Fred Glover, OptTek Systems, Inc., USA

Scatter search (SS) and path relinking (PR) are evolutionary methods that have been successfully applied to a wide range of hard optimization problems. The fundamental concepts and principles of the methods were first proposed in the 1970s and 1980s, and were based on formulations, dating back to the 1960s, for combining decision rules and problem constraints. The methods use strategies for search diversification and intensification that have proved effective in a variety of optimization problems and that have sometimes been embedded in other evolutionary methods to yield improved performance. This paper examines the scatter search and path relinking methodologies from both conceptual and practical points of view, and identifies certain connections between their strategies and those adopted more recently by particle swarm optimization. The authors describe key elements of the SS & PR approaches and apply them to a hard combinatorial optimization problem: the minimum linear arrangement problem, which has been used in applications of structural engineering, VLSI and software testing.

Chapter 2

Peng-Yeng Yin, National Chi Nan University, Taiwan
Fred Glover, OptTek Systems, Inc., USA
Manuel Laguna, University of Colorado, USA
Jia-Xian Zhu, National Chi Nan University, Taiwan

A recent study (Yin et al., 2010) showed that combining particle swarm optimization (PSO) with the strategies of scatter search (SS) and path relinking (PR) produces a Cyber Swarm Algorithm that creates a more effective form of PSO than methods that do not incorporate such mechanisms. This paper proposes a Complementary Cyber Swarm Algorithm (C/CyberSA) that performs in the same league as the original Cyber Swarm Algorithm but adopts different sets of ideas from the tabu search (TS) and the SS/PR template. The C/CyberSA exploits the guidance information and restriction information produced in the history of swarm search and the manipulation of adaptive memory. Responsive strategies using long term memory and path relinking implementations are proposed that make use of critical events encountered in the search. Experimental results with a large set of challenging test functions show that the C/CyberSA outperforms two recently proposed swarm-based methods by finding more optimal solutions while simultaneously using a smaller number of function evaluations. The C/CyberSA approach further produces improvements comparable to those obtained by the original CyberSA in relation to the Standard PSO 2007 method (Clerc, 2008).

Chapter 3

Volodymyr P. Shylo, Institute of Cybernetics NAS of Ukraine, Ukraine
Oleg V. Shylo, University of Pittsburgh, USA

In this paper, the potential of the path relinking method for the maximum cut problem is investigated. This method is embedded within global equilibrium search to utilize the set of high quality solutions provided by the latter. The computational experiment on a set of standard benchmark problems is provided to study the proposed approach. The empirical experiments reveal that the large sizes of the elite set lead to restart distribution of the running times, i.e., the algorithm can be accelerated by simply removing all of the accumulated data (set P) and re-initiating its execution after a certain number of elite solutions is obtained.

Chapter 4

Tabitha James, Virginia Tech, USA
Cesar Rego, University of Mississippi, USA

This paper introduces a new path relinking algorithm for the well-known quadratic assignment problem (QAP) in combinatorial optimization. The QAP has attracted considerable attention in research because of its complexity and its applicability to many domains. The algorithm presented in this study employs path relinking as a solution combination method incorporating a multistart tabu search algorithm as an improvement method. The resulting algorithm has interesting similarities and contrasts with particle swarm optimization methods. Computational testing indicates that this algorithm produces results that rival the best QAP algorithms. The authors additionally conduct an analysis disclosing how different strategies prove more or less effective depending on the landscapes of the problems to which they are applied. This analysis lays a foundation for developing more effective future QAP algorithms, both for methods based on path relinking and tabu search, and for hybrids of such methods with related processes found in particle swarm optimization.

Chapter 5

Gary G. Yen, Oklahoma State University, USA
Wen-Fung Leong, Oklahoma State University, USA

Constraint handling techniques are mainly designed for evolutionary algorithms to solve constrained multiobjective optimization problems (CMOPs). Most multiojective particle swarm optimization (MOPSO) designs adopt these existing constraint handling techniques to deal with CMOPs. In the proposed constrained MOPSO, information related to particles' infeasibility and feasibility status is utilized effectively to guide the particles to search for feasible solutions and improve the quality of the optimal solution. This information is incorporated into the four main procedures of a standard MOPSO algorithm. The involved procedures include the updating of personal best archive based on the particles' Pareto ranks and their constraint violation values; the adoption of infeasible global best archives to store infeasible nondominated solutions; the adjustment of acceleration constants that depend on the personal bests' and selected global best's infeasibility and feasibility status; and the integration of personal bests' feasibility status to estimate the mutation rate in the mutation procedure. Simulation to investigate the proposed constrained MOPSO in solving the selected benchmark problems is conducted. The simulation results indicate that the proposed constrained MOPSO is highly competitive in solving most of the selected benchmark problems.

Chapter 6

Shi Cheng, University of Liverpool, UK
Yuhui Shi, Xi'an Jiaotong-Liverpool University, China
Quande Qin, Shenzhen University, China

Premature convergence happens in Particle Swarm Optimization (PSO) for solving both multimodal problems and unimodal problems. With an improper boundary constraints handling method, particles may get "stuck in" the boundary. Premature convergence means that an algorithm has lost its ability of exploration. Population diversity is an effective way to monitor an algorithm's ability of exploration and exploitation. Through the population diversity measurement, useful search information can be obtained. PSO with a different topology structure and a different boundary constraints handling strategy will have a different impact on particles' exploration and exploitation ability. In this paper, the phenomenon of particles gets "stuck in" the boundary in PSO is experimentally studied and reported. The authors observe the position diversity time-changing curves of PSOs with different topologies and different boundary constraints handling techniques, and analyze the impact of these setting on the algorithm's ability of exploration and exploitation. From these experimental studies, an algorithm's ability of exploration and exploitation can be observed and the search information obtained; therefore, more effective algorithms can be designed to solve problems.

Chapter 7

Xin-She Yang, National Physical Lab, UK

Many metaheuristic algorithms are nature-inspired, and most are population-based. Particle swarm optimization is a good example as an efficient metaheuristic algorithm. Inspired by PSO, many new algorithms have been developed in recent years. For example, firefly algorithm was inspired by the flashing behaviour of fireflies. In this paper, the author extends the standard firefly algorithm further to introduce chaos-enhanced firefly algorithm with automatic parameter tuning, which results in two more variants of FA. The author first compares the performance of these algorithms, and then uses them to solve a benchmark design problem in engineering. Results obtained by other methods will be compared and analyzed.

Chapter 8

Yuhui Shi, Xi'an Jiaotong-Liverpool University, China

In this paper, the human brainstorming process is modeled, based on which two versions of Brain Storm Optimization (BSO) algorithm are introduced. Simulation results show that both BSO algorithms perform reasonably well on ten benchmark functions, which validates the effectiveness and usefulness of the proposed BSO algorithms. Simulation results also show that one of the BSO algorithms, BSO-II, performs better than the other BSO algorithm, BSO-I, in general. Furthermore, average inter-cluster distance D_c and inter-cluster diversity D_e are defined, which can be used to measure and monitor the distribution of cluster centroids and information entropy of the population over iterations. Simulation results illustrate that further improvement could be achieved by taking advantage of information revealed by D_c and/or D_e, which points at one direction for future research on BSO algorithms.

Section 2
Swarm Intelligence Applications

Chapter 9

Andreas Janecek, University of Vienna, Austria
Ying Tan, Peking University, China

The Non-negative Matrix Factorization (NMF) is a special low-rank approximation which allows for an additive parts-based and interpretable representation of the data. This article presents efforts to improve the convergence, approximation quality, and classification accuracy of NMF using five different meta-heuristics based on swarm intelligence. Several properties of the NMF objective function motivate the utilization of meta-heuristics: this function is non-convex, discontinuous, and may possess many local minima. The proposed optimization strategies are two-fold: On the one hand, a new initialization strategy for NMF is presented in order to initialize the NMF factors prior to the factorization; on the other hand, an iterative update strategy is proposed, which improves the accuracy per runtime for the multiplicative update NMF algorithm. The success of the proposed optimization strategies are shown by applying them on synthetic data and data sets coming from the areas of spam filtering/email classification, and evaluate them also in their application context. Experimental results show that both optimization strategies are able to improve NMF in terms of faster convergence, lower approximation error, and better classification accuracy. Especially the initialization strategy leads to significant reductions of the runtime per accuracy ratio for both, the NMF approximation as well as the classification results achieved with NMF.

Chapter 10

Paweł Paduch, Kielce University of Technology, Poland
Krzysztof Sapiecha, Kielce University of Technology, Poland

This paper presents a new algorithm for solving the generalized watchman problem. It is the problem of mobile robot operators that must find the shortest route for the robot to see the whole area with many obstructions. The algorithm adapts the well-known ant algorithm to the new problem. An experiment where the algorithm is applied to an area containing more than 10 obstructions is described. It proves that efficiency and accuracy of the algorithm are high.

Hongwei Mo, Harbin Engineering University, China

Yujing Yin, Harbin Engineering University, China

This paper addresses the issue of image segmentation by clustering in the domain of image processing. The clustering algorithm taken account here is the Fuzzy C-Means which is widely adopted in this field. Bacterial Foraging Optimization Algorithm is an optimal algorithm inspired by the foraging behavior of E.coli. For the purpose to reinforce the global search capability of FCM, the Bacterial Foraging Algorithm was employed to optimize the objective criterion function which is interrelated to centroids in FCM. To evaluate the validation of the composite algorithm, cluster validation indexes were used to obtain numerical results and guide the possible best solution found by BF-FCM. Several experiments were conducted on three UCI data sets. For image segmentation, BF-FCM successfully segmented 8 typical grey scale images, and most of them obtained the desired effects. All the experiment results show that BF-FCM has better performance than that of standard FCM.

Jing Liu, Xidian University, China

Jinshu Li, Xidian University, China

Weicai Zhong, Northwest A&F University, China

Li Zhang, Soochow University, China

Ruochen Liu, Xidian University, China

In frequency assignment problems (FAPs), separation of the frequencies assigned to the transmitters is necessary to avoid the interference. However, unnecessary separation causes an excess requirement of spectrum, the cost of which may be very high. Since FAPs are closely related to T-coloring problems (TCP), multiagent systems and evolutionary algorithms are combined to form a new algorithm for minimum span FAPs on the basis of the model of TCP, which is named as Multiagent Evolutionary Algorithm for Minimum Span FAPs (MAEA-MSFAPs). The objective of MAEA-MSFAPs is to minimize the frequency spectrum required for a given level of reception quality over the network. In MAEA-MSFAPs, all agents live in a latticelike environment. Making use of the designed behaviors, MAEA-MSFAPs realizes the ability of agents to sense and act on the environment in which they live. During the process of interacting with the environment and other agents, each agent increases the energy as much as possible so that MAEA-MSFAPs can find the optima. Experimental results on TCP with different sizes and Philadelphia benchmark for FAPs show that MAEA-MSFAPs have a good performance and outperform the compared methods.

Gomaa Zaki El-Far, Menoufia University, Egypt

This paper presents a robust instrument fault detection (IFD) scheme based on modified immune mechanism based evolutionary algorithm (MIMEA) that determines on line the optimal control actions, detects faults quickly in the control process, and reconfigures the controller structure. To ensure the capability of the proposed MIMEA, repeating cycles of crossover, mutation, and clonally selection are included through the sampling time. This increases the ability of the proposed algorithm to reach the global optimum performance and optimize the controller parameters through a few generations. A fault diagnosis logic system is created based on the proposed algorithm, nonlinear decision functions, and its derivatives with respect to time. Threshold limits are implied to improve the system dynamics and sensitivity of the IFD scheme to the faults. The proposed algorithm is able to reconfigure the control law safely in all the situations. The presented false alarm rates are also clearly indicated. To illustrate the performance of the proposed MIMEA, it is applied successfully to tune and optimize the controller parameters of the nonlinear nuclear power reactor such that a robust behavior is obtained. Simulation results show the effectiveness of the proposed IFD scheme based MIMEA in detecting and isolating the dynamic system faults.

This paper examines the problem of distributed coverage of an initially unknown environment using a multi-robot system. Specifically, focus is on a coverage technique for coordinating teams of multiple mobile robots that are deployed and maintained in a certain formation while covering the environment. The technique is analyzed theoretically and experimentally to verify its operation and performance within the Webots robot simulator, as well as on physical robots. Experimental results show that the described coverage technique with robot teams moving in formation can perform comparably with a technique where the robots move individually while covering the environment. The authors also quantify the effect of various parameters of the system, such as the size of the robot teams, the presence of localization, and wheel slip noise, as well as environment related features like the size of the environment and the presence of obstacles and walls on the performance of the area coverage operation.

Preface

Swarm intelligence algorithms are a collection of population-based stochastic optimization algorithms which are generally categorized under the big umbrella of evolutionary computation algorithms. There is no standard definition that defines a swarm intelligence algorithm and differentiates it from other population-based optimization algorithms. In the literature, there are a lot of swarm intelligence algorithms which have been reported and introduced, for example, ant colony optimization, artificial immune system, bacterial foraging optimization algorithm, bee colony optimization algorithm, brain storm optimization algorithm, firefly optimization algorithm, firework optimization algorithm, fish school search optimization algorithm, particle swarm optimization algorithm, shuffled frog-leaping algorithm, to name just a few. Generally speaking, a swarm intelligence algorithm is a population-based stochastic optimization algorithm that is inspired or motivated by the collective behavior of small and simple objects such as the ants in ant colony optimization algorithm, fishes in fish school search optimization algorithms, and birds in particle swarm optimization algorithm. Collectively and cooperatively, a population of individuals in a swarm intelligence algorithm, each of which represents a possible solution to the problem to be solved, is updated or generated iteration over iteration in the hope that the better and better population of individuals will be generated over iterations and finally a good enough solution will be found. Originally, a swarm optimization algorithm usually was designed or introduced to be simple in concept which was at least one reason that the swarm intelligence algorithm attracted attentions initially. With the successes and wide studies of a swarm intelligence algorithm, it has been and will be applied to solve more and more complicated problems which are at least difficult, if not impossible, for traditional algorithms such as hill-climbing algorithms to solve. As a consequence of solving more complicated optimization problems, the swarm intelligence algorithm itself has been under extensive modifications and studies. One tendency of researches on swarm intelligence algorithms is to combine an original or a modified swarm intelligence algorithm with another optimization algorithm in the hope that the hybrid algorithm can be better than any component algorithm itself in general or in solving one specific problem. One common goal of a hybrid algorithm is to have one component algorithm focus on global search while another component algorithm focuses on local search so that the hybrid algorithm has better balance between exploration capability and exploitation capability and therefore has more capability to avoid premature convergence and to find better and good enough solution(s). One example is the complementary cyber swarm intelligence introduced in the chapter "A Complementary Cyber Swarm Algorithm" in this book. This is also one of common purposes of researches on memetic algorithms which, in the aspects of swarm intelligence researches, combine a swarm intelligence algorithm with another swarm intelligence algorithm or one of other non-swarm intelligence algorithms.

In addition to hybrid swarm intelligence algorithms, another way for an swarm intelligence algorithm to have balance between an swarm intelligence algorithm's exploration capability and exploitation capability is to design the swarm intelligence algorithm to be able to converge to a local minimum or to diverge from a local minimum when it is necessary. For example, a swarm intelligence algorithm needs to have the capability to converge so that the swarm intelligence algorithm can converge to (or find) a good enough solution. But for complicated, nonlinear, especially multimodal problems, it is easy for an swarm intelligence algorithm to be trapped into a local minimum, therefore, the swarm intelligence algorithm needs to be able to jump out of the local minimum, that is, to diverge from the local minimum so that the swarm intelligence algorithm can start another round of convergent search process in the hope to find a better and good enough solution. One way to design a swarm intelligence algorithm to be able in either convergent search process or divergent search process is to establish a relationship between at least one parameter of the swarm intelligence algorithm and the search process of the swarm intelligence algorithm. For example, for a parameter of an swarm intelligence algorithm, if the parameter is within one range of values, the search process of the swarm intelligence algorithm is in convergent search process while in another range of values, the search process is in divergent search process, then the swarm intelligence algorithm can be put into either convergent or divergent search process by simply changing the value of the parameter. A good example is the chaos-enhanced firefly algorithm proposed in the chapter "Chaos-Enhanced Firefly Algorithm with Automatic Parameter Tuning." Another way is to design a swarm intelligence algorithm to have both convergent operation and divergent operation during each iteration so that the search process of the swarm intelligence algorithm involves both convergent search operation and divergent search operation; therefore, intuitively, the swarm intelligence algorithm has higher potential to escape from local minima which represent not-good enough solutions. A good example is the brain storm optimization algorithm discussed in the chapter "An Optimization Algorithm Based on Brainstorming Process" in this book.

Another trend for the research on swarm intelligence algorithms is to specially design or modify a swarm intelligence algorithm to be able to solve one kind of optimization problems more effectively and/or more efficiently. For example, for the multi-objective optimization problems with constraints, special care could and should be taken for particle swarm optimization algorithms to solve them, such as how to take care of feasible and infeasible solutions. Another example is to use an optimization algorithm to solve optimization problems with boundary constraints. Special techniques have to be designed and implemented to take care of boundary constraints violations. Also, certain performance metrics could be defined and measured to monitor the search process of the optimization algorithm, such as the population diversity defined in particle swarm optimization algorithms.

One major purpose of the research on swarm intelligence algorithms is to be able to apply these swarm intelligence algorithms to solve real-world problems. So far, swarm intelligence algorithms have been applied to successfully solve wide range of application problems. Successful applications of these swarm intelligence algorithms are the major vitality to keep the researches on swarm intelligence algorithms to be active and attract attentions from wider and wider range of applications. Therefore, the application of swarm intelligence algorithms to effectively and efficiently solve real-world problems is another important and critical research direction on swarm intelligence in addition to the research direction on swarm intelligence algorithms.

WHAT IS THE BOOK ABOUT?

This book volume does not intend to cover all aspects of research on swarm intelligence algorithms and their applications. It is a snapshot of current research on swarm intelligence algorithms and their applications which are included and/or covered in the 2011 issues of the *International Journal of Swarm Intelligence Research*. It may reflect a research tendency in the research areas of swarm intelligence algorithms. This book volume can be a good reference book for researchers who have been conducting research work on swarm intelligence algorithms or at least are interested in the research areas of swarm intelligence algorithms. It can also be used as a reference book for graduate students and senior undergraduate students who are going to conduct researches on swarm intelligence algorithms and/or their applications.

ORGANIZATION OF THE BOOK

This book volume consists of 14 chapters which are organized into two sections for the convenience of reference. Section 1 includes 8 chapters which are about current research works on swarm intelligence algorithms. Section 2 includes 6 chapters which are about the applications of swarm intelligence algorithms.

Section 1: Swarm Intelligence Algorithms

Scatter search algorithm was introduced by Glover in 1977. It is a population-based search algorithm originally designed for solving general integer problems. The scatter search algorithm can be implemented as an integration of five basic components, which are: diversification-generation component, improvement component, reference-set update component, subset-generation component, and solution-combination component. The reference-set is usually a smaller subset of the population of individuals with better qualities, and plays a central role in the algorithm. Path relinking was also introduced by Glover in 1989. It used the neighborhood space instead of Euclidean space in scatter search. The search algorithms can be considered as forming path between and/or beyond existing solutions. In the chapter "Scatter Search and Path Relinking: A Tutorial on the Linear Arrangement Problem," Marti *et al.* reviewed the scatter search algorithm and path relinking process, and applied them to solve the minimum linear arrangement problem, which is a NP-hard combinatorial optimization problem, in order to illustrate how the algorithms work. The authors also discussed the relationship between scatter search/path relinking, and the recent particle swarm optimization algorithm introduced by Kennedy and Eberhart in 1995 through pointing out the differences and similarities between them.

Hybrid algorithms combine one algorithm with another algorithm by taking advantage of strength of all involved algorithms. A cyber swarm algorithm is a combination of particle swarm optimization algorithm with scatter search algorithm embedded with path relinking process. It intends to make the particle swarm optimization algorithm more effective than those without combing scatter search with path relinking process by better balancing between intensification and diversification. In the chapter "A Complementary Cyber Swarm Intelligence," Yin *et al.* proposed a complementary cyber swarm algorithm which makes use a different set of ideas from the Tabu search in addition to the scatter search with path relinking process. It can better utilize the history search information to guide or restrict the search for better exploitation of the search area and for better manipulation of adaptive memory which consists of best solutions observed throughout search process derived from Tabu search. Experimental results demonstrated that the proposed complementary cyber swam algorithm performs better than the original cyber swarm intelligence and the standard PSO proposed by Clerc at least with regards to the benchmark functions tested.

Max-cut problem is a NP-hard optimization problem. Its objective is to find a cut in a graph which has the maximum sum of the edge weights. Path relinking method involves a pair of solutions, an initiating solution and a guiding solution, and generates a set of solutions that lie on a path between or beyond the pair of solutions. Global equilibrium search algorithm generates a set of initial solutions at each different temperature value, which is similar to that in the simulated annealing method, for other local search methods as starting solutions. In the Chapter "Path Relinking Scheme for the Max-Cut Problem within Global Equilibrium Search," Shylo and Shylo propose a hybrid search algorithm which embeds the path relinking method into the global equilibrium search algorithm to take advantages from both approaches, that is, maintaining high quality of solutions by the global equilibrium search algorithm, and combining existing high quality solutions to form a new enhanced solution by path relinking method. The proposed hybrid algorithm was applied to solve max-cut problem. Experimental results show that the proposed approach can provide solutions with better quality within less time.

In the chapter "Path Relinking with Multi-Start Tabu Search for the Quadratic Assignment Problem," James and Rego proposed a hybrid optimization algorithm for solving quadratic assignment problem. Their proposed algorithm is a combination of path relinking algorithm and the Tabu search method. Path relinking algorithm forms a path between an initiating solution and one or more guiding solutions by selecting high quality solutions from a set of best solutions obtained in the history of search process, which is similar to the concept of personal, local, and/or global best positions in a particle swarm optimization algorithm. Tabu search is a neighborhood search technique which can provide higher quality solutions from a starting solution. By selecting different tabu restriction and aspiration criteria, the Tabu search method can make a trade-off between intensification (exploitation) and diversification (exploration). In this chapter, the authors utilized a Tabu search with multi-starts as the improvement method component in the path relinking algorithm to further improve the solutions on the path between an initiating solution and guiding solutions. The outcome solutions with better quality from the Tabu search in return will be used as new initiating and guiding solutions by the path relinking methods. The proposed algorithm was tested on the quadratic assignment problem (QAP) which is a classical NP-hard combinatorial optimization problem. In addition, the authors analyzed different strategies and their effectiveness on solving QAP problems with different landscapes, and therefore provided a guidance to integrate these components to design more effective QAP algorithms. The authors also compared the proposed algorithm with the particle swarm optimization algorithm and pointed out their differences and similarities.

For most real world multi-objective optimization problems, there are constraints which define the feasibility of potential solutions. The only feasible solutions are acceptable solutions, and infeasible solutions are those which need to be avoided. There are several existing techniques to handle constraints. For example, 1) higher priority is given to constraints so that feasible solution areas will more likely be searched compared with infeasible solution areas; 2) genetic operators are designed to allow only feasible solutions surviving into next generation; 3) dominance principles are defined to rank all individuals including both feasible and infeasible solutions so that higher rank solutions will be preferred over generations; et cetera. These existing constraints handling techniques have been adopted by multiobjective particle swarm optimization (MOPSO) algorithms to handle multi-objective problems with constraints. In the chapter "A Multiobjective Particle Swarm Optimizer for Constrained Optimization," the authors proposed to convert constraints into one extra objective the purpose of which is to have zero constraint violation after going through an evolutionary process. For example, a k-objective optimization problem with constraints will be converted into a (k+1)-objective optimization problem without constraints. The additional objective is defined as the constraint violation which is then a minimization objective function. The essential goals of the proposed MOPSO are 1) to search for feasible solutions through guiding obtained infeasible solutions towards feasible solutions over generations; 2) to converge to feasible optimal solution or Pareto front eventually. In order to achieve the above goals, the proposed constrained MOPSO modified a standard MOPSO in the following aspects, 1) a rank-constraint violation indicator and a feasibility ration are defined for the step of updating particles' personal best memory; 2) two fixed size archives are designed to hold feasible global best solutions and infeasible global best solutions, respectively so that the infeasible solutions can be used as bridges to explore feasible solution areas; 3) the global best is selected equally from the above two archives and by applying tournament selection with the use of dynamic crowing distance values; 4) the particles are updated by taking consideration of the constraint violation and the feasibility ratio; 5) applying both uniform mutation and Gaussian mutation operations. Simulation results on the benchmark functions illustrated that the proposed MOPSO is highly competitive by comparing with other three existing algorithms, i.e., NSGA-II, GZHW, and WTY algorithms.

When a particle swarm optimization algorithm applies to solve a multimodal problem, premature convergence may happen. The designs of various particles swarm optimization algorithms for multimodal problems have to take and have taken this into consideration. This consideration may be also necessary for designing particle swarm optimization algorithms for unimodal problems. For example, for a unimodal problem with boundary constraints, premature convergence may occur if boundary constraints are handled improperly. In the chapter "Experimental Study on Boundary Constraints Handling in Particle Swarm Optimization: From Population Diversity Perspective" Cheng *et al.* experimentally studied boundary constraints handling techniques in particle swarm optimization algorithms with different topology structures. In this chapter, population diversity, which is a way to measure the distribution of particles in the search space, is utilized to monitor the search process of particle swarm optimization algorithms with different topology structures and different boundary handling techniques. The topology structure of a particle swarm optimization algorithm determines the information propagation method and speed. A good particle swarm optimization algorithm generally should possess a good balance between its exploration capability and exploitation capability over its entire search process. The topology structure of a particle swarm optimization algorithm determines the information propagation method and speed, therefore different boundary handling technique may be required for a particle swarm optimization algorithm with a different topology structure. The topology structures studied in the chapter include star structure, ring structure, four cluster structure, and von Neumann structure. The boundary constraints handling techniques studied include classical strategy, deterministic strategy, stochastic strategy, and modified stochastic strategy. Experimental results and observations revealed the tendency of particles' exploration capability and exploitation capability during the search process. For example, a deterministic boundary handling technique may improve the search performance of the particle swarm optimization algorithm with ring, four clusters, or Von Neumann structure, but not the star structure; Stochastic boundary handling technique can have good exploration capability, and therefore, by further including the method of resetting particles in a small or decreased region, the particle swarm optimization algorithm will also retain good exploitation ability so that better performance can be achieved by the particle swarm optimization algorithm. In general, from the search tendency revealed by the population diversity, a more effective and efficient particle swarm optimization algorithm could be designed for solving an optimization problem by considering, say, boundary handling technique and topology structure together.

Firefly optimization algorithm is a population-based algorithm which is inspired by flashing behavior of fireflies. Like other swarm intelligence algorithms, premature convergence may occur in firefly optimization algorithm, and firefly optimization algorithm may be trapped in any local minima which is not a good enough solution to the problem to be solved. A critical feature for an optimization algorithm to have is to have the capability to escape from local minimum, therefore to have more chances to search other local minima and eventually find at least a local minima, if not a global optima, which represents a good enough solution to the problem to be solved. Traditionally, an optimization algorithm is designed to have the ability to avoid instability or chaotic behavior. In the chapter "Chaos-Enhanced Firefly Algorithm with Automatic Parameter Tuning," Yang analyzed the original firefly optimization algorithm and observed that by changing a parameter of the simplified firefly algorithm's equation with a single agent (individual), chaotic behavior can be observed. It is then reasonable to believe that chaotic behavior should appear in the original firefly optimization algorithm by changing its parameter. As a consequence, the firefly optimization algorithm can enter either a stable and convergent search process or a chaotic and divergent search process by intensively controlling or adjusting this parameter, therefore, the firefly optimization algorithm can be modified to interchangeably enter either convergent search process or divergent search process. That means at least theoretically the firefly optimization algorithm can be made to balance between its exploration capability and exploitation capability. In the chapter, the author further discussed the automatic parameter tuning for the proposed chaos-enhanced firefly optimization algorithm.

There are a lot of swarm intelligence algorithms reported in the literature so far, such as particle swarm optimization algorithm, ant colony optimization algorithm, fish school search optimization algorithm, bacterial foraging optimization algorithm, firework optimization algorithm, and firefly optimization algorithm, to name just a few. Most of these swarm intelligence algorithms are inspired by objects with low level intelligence at individual level, for example, birds in particle swarm optimization algorithm, ants in ant colony optimization algorithm, fishes in fish school search optimization algorithm, et cetera. The collective collaboration of these objects with low level intelligence inspired the designs of these optimization algorithms, which have shown good search capability. It is natural and intuitive to expect that an optimization algorithm inspired by the collective collaboration of human being should be at least competitive with, if not superior to, these swarm intelligence algorithms inspired by the collective collaboration of these objects with low level intelligence, because human being are the most intelligent animal in this world. In the chapter "An Optimization Algorithm Based on Brainstorming Process," Shi proposed a new population-based stochastic optimization algorithm called the brain storm optimization algorithm, which is inspired by the human being brainstorming process. Brainstorming process is often utilized by a group of people to brain storm good ideas to solve problems that is very difficult, if not impossible, for a single person to solve. In the chapter, Shi first introduced one type of brainstorming process, which is then modeled. The brainstorming process model is then standardized and abstracted as a flow chart based on which two versions of brain storm optimization algorithms are designed and implemented. A brain storm optimization algorithm basically consists of two kind major operations within each iteration: the clustering operation and the individual updating operation. The clustering operation focuses more on convergence of the search process while the individual generation operation focuses more on divergence of search process. In other words, each iteration of the brain storm optimization algorithm involves both expansion operation and contraction operation. The two versions of brain storm optimization algorithms are tested on ten benchmark functions. The experimental results validated and illustrated the effectiveness and efficiency of the proposed brain storm optimization algorithms. Furthermore, in the chapter, two measurement metrics are defined: the average inter-cluster distance and the inter-cluster diversity. The average inter-cluster distance measures and/or monitors the distribution of cluster centers, while the inter-cluster diversity can be looked as a measurement of information entropy for the population of individuals in the brain storm optimization algorithm. The two metrics can be further utilized to monitor and control the search process of a brain storm optimization algorithm so that better performed brain storm optimization algorithm can be achieved.

Section 2: Swarm Intelligence Applications

In applications such as text mining, web classification, etc., there are huge amount of data items which have been and will be continually collected. Furthermore, each data item represents a point in a high-dimensional space. For example, in web classification, each web can be represented by a vector of occurrence frequencies of all words that are possible to occur in any web page. These high-dimensional data vectors together form a data matrix which usually is a sparse matrix. Therefore, for the web classification problem, a good way is to greatly reduce its dimension through low-rank approximation approaches. Most commonly used low rank approximation approaches are singular value decomposition, principal component analysis, factor analysis, independent components analysis, and multidimensional scaling, to name just a few. Among them, singular value decomposition and principal component analysis approaches provide best approximation in the sense that Frobenius norm is the smallest. However, the low rank approximations obtained by singular value decomposition and principal component analysis contain elements with both positive and negative values. For many applications, negative values in a low rank approximation are not meaningful; therefore, a low rank approximation with all non-negative elements are sought, called non-negative matrix factorization (NMF). One goal of NMF as in the web classification is to reduce dimensionality so that the classification task can be easier to achieve, and at the same time, the classification accuracy can be higher. Another more general goal of NMF is to find a good enough non-negative matrix approximate for large sparse matrix such as that generated in the web classification application which usually will be modeled as an optimization problem with nonlinear, no-convex, discontinuous, and multimodal objective function. The population-base algorithms such as swarm intelligence algorithms are good choices to solve this kind of optimization problems. In the chapter "Swarm Intelligence for Non-Negative Matrix Factorization," Janecek and Tan utilized five different population-based algorithms as the NMF approaches, which are: particle swarm optimization algorithm, genetic algorithm, fish school search algorithm, differential evolution, and firework algorithm. Among them, three are swarm intelligence algorithms. To improve convergence speed and increase classification accuracy, two optimization strategies for initialization and iterative update are designed and implemented in the five population-based optimization algorithms.

A watchman route problem (WRP) is a problem that is to find the shortest route in a polygon with holes under the condition that all points inside the polygon are visible from the route. The generalized watchman route problem is a problem that mobile robot operator should find the shortest route for the robot to oversee the whole area with holes. Both the WRP and generalized WAP problems are NP-hard problems. Ant colony optimization algorithm is a nature-inspired optimization algorithm that was abstracted and modeled from what ants do. Simulated ants intend to find the shortest path by following the path that has the stronger smell of pheromone. In the chapter "How Ants Can Efficiently Solve the Generalized Watchman Route Problem," Paduch and Sapiecha proposed to use ant colony optimization algorithm to solve generalized watchman route problem.

Image segmentation is a problem to label every pixel of an image so that the image can be simplified or be changed into a different image which is more meaningful and easier to understand. Fuzzy C-Means algorithm is a clustering algorithm that is widely used for image segmentation. Bacterial foraging optimization algorithm is a stochastic optimization algorithm that is motivated by the bacterial foraging behavior of E. coli. In the chapter "Image Segmentation Based on Bacterial Foraging and FCM Algorithm," Mo and Yin proposed a hybrid algorithm, which combines the bacterial foraging optimization algorithm and fuzzy c-means algorithm to solve the image segmentation problems. Image segmentation problem is first represented as an optimization problem. Then the fuzzy-c-means algorithm is used to solve the optimization problem, and the bacterial foraging optimization algorithm is used to reinforce the global search capability of fuzzy c-means algorithm so that it can overcome the original fuzzy c-means algorithm's poor global search capability, and therefore can avoid its converging into local minima. The proposed hybrid algorithm is tested on several image segmentation problems. Experimental results illustrated the good performance of the proposed algorithm.

Frequency assignment problem (FAP) is a problem to assign frequency to transmitters in a wireless communication network with at most acceptable interference among channels. Due to the limited available radio spectrum, FAP is a difficult, challenging, and practical problem. FAP will usually be represented as a strongly NP-hard optimization problem which optimization algorithms are designed to solve. In the chapter "Minimum Span Frequency Assignment Based on a Multiagent Evolutionary Algorithm," Liu *et al.* proposed a hybrid algorithm, which is a combination of multi-agent system and evolutionary algorithm, to solve minimum span FAP problems the objective of which is to minimize the required frequency spectrum to meet a given level of reception quality over the network. Agents live in a lattice-like environment while evolutionary algorithm is utilized to evolve the agents' behaviors so that to increase their energies, which correspond to better frequency assignment with minimum span. The proposed algorithm was tested on T-coloring problems, which is very closely related to the FAP problems, with different sizes and Philadelphia benchmark for FAPs. Experimental results illustrated the good performance of the proposed algorithm.

The control of a nuclear reactor usually is based on data from a set of sensors. In order to control the nuclear system, which can be modeled as a nonlinear system, the control system needs to be reliable, robust, and stable, which means the control system needs to be a redundant control system in order to be able to detect and react to sensors' failures quickly. One way to add redundancy is using hardware redundancy, for example, with redundant sensors. One possible problem with the redundant sensor strategy is that the lifetime expectation for all sensors is similar, therefore with one sensor fails, the other sensors are also like to fail soon. The other way is to add detect system to detect any possible failure and react to the detected failure. In the chapter "Design of Robust Approach for Failure Detection in Dynamic Control Systems," Zaki Ei-Far proposed a robust instrument fault detection (IFD) algorithm based on a modified immune mechanism based evolutionary algorithm. Based on the proposed IFD algorithm, a fault diagnosis logic system is further created on the purpose to be able to determine on line optimal control action, quick fault detection, and controller structure reconfigurations. Through a sampling time, cycles of genetic operators are performed to ensure the capability of the proposed algorithm. The proposed IFD algorithm is applied to the control system of a nonlinear nuclear power reactor to illustrate the performance of the proposed algorithm. Experimental results showed that the designed fault diagnosis logic system is capable of detecting the fault and reconfiguring the controller system under situations with system parameters uncertainties and noisy data.

In applications such as surveillance operations, automated lawn mowing, and automated vacuum cleaning, distributed area coverage using multi-robot system is an important research topic in which multiple robots are teamed up to cover and/or explore an environment which may be initially unknown. Numerous area coverage algorithms exist to solve this kind of coverage problems in which usually, the entire environment should be covered or explored by at least one robot. For most existing coverage techniques, they consider the coverage problem independently, for example, each robot performs its action individually, while in reality, there are numerous different scenarios out there. For example, robots may be equipped with different sensors, and therefore, have different functionalities. Several robots with different functionalities should team up to perform one single task. Therefore for this kind of task, a more efficient solution is to consider the coverage problem together with the multi-robot formation problem. In the chapter "Effects of Multi-Robot Team Formations on Distributed Area Coverage," Dasgupta, *et al*. combined the multi-robot formation techniques and area coverage techniques together so that an initially unknown environment can be efficiently covered by maintaining effective team formation of multiple robots. The authors theoretically analyzed their approach and conducted extensive experiments on the Webots robotic simulation platform in addition to using physical robots within an indoor environment.

Yuhui Shi
Xi'an Jiaotong-Liverpool University, China

Acknowledgment

I would like to thank all chapter authors and reviewers for their contributions and supports. They retain the quality of the book volume. I would also like to take this opportunity to thank the National Natural Science Foundation of China and the Suzhou Science and Technology Bureau for their supports under Grant Number 60975080 and SYJG0919, respectively. Last but not least, my thanks go to the team, Heather Probst, Jamie Wilson, and Jan Travers, at the IGI Global Publishers for their support and patience. They worked diligently with me throughout the process of editing and production. It has been a pleasure and a learning experience for me to work with them. They made the book a reality.

Section 1
Swarm Intelligence Algorithms

Chapter 1
Scatter Search and Path Relinking:
A Tutorial on the Linear Arrangement Problem

Rafael Martí
Universidad de Valencia, Spain

Juan-José Pantrigo
Universidad Rey Juan Carlos, Spain

Abraham Duarte
Universidad Rey Juan Carlos, Spain

Vicente Campos
Universidad de Valencia, Spain

Fred Glover
OptTek Systems, Inc., USA

ABSTRACT

Scatter search (SS) and path relinking (PR) are evolutionary methods that have been successfully applied to a wide range of hard optimization problems. The fundamental concepts and principles of the methods were first proposed in the 1970s and 1980s, and were based on formulations, dating back to the 1960s, for combining decision rules and problem constraints. The methods use strategies for search diversification and intensification that have proved effective in a variety of optimization problems and that have sometimes been embedded in other evolutionary methods to yield improved performance. This paper examines the scatter search and path relinking methodologies from both conceptual and practical points of view, and identifies certain connections between their strategies and those adopted more recently by particle swarm optimization. The authors describe key elements of the SS & PR approaches and apply them to a hard combinatorial optimization problem: the minimum linear arrangement problem, which has been used in applications of structural engineering, VLSI and software testing.

DOI: 10.4018/978-1-4666-2479-5.ch001

1. INTRODUCTION

Scatter search (SS) was first introduced in Glover (1977) as a heuristic approach for general integer programming problems. SS systematically generates and updates a set of reference points that includes good solutions obtained by prior problem-solving efforts together with solutions that are screened to add diversity to the reference set. Path relinking (PR) was subsequently proposed in Glover (1989) and Glover and Laguna (1993) as an analog making use of neighborhood spaces in place of Euclidean spaces. Interesting relationships exist between the SS/PR approaches and the more recent particle swarm optimization methodology introduced by Kennedy and Eberhart (1995).

The SS and PR template (Glover, 1997) has served as a foundation for most of the SS and PR implementations to date, underscoring processes to take advantage of the flexibility of the SS and PR methodologies. Through these processes, each of the basic components can be implemented in a variety of ways and degrees of sophistication, and hence can be adapted conveniently to a variety of different problem settings. Advanced options derive from the way that five pivotal elements of the methods are implemented. We can find a large number of papers on both the SS method and the PR method and their applications. Glover and Laguna (1997) provide overviews and a variety of references on these methods and the monographic book on Scatter Search (Laguna & Martí, 2003) together with the feature cluster of the European Journal of Operational Research (Martí, 2006), which includes 19 papers, provide the reader with the elements to design successful SS implementations. A recent survey of SS and PR methods appears in Resende et al. (2010).

The following principles summarize the foundations of the scatter search and path relinking methodologies as evolved from its origins:

- Useful information about the form (or location) of optimal solutions is typically contained in a suitably diverse collection of elite solutions.

- When solutions are combined as a strategy for exploiting such information, it is important to provide mechanisms capable of constructing combinations that extrapolate beyond the regions spanned by the solutions considered.

- The manner of combining solutions may be viewed as forming paths between (and beyond) them (using Euclidean spaces in SS and neighborhood spaces in PR). Each path results in introducing attributes of one elite solution into another, by a process where the trajectory for a given solution is influenced by the guidance of other solutions.

- It is likewise important to incorporate heuristic processes to map combined solutions into new solutions. The purpose of these combination mechanisms is to incorporate both diversity and quality.

- Taking account of multiple solutions simultaneously, as a foundation for creating combinations, enhances the opportunity to exploit information contained in the union of elite solutions.

A connection between the SS & PR approaches and particle swarm optimization (PSO) arises through the SS & PR strategy of combining solutions in a manner that may be interpreted as generating trajectories of selected elite solutions by reference to directions determined by other elite solutions (called guiding solutions in path relinking). In contrast to PSO, the solutions guided by SS & PR are initially generated and subsequently updated after the combination process by the application of associated heuristic or metaheuristic processes. PSO methods characteristically guide the progress of solutions in different streams of search by reference to the personal best of each stream and the global best overall streams.

The evolving reference set of elite solutions used by SS & PR always includes the global best, and hence each solution in the set likewise enters into combinations with the global best to provide one of the influences on its trajectory, inviting a direct comparison with the PSO approach. However, each solution in SS & PR also enters into combinations with other members of the reference set, as would be analogous to a form of PSO guided by additional personal best solutions beyond those deriving from a single stream in question. Another apparent contrast is that SS & PR employ solution streams outside of those guided by other elite solutions, drawing on improving methods (such as iterated descent or tabu search) to yield new members to enter the elite reference set. Parallel versions of SS & PR which generate such streams simultaneously set up a master slave relationship where the maintenance of the reference set and the combinations produced from it yield the master processes than spawn candidate solutions passed to the slaves employing local search. Aside from the differences in strategic detail, there are evidently intriguing similarities in overall conceptual design between SS & PR approaches and PSO methods when viewed from a higher level.

In this paper we consider the scatter search and path relinking methodologies applied to solve combinatorial optimization problems by targeting an NP-hard problem based on graphs; the minimum linear arrangement problem. We adapt three elements from the five in the SS and PR template that are context-dependent (i.e., that are conveniently susceptible to being customized for specific problem settings): the diversification generation method, the improvement method and the combination method. Accompanying this, we apply a standard design for the other two methods (which usually are context-independent): the reference set update and the subset generation methods. We begin by focusing on the SS method and later include elements of the PR method.

2. PROBLEM FORMULATION

The minimum linear arrangement problem may be described as follows. Let $G=(V,E)$ be a graph with a vertex set $V(|V|=n)$ and an edge set $E(|E|=m)$. A labeling or linear layout f of G assigns the integers 1, 2, ..., n to the vertices of G. Let $f(v)$ be the label of vertex v, where each vertex has a different label. The contribution of a vertex v, $L(v,f)$, to the objective function is the sum of the absolute values of the differences between $f(v)$ and the labels of its adjacent vertices. That is:

$$L(v,f) = \sum_{u \in N(v)} \left| f(v) - f(u) \right|$$

where $N(v)$ is the set of vertices adjacent to v. The value of a linear arrangement of a graph G with respect to a labeling f is then:

$$LA(G,f) = \frac{1}{2} \sum_{v \in V} L(v,f)$$

Figure 1 shows an example of a linear arrangement and the associated computation of the objective function value. The optimum linear arrangement $LA(G)$ of graph G is then the minimum $LA(G,f)$ value over all possible labelings f – i.e., the Linear Arrangement Minimization problem (MinLA) consists of finding a labeling f that minimizes $LA(G,f)$. This NP-hard problem (Garey & Johnson, 1979) is related to two other well-known layout problems, the bandwidth and profile minimization problems. However, as pointed out by McAllister (1999), an optimal solution for one of these problems is not necessarily optimal for the other related problems.

The MinLA problem was first stated by Harper (1964), and through the years many different algorithms have been proposed for solving it, with varying degrees of success.

The remainder of this paper is organized as follows. In Section 3 we first give a brief sum-

Figure 1. Objective function computation for a graph G and an arrangement f

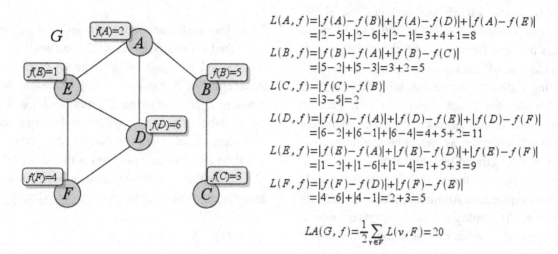

$$L(A,f)=|f(A)-f(B)|+|f(A)-f(D)|+|f(A)-f(E)|$$
$$=|2-5|+|2-6|+|2-1|=3+4+1=8$$

$$L(B,f)=|f(B)-f(A)|+|f(B)-f(C)|$$
$$=|5-2|+|5-3|=3+2=5$$

$$L(C,f)=|f(C)-f(B)|$$
$$=|3-5|=2$$

$$L(D,f)=|f(D)-f(A)|+|f(D)-f(E)|+|f(D)-f(F)|$$
$$=|6-2|+|6-1|+|6-4|=4+5+2=11$$

$$L(E,f)=|f(E)-f(A)|+|f(E)-f(D)|+|f(E)-f(F)|$$
$$=|1-2|+|1-6|+|1-4|=1+5+3=9$$

$$L(F,f)=|f(F)-f(D)|+|f(F)-f(E)|$$
$$=|4-6|+|4-1|=2+3=5$$

$$LA(G,f)=\frac{1}{2}\sum_{v\in V}L(v,F)=20$$

mary of some of the leading methods previously developed from the MinLA problem. Section 4 covers the basics of the scatter search procedure, introducing the SS methodology and describing how we apply it to solve the MinLA problem. Section 5 describes the diversification generation methods we have incorporated which are based on the GRASP methodology and in Section 6 we describe an improvement method based on local search. Section 7 presents a mechanism to selectively apply the improvement method within Scatter Search in order to save computational effort. Finally, Section 8 introduces a path relinking procedure which fulfills the role of a combination method in our scatter search algorithm. The paper finishes with the computational experiments in Section 9 and associated conclusions in Section 10.

3. BRIEF SUMMARY OF PREVIOUS MINLA METHODS

We chiefly restrict attention to more modern solution approaches proposed since 1990.

Juvan and Mohar (1992) introduced the Spectral Sequencing method (SSQ). This method computes the eigenvectors of the Laplacian matrix of G. It then orders the vertices according to the second smallest eigenvector. As stated by Petit (2003a), the rationale behind the SSQ heuristic is that vertices connected with an edge will tend to be assigned numbers that are close to each other, thus providing a good solution to the MinLA problem.

McAllister (1999) proposed a heuristic method for the MinLA which basically consists of a constructive procedure that labels vertices in a sequential order. Vertices are selected according to their degree with respect to previously labeled vertices. This method compares favorably with previous methods for this and related problems.

Petit (2003a) reviewed lower bounds and heuristic methods, proposed new ones and introduced a set of 21 small and medium size instances (62 $\leq n \leq 10240$) for the MinLA problem. Among the methods reviewed were the Juvan-Mohar method (Juvan & Mohar, 1992), the Gomory-Hu tree method (Adolphson and Hu 1973), and the Edge method, to which he added a Degree method for improved lower bounds. Petit concluded that the Juvan-Mohar method and the Degree method provide the best lower bounds; however, their values are far from those of the best known solutions, and therefore they are of very limited interest from a practical point of view. Petit additionally introduced both a constructive and a local search procedure. The Successive Augmentation (SAG) is a greedy heuristic that constructs step by step a solution extending a partial layout until all vertices have been enumerated. At each step, the best free label is assigned to the current vertex. Vertices are examined in the order given by a breadth-first search. Once a solution has been constructed, different improvement methods are considered. The author studied three different heuristics based on local search: Hill-climbing, Full-search and Simulated Annealing (SA). In the Hill-climbing method moves are selected at random; in the Full-search the entire neighborhood of a solution is examined, at each iteration, in search of the best available move. Finally, the SA algorithm implements the temperature parameter as described in Kirkpatrick, Gelatt, and Vecchi (1983) for move selection. Petit considered two neighborhoods, called flip2 and flip3. The former exchanges the label of two vertices, while the latter "rotates" the label of three vertices.

The experimentation in Petit (2003a) shows that the neighborhood based on the exchange of two labels (flip2) produces better results than the rotation (flip3). Overall experimentation concludes that the SA method outperforms the others, although it employs much longer running times (not reported in the paper). Therefore, the author recommends employing the Hill-climbing as well as the Spectral Sequencing methods. In Petit (2003b), a more elaborate Simulated Annealing algorithm is proposed. The author introduces a new neighborhood, flipN, based on the Normal distribution of the distances between the labels of vertices. The Simulated Annealing algorithm based on the flipN neighborhood (SAN) improves upon the previous SA method. Moreover, to speed up the method, the initial solution is obtained with the SSQ algorithm. The combined method, SSQ+SAN, is able to outperform previous methods.

Rodriguez-Tello, Hao, and Torres-Jimenez (2008) proposed a new algorithm based on the Simulated Annealing methodology. The Two-Stage Simulated Annealing (TSSA) performs two steps. In the first one a solution is constructed with the procedure by McAllister (1999); then in the second step it performs a Simulated Annealing procedure based on exchanges of labels. This method introduces two new elements to solve the MinLA: a combined neighborhood and a new evaluation function. Given a vertex v, the first neighborhood, selected with a probability of 0.9, examines the vertices u such that their label $f(u)$ is close to the median of the vertices' labels adjacent to v (at a maximum distance of 2). The second neighborhood, selected with a probability 0.1, exchanges the labels of two vertices selected at random with diversification (exploration) purposes. The method evaluates the solutions with a function that is more discriminating than the original LA. The authors compared their TSSA method with the best known algorithms and they concluded that their method outperforms previous algorithms.

4. SCATTER SEARCH METHODOLOGY

We begin by summarizing the "five-method template" for implementing SS and then discuss the relationships among its component processes. These key components are as follows:

1. A *diversification-generation method* to generate a collection of diverse trial solutions, using an arbitrary trial solution (or seed solution) as an input.

2. An *improvement method* to transform a trial solution into one or more enhanced trial solutions. Neither the input nor the output solutions are required to be feasible, though the output solutions will more usually be

expected to be so. If no improvement of the input trial solution results, the "enhanced" solution is considered to be the same as the input solution.

3. A *reference-set update method* to build and maintain a *reference set* consisting of the *b* "best" solutions found (where the value of *b* is typically small, e.g. no more than 20), organized to provide efficient accessing by other parts of the method. Solutions gain membership to the reference set according to their quality or their diversity.

4. A *subset-generation method* to operate on the reference set, to produce several subsets of its solutions as a basis for creating combined solutions.

5. A *solution-combination method* to transform a given subset of solutions produced by the Subset Generation Method into one or more combined solution vectors.

Figure 2 shows the interaction among these five components and highlights the central role of the reference set. This basic design starts with the creation of an initial set of solutions *P*, and then extracts the reference set (*RefSet*) of solutions from it. The shaded circles represent improved solutions resulting from the application of the improvement method.

The diversification-generation method is used to build a large set *P* of diverse solutions. The size of *P* (*PSize*) is typically at least 10 times the size of *RefSet*. The initial reference set is built according to the reference-set-update method, which takes the *b* "best" solutions from *P* to compose the *RefSet*, which typically is of modest size, e.g., containing between 10 and 30 solutions in all. The qualifier "best" is not restricted to referring to solution quality (i.e., the objective function value of a solution), but often embraces an expanded form of evaluation that accounts for

Figure 2. Schematic representation of a basic SS design

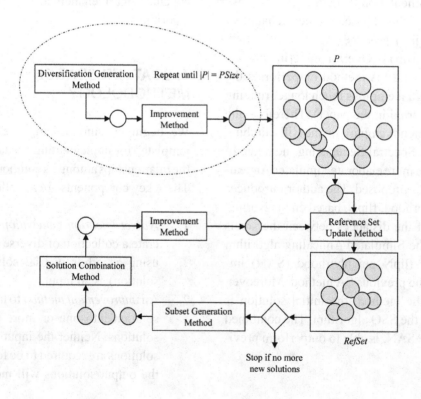

diversity. This evaluation can change throughout the application of the procedure. For example, during a phase that is specifically devoted to diversification, the reference-set update method can consist of selecting b distinct and maximally diverse solutions from P. Regardless of the rules used to select the reference solutions, the solutions in *RefSet* are ordered according to quality, where the best solution is the first one in the list.

The search is then initiated by applying the subset-generation method that, in its simplest form, involves generating all pairs of reference solutions. The pairs of solutions in *RefSet* are selected one at a time and the solution-combination method is applied to generate one or more trial solutions which are subjected to the improvement method. The reference-set update method is applied once again to build the new *RefSet* with the best solutions, according to the objective function value, from the current *RefSet* and the set of trial solutions. The basic procedure terminates after all the subsets generated are subjected to the combination method and none of the improved trial solutions are admitted to *RefSet* under the rules of the reference-set-update method.

In our approach, we use a simple mechanism to construct an initial reference set and then update it during the search. The size of the reference set is denoted by $|RefSet| = b_1 + b_2 = b$. The construction of the initial reference-set starts with the selection of the best b_1 solutions from P. These solutions are added to *RefSet* and deleted from P. For each solution in $P \setminus RefSet$, the minimum of the distances to the solutions in *RefSet* is computed. The solution with the maximum of these minimum distances is then selected. This solution is added to the *RefSet* and deleted from P, and the minimum distances are updated. The process is repeated b_2 times, where $b_2 = b - b_1$. The resulting reference set has b_1 high-quality solutions and b_2 diverse solutions.

Of the five SS components, only four are strictly required. The improvement method is usually needed if high-quality outcomes are desired, but an

SS procedure can be implemented without it. On the other hand, the SS method could incorporate tabu search or another complex metaheuristic as the improvement method (usually demanding more running time).

5. DIVERSIFICATION GENERATION METHODS

A straightforward scheme to construct a solution consists of performing n steps, labeling a vertex at each step with the lowest available label. At a higher level of sophistication, the so-called Frontal Increase Minimization (FIM) starts by creating a list of unlabeled vertices U, which at the beginning consists of all the vertices in the graph (i.e. initially $U=V$). The first vertex v is randomly selected from all those vertices in U and labeled as 1. In subsequent construction steps, the candidate list CL consists of all the vertices in U that are adjacent to at least one labeled vertex. A vertex v is randomly selected from CL, labeled with the next available label and deleted from U. The method finishes after n steps, when all the vertices have received a label.

McAllister (1999) proposed the following refinement of the FIM construction. Let L be the set of labeled vertices and let $d(v)$ be the degree of vertex v, then $d_L(v)$ represents the number of labeled vertices adjacent to v and $d_U(v)$ represents the number of unlabeled vertices adjacent to v. This variant of the FIM construction is based on the computation of $sf(v) = d_U(v) - d_L(v)$ as a way to measure the attractiveness of vertex v for selection. Figure 3 shows a pseudo-code of this method, denoted C1, in which the vertex with the lowest sf-value is selected from CL and assigned the lowest available label in each construction step. The procedure specifies a tie-breaking mechanism in step 7 of Figure 3. When more than one vertex in CL has the minimum sf-value, the method selects the oldest one (the vertex with maximum number

Figure 3. Pseudo-code of the constructive method C1

---

1. Initially $L = \varnothing$ and $U=V$.
2. Select a vertex u randomly from U.
3. Assign the label l=1 to u. $L = \{u\}$, $U = U \setminus \{u\}$
WHILE $(U \neq \varnothing)$
4. $l = l+1$
     5. Construct CL = $\{ v \in U / (w,v) \in E, w \in L \}$
6. Compute $sf(v) = d_U(v)-d_L(v)$ for all v in CL
7. Select the vertex u in CL with minimum $sf(u)$
8. Label u with the label l
9. $U = U \setminus \{u\}$, $L = L \cup \{u\}$
ENDWHILE

Figure 4. Pseudo-code of the constructive method C2

---

1. Initially $L = \varnothing$ and $U=V$.
2. Select a vertex u randomly from U.
3. Assign the label l=1 to u. $L = \{u\}$, $U = U \setminus \{u\}$
WHILE $(U \neq \varnothing)$
4. $l = l+1$
     5. Construct CL = $\{ v \in U / (w,v) \in E, w \in L \}$
6. Compute $sf(v) = d_U(v)-d_L(v)$ for all v in CL
7. Construct RCL= $\{ v \in CL / sf(v) \leq th \}$
8. Select a vertex u randomly in RCL
9. Label u with the label l
10. $U = U \setminus \{u\}$, $L = L \cup \{u\}$
ENDWHILE

---

of iterations in CL). McAllister (1999) tested this method against previous constructive methods based on the FIM strategy, showing its superiority.

We propose now a GRASP construction based on the computation of $sf(v)$. GRASP, Greedy Randomized Adaptive Search Procedure, is a multi-start or iterative process in which each iteration consists of two phases: construction and local search. The construction phase builds a feasible solution, whose neighborhood is explored until a local optimum is found after the application of the local search phase (Resende & Ribeiro, 2003). At each iteration of the construction phase, GRASP maintains a set of candidate elements CL that can be feasibly added to the partial solution under construction. All candidate elements are evaluated according to a greedy function ($sf(v)$ in our case) in order to select the next element to be added to the construction. A restricted candidate list (RCL) is created with the best elements in CL. This is the greedy aspect of the method. The element to be added to the partial solution is randomly selected from those in the RCL. This is the probabilistic aspect of the heuristic. Once the selected element is added to the partial solution, the candidate list CL is updated and its elements evaluated. This is the adaptive aspect of the heuristic. Figure 4 shows the pseudo-code of this GRASP construction, which we will call C2.

In the GRASP construction above, the parameter th represents a threshold on the quality of the elements. Specifically, the elements in CL with an sf-value lower than th are admitted to become part of RCL. This search parameter is computed as a fraction α of the rank of sf in CL:

$$th = msf + \alpha (Msf-msf)$$

$$msf = \min_{v \in CL} sf(v)$$

$$Msf = \max_{v \in CL} sf(v)$$

Note that if α is equal to 0, then $th=msf$, and the GRASP construction is equivalent to the McAllister method. On the other hand, if α is equal to 1, then RCL=CL and the GRASP construction is equivalent to the FIM strategy. In the computational study reported in Section 9, we test the effect of changes in α to the solutions with this method.

In the adaptation above of the GRASP construction to the MinLA problem, we only consider the evaluation given by the sf function. We now propose a second variant, C3, in which we include the contribution of the selected vertex to the objective function. Specifically, let $C(v,l)$ be the contribution of v, when v is labeled with label l, to the current solution (and the labels 1 to l-1 have already been assigned). In mathematical terms:

$$C(v,l) = \sum_{u \in N(v) \cap L} \left| f(u) - l \right|$$

The GRASP construction C3 only considers the vertices with minimum sf-value at each step. The restricted candidate list RCL is now formed with the vertices with minimum sf-value and with a C-value below a threshold th_C. In this way we can say that the C-value is used as a tie-breaking mechanism when more than one vertex in CL reaches the minimum sf-value. Figure 5 shows the pseudo-code of this construction.

The parameter th_C in C3 is the threshold that establishes the vertices with a relatively low contribution to the current solution. It is computed as a fraction β of its range in the candidate list CLmsf:

$$th_C = dm_L + \beta \left(dM_L - dm_L \right)$$

$$dm_L = \min_{v \in CLmsf} C(v,l)$$

$$dM_L = \max_{v \in CLmsf} C(v,l)$$

Figure 5. Pseudo-code of the constructive method C3

---

1. Initially $L = \varnothing$ and $U=V$.
2. Select a vertex u randomly from U.
3. Assign the label l=1 to u. $L = \{u\}$, $U = U \setminus \{u\}$
WHILE ($U \neq \varnothing$)
4. $l = l+1$
     5. Construct CL = $\{ v \in U / (w,v) \in E, w \in L \}$
6. Compute $sf(v) = d_U(v) - d_L(v)$ for all v in CL
7. Construct CLmsf = $\{ v \in CL / sf(v) = msf \}$
8. Construct RCL= $\{ v \in CLmsf / C(v) \leq th_C \}$
9. Select a vertex u randomly in RCL
10. Label u with the label l
11. $U = U - \{u\}$, $L = L \cup \{u\}$
ENDWHILE

If the parameter β in C3 takes the value 1, th_C equals dM_L and all the vertices in CLmsf are in RCL, thus resulting in a random selection among them. On the other hand, if it takes the value 0, th_C equals dm_L, thus resulting in a greedy selection. In Section 9 we will compare the three constructive methods C1, C2 and C3 described in this section and study the influence of their parameters on their performance.

6. IMPROVEMENT METHOD

Exchanges are used as the primary mechanism to move from one solution to another in our implementation. We have considered an improvement method based on the ejection chain methodology often used in association with tabu search (see Glover and Laguna, 1997). As a basis for describing our approach, it is useful to first discuss a type of move commonly used in heuristics for the MinLA problem.

Given a labeling f and two vertices u and v with labels $f(u)$ and $f(v)$ respectively, we define $move(u,v)$ as the exchange of the labels $f(u)$ and $f(v)$. Let g be the resulting labeling when $move(u,v)$ is performed. We can then compute the value of g, $LA(G,g)$, from the value of f, $LA(G,f)$, as:

$$LA(G,g) = LA(G,f) - MoveValue(u,v)$$

where

$$MoveValue(u,v) = L(u,f) + L(v,f) - L(u,g) - L(v,g)$$

Therefore, the larger the *MoveValue*, the better the move. Previous heuristics for MinLA based on this exchange move include the approach by Rodríguez-Tello et al. (2008), which, given a vertex u, considers the median of the vertices' labels adjacent to u as the best label for exchange. Although assigning the median label med(u) to u minimizes the sum of the absolute values of differences between this label and the labels of adjacent vertices, it is of course necessary to give u a label different from $med(u)$ unless the adjacent vertex v with $f(v) = med(u)$ is given a new assignment different from $med(u)$. This will occur if vertex u and vertex v exchange labels, but then the rationale of reassigning u the label $med(u)$ is destroyed[1]. The following example (see Figure 6) illustrates that an exchange with the "median label" is not necessarily the best choice.

Consider the partial graph depicted in Figure 6 in which vertex u has a relatively large contribution value $LA(u,f)= |23-2|+ |23-7|+ |23-14|=46$, and we consider exchanging its label, 23, with another one. According to the rule above, we would consider the median of the labels of its adjacent vertices, $med(u)$, as the best label for exchange. In this example, $med(u)$ is 7 and corresponds to vertex v. Let g be the labelling after the exchange ($g(v) = 23$ and $g(u) = 7$); we then obtain $LA(u,g) = 28$, thus reducing the contribution of u to the objective function LA. However, if we assign label 8 to vertex u (instead of 7), the contribution of u will be $|8-2|+ |8-7|+ |8-14|=13$. This motivates an exchange between $f(u)$ and a label $f(v^*)$, where v^* is not adjacent to u and where $f(v^*)$ is close to the value $med(u)$. (In the present case, $f(u) = 23$ and $f(v^*) = 8$.) Of course, this is only a first order consideration, because it would be entirely possible that exchanging the indicated $f(u)$ and $f(v^*)$ could produce an unfavourable

Figure 6. Move illustration

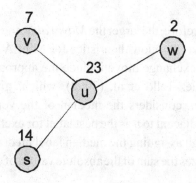

result – as where, for example, the vertices adjacent to v^* contain the labels 5, 6, 9 and 10. (Then assigning the label 23 to $f(v^*)$ would cause the new labeling of v^* to increase its LA value by 62, causing the value of the complete solution to deteriorate significantly.) Nevertheless, we abide by the principle that it is usually better to consider a label close to the "median-label" and not assigned to an adjacent vertex, than the "median-label" itself.

The situation illustrated in Figure 6 appears in all the cases in which the vertex considered for exchange has an odd degree (and thus the median value corresponds to the label of one of its adjacent vertex). This can be particularly problematic when the vertex u has only one adjacent vertex ($|N(u)|=1$). In that case, the selection of the median-label could even cycle the search. In line with this, previous papers (Rodríguez-Tello et al., 2008), do not limit the move to only considering $med(u)$, but examine a set of candidate labels close to the median at a maximum distance of 2. Therefore, they indirectly overcome this situation. We now propose to extend this set of "good labels" for exchanging including a search parameter *width* and avoiding the labels of adjacent vertices. The set CL(u) contains the candidate labels for u:

$$CL(u)=\{l \;/\; |l-med(u)|\leq width, l \neq f(v) \; \forall v \in N(u)\}$$

The ejection chain methodology we employ follows the general form indicated in Glover (1992) and Glover (1996), which is "based on the notion of generating compound sequences of moves, leading from one solution to another, by linked steps in which changes in selected elements cause other elements to be *ejected from* their current state, position or value assignment." In this section we make use of this notion as follows:

In the MinLA problem, suppose that we want to exchange the label of a vertex u with the label $f(v)$ of another vertex v because this exchange results in a reduction of $LA(u,f)$. However, this exchange could produce an increase in $LA(v,f)$, thus resulting in a non-improving move ($MoveValue(u,v)<0$). We can therefore consider labeling v with $f(u)$ but, instead of labeling u with $f(v)$, examine another vertex w and check whether the label $f(v)$ may be advantageously assigned to w and whether, to complete the process, the label $f(w)$ is appropriate to assign to u (as by reducing $LA(u,f)$). In terms of ejection chains, we may say that the assignment of $f(u)$ to v caused $f(v)$ to be "ejected" from v to w (and concluding by assigning $f(w)$ to u). The outcome defines a compound move of depth two that we can represent as $move(u,v)+move(v,w)$). We can then repeat this logic to build longer chains.

In our local search procedure based on ejection chains, EC, we define $move_{EC}(u,depth)$ as the ejection chain that starts the chain building process from vertex u. To restrict the search and to make it more efficient, we only scan the labels in $CL(u)$. Let v be the vertex with an associated label $f(v)\in CL(u)$ with a maximum $MoveValue(u,v)$. The chain starts by making $move_{EC}(u,depth) = move(u,v)$, thus exchanging the labels $f(u)$ and $f(v)$. If $move(u,v)$ is an improving one, it is executed and the chain stops. Otherwise, we select the vertex v in $CL(u)$ so that, when assigning its label $f(v)$ to u, the contribution of u to the objective function, $LA(u,f)$ is minimized. We then search for a vertex w with a label $f(w)$ in $CL(v)$ which is adequate for v. We select the label $f(w)$ in $CL(v)$ with maximum $MoveValue(v,w)$. If the compound move of depth two, $move(u,v)+ move(v,w)$, is an improving one ($MoveValue(u,v)+ MoveValue(v,w)\geq0$), the move is executed and the chain stops; otherwise the chain continues until the compound move becomes an improving one or the length of the chain reaches the pre-specified limit $depth$. If none of the compound moves from depth 1 to $depth$ examined in $move_{EC}(u,depth)$ is an improving move, no move is performed and the exploration continues with the next vertex to be considered for movement.

Note that we perform a move even when its value is 0. We have empirically found that this strategy permits the exploration of a larger number of solutions (compared to an implementation in which only moves with a positive value are performed), thus obtaining improved outcomes. On the other hand, we have also found that when we apply a move, we usually change a relatively large number of labels, and it is useful to apply the ejection chain from the same vertex again. Therefore, we move to the next vertex considered for movement when no exchange is performed in the ejection chain.

A global iteration of the EC method consists of first ordering the vertices in the opposite order to their labeling in the construction. We then examine the vertices in this order in search of an improving $move_{EC}$ move. The rationale behind this ordering is to give priority to those vertices which are more constrained in the construction process. We have also considered a variant in which the vertices are ordered according to their contribution $LA(u,f)$. However, this variant produces lower quality results compared with the former one. The method continues iterating only if in the previous iteration (i.e. the examination of all nodes) at least one improving move is performed. Otherwise, EC stops.

In addition to the parameter $depth$ our ejection chain method, EC includes the parameter $width$ described previously. By this means we control both the number of vertices involved in the move and the distance between the labels. Both parameters together permit the application of EC with a moderate running time; however, they constrain the search to "small" moves in the sense that it only considers candidate labels close to the neighbor's labels of the vertex selected for movement. In order to diversify the search and try more aggressive moves, we apply the Hill Climbing method (Petit, 2003a) in which moves are selected at random at the end of EC as a post-processing of the ejection chain for $iter\_Hc$ iterations. Section 9 reports on the experimentation in which we study these search parameters.

7. FILTERING SOLUTIONS

After a number of iterations, it is possible to estimate the fractional improvement achieved by the application of the improvement phase and use this information to increase the efficiency of the search (Laguna & Martí, 1999). Define the fractional improvement in the iteration i as:

$$P(i) = \frac{LA(G, f_i) - LA(G, f_i^*)}{LA(G, f_i^*)}$$

where f_i is the solution (labeling) constructed at iteration i, $LA(G, f_i)$ is its value, and f_i^* is the improved solution obtained applying the improvement method EC to f_i (and $LA(G, f_i^*)$ is its value). After n iterations, the mean μ_P and standard deviation σ_P of P can be estimated as:

$$\hat{\mu}_P = \frac{\sum_{i=1}^{n} P(i)}{n}$$

$$\hat{\sigma}_P = \sqrt{\frac{\sum_{i=1}^{n} (P(i) - \hat{\mu}_P)^2}{n-1}}$$

Then, at a given iteration i, these estimates can be used to determine whether it is "likely" that the improvement phase will be able to improve the current construction enough to produce a better solution than the current best, f_{best}. In particular, we calculate the minimum fractional improvement $imp(i)$ that is necessary for a construction f_i to be better than f_{best}, as:

$$imp(i) = \frac{LA(G, f_i) - LA(G, f_{best})}{LA(G, f_i)}$$

If the value of $imp(i)$ is close to the estimation of μ_P, we can consider that when we apply the improvement method EC to the current solution f_i, we will probably obtain a solution f_i^* which is better than f_{best}. Therefore, in order to save computational time, we only apply EC to promising solutions f_i according to this estimation. In mathematical terms, if $imp(i) < \hat{\mu}_P + \delta\hat{\sigma}_P$, then we apply EC to f_i; otherwise, we discard f_i. The value of δ is a search parameter representing a threshold on the number of standard deviations away from the estimated mean percentage improvement. In Section 9, we perform a set of preliminary experiments to test the effect of different δ values on solution quality and speed.

8. COMBINATION METHOD BASED ON PATH RELINKING

We consider a reference set with $b = 10$ solutions and apply a combination method to them. In our implementation for the linear arrangement problem we have considered the path relinking methodology to elaborate our combination method.

The initial reference set (*RefSet*) in standard scatter search implementations is constructed by selecting the |*RefSet*|/2 best solutions from a population of solutions P and adding to *RefSet* the |*RefSet*|/2 most diverse solutions in $P \setminus RefSet$ one-by-one, where the concept of diversity is defined below. Instead of this one-by-one selection of diverse solutions we consider here solving the maximum diversity problem (MDP) in order to obtain the five most diverse solutions in $P \setminus RefSet$.

The MDP consists of finding, from a given set of elements and corresponding distances between elements, the most diverse subset of a given size. The diversity of the chosen subset is given by the sum of the distances between every pair of elements. Since the MDP is a computationally hard problem, we employ the GC_2 method (Duarte &

Martí, 2007) because it provides a good balance between solution quality and speed, attributes that are important in order to embed it as part of the overall solving procedure.

In order to define a distance function we need to consider that *reverse* labelings (permutations) define equivalent MinLA solutions. In mathematical terms, let $p = (p_1, p_2, ..., p_n)$ and $q = (q_1, q_2, ..., q_n)$ be two labelings of a set of n vertices in which $q_i = n - p_i + 1$, then we say that p and q are *reverse* permutations and equivalent MinLA solutions with the same value (it is easy to check that $LA(G,p) = LA(G,q)$). In order to measure the distance between pairs of MinLA solutions, we want equivalent solutions to have a distance of 0. We then propose the following function:

$$d(p,q) = \sum_{i=1}^{n} \partial_i$$

where

$$\partial_i = \begin{cases} 1 \ if \ p_i \neq q_i \quad and \quad p_i \neq n - q_i + 1 \\ 0 \ otherwise \end{cases}$$

To illustrate this distance function, consider for example $p = (6,1,2,3,4,5)$ and $q = (1,2,3,4,5,6)$, then $d(p,q) = 0 + 1 + 1 + 0 + 1 + 1 = 4$. Therefore, we build the *RefSet* with the five best solutions and the five most diverse solutions (according to the distance above) from the set of solutions P obtained with the application of the GRASP method.

We apply the relinking process to each pair of solutions in the *RefSet*. Given the pair (f,g), we consider the path from f to g (where f is the initiating solution and g the guiding one). In this path we basically assign each vertex label one by one in the guiding solution to the initiating solution. Given the pair (f,g), let $C(f,g)$ be the candidate list of vertices to be examined in the relinking process from f to g. At each step in this process, a vertex v is chosen from $C(f,g)$ and labeled in the initiating solution with its label $g(v)$ in the guiding solution. To do this, in the initiating solution we look for the vertex u with label $g(v)$ and perform $move(u,v)$, then vertex v is removed from $C(f,g)$. The candidate set $C(f,g)$ is initialized with a randomly selected vertex. In subsequent iterations, each time a vertex is selected and removed from $C(f,g)$, its adjacent vertices are included in this candidate set of vertices.

In the Path Relinking methodology, it is convenient to add a local search exploration from some of the solutions visited in order to produce improved outcomes (Laguna & Martí, 1999; Piñana et al., 2004). We have applied the local search method based on ejection chains EC to some of the solutions generated in the path. Note that two consecutive solutions after a relinking step only differ in the labeling of two vertices. Therefore, it does not seem efficient to apply the local search exploration at every step of the relinking process. We introduce the parameter *pr* to control the application of the EC method. In particular, EC is applied *pr* times in the relinking process. We report on the effectiveness of the procedure with different values of this parameter in the computational testing that follows. After the application of the Path Relinking strategy, we return the best solution found as the output of the method.

9. COMPUTATIONAL EXPERIMENTS

This section describes the computational experiments that we performed to compare our proposed procedure with previous methods for solving the MinLA problem. We first describe our preliminary experimentation to compare the alternative solving methods proposed in previous sections. We also adjust the search parameters in order to establish a good combination of the proposed elements and strategies in our "final" algorithm. All experiments were performed on a personal computer with a 3.2 GHz Intel Xenon processor and 2.0 GB of RAM. We consider a set of twenty one instances ($62 \leq n \leq 10,240$ and $125 \leq m \leq 30,380$) introduced in Petit (2003a). They are designed to be difficult; i.e. in that they cannot be optimally solved by an explicit enumeration of all their feasible solutions. This set includes random graphs and three families of "real-world" graphs: VLSI, graph-drawing and engineering (fluid-dynamics and structural mechanics).

We perform the preliminary experimentation on four instances: randomA1, c1y, bintree10 and mesh33x33 selected at random from the original set. In our first preliminary experiment we compare the previous constructive method C1 (McAllister, 1999) with our two methods C2(α) and C3(β) described in Section 5. We test five values for the search parameters α and β: 0.1, 0.2, 0.3, 0.4 and 0.5. We also test a variant C2(rand) in which the value of α is randomly selected from among these five values in each construction (and similarly with β in C3(rand)). Table 1 shows the results of these three methods on the four Petit

instances mentioned above. We construct 100 solutions with each method on each instance and report the average across the four instances of the best solution found, Best, and the average of the worst solution found, Worst. We also report the average percentage deviation of the best solution obtained with each method from the best known solution, Dev. Best, as well as the average running time, Time.

The results in Table 1 indicate that the two proposed methods, C2 and C3, obtain better solutions than the previous method C1. Moreover, as shown in the average percentage deviation, the best results are obtained with the C3 method with a random selection of the parameter β (C3(rand)). However, in this experiment we have empirically found that some methods systematically obtain better solutions on some instances than other methods (although on average, across all the instances C3, is the best one). For example, C1 always obtains the best solutions in the bintree instances and C2 always obtains the best in the random ones. Therefore we have considered a mixed method, called C4, in which we randomly select C1, C2(rand) or C3(rand) in each construc-

Table 1. Comparison of constructive methods

Method	Best	Worst	Dev. Best	Time (seconds)
C1	53,9734.5	365,513.4	174.79%	2.25
C2(rand)	279,603.8	313,168.7	16.50%	2.75
C2(0.1)	279,516.6	313,168.7	16.50%	2.50
C2(0.2)	279,331.3	312,248.5	20.12%	2.75
C2(0.3)	279,401.6	312,932.7	19.97%	2.75
C2(0.4)	279,401.6	312,932.7	19.97%	2.75
C2(0.5)	279,344.8	313,168.2	16.50%	2.75
C3(rand)	282,040.0	327,343.5	13.77%	2.75
C3(0.1)	266,755.0	315,570.2	29.04%	2.50
C3(0.2)	266,852.7	322,400.5	31.71%	2.75
C3(0.3)	266,534.5	320,361.7	39.10%	2.75
C3(0.4)	265,768.2	321,176.7	36.76%	2.75
C3(0.5)	262,767.2	324,549.7	37.04%	2.75

tion. C4 is able to obtain an average percentage deviation of 11.26% across the four problems of our preliminary experimentation, thus improving upon the other methods. We will then consider C4 as the constructive method in the rest of our experimentation.

In our second preliminary experiment we undertake to compare the effectiveness of the improvement method described in Section 5. As a baseline method, we consider the construction method C4 without any improvement run for 500 seconds. We compare it with the combination of C4 and the ejection-chain-based improvement method EC with several values for its two parameters: *width* and *depth*. To do this, we run C4+EC(*width,depth)* for 500 seconds on each instance and report, as in the previous experiment, the Best, Worst and Dev. Best average values. Table 2 shows that the best combination of the search parameters is obtained with *width*=10 and *depth*=5 in our ejection-chain procedure, since C4+EC(10,5) presents an average percentage deviation from the best known solution of

10.37. It should be noted that previous studies (Rodriguez-Tello et al., 2008) are limited to a *width* value of 5 in the local search method, and we are obtaining the best results with *width* set to 10. On the other hand, the variant C4+EC(1,1) is simply C4 plus a local search and surprisingly obtains worse solutions (13.34 average percentage deviation from best) than C4 by itself (which as shown in the previous experiment obtains an 11.26 average percentage deviation from best). This is explained by the fact that the local search method is extremely time-consuming in this problem, and within 500 seconds the method can only construct and improve less than 50 solutions in some instances.

As described in Section 5 the application of the improvement method finishes with a post-processing consisting of the Hill climbing method (HC). It is performed for *iter_Hc* iterations. Table 3 reports the statistics Best, Worst, Dev. Best as well as the CPU running time, Time, of the C4+EC+HC procedure with iter_Hc=0, |V| /20, |V| /15, |V| /10 and |V| /5.

Table 2. Comparison of C4 coupled with different improvement methods with a time limit of 500 sec

Method	Best	Worst	Dev. Best
C4	263,636.7	509,565.2	11.26%
C4+EC(1,1)	264,574.5	457,632.0	13.34%
C4+EC(1,5)	263,224.8	327,512.8	13.15%
C4+EC(1,10)	262,739.3	370,197.0	13.19%
C4+EC(1,15)	264,512.5	319,452.0	13.58%
C4+EC(1,20)	262,872.3	316,349.0	13.05%
C4+EC(5,1)	262,025.0	454,472.5	11.45%
C4+EC(5,5)	261,836.8	309,190.0	11.21%
C4+EC(5,10)	263,258.3	303,643.8	11.23%
C4+EC(5,15)	260,298.3	324,966.8	11.14%
C4+EC(5,20)	262,929.3	332,535.3	11.30%
C4+EC(10,1)	261,698.0	302,020.5	10.51%
C4+EC(10,5)	260,345.3	313,030.5	10.37%
C4+EC(10,10)	263,572.3	439,862.0	10.88%
C4+EC(10,15)	262,983.8	311,830.8	10.84%
C4+EC (10,20)	261,869.8	452.744.8	10.91%

Table 3. Hill climbing post-processing in the improvement method

iter_Hc	Best	Worst	Dev. Best	Time
0	261,538.5	434,911.3	10.12%	505.8
$|V|/20$	255,043.3	288,956.0	10.02%	502.0
$|V|/15$	254,594.5	298,544.3	9.64%	504.8
$|V|/10$	255,680.8	285,602.0	10.47%	508.5
$|V|/5$	253,935.5	284,989.3	9.96%	505.3

Table 3 clearly shows that the application of the HC post-processing in the EC improvement method presents a marginal improvement in the final quality of the solution. Specifically, the application of the Hill climbing method for n/15 iterations reduces the average percentage deviation from 10.12% to 9.64% consuming the same running time. In the reminder of our experimentation we select the constructive method C4 and the improvement method EC(10,5) with the post-processing HC.

In the third preliminary experiment we test the effect of the filter mechanism described in Section 7 to skip the improvement method when the value of the construction recommends it. During the first 20 constructions the method stores the fractional improvement achieved with the local search procedure EC. Then, when a solution is constructed, it computes its minimum fractional improvement *imp* that is necessary to improve the best solution known so far. If $imp < \hat{\mu}_P + \delta\hat{\sigma}_P$ we apply the improvement method; otherwise it is skipped, where $\hat{\mu}_P$ and $\hat{\sigma}_P$ are the average and the standard deviation estimations of the percentage improvement. The parameter δ controls the number of standard deviations away from the estimated mean percentage improvement. To measure the effectiveness of this strategy and the best choice of δ, we populate the *RefSet* with 100 solutions and apply this filter from iteration 21 to 100. Table 4 reports the average, across the instances in the preliminary experimentation, of the number of iterations in which the test recommends not applying the improvement, Skip, the average percentage deviation from the best known solution, Dev. Best and the average running time of the methods, Time.

Table 4 shows that as δ decreases the number of skipped improvement iterations increases. This is to be expected by definition of δ. However, the average percentage deviation from the best solution known, Dev. Best, does not present significant changes across different values of δ, thus indicating the robustness of the filter (i.e. solutions skipped for improvement hardly modify the final result). The best value for δ is 0.5, since it provides

Table 4. Filtering solutions

δ	# Skip	Dev. Best	Time
0.5	51.7	10.51%	292.0
1	37.5	10.40%	550.2
1.5	30.0	10.90%	485.2
2	25.7	10.86%	485.7

a saving in the CPU time without a significant deterioration of the quality of the final solution.

In our final preliminary experiment we test the path relinking (PR) algorithm to measure the contribution of the combination method within our scatter search procedure. We populate the *RefSet* with the solutions obtained by applying our GRASP algorithm for 100 iterations. We then apply the PR to all the pairs in *RefSet* and report the best solution found. As described in Section 8, we apply the improvement method (EC(10,5)+HC) to some of the solutions in the paths. In particular, it is applied *pr* times in each path. Table 5 reports the statistics Best, Dev. Best and Time of the SS+PR algorithm with different values of the *pr* parameter.

Results in Table 5 show that as *pr* increases, the SS+PR algorithm is able to marginally improve the quality of the final solution. However, as expected, running times also increase since, as we have already mentioned, the application of the improvement method is time-consuming. We set *pr*=15 because it represents a good balance between solution quality and speed.

In the final experiment we compare our SS+PR algorithm with the best published methods: the McAllister constructive method C1 coupled with the Hill-climbing algorithm HC (Petit, 2003a), C1+HC, the simulated annealing SAN (Petit, 2003) and the two stage simulated annealing TSSA (Rodriguez-Tello et al., 2008). Table 6 shows the results in the 21 Petit instances. We run these methods once on each instance (with the exception of C1+HC that, considering its simplicity, is executed

1000 times) with their parameters adjusted to run for about 1000 seconds of CPU time.

Table 6 is split into two parts. In the upper part we can find the results of each algorithm on each particular instance in the Petit set. Specifically, we report the value of the best solution found, Value, and the percentage deviation, Dev., between Value and the value of the best solution found with the four methods under consideration. In the lower part of Table 6 we report the average running time of each method across the 21 instances, Avg. Time, as well as the average percentage deviation, Avg. Dev., and the number of best solutions, #Best that each method is able to obtain.

Table 6 shows that C4+HC and SAN are clearly inferior to the other two methods considered in this comparison, since they obtain an average percentage deviation from the best known solution of 49.89 and 55.17 respectively. Our SS+PR method obtains the greatest number of best solutions found by any of the methods, 11, followed by the TSSA method which obtains 9 best solutions. SS+PR and TSSA obtain an average percentage deviation of 3.03 and 2.97 respectively. It should be noted that our SS+PR algorithm presents a running time of 529.14 seconds on average, which compares favorably with the 870.57 seconds of TSSA. Moreover, TSSA would demand more than four hours of CPU time in some instances if we adjusted its parameters as in Rodriguez-Tello et al. (2008), although the average percentage deviation from employing such lengthy runs would be reduced to 0.05.

Table 5. Scatter search with path relinking (SS+PR)

pr	best	Dev. Best	Time
5	254,964.5	9.59%	824.5
10	253,773.5	8.51%	1,041.7
15	253,516.5	8.00%	1,268.0
20	252,476.5	8.04%	1,521.7

Table 6. Comparison of best methods

	SS+PR		C4+HC		SAN		TSSA	
	Value	Dev.	Value	Dev.	Value	Dev.	Value	Dev.
randomA1	914882	2.31	950394	6.28	894205	0.00	948868	6.11
randomA2	6572444	0.00	6708192	2.07	6596880	0.37	6625307	0.80
randomA3	14336736	0.00	14463797	0.89	14346700	0.07	14441751	0.73
randomA4	1779181	1.17	1824564	3.75	1758560	0.00	1816732	3.31
randomG4	179138	0.00	206123	15.06	299571	67.23	185912	3.78
bintree10	4267	0.00	13951	226.95	14247	233.89	4440	4.05
hc10	523776	0.00	538116	2.74	540512	3.20	523776	0.00
mesh33x33	32703	0.00	35509	8.58	38481	17.67	33464	2.33
3elt	431737	0.00	1369880	217.30	867560	100.95	509337	17.9
airfoil1	322611	0.00	867560	168.92	1369880	324.62	392989	21.8
whitaker3	1307540	0.00	4857190	271.48	4857190	271.48	1313857	0.48
c1y	65084	4.23	70896	13.54	73867	18.30	62441	0.00
c2y	82665	4.38	89029	12.41	89029	12.41	79199	0.00
c3y	136103	9.66	144902	16.75	163785	31.96	124117	0.00
c4y	125720	9.19	146651	27.36	146651	27.36	115144	0.00
c5y	109279	12.71	122652	26.51	123891	27.79	96952	0.00
gd95c	506	0.00	529	4.55	506	0.00	507	0.20
gd96a	114377	18.83	107945	12.15	111144	15.47	96253	0.00
gd96b	1421	0.35	1527	7.84	1483	4.73	1416	0.00
gd96c	519	0.00	531	2.31	519	0.00	523	0.77
gd96d	2414	0.84	2399	0.21	2421	1.13	2394	0.00
Avg. Time	529.14		552.90		1274.14		870.57	
Avg. Dev.	3.03%		49.89%		55.17%		2.97%	
#Best	11		0		4		9	

We finish our experimentation studying the contribution of the different SS elements in the evolution of the best solution. Specifically, Figure 7 depicts, for each SS iteration, the value of the best solution in the *RefSet* (Best RefSet), the value of the best solution obtained with the combination of the solutions in the *RefSet* (Best Comb), and the value of the best solution resulting from the application of the improvement method to the combined solutions (BestLS).

Figure 7 shows the contribution of the combination and improvement methods to the best solution found. This figure clearly shows that the solutions obtained by combination are not able to improve themselves the value of the best solution in the *RefSet*; however, they constitute good seeds for the application of the improvement method. This is especially true in iterations 1, 2 and 7 in which the application of the improvement method to the combined solutions is able to improve the best solution in the *RefSet*, thus generating a new best solution overall.

Figure 7. Evolution of the best SS solution

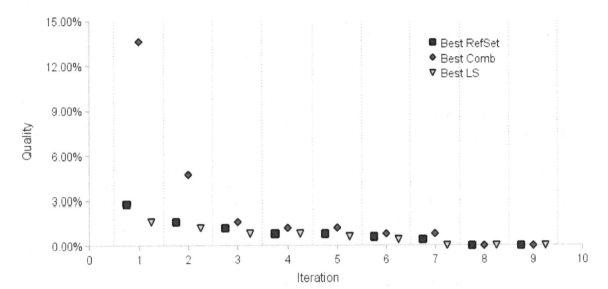

10. CONCLUSION

We have developed a heuristic procedure based on the SS methodology to illustrate how this methodology can be applied to an intensively studied problem in combinatorial optimization – the linear arrangement minimization problem. Although our development is tutorial in nature, our illustrative method nevertheless performs highly effectively compared to the leading methods in the literature.

Overall experiments with previously reported instances were performed to first identify the contribution of the different elements in our procedure and then to compare the outcomes with those of previous methods. Our preliminary experiments illustrate the merit of the proposed mechanisms, such as the use of ejection chains (Section 6), the filter of low quality constructions (Section 7) and the selection of diverse solutions for Path Relinking (Section 8), that we hope other researchers might find useful in different combinatorial optimization problems. The efficacy of the resulting scatter search with path relinking implementation is demonstrated by surpassing the best procedures in the literature in the number of best solutions obtained when solving the problem within moderate running times (1000 seconds on medium sized instances). An immediate opportunity for obtaining still better results may be noted to arise by employing a self-adjusting mechanism for choosing parameter values, rather than relying on fixed values that represent a compromise between competing considerations. To carry the basic foundations of this work further, a sequel will examine more finely tuned versions of the illustrated strategies, and additionally focus on longer term strategies, thus exposing options for obtaining improved solutions when time limits are made substantially longer.

ACKNOWLEDGMENT

This research has been partially supported by the *Ministerio de Ciencia e Innovación* of Spain (TIN2009-07516). The authors thank professors Rodriguez-Tello, Hao and Torres-Jimenez for sharing their results.

REFERENCES

Adolphson, D., & Hu, T. C. (1973). Optimal linear ordering. *SIAM Journal on Applied Mathematics*, *25*(3), 403–423. doi:10.1137/0125042

Garey, M. R., & Johnson, D. S. (1979). *Computers and intractability: A guide to the theory of completeness*. New York, NY: W. H. Freeman and Company.

Glover, F. (1977). Heuristics for integer programming using surrogate constraints. *Decision Sciences*, *8*, 156–166. doi:10.1111/j.1540-5915.1977.tb01074.x

Glover, F. (1982). *Ejection chains, reference structures and alternating path methods*. Boulder, CO: University of Colorado.

Glover, F. (1989). Tabu search - Part I. *ORSA Journal on Computing*, *1*(3) 190-206.

Glover, F. (1996). Ejection chains, reference structures and alternating path methods for traveling salesman problems. *Discrete Applied Mathematics*, *65*(1-3), 223–253. doi:10.1016/0166-218X(94)00037-E

Glover, F. (1997). A template for scatter search and path relinking. In J.-K. Hao, E. Lutton, E. Ronald, M. Schoenauer, & D. Snyers (Eds.), *Proceedings of the Conference on Artificial Evolution* (LNCS 1363, pp. 13-54).

Glover, F., & Laguna, M. (1993). Tabu search. In Reeves, C. (Ed.), *Modern heuristic techniques for combinatorial problems* (pp. 71–140). Oxford, UK: Blackwell Scientific.

Glover, F., & Laguna, M. (1997). *Tabu search*. Boston, MA: Kluwer Academic.

Harper, L. H. (1964). Optimal assignment of numbers to vertices. *SIAM Journal on Applied Mathematics*, *12*(1), 131–135. doi:10.1137/0112012

Juvan, M., & Mohar, B. (1992). Optimal linear labelings and eigenvalues of graphs. *Discrete Applied Mathematics*, *36*(2), 153–168. doi:10.1016/0166-218X(92)90229-4

Kennedy, J., & Eberhart, R. C. (1995). Particle swarm optimization. In. *Proceedings of the IEEE International Conference on Neural Networks*, *4*, 1942–1948. doi:10.1109/ICNN.1995.488968

Kirkpatrick, S., Gelatt, C., & Vecchi, M. (1983). Optimization by simulated annealing. *Science*, *220*, 671–680. doi:10.1126/science.220.4598.671

Laguna, M., & Martí, R. (1999). GRASP and path relinking for 2-layer straight line crossing minimization. *INFORMS Journal on Computing*, *11*(1), 44–52. doi:10.1287/ijoc.11.1.44

Laguna, M., & Martí, R. (2003). *Scatter search: Methodology and implementations in C*. Boston, MA: Kluwer Academic.

Martí, R. (Ed.). (2006). Feature cluster on scatter search methods for optimization. *European Journal of Operational Research*, *169*(2), 351–698. doi:10.1016/j.ejor.2004.08.003

Martí, R., Laguna, M., Glover, F., & Campos, V. (2001). Reducing the bandwidth of a sparse matrix with tabu search. *European Journal of Operational Research*, *135*(2), 211–220. doi:10.1016/S0377-2217(00)00325-8

McAllister, A. J. (1999). *A new heuristic algorithm for the linear arrangement problem* (Tech. Rep. No. TR-99-126a). New Brunswick, CA: University of New Brunswick.

Petit, J. (2003a). Combining spectral sequencing and parallel simulated annealing for the MinLA problem. *Parallel Processing Letters*, *13*(1), 71–91. doi:10.1142/S0129626403001161

Petit, J. (2003b). Experiments on the minimum linear arrangement problem. *ACM Journal of Experimental Algorithmics, 8*.

Piñana, E., Plana, I., Campos, V., & Martí, R. (2004). GRASP and path relinking for the matrix bandwidth minimization. *European Journal of Operational Research, 153*, 200–210. doi:10.1016/S0377-2217(02)00715-4

Resende, M. G. C., & Ribeiro, C. C. (2003). Greedy randomized adaptive search procedures. In Glover, F., & Kochenberger, G. A. (Eds.), *Handbook of metaheuristic* (pp. 219–249). Boston, MA: Kluwer Academic.

Resende, M. G. C., Ribeiro, C. C., Glover, F., & Martí, R. (2010). Scatter search and path-relinking: Fundamentals, advances, and applications. In Gendreau, M., & Potvin, J. Y. (Eds.), *Handbook of metaheuristics* (2nd ed., pp. 87–108). Boston, MA: Kluwer Academic. doi:10.1007/978-1-4419-1665-5_4

Rodriguez-Tello, E., Hao, J., & Torres-Jimenez, J. (2008). An effective two-stage simulated annealing algorithm for the minimum linear arrangement problem. *Computers & Operations Research, 35*(10), 3331–3346. doi:10.1016/j.cor.2007.03.001

ENDNOTES

[1] In the case where a vertex has an even number of adjacent neighbors, so that the labels of two of these neighbors could be considered candidates for a median, then selecting any value between and including the two candidates will minimize the sum of the absolute values of the differences. This property is not restricted to label values that are positive integers, but holds for any finite collection of real valued labels.

This work was previously published in the International Journal of Swarm Intelligence Research, Volume 2, Issue 2, edited by Yuhui Shi, pp. 1-21, copyright 2011 by IGI Publishing (an imprint of IGI Global).

Chapter 2
A Complementary Cyber Swarm Algorithm

Peng-Yeng Yin
National Chi Nan University, Taiwan

Fred Glover
OptTek Systems, Inc., USA

Manuel Laguna
University of Colorado, USA

Jia-Xian Zhu
National Chi Nan University, Taiwan

ABSTRACT

A recent study (Yin et al., 2010) showed that combining particle swarm optimization (PSO) with the strategies of scatter search (SS) and path relinking (PR) produces a Cyber Swarm Algorithm that creates a more effective form of PSO than methods that do not incorporate such mechanisms. This paper proposes a Complementary Cyber Swarm Algorithm (C/CyberSA) that performs in the same league as the original Cyber Swarm Algorithm but adopts different sets of ideas from the tabu search (TS) and the SS/PR template. The C/CyberSA exploits the guidance information and restriction information produced in the history of swarm search and the manipulation of adaptive memory. Responsive strategies using long term memory and path relinking implementations are proposed that make use of critical events encountered in the search. Experimental results with a large set of challenging test functions show that the C/CyberSA outperforms two recently proposed swarm-based methods by finding more optimal solutions while simultaneously using a smaller number of function evaluations. The C/CyberSA approach further produces improvements comparable to those obtained by the original CyberSA in relation to the Standard PSO 2007 method (Clerc, 2008).

DOI: 10.4018/978-1-4666-2479-5.ch002

1. INTRODUCTION

Metaheuristics are master strategies that guide and modify slave heuristics to produce solutions beyond those that are normally generated for local optimality. Effective metaheuristics make a search plan of intensification and diversification to reach a good trade-off between solution quality and computational effort. Intensification exploits information about elite solutions that were previously found as a basis for focusing the search in regions anticipated to harbor additional solutions of high quality. Diversification promotes the exploration of regions appreciably different from those previously examined in order to produce new solutions with characteristics that depart from those already seen. Intensification and diversification work together to identify new promising regions when the slave heuristics stagnate in the executed search courses. Many intelligent algorithms fall in the territory of metaheuristics. Some exemplary algorithms (Luke, 2009) are genetic algorithms (GA), simulated annealing (SA), ant colony optimization (ACO), tabu search (TS), particle swarm optimization (PSO), scatter search (SS), greedy randomized adaptive search procedure (GRASP), variable neighborhood search (VNS), to name a few. A recent survey and descriptive analysis of metaheuristic algorithms can be found in Sorensen and Glover (2010).

Slave heuristics embedded in metaheuristic methods often adopt solution combination or neighborhood exploration processes to generate new solutions based on the current state of search. Solution combination approaches produce new solutions by exchanging information between candidate solutions (for example, crossover operation executed in GA) or by using candidate solutions as guiding points for producing new solutions (for example, by reference to the best experiences in PSO or the path relinking (PR) process used in SS). Alternatively, neighborhood exploration employs incremental changes, called moves, which progress from one solution to an-

other within local regions called neighborhoods that are considered relevant to the search (as by changing one or a small number of elements within a current solution). Sophisticated neighborhood concepts like ejection chains (Glover, 1996b; Rego & Glover, 2009) have been proposed for tackling a variety of complex problems and various types of multiple neighborhood strategies (Glover, 1996a; Mladenovic & Hansen, 1997; Sörensen, Sevaux, & Schittekat, 2008; Lu, Hao, & Glover, 2010) have been proposed for enriching the set of moves employed during the search. To avoid reversing the search course and prevent getting trapped in local optima, some solution attributes and move directions may be forbidden by means of tabu restrictions as proposed in tabu search, or multi-start mechanisms may be employed to initiate a new search thread in an uncharted region. There are other metaheuristic methods employing gradient-based or derivative-free supplementary procedures. The best of these methods are provided by Hedar and Fukushima (2006) and Duarte et al. (2007) for problems of moderate dimension, and by Hvattum and Glover (2009) and Vaz and Vicente (2007) for problems of large dimension. Duarte et al. (2011b) analyzes the performance of two path relinking variants: the static and the evolutionary path relinking. Both are based on the strategy of creating trajectories of moves passing through high quality solutions in order to incorporate their attributes to the explored solutions.

Methods that employ both solution combination and neighborhood exploration perform more effectively by carefully coordinating the slave heuristics with the master strategy employed. An illustration of this is provided, for example, by methods that integrate tabu search with classical direct search for global function optimization. Chelouah and Siarry (2005) proposed a continuous tabu simplex search (CTSS) method that uses the Nelder-Mead simplex algorithm to accelerate convergence towards a minimum within a detected promising region, while maintaining the tabu search (TS) restriction as a mechanism to search uncharted solution space. Hedar and Fukushima (2006) introduced a directed TS (DTS) method for non-linear global optimization which, instead of identifying promising regions before the application, immediately applies the Nelder-Mead method at every non-improving trial point obtained by the TS neighborhood search. A study of larger problems by Hvattum and Glover (2009) shows that the use of direct search methods different from the Nelder-Mead procedure can produce superior results.

Another approach (Nakano et al., 2007; Shen et al., 2008; Wang et al., 2007) akin to this research direction is the hybridization of PSO and TS. The TS processes for managing adaptive memory via responsive strategies enables PSO to implement intensification and diversification searches more effectively. On the one hand, the attribute values which produced high quality solutions in TS recency memory can be reserved for other particles in the future. On the other hand, less fit attribute values contained in the adaptive memory are designated as tabu-active and the particles are pulled away from these attribute values. The particle swarm and pattern search method (Vas and Vicente, 2007) referred to as PSwarm is a pattern search method incorporating particle swarm search as a step within its framework. In additional to the original mesh search, the particle swarm search can explore the nonconvexity of the objective function. More recently, Yin et al. (2010) introduced a Cyber Swarm Algorithm (CyberSA) as the marriage of PSO and the scatter search/path relinking (SS/PR) template that obtains improved outcomes. With the addition of an external memory, embodied in a reference set consisting of the best solutions observed throughout the evolution history, useful information is produced and maintained that is not attainable by relying on traditional PSO mechanisms involving particle experiences.

We propose a restricted variant of the CyberSA by strategically exploring special guidance and restriction information. The contributions of this work are: (1) the augmentation of the search capability of CyberSA by considering additional ideas from TS and SS/PR, (2) a multi-level (short term, middle term, and long term) memory manipulations designed to reinforce the search process, and (3) extensive performance evaluation of the proposed method with a large set of diverse benchmark functions.

The remainder of this paper is organized as follows. Section 2 presents a literature review of fundamental PSO methods relevant to our work. Section 3 proposes the Complementary Variant of the Cyber Swarm Algorithm and describes its salient features. Section 4 presents experimental results together with an analysis of their implications. Finally, concluding remarks and discussions are given in Section 5.

2. PSO LITERATURE REVIEW

The introduction of particle swarm optimization (PSO) has motivated many researchers to develop various swarm algorithms by drawing fruitful notions from other domains. These development efforts include two main types: the exploitation of guidance information and the hybridization with other intelligent search strategies.

2.1. Exploitation of Guidance Information

The PSO proposed by Kennedy and Eberhart (1995) has exhibited effectiveness and robustness in many applications, such as evolving artificial neural networks (Eberhart & Shi, 1998), reactive power and voltage control (Yoshida & Kawata, 1999), state estimation for electric power distribution systems (Shigenori et al., 2003), and image compression (Feng et al., 2007). PSO has drawn on a sociocognition model to gain recognition as a useful global optimizer. A swarm of particles is assumed to follow the social norm manifest of convergent behaviors. The social norm consists of quality experiences by comparing search trajectories of individual particles. This is an auto-catalytic process that the social norm influences the individual behaviors which in turn collectively improve the social norm.

The original version of PSO is quite simple. A swarm of particles iteratively update their positional vectors by reference to previous positions and two forms of the best trajectory experience, namely, the personal best (*pbest*) and the global best (*gbest*). The personal best is the best position that a particle has experienced, while the global best is the best position ever experienced by the particles in the swarm. Let the optimization problem be formulated with R decision variables and a particle $P_i = (p_{i1}, p_{i2}, ..., p_{iR})$ representing a candidate solution whose search trajectory is iteratively determined by adding a velocity vector $V_i = (v_{i1}, v_{i2}, ..., v_{iR})$ to its previous position. According to Clerc's Stagnation Analysis (Clerc & Kennedy, 2002), the convergence of the particles' trajectories is mathematically guaranteed by the following equations:

$$v_{ij} \leftarrow K \begin{pmatrix} v_{ij} + \varnothing_1 \mathrm{rand}_1 \left(pbest_{ij} - p_{ij} \right) \\ + \varnothing_2 \mathrm{rand}_2 \left(gbest_{ij} - p_{ij} \right) \end{pmatrix} \quad (1)$$

$$K = \frac{2}{\left| 2 - \left(\phi_1 + \phi_2 \right) - \sqrt{\left(\phi_1 + \phi_2 \right)^2 - 4 \left(\phi_1 + \phi_2 \right)} \right|}$$
$$\left(\text{with the constraint } \varnothing_1 + \varnothing_2 > 4 \right)$$
$$\quad (2)$$

$$p_{ij} \leftarrow p_{ij} + v_{ij} \quad (3)$$

where φ_1 and φ_2 are the cognitive coefficients, *rand₁* and *rand₂* are random real numbers drawn from $U(0, 1)$, and K is the constriction coefficient. In essence, the particle explores a potential region defined by *pbest* and *gbest*, while the cognitive coefficients and the random multipliers change the weightings for the two best solutions in every iteration.

As indicated by the term "small world" in sociology, two people indirectly share information via the social network. The speed on which the information spreads depends upon the structure of the social network. Kennedy (1999) has studied the effects of neighborhood topologies on particle swarm performance. The local best leader (*lbest*), the best position visited by any member in the neighborhood of a designated given particle, is used as a substitute for *gbest*. He found that the best neighborhood topology depends on the problem context. The Star topology (the *gbest* version where each particle is connected to all particles in the swarm) spreads the individual information throughout the swarm most quickly and can expedite the convergence of explored solutions in unimodal function optimization problems. However, the Ring topology (each particle is connected to exactly two other particles) can usually produce better solutions on multimodal functions than the Star topology because the former structure postpones the information transmission between two arbitrary particles and is more effective in avoiding being trapped in local optimality. The performance of other topologies, such as Wheel or Pyramid, varies from problem to problem.

Miranda et al. (2007) proposed a Stochastic Star topology where a particle is informed by *gbest* with a predefined probability *p*. Their experimental results showed that the Stochastic Star topology leads in many cases to better results than the original Star topology. The standard PSO 2007 (Clerc, 2008) regenerates a random permutation of particles before each iteration. Hence, the resulting neighborhood structure is in essence a random topology.

While most of the PSO algorithm variants conduct the swarm evolution using two particle leaders, Clerc's Stagnation Analysis (Clerc & Kennedy, 2002) does not limit consideration to two cognitive coefficients, but only requires that the parts sum to a value that is appropriate for the constriction coefficient K. Mendes et al. (2004) have proposed to combine all neighbors' information instead of only using *lbest*. Let Ω_i be the set of neighbors' indices of particle i and let ω_k be an estimate of the relevance of particle k as being an informant of particle i. Then the velocity can be updated by

$$v_{ij} \leftarrow K(v_{ij} + \varphi \, (mbest_{ij} - p_{ij})) \qquad (4)$$

and

$$mbest_{ij} = \frac{\sum_{k \in \Omega_i} \omega_k \phi_k pbest_{kj}}{\sum_{k \in \Omega_i} \omega_k \phi_k}$$

$$\phi = \sum_{k \in \Omega_i} \phi_k \qquad (5)$$

$$\phi_k \in U\left[0, \frac{\phi_{\max}}{|\Omega_i|}\right]$$

As all the neighbors contribute to the velocity update, the focal particle is fully informed.

The Cyber Swarm Algorithm (CyberSA), which has produced better results than the standard PSO 2007 method, uses three leaders in the velocity adjustment and extends the neighborhood topology by additionally including the reference set construction of the SS/PR template. The reference set is not restricted simply to neighbors, but consists of the best solutions observed throughout the evolution history. The CyberSA reinstates *pbest* and *gbest* in the group of leaders and systematically selects each member from the reference set as the third leader. Additional details of this method are discussed subsequently.

2.2. Hybridization with Outsource Strategies

Researchers have proposed that PSO may be extended by taking into account useful strategies from other methodologies. The obvious advantage of hybridizing PSO is the potential for enhancing the intensification/diversification synergy and improving the regions selected to be explored in the course of the search. Often, hybrid algorithms exhibit better performance when solving complex problems, such as the optimization of difficult multimodal functions. These mechanisms are mainly found within the framework of evolutionary algorithms and adaptive memory programming concepts derived from tabu search.

In the hybrid algorithm proposed by Angeline (1999) particles with low fitness are replaced by those with high fitness using natural selection while these particles preserve their original best experience. This approach is reported to facilitate the exploration of highly promising regions while maintaining experience diversity. Lovbjerg et al. (2001) implement a hybrid approach by inserting a breeding (recombination) step after the movement of all particles. Particles are selected with equal probability to become parents and in turn are replaced by offspring that are generated using the arithmetic crossover operator. In order to keep diversity in the gene pool, particles are divided into subpopulations and the breeding is allowed both within a given subpopulation and between different subpopulations.

A hybridization of generalized pattern search (Audet & Dennis, 2003) with PSO is proposed by Vas and Vicente (2007) to produce the PSwarm algorithm that consists of alternating iterations of search and poll steps. The search enforces a step of particle swarm search (and expands the mesh size parameter) if such a step causes the individual bests of the particles to improve. Otherwise, the poll step is activated, consisting of applying one step of local pattern search (along the canonical mesh) on the best particle of the entire swarm. The mesh size parameter is either expanded or contracted according to whether the pattern search improves the best particle. PSwarm has been shown to outperform several optimizers on an experiment over a set of 122 benchmark functions.

A number of effective hybrids have been produced by incorporating various elements of tabu search. Nakano et al. (2007) divide the particles into two sub-swarms that play the roles of intensification and diversification, respectively. When an attribute value in the global best solution is not updated for a number of iterations, the attribute value is designated as tabu. The particles from the intensification sub-swarm fix the attribute values as specified by the tabu restrictions and contained in the global best solution, while the particles in the diversification sub-swarm are encouraged to pull away from solutions containing the tabu attributes. Shen et al. (2008) propose an approach called HPSOTS which enables the PSO to leap over local optima by restraining the particle movement based on the use of tabu conditions. Wang et al. (2007) enhances the diversification capability of PSO by setting the less fit attributes contained in the global best solution as tabu-active and repelling the particles from the tabu area.

The Cyber Swarm Algorithm (CyberSA) of Yin et al. (2010) creates an enhanced form of swarm algorithms by incorporating three features: (1) augmenting the information sharing among particles by learning from the reference set members, (2) systematically generating dynamic social networks in order to choose various solutions as the leaders such that the search can adapt to different functional landscape, and (3) executing diversification strategies based on path relinking approaches as a response to the status of the adaptive memory. The success of this method has motivated us to examine another variant that draws on alternative ideas from the same sources.

3. COMPLEMENTARY VARIANT OF CYBER SWARM ALGORITHM

As disclosed in the literature discussed in Section 2, the performance of PSO can be improved by exploiting the guidance information and hybridizing the method with outsource strategies. Following this theme, the CyberSA creates an effective form of PSO by carefully selecting leading solutions and embedding scatter search/path relinking (SS/PR) strategies. The Complementary Cyber Swarm Algorithm (C/CyberSA) proposed here uses different sets of ideas from the adaptive memory programming perspective of tabu search and scatter search. As we show, the C/CyberSA can produce improvements comparable to those obtained by the original CyberSA in relation to those PSO methods that do not incorporate adaptive memory programming ideas.

3.1. Using Guidance Information

As previously noted, the choice of neighborhood topologies and leading solutions significantly affects the particle swarm performance. The literature discloses that the use of a dynamic neighborhood (Miranda et al., 2007; Clerc, 2008; Yin et al., 2010) and the local best solution *lbest* (Kennedy, 1999; Clerc, 2008) leads to a better performance. These notions create a form of multiple neighborhood search in which the neighboring particles (each maintaining a search trajectory) are selected at random or systematically and the local optimum corresponds to the best solution encountered by the multiple search trajectories.

Our proposed C/CyberSA method generates a random permutation of particles on a Ring topology before performing each iteration, so the neighboring particles are very likely different from those assigned at previous iterations. The three leaders, the local best solution (*lbest*) observed by the neighboring particles, the overall best solution (*gbest*) found by the entire swarm, and the individual best experience (*pbest*) for the operating particle, are used as the guiding solutions. More precisely, the C/CyberSA uses the velocity updating formula for the *i*th particle shown in Box 1. The weight ω_i is selected to be the same for each of the three guiding solutions.

The advantage of using three guiding solutions has been empirically verified in several relevant studies. For example, Campos et al. (2001) found that in scatter search most of the high quality solutions come from combinations using at most 3 reference solutions. Mendes et al. (2004) have also more recently found that their FIPS algorithm (which treats the previous bests of all neighbors as guiding solutions) performs best when a neighborhood size of 2 to 4 neighbors is used, and increasing the neighborhood size causes the overall performance to deteriorate. The CyberSA method also achieves particularly good outcomes when using three strategically selected guiding solutions.

3.2. Using Restriction Information

The adaptive memory programming perspective of tabu search provides a fruitful basis for generating incentives and restrictions to guide the search towards more promising regions. The central idea is to compare previous states (e.g., selected solution attributes) stored in the adaptive memory to those states of new candidate solutions currently contemplated.

Our C/CyberSA approach uses multiple levels of adaptive memory to exploit the benefits of restriction information. Three categories of adaptive memory are employed: (1) a short-term memory (STM) that records the solutions visited by individual particles within a short span of recent

history; (2) a middle-term memory (MTM) that tallies the solutions that pass a certain acceptance threshold dynamically changed according to the current state; and (3) a long-term memory (LTM) that tracks the frequency or duration of critical events and activates appropriate reactions. Immediately following, we present the implementation for STM and MTM, and the description for LTM is given in Subsection 3.3.

In PSO, a swarm of particles construct their individual search courses to accumulate rewarded experiences and there is no additional value in allowing particles to be transformed into recent previous solutions. We therefore use STM to prevent individual particles from reversing recent moves as they undergo the transformation to produce new particles. The notion of a "tabu ball" proposed by Chelouah and Siarry (2000) is adopted in our implementation. When a particle is replaced by a new solution based on Equation 6, the solution is designated as tabu-active with a tabu tenure. A tabu ball centered at this solution with radius r is created and prohibits the acceptance of new solutions produced inside this ball during its tabu tenure. Let the set of centers of currently STM active tabu balls be $\pi_{STM} = \{s_1, s_2, ..., s_T\}$, a new solution s' is rejected (tabu) if it is contained within any of the tabu balls, i.e., $\|s' - s_i\| \leq r, \forall s_i \in \pi_{STM}$, where $\|\cdot\|$ denotes the Euclidean norm (additional ways to generate "tabu regions" along with the possibility to use other distance norms are proposed in Glover, 1994). However, the tabu restriction can be overruled if s' meets some aspiration criterion. The *Aspiration_by_objective* rule stipulates that a tabu solution s' can be accepted if its objective value is

Box 1. Velocity updating formula

$$v_{ij} \leftarrow K\left(v_{ij} + (\phi_1 + \phi_2 + \phi_3)\left(\frac{\omega_1\phi_1 pbest_{ij} + \omega_2\phi_2 lbest_{ij} + \omega_3\phi_3 gbest_j}{\omega_1\phi_1 + \omega_2\phi_2 + \omega_3\phi_3} - p_{ij}\right)\right) \tag{6}$$

better than that of the overall best solution. To introduce a form of vigor into the search that accommodates varying widths of local minima, the tabu tenure of a tabu ball is determined dynamically and drawn randomly from a pre-specified range, motivated by the fact that a dynamic tabu tenure typically performs better than a constant tabu tenure in TS implementations. To finely tune the size of the tabu ball in accordance with different phases of the search, the ball radius r is reduced by a ratio β upon the detection of stagnation as noted in the next subsection.

For the implementation of tabu restrictions with MTM, we prevent a particle from updating its personal best (*pbest*) if the candidate solution is too close to the recent best of any particle. Again, a tabu ball is created for a newly produced *pbest* solution and the update of *pbest* is prohibited for any particle inside this tabu ball during its tabu tenure. Denote the set of centers of currently MTM active tabu balls by π_{MTM}. The MTM incorporates the same rules for the aspiration criterion, dynamic tabu tenure, and tabu ball radius reduction as enforced in the STM mechanism.

We do not impose a tabu restriction on the update of the overall best (*gbest*) because it is always beneficial to obtain a better overall best solution during the search (and such a solution automatically satisfies the aspiration criterion in any case).

3.3. Responsive Strategies

Longer term strategies responding to detections of critical changes in LTM are invoked when a short term strategy has lost its search efficacy. Successful applications of this principle have been seen in both static and dynamic optimization problems (James et al., 2009; Lepagnot et al., 2010), reinforcing the supposition that promising solutions having features differing from those previously seen are likely to be obtained by using longer term strategies.

One of the effective longer term strategies is path relinking (PR). (For recent surveys, see Ho & Gendreau, 2006; Rego & Glover, 2008.) PR is a search process which constructs a link between two or more strategically selected solutions. The construction starts with one solution (called the initiating solution) and moves to or beyond a second solution (referred to as the guiding solution). PR transforms the initiating solution into the guiding solution by generating moves that successively replace an attribute of the initiating solution that is contained in the guiding solution. The link can be constructed in both directions by interchanging the roles of the initiating and guiding solutions, or can proceed from both ends toward the middle.

PR can emphasize either intensification or diversification. For example, intensification strategies may choose reference solutions to be the best solutions encountered in a common region while diversification strategies can select reference solutions that lie within different regions. Reference solutions are selected according to their status in the LTM and the appropriate PR strategies are triggered upon the detections of critical events. We propose two responsive PR strategies and the corresponding triggering critical events in the following.

1. **Diversification PR Strategy – Particle Restarting:** The C/CyberSA manages multiple particle search threads exploring promising regions in the solution space. The identified promising regions are located by using *pbest* which in turn is used to identify the particles to exploit these regions. A critical event arises when *pbest* has not improved for t_2 successive search iterations. This indicates the region has been over-exploited and the corresponding particle should be repositioned in an uncharted region to start a new round of search. In light of this, PR can focus on identifying new promising regions. We do this by selecting two reference solu-

tions from two under-exploited regions, using the biased random approach proposed in the original CyberSA method. This approach generates a biased-random solution which is likely to be in a position at a maximal distance from all previous trial solutions. Let the two reference solutions be $RandSol_1$ and $RandSol_2$, respectively. The diversification PR strategy is triggered by the critical event to construct a link $PR(RandSol_1, RandSol_2)$ between the two reference solutions. The best solution observed over the constructed link is designated as the initiating particle for restarting a new search thread. It is noted that although the particle has been repositioned, the content of the adaptive memory (such as *pbest*, *gbest*, tabu list, tabu tenure, and tabu ball radius) is retained.

The diversification PR strategy not only diversifies the search (by creating a new thread that has not been targeted before) but also tunnels through different regions that have contrasting features. This strategy is designed based on the anticipation that the solutions with fruitful information for the current search state are those contained in uncharted regions or near the boundaries between regions having contrasting features.

2 **Intensification PR Strategy – Swarm Shrinking:** The other critical event is the detection of swarm stagnation. This happens when the distributed particles have exhausted their search efficacy and the swarm overall best solution *gbest* has not improved for t_1 successive search iterations. We propose an intensification PR strategy named swarm shrinking which regenerates a new swarm within the neighborhood proximity of *gbest* to replace the original population of particles in order to intensify the search in the overall best region. Each particle in the new swarm is generated by applying a truncated PR process, Truncated_PR($gbest, RandSol_1$), using *gbest* as the initiating solution and, again,

employing a solution $RandSol_1$ produced by the biased random approach as the guiding solution. The truncated PR process starting with the initiating solution performs a few moves and only constructs a partial link. In our implementation, we terminate the link construction when one tenth of the number of attributes in *gbest* have been replaced (at least one attribute has been replaced if *gbest* has less than 10 attributes). The best solution observed on the partial link is used to replace the original particle.

In the process of swarm shrinking, all the elements excluding the tabu ball radius in the adaptive memory hold their original values. The length of the tabu ball radius is halved to facilitate a finer search with the shrunken swarm.

3.4. C/CyberSA Pseudo Code

The C/CyberSA design is elaborated in the pseudo codes shown in Figure 1. The three important features (guidance information, restriction information, and responsive strategies) of the C/CyberSA are in boldface to emphasize these features within the algorithm. In the initialization phase (Step 1) the initial values for particle positions and velocities and the values for the elements (*pbest*, *gbest*, tabu ball radius, etc.) stored in the adaptive memory are given. In the main-loop iterations (Step 2), the swarm conducts its search using these three components. To generate a dynamic neighborhood, the particles are randomly arranged on a Ring topology. Each particle moves with the guidance information provided by $pbest_i$, $lbest_i$ and *gbest* (Step 2.2.1). However, any movement leading into a tabu ball stored in STM is prohibited (Step 2.2.3). The individual $pbest_i$ is updated if a better solution is produced by the movement which is not tabu by the MTM restriction (Step 2.2.4). Finally, as shown in Step 2.4, the intensification PR strategy is executed if *gbest* has not improved for a number of standing

Figure 1. Pseudo codes for the Complementary Cyber Swarm Algorithm (C/CyberSA)

1 Initialize.
   1.1   Generate N particle solutions, $P_i = (p_{i1}, p_{i2}, ..., p_{iR})$, $1 \leq i \leq N$, at random.
   1.2   Generate N velocity vectors, $V_i = (v_{i1}, v_{i2}, ..., v_{iR})$, $1 \leq i \leq N$, at random.
   1.3   Evaluate the fitness of each particle *fitness*(P_i), and set previous best solution *pbest*$_i$ to P_i. Determine the overall best solution *gbest* as the best among all *pbest*$_i$.
   1.4   Set initial tabu ball radius r
2 Repeat until a stopping criterion is met.
   2.1   Generate a random permutation of particles on a Ring topology to determine local bests *lbest*$_i$, $\forall i = 1, ..., N$.
   2.2   For each particle P_i, $\forall i = 1, ..., N$, Do
   2.2.1 **Guidance:** Compute the velocity using the three strategically selected guiding solutions.

$$v_{ij} \leftarrow K\left(v_{ij} + (\varphi_1 + \varphi_2 + \varphi_3)\left(\frac{\omega_1\varphi_1 pbest_{ij} + \omega_2\varphi_2 lbest_{ij} + \omega_3\varphi_3 gbest_j}{\omega_1\varphi_1 + \omega_2\varphi_2 + \omega_3\varphi_3} - p_{ij}\right)\right)$$

   2.2.2 Compute the tentative movement $P_i' = P_i + V_i$.
   2.2.3 **STM restriction:** If $\|P_i' - s_i\| \leq r, \forall s_i \in \pi_{STM}$ and P_i' does not satisfy the aspiration criterion, goto Step 2.2.1.
   2.2.4 **MTM restriction:** If P_i' is better than *pbest*$_i$ and $\|P_i' - s_i\| > r, \forall s_i \in \pi_{MTM}$, or P_i' satisfies the aspiration criterion,
           $pbest_i \leftarrow P_i'$
   2.3   Determine the overall best solution *gbest* as the best among all *pbest*$_i$, $\forall i = 1, ..., N$.
   2.4   **Intensification PR strategy (swarm shrinking):** If *gbest* has not improved for t_1 iterations, reinitiate all particles and halve the tabu ball radius by
           $P_i \leftarrow \text{Truncated\_PR}(gbest, RandSol_1), \forall i = 1, ..., N$
           $r \leftarrow 0.5r$
           Diversification PR strategy (particle restarting): Else if a particular *pbest*$_i$ has not improved for t_2 iterations, replace its particle by
           $P_i \leftarrow PR(RandSol_1, RandSol_2)$

iterations. Otherwise, the diversification strategy is performed if a particular *pbest*$_i$ stagnates during the attempted improvement process.

4. EXPERIMENTAL RESULTS AND ANALYSIS

We have conducted extensive experiments to evaluate the performance of the C/CyberSA. The experimental results disclose several interesting outcomes in addition to establishing the effectiveness of the proposed method. The platform for conducting the experiments is a PC with a 1.8 GHz CPU and 1.0 GB RAM. All programs are coded in C++ language.

4.1. Performance Measures and Competing Algorithms

We measure the performance of competing algorithms in terms of effectiveness and efficiency. Effectiveness measures how close the quality of the obtained solution is to that of the optimal solution while efficiency assesses how fast a given algorithm can obtain a solution with a target quality.

The effectiveness measure is gauged by reference to the best objective value obtained by a competing algorithm that has been allowed to consume a maximum number of function evaluations equal to 160,000. (We selected this number because we observed the competing algorithms converge for most of the test functions after performing 160,000 evaluations.) When comparing the effectiveness of a target algorithm against a reference algorithm, a relative measure called merit is often used and defined as merit $= (f_p - f^* + \varepsilon)/(f_q - f^* + \varepsilon)$, where f_p and f_q are the mean best objective value obtained by the target algorithm and the reference algorithm, respectively, f^* is the known global optimum of the test function, and ε is a small constant equal to 5×10^{-7}. Without loss of generality, we consider all the test functions to involve minimization, and stipulate that the target algorithm outperforms the reference algorithm if the value of merit is less than 1.0 (where smaller values represent greater differences in favor of the target algorithm.)

We employ the policy widely adopted in the literature of representing the efficiency measure as the mean number of function evaluations required by a given algorithm in order to obtain an objective value that is sufficiently close to the known global optimum by reference to a specified gap.

Yin et al. (2010) have shown the advantages of the original CyberSA by comparing it with several other metaheuristics such as the Standard PSO 2007 (Clerc, 2008), C-GRASP (Hirsch et al., 2007), Direct Tabu Search, (Hedar & Fukushima, 2006), Scatter Search (Laguna & Marti, 2005), and Hybrid Scatter Tabu Search (Duarte et al., 2011a). In our present comparison we also include the PSwarm algorithm of Vaz and Vicente (2007), which embeds the swarm algorithm into the pattern search framework.

The parameter values used by the C/CyberSA have been determined based on preliminary experiments with a variety of test values, which led us to select the following settings. The size of the swarm is set to consist of 40 particles. At most five trial particles are produced by each "particle move" operation. The first non-tabu trial particle is accepted to be the next position of the focal particle, and the new position is marked as tabu with a dynamic tenure drawing a random value from the range [5, 15]. If all the five trial particles are tabu, the default aspiration chooses the one with the shortest tabu tenure to be released and

accessed. The radius of the tabu ball is initialized to one percent of the mean range of variable values. The responsive longer term strategies (swarm shrinking and particle restarting) are executed when critical events are observed with the parameter settings of $t_1 = 100$ and $t_2 = 200$. As for the other competing algorithms, the parameter values are set to the suggested values according to their original papers.

4.2. Performance

4.2.1. Experiment 1

Our first experiment evaluates the effectiveness of the C/CyberSA with a set of 30 test functions that are widely used in the literature (Laguna & Marti, 2003; Hedar & Fukushima, 2006; Hirsch et al., 2007; Yin et al., 2010). All these functions are continuous and together they present a wide variety of different landscapes. A hundred repetitive runs are executed for each of the three methods compared: the Standard PSO 2007, CyberSA, and C/CyberSA. Each run of a given algorithm is terminated when 160,000 function evaluations have been exhausted and the best function value obtained is considered as the outcome of this run.

The mean best function value over the 100 independent runs and the merit value relative to the mean best result of the Standard PSO 2007 are shown in Table 1. The numerical values in the parentheses correspond to the standard deviation of the best function values over the 100 repetitions. We observe that, except for the simple functions where all competing algorithms can obtain the global optimum, CyberSA is more effective than the Standard PSO 2007 by being able to obtain a lower mean best function value for the test functions. The product of the merit values for the CyberSA is equal to 1.15E-36. The best function value reported by the CyberSA is significantly closer to the global optimum than that obtained by the Standard PSO 2007.

Table 1. Mean best function value with standard deviation and the merit value for the competing algorithms

R	Test Function	Standard PSO 2007	CyberSA	CyberSA Merit	C/CyberSA	C/CyberSA Merit
2	Easom	-0.9999 (0.0000)	-1.0000 (0.0000)	0.3333	-1.0000(0.0000)	0.33333
2	Shubert	-186.7202 (0.0071)	-186.7309 (0.0000)	4.67 E-5	-186.7309(0.0000)	4.67E-5
2	Branin	0.3979 (0.0000)	0.3979 (0.0000)	1.0000	0.3979 (0.0000)	1.0000
2	Goldstein-Price	3.0001 (0.0001)	3.0000 (0.0000)	0.0050	3.0000 (0.0000)	0.0050
2	Rosenbrock(2)	0.0000 (0.0000)	0.0000 (0.0000)	1.0000	0.0000(0.0000)	1.0000
2	Zakharov(2)	0.0000 (0.0000)	0.0000 (0.0000)	1.0000	0.0000(0.0000)	1.0000
3	De Jong	0.0000 (0.0000)	0.0000 (0.0000)	1.0000	0.0000(0.0000)	1.0000
3	Hartmann(3)	-3.8626 (0.0000)	-3.8628 (0.0000)	0.0025	-3.8628 (0.0000)	0.0025
4	Shekel(4, 5)	-10.1326 (0.0004)	-10.1332 (0.0000)	0.0008	-10.0038(0.7469)	248.8032
4	Shekel(4, 7)	-10.4019 (0.0008)	-10.4029 (0.0000)	0.0005	-10.3264(0.7612)	76.4323
4	Shekel(4, 10)	-10.5363 (0.0001)	-10.5364 (0.0000)	0.0050	-10.5364(0.0000)	0.0050
5	Rosenbrock(5)	0.4324 (1.2299)	0.0000 (0.0000)	1.16E-6	0.0000 (0.0000)	1.16E-6
5	Zakharov(5)	0.0000 (0.0000)	0.0000 (0.0000)	1.0000	0.0000 (0.0000)	1.0000
6	Hartmann(6)	-3.3150 (0.0283)	-3.3224 (0.0000)	6.76E-5	-3.3224 (0.0000)	6.76E-5
10	Sum-Squares(10)	0.0000 (0.0000)	0.0000 (0.0000)	1.0000	0.0000 (0.0000)	1.0000
10	Sphere(10)	0.0000 (0.0000)	0.0000 (0.0000)	1.0000	0.0000(0.0000)	1.0000
10	Rosenbrock(10)	0.9568 (1.7026)	0.1595 (0.7812)	0.1667	0.0000(0.0000)	5.23E-7
10	Rastrigin(10)	4.9748 (2.7066)	0.7464 (0.8367)	0.1500	0.3283(0.4667)	0.0660
10	Griewank(10)	0.0532 (0.0310)	0.0474 (0.0266)	0.8915	0.0426(0.0184)	0.8002
10	Zakharov(10)	0.0000 (0.0000)	0.0000 (0.0000)	1.0000	0.0000(0.0000)	1.0000
20	Sphere(20)	0.0000 (0.0000)	0.0000 (0.0000)	1.0000	0.0000(0.0000)	1.0000
20	Rosenbrock(20)	3.9481 (15.1928)	0.4788 (1.2955)	0.1213	0.0013(0.0078)	0.0003
20	Rastrigin(20)	24.9071 (6.7651)	6.8868 (3.0184)	0.2765	0.7960(1.2833)	0.0319
20	Griewank(20)	0.0129 (0.0137)	0.0128 (0.0130)	0.9910	0.0202(0.0195)	1.5682
20	Zakharov(20)	0.0000 (0.0000)	0.0000 (0.0000)	1.0000	0.0000(0.0000)	1.0000
30	Sphere(30)	0.0000 (0.0000)	0.0000 (0.0000)	1.0000	0.0000(0.0000)	1.0000
30	Rosenbrock(30)	8.6635 (6.7336)	0.3627 (1.1413)	0.0419	0.0632(0.0629)	0.0073
30	Rastrigin(30)	45.1711 (15.8998)	11.9425 (3.9591)	0.2644	1.4327(3.2848)	0.0317
30	Griewank(30)	0.0134 (0.0185)	0.0052 (0.0080)	0.3907	0.0187(0.0163)	1.3980
30	Zakharov(30)	0.9086 (4.8932)	0.0000 (0.0000)	5.5E-7	0.0000(0.0000)	5.5E-7

The C/CyberSA exhibits similar effectiveness as observed from its mean best function value and merit value. The product of the merit values for the C/CyberSA is 1.07E-40 which is even somewhat better than the corresponding product for the C/CyberSA. However, the C/CyberSA is less effective than CyberSA in finding the global optimum for the four functions Shekel(4, 5), Shekel(4, 7), Griewank(20), and Griewank(30). This is compensated by the fact that the C/CyberSA demonstrates significantly greater effectiveness than the CyberSA in tackling the difficult functions like Rosenbrock and Rastrigin having ten or more variables. These findings motivate future investigations of Cyber Swarm methods that combine features of the original CyberSA and the C/CyberSA as a basis for creating a method that may embody the best features of both approaches. To get a rough indication of the promise of such an approach, we examined a "trivial combination" of the two methods as follows. Of the eleven functions that are not solved optimally by both CyberSA and C/CyberSA, we observe that CyberSA obtains better solutions on Shekel(4, 5), Shekel(4, 7), Griewank(20), and Griewank(30), while C/CyberSA obtains better solutions on Rosenbrock(10), Rastrigin(10), Griewank(10), Rosenbrock(20), Rastrigin(20), Rosenbrock(30) and Rastrigin(30). The maximum number of function evaluations required by CyberSA to find its best solution to any of the problems where it performs better is 104,416, while the maximum number of function evaluations required by C/CyberSA to find its best solution to any of the problems where it performs better is 137,504. Consequently, a "trivial combination" of the two methods that runs CyberSA for 104,416 function evaluations and C/CyberSA for 137,504 function evaluations would yield a method that provides the best solutions on all of these problems within a total number of 241,920 function evaluations. We have allotted a maximum of 250,000 function evaluations for the Standard PSO 2007 as a basis for fair comparison. The resulting version of Standard PSO 2007 does not perform much better than when the method is allotted 160,000 function evaluations, although it can solve Rosenbrock(5) and Zakharov(30) to optimality with 250,000 function evaluations. Consequently, the "trivial combination" of CyberSA and C/CyberSA likewise dominates the Standard PSO 2007 method when the latter is permitted to use 250,000 function evaluations, obtaining better solutions than the Standard PSO method on 16 test problems and matching the Standard PSO 2007 method on the remaining 14 problems. A more sophisticated way of combining the strategies employed by CyberSA and C/CyberSA would undoubtedly

perform still better, thus reinforcing the motivation for future research to examine ways of integrating the TS and SS/PR strategies embodied in the CyberSA and C/CyberSA methods.

Finally, the value of the standard deviation listed in Table 1 also discloses that the computational results obtained by CyberSA and C/CyberSA from 100 independent runs are more consistent than those produced by the standard PSO 2007, recommending the use of the CyberSA and C/CyberSA from the worst-case analysis perspective.

4.2.2. Experiment 2

In the second experiment, we compare C/CyberSA with the Standard PSO 2007 and the PSwarm algorithm (Vaz & Vicente, 2007) with an extended set of test functions. The original set from Vaz and Vicente contains 122 test functions, although global optimum solutions were not identified for twelve of these to enable algorithmic performance to be evaluated in these cases. We thus solve the remaining 110 test functions by reference to the experimental setting used in Vaz and Vicente (2007). Thirty runs are executed for each competing algorithm, recording the number of function evaluations consumed when reaching the specified gap to the global optimum, with the limitation that the maximum number of function evaluations for each run is set to 10,000. For each test function, the best result (in terms of the number of function evaluations) obtained among the 30 runs is reported.

Table 2 lists the specified gap and the best result. The value in parentheses indicates the number of times among the 30 runs that the function value obtained by the algorithm reaches the specified gap. (The result for PSwarm does not include this success rate information because it was not provided in the original paper.) Overall, there are twelve test functions containing either 114, or 225, or 294 variables, which is extremely large by the usual standards for global function optimization. In these challenging cases all the competing algorithms fail to obtain a within-gap function value within 10,000 function evaluations. The function value finally obtained is marked with an asterisk (*) and is reported under the column of the corresponding algorithm. For these large and challenging test functions, the C/CyberSA method obtains the best function values with the same maximal number of function evaluations as the other methods. The Standard PSO 2007 ranks in second position while the PSwarm obtains the worst objective values for these functions. For the remaining 98 test functions which contain no more than 30 variables, we compare the number of test functions for each of the competing algorithms where the algorithm is unable to reach the specified gap within 10,000 function evaluations. Table 2 shows that the Standard PSO 2007 is less efficient than the other two methods and it fails to solve 17 test functions with satisfactory function values within the 10,000 function evaluation limit. PSwarm performs somewhat better by failing to reach the gap for only 13 test functions and the C/CyberSA method performs the best by solving all but 12 test functions.

Next we compare the efficiency for the test functions where the three competing methods can successfully solve to reaching the gap. We consider the number of function evaluations divided by 10,000 (excluding the cases where the algorithm fails to solve the test function) as the probability p_i that the corresponding algorithm fails to efficiently solve the test function i. Then the geometric mean of the efficiency probability $(1 - p_i)$ over the successfully solved cases can be derived by

$$\sqrt[|S|]{\prod_{i \in S}\left(1 - p_i\right)} \tag{7}$$

where S denotes the set of test functions where the corresponding algorithm successfully reaches the gap. We obtain the efficiency probability for the C/CyberSA, PSwarm, and Standard PSO 2007 as being 98.91%, 88.60%, and 83.23%, respectively,

thus disclosing that the C/CyberSA is able to solve a wider range of test functions more efficiently than the other two algorithms. Moreover, the result also discloses that the PSwarm ranks as more efficient than the Standard PSO 2007 for this set of test functions.

Finally, we compare the success rate (the ratio of the 30 runs that the obtained function value reaches the specified gap) for the Standard PSO 2007 and the C/CyberSA. The success rate for the PSwarm is not available from its original paper. By excluding the failure cases where none of the 30 runs produces a solution that satisfies the gap, the overall success rate can be estimated by the geometric mean of individual rates. The over success rate for the Standard PSO 2007 and the C/CyberSA is derived according to the numbers listed in parentheses in Table 2, being 80.98% and 84.95%, respectively. In addition to solving five more test functions than the Standard PSO 2007, the C/CyberSA also manifests a higher success rate for the successfully solved cases. Consequently the C/CyberSA is more effective than the Standard PSO 2007 on all measures.

5. CONCLUDING REMARKS

Our Complementary Cyber Swarm Algorithm (C/CyberSA) draws on the basic principles underlying the original C/CyberSA method, but adopts different sets of ideas from tabu search (TS) and scatter search/path relinking (SS/PR). Extensive empirical tests with a set of 110 test functions shows that the C/CyberSA can produce improvements comparable to those provided by the CyberSA in relation to PSO methods that do not incorporate such ideas. The C/CyberSA exploits guidance and restriction information derived by applying adaptive memory strategies from TS to the history of swarm search and incorporates path relinking as an essential component to yield two long-term strategies as responses to the detection of critical events encountered in the search,

Table 2. Number of function evaluations to reach the specified gap to the global optimum by the competing algorithms

R	Test Function	gap	Standard PSO 2007	PSwarm	C/CyberSA
10	ack	2.171640E-01	10000(0)	1797	84(27)
2	ap	8.600000E-05	440(30)	207	200(8)
2	bf1	0.000000E+00	2560(30)	204	86(30)
2	bf2	0.000000E+00	2240(30)	208	88(30)
2	bhs	1.384940E-01	80(30)	218	80(30)
2	bl	0.000000E+00	1000(30)	217	84(30)
2	bp	0.000000E+00	1440(30)	224	84(30)
2	cb3	0.000000E+00	1040(30)	190	84(30)
2	cb6	2.800000E-05	10000(0)	211	10000(0)
2	cm2	0.000000E+00	1160(30)	182	159(30)
4	cm4	0.000000E+00	2000(30)	385	84(30)
2	da	4.816600E-01	2720(30)	232	84(30)
10	em_10	1.384700E+00	10000(0)	4488	10000(0)
5	em_5	1.917650E-01	4480(2)	823	130(4)
2	ep	0.000000E+00	2320(30)	227	260(30)
10	exp	0.000000E+00	3240(30)	1434	84(30)
2	fls	3.000000E-06	10000(0)	227	10000(0)
2	fr	0.000000E+00	1160(29)	337	84(30)
10	fx_10	8.077291E+00	10000(0)	1773	10000(0)
5	fx_5	6.875980E+00	440(1)	799	10000(0)
2	gp	0.000000E+00	1840(30)	190	163(30)
3	grp	0.000000E+00	280(30)	1339	135(30)
10	gw	0.000000E+00	10000(0)	2296	10000(0)
3	h3	0.000000E+00	1280(30)	295	156(30)
6	h6	0.000000E+00	2680(14)	655	10000(0)
2	hm	0.000000E+00	1520(30)	195	84(30)
1	hm1	0.000000E+00	120(30)	96	84(30)
1	hm2	1.447000E-02	80(30)	141	80(30)
1	hm3	2.456000E-03	80(30)	110	80(30)
2	hm4	0.000000E+00	1480(30)	198	84(30)
3	hm5	0.000000E+00	960(30)	255	159(30)
2	hsk	1.200000E-05	120(30)	204	170(30)
3	hv	0.000000E+00	2560(30)	343	84(30)
4	ir0	0.000000E+00	5280(30)	671	114(27)
3	ir1	0.000000E+00	1480(30)	292	90(30)
2	ir2	1.000000E-06	1680(30)	522	144(30)
5	ir3	0.000000E+00	320(30)	342	172(30)

continued on following page

Table 2. Continued

R	Test Function	gap	Standard PSO 2007	PSwarm	C/CyberSA
30	ir4	1.587200E-02	560(30)	8769	84(30)
4	kl	4.800000E-07	680(30)	1435	148(30)
1	ks	0.000000E+00	80(30)	92	80(30)
114	lj1_38	4.000000E-07	-65.83*	140.92*	-83.13*
225	lj1_75	4.000000E-07	18838.57*	35129.64*	5958.58*
294	lj1_98	4.000000E-07	134854.88*	193956.8*	35613.6*
114	lj2_38	4.000000E-07	146.48*	372.77*	161.2*
225	lj2_75	4.000000E-07	25227.97*	32450.09*	8302.73*
294	lj2_98	4.000000E-07	112291.68*	170045.2*	52087.07*
114	lj3_38	4.000000E-07	588.51*	1729.29*	283.24*
225	lj3_75	4.000000E-07	499130*	1036894*	118721*
294	lj3_98	4.000000E-07	7667493*	15188010*	2562334*
3	lm1	0.000000E+00	1760(30)	335	84(30)
10	lm2_10	0.000000E+00	4920(28)	1562	162(30)
5	lm2_5	0.000000E+00	2640(30)	625	84(30)
3	lv8	0.000000E+00	1560(30)	310	84(30)
2	mc	7.700000E-05	160(30)	211	84(30)
4	mcp	0.000000E+00	200(30)	248	164(30)
2	mgp	2.593904E+00	80(30)	193	80(30)
10	mgw_10	1.107800E-02	240(30)	10007	173(30)
2	mgw_2	0.000000E+00	80(30)	339	84(30)
20	mgw_20	5.390400E-02	560(27)	10005	133(28)
10	ma_10	0.000000E+00	10000(0)	2113	10000(0)
5	ml_5	0.000000E+00	2640(8)	603	135(15)
3	mr	1.860000E-03	560(27)	886	84(30)
2	mrp	0.000000E+00	1720(18)	217	185(24)
4	nf2	2.700000E-05	320(30)	2162	156(30)
10	nf3_10	0.000000E+00	10000(0)	4466	86(23)
15	nf3_15	7.000000E-06	10000(0)	10008	90(18)
20	nf3_20	2.131690E-01	10000(0)	10008	85(19)
25	nf3_25	5.490210E-01	10000(0)	10025	94(9)
30	nf3_30	6.108021E+01	10000(0)	10005	98(14)
10	osp_10	1.143724E+00	480(19)	1885	132(11)
20	osp_20	1.143833E+00	80(30)	5621	80(30)
114	plj_38	4.000000E-07	486.37*	774.64*	299.12*
225	plj_75	4.000000E-07	21733.21*	37284.11*	10953.88*
294	plj_98	4.000000E-07	111878.79*	179615.0*	39135.69*

continued on following page

Table 2. Continued

R	Test Function	gap	Standard PSO 2007	PSwarm	C/CyberSA
10	pp	4.700000E-04	2320(30)	1578	84(30)
2	prd	0.000000E+00	1440(26)	400	126(30)
9	ptm	3.908401E+00	4280(2)	10009	10000(0)
4	pwq	0.000000E+00	2880(30)	439	84(30)
10	rb	1.114400E-02	10000(0)	10003	84(16)
10	rg_10	0.000000E+00	10000(0)	4364	170(9)
2	rg_2	0.000000E+00	1120(29)	210	84(30)
4	s10	4.510000E-03	1560(12)	431	84(30)
4	s5	3.300000E-03	1480(9)	395	10000(0)
4	s7	3.041000E-03	1400(17)	415	84(30)
10	sal_10	3.998730E-01	1400(30)	1356	84(30)
5	sal_5	1.998730E-01	800(30)	452	85(30)
2	sbt	9.000000E-06	1480(30)	305	129(30)
2	sf1	9.716000E-03	320(30)	210	84(30)
2	sf2	5.383000E-03	3280(30)	266	90(30)
1	shv1	1.000000E-03	80(30)	101	80(30)
2	shv2	0.000000E+00	640(30)	196	154(30)
10	sin_10	0.000000E+00	4560(29)	1872	85(30)
20	sin_20	0.000000E+00	8360(25)	5462	84(29)
17	st_17	3.081935E+06	4160(5)	10011	127(30)
9	st_9	7.516622E+00	10000(0)	10001	10000(0)
1	stg	0.000000E+00	80(30)	113	84(30)
10	swf	1.184385E+02	10000(0)	2311	10000(0)
1	sz	2.561249E+00	80(30)	125	80(29)
1	szzs	1.308000E-03	80(30)	112	80(30)
4	wf	2.500000E-05	10000(0)	10008	84(17)
10	zkv_10	1.393000E-03	3920(30)	10003	84(30)
2	zkv_2	0.000000E+00	1120(30)	212	84(30)
20	zkv_20	3.632018E+01	840(29)	10018	171(30)
5	zkv_5	0.000000E+00	3280(30)	1318	84(30)
1	zlk1	4.039000E-03	200(30)	119	126(30)
1	zlk2a	5.000000E-03	80(30)	130	80(30)
1	zlk2b	5.000000E-03	80(30)	113	80(30)
2	zlk4	2.112000E-03	240(30)	224	162(9)
3	zlk5	2.782000E-03	200(30)	294	166(5)
1	zzs	4.239000E-03	80(30)	120	80(23)

Our experimental results show that the C/CyberSA outperforms the PSwarm and the Standard PSO 2007 methods by finding more optimal solutions of the test problems and by simultaneously using a smaller number of function evaluations. In addition, we find that a "trivial combination" of C/CyberSA and CyberSA that runs for 250,000 function evaluations strongly dominates the Standard PSO 2007 method when the latter method is allotted this number of function evaluations, obtaining better solutions on 16 out of 30 basic test cases and matching the quality of solutions obtained by the Standard PSO 2007 on the remaining 14 cases. These findings motivate future investigations of Cyber Swarm methods that combine features of both the original and complementary variants and incorporate additional strategic notions from SS and PR.

REFERENCES

Angeline, P. J. (1999). Using selection to improve particle swarm optimization. In *Proceedings of the IEEE International Joint Conference on Neural Networks* (pp. 84-89).

Audet, C., & Dennis, J. E. (2003). Analysis of generalized pattern searches. *SIAM Journal on Optimization*, *13*, 889–903. doi:10.1137/S1052623400378742

Campos, V., Glover, F., Laguna, M., & Martí, R. (2001). An experimental evaluation of a scatter search for the linear ordering problem. *Journal of Global Optimization*, *21*(4), 397–414. doi:10.1023/A:1012793906010

Chelouah, R., & Siarry, P. (2000). Tabu search applied to global optimization. *European Journal of Operational Research*, *123*, 256–270. doi:10.1016/S0377-2217(99)00255-6

Chelouah, R., & Siarry, P. (2005). A hybrid method combining continuous tabu search and Nelder–Mead simplex algorithms for the global optimization of multiminima functions. *European Journal of Operational Research*, *161*, 636–654. doi:10.1016/j.ejor.2003.08.053

Clerc, M. (2008). *Particle swarm programs.* Retrieved from http://www.particleswarm.info/Programs.html

Clerc, M., & Kennedy, J. (2002). The particle swarm explosion, stability, and convergence in a multidimensional complex space. *IEEE Transactions on Evolutionary Computation*, *6*, 58–73. doi:10.1109/4235.985692

Duarte, A., Marti, R., & Glover, F. (2007). *Adaptive memory programming for global optimization.* Valencia, Spain: University of Valencia.

Duarte, A., Marti, R., & Glover, F. (2011a). Hybrid scatter-tabu search for unconstrained global optimization. *Annals of Operations Research*, *183*, 95–123. doi:10.1007/s10479-009-0596-2

Duarte, A., Marti, R., & Glover, F. (2011b). Path relinking for large scale global optimization. *Soft Computing*, 15.

Eberhart, R. C., & Shi, Y. (1998). Evolving artificial neural networks. In *Proceedings of the International Conference on Neural Networks and Brain* (pp. 5-13).

Feng, H. M., Chen, C. Y., & Ye, F. (2007). Evolutionary fuzzy particle swarm optimization vector quantization learning scheme in image compression. *Expert Systems with Applications*, *32*, 213–222. doi:10.1016/j.eswa.2005.11.012

Glover, F. (1986). Future paths for integer programming and links to artificial intelligence. *Computers & Operations Research*, *13*, 533–549. doi:10.1016/0305-0548(86)90048-1

Glover, F. (1994). Tabu search for nonlinear and parametric optimization (with links to genetic algorithms). *Discrete Applied Mathematics, 49,* 231–255. doi:10.1016/0166-218X(94)90211-9

Glover, F. (1996a). Tabu search and adaptive memory programming - advances, applications and challenges. In Barr, R. S., Helgason, R. V., & Kennington, J. L. (Eds.), *Interfaces in computer science and operations research* (pp. 1–75). Boston, MA: Kluwer Academic.

Glover, F. (1996b). Ejection chains, reference structures and alternating path methods for traveling salesman problems. *Discrete Applied Mathematics, 65,* 223–253. doi:10.1016/0166-218X(94)00037-E

Glover, F. (1998). A template for scatter search and path relinking. In J.-K. Hao, E. Lutton, E. M. A. Ronald, M. Schoenauer, & D. Snyers (Eds.), *Proceedings of the Third European Conference on Artificial Evolution* (LNCS 1363, pp. 3-54).

Glover, F., & Laguna, M. (1997). *Tabu search.* Boston, MA: Kluwer Academic.

Hedar, A., & Fukushima, M. (2006). Tabu search directed by direct search methods for nonlinear global optimization. *European Journal of Operational Research, 170*(2), 329–349. doi:10.1016/j.ejor.2004.05.033

Hirsch, M. J., Meneses, C. N., Pardalos, P. M., & Resende, M. G. C. (2007). Global optimization by continuous grasp. *Optimization Letters, 1*(2), 201–212. doi:10.1007/s11590-006-0021-6

Ho, S. C., & Gendreau, M. (2006). Path relinking for the vehicle routing problem. *Journal of Heuristics, 12,* 55–72. doi:10.1007/s10732-006-4192-1

Hvattum, L. M., & Glover, F. (2009). Finding local optima of high-dimensional functions using direct search methods. *European Journal of Operational Research, 195,* 31–45. doi:10.1016/j.ejor.2008.01.039

James, T., Rego, C., & Glover, F. (2009). Multistart tabu search and diversification strategies for the quadratic assignment problem. *IEEE Transactions on Systems, Man, and Cybernetics. Part A, Systems and Humans, 39*(3). doi:10.1109/TSMCA.2009.2014556

Kennedy, J. (1999, July). Small world and megaminds: Effects of neighbourhood topology on particle swarm performance. In *Proceedings of the Congress on Evolutionary Computation* (pp. 1931-1938).

Kennedy, J., & Eberhart, R. C. (1995). Particle swarm optimization. In. *Proceedings of the IEEE International Conference on Neural Networks, IV,* 1942–1948. doi:10.1109/ICNN.1995.488968

Laguna, M., & Marti, R. (2003). *Scatter search: Methodology and implementation in C.* Boston, MA: Kluwer Academic.

Laguna, M., & Marti, R. (2005). Experimental testing of advanced scatter search designs for global optimization of multimodal functions. *Journal of Global Optimization, 33,* 235–255. doi:10.1007/s10898-004-1936-z

Lepagnot, J., Nakib, A., Oulhadj, H., & Siarry, P. (2010). A new multiagent algorithm for dynamic continuous optimization. *International Journal of Applied Metaheuristic Computing, 1*(1), 16–38. doi:10.4018/jamc.2010102602

Lovbjerg, M., Rasmussen, T. K., & Krink, T. (2001). Hybrid particle swarm optimizer with breeding and subpopulations. In *Proceedings of the Genetic and Evolutionary Computation Conference.*

Lu, Z., Hao, J.-K., & Glover, F. (2010). Neighborhood analysis: A case study on curriculum-based course timetabling. *Journal of Heuristics.*

Luke, S. (2009). *Essentials of metaheuristics.* Retrieved from http://cs.gmu.edu/~sean/book/metaheuristics/

Mendes, R., Kennedy, J., & Neves, J. (2004). The fully informed particle swarm: Simpler, maybe better. *IEEE Transactions on Evolutionary Computation, 8*, 204–210. doi:10.1109/TEVC.2004.826074

Miranda, V., Keko, H., & Jaramillo, A. (2007). EPSO: Evolutionary particle swarms. *Studies in Computational Intelligence, 66*, 139–167. doi:10.1007/978-3-540-72377-6_6

Mladenovic, N., & Hansen, P. (1997). Variable neighborhood search. *Computers & Operations Research, 24*, 1097–1100. doi:10.1016/S0305-0548(97)00031-2

Nakano, S., Ishigame, A., & Yasuda, K. (2007). Particle swarm optimization based on the concept of tabu search. In *Proceedings of the IEEE Congress on Evolutionary Computation* (pp. 3258-3263).

Rego, C., & Glover, F. (2009). Ejection chain and filter-and-fan methods in combinatorial optimization. *Annals of Operations Research, 175*(1), 77–105. doi:10.1007/s10479-009-0656-7

Shen, Q., Shi, W. M., & Kong, W. (2008). Hybrid particle swarm optimization and tabu search approach for selecting genes for tumor classification using gene expression data. *Computational Biology and Chemistry, 32*(1), 52–59. doi:10.1016/j.compbiolchem.2007.10.001

Shigenori, N., Takamu, G., Toshiku, Y., & Yoshikazu, F. (2003). A hybrid particle swarm optimization for distribution state estimation. *IEEE Transactions on Power Systems, 18*, 60–68. doi:10.1109/TPWRS.2002.807051

Sörensen, K., & Glover, F. (2010). Metaheuristics. In Gass, S., & Fu, M. (Eds.), *Encyclopedia of operations research* (3rd ed.). New York, NY: Springer.

Sörensen, K., Sevaux, M., & Schittekat, P. (2008). Multiple neighbourhood search in commercial VRP packages: Evolving towards self-adaptive methods. *Studies in Computational Statistics, 136*, 239–253.

Vaz, A. I. F., & Vicente, L. N. (2007). A particle swarm pattern search method for bound constrained global optimization. *Journal of Global Optimization, 39*, 197–219. doi:10.1007/s10898-007-9133-5

Wang, Y. X., Zhao, Z. D., & Ren, R. (2007). Hybrid particle swarm optimizer with tabu strategy for global numerical optimization. In *Proceedings of the IEEE Congress on Evolutionary Computation* (pp. 2310-2316).

Yin, P. Y., Glover, F., Laguna, M., & Zhu, J. X. (2010). Cyber swarm algorithms – improving particle swarm optimization using adaptive memory strategies. *European Journal of Operational Research, 201*(2), 377–389. doi:10.1016/j.ejor.2009.03.035

Yoshida, H., Kawata, K., Fukuyama, Y., & Nakanishi, Y. (1999). A particle swarm optimization for reactive power and voltage control considering voltage stability. In *Proceedings of the International Conference on Intelligent System Application to Power Systems* (pp. 117-121).

This work was previously published in the International Journal of Swarm Intelligence Research, Volume 2, Issue 2, edited by Yuhui Shi, pp. 22-41, copyright 2011 by IGI Publishing (an imprint of IGI Global).

Chapter 3
Path Relinking Scheme for the Max–Cut Problem within Global Equilibrium Search

Volodymyr P. Shylo
Institute of Cybernetics NAS of Ukraine, Ukraine

Oleg V. Shylo
University of Pittsburgh, USA

ABSTRACT

In this paper, the potential of the path relinking method for the maximum cut problem is investigated. This method is embedded within global equilibrium search to utilize the set of high quality solutions provided by the latter. The computational experiment on a set of standard benchmark problems is provided to study the proposed approach. The empirical experiments reveal that the large sizes of the elite set lead to restart distribution of the running times, i.e., the algorithm can be accelerated by simply removing all of the accumulated data (set P) and re-initiating its execution after a certain number of elite solutions is obtained.

PATH RELINKING SCHEME FOR THE MAX-CUT PROBLEM WITHIN GLOBAL EQUILIBRIUM SEARCH

The maximum cut problem is a well-known NP-hard problem (Karp, 1972), which recently gathered a lot of interest due to a number of important practical applications (Barahona, Grotschel, Junger, & Reinelt, 1988; Chang & Du, 1988). The input for the maximum cut problem is an undirected graph $G = G(V,E)$, where each edge $(i, j) \in E$ is assigned a certain weight w_{ij}. Let (V_1, V_2) be a partition of the set of vertices V into two disjoint subsets. A cut (V_1, V_2) in G is any subset of edges $(i, j) \in E$, such that $i \in V_1$ and $j \in V_2$. The maximum cut problem is to find a cut in graph G with the maximum sum of the edge weights.

In the current paper we consider an extension of the algorithm for the maximum cut problem based on global equilibrium search (GES). The

DOI: 10.4018/978-1-4666-2479-5.ch003

comparison with other available algorithms using a set of benchmark problems revealed that GES dominates other approaches in terms of computational speed and solution quality (Shylo & Shylo, 2010). The implementation of GES maintains a set of solutions, which are used to prevent algorithm from converging to previously visited areas in the search space. Since this set contains high quality solutions, it is desirable to use it in a more efficient manner. Assuming that high quality solutions share some common structure, one can try to combine their components in an attempt to find an enhanced solution. In the current paper, we propose an extension of path relinking to GES to achieve this goal.

Path relinking method organizes a search for an improvement based on some population of solutions (Glover, Laguna, & Marti, 2000). The most common path relinking scheme involves a pair of solutions: an initiating solution and a guiding solution. A set of moves (transformations) are applied starting in the initiating solution that sequentially introduce the attributes of the guiding solution. Usually, such moves results in a set of solutions that lie on a path in the search space between the initial solution pair.

METHOD

Assuming that the weights are non-negative, the maximum cut problem can be formulated by the following mixed-integer program (Kahruman, Kolotoglu, Butenko, & Hicks, 2007):

$$\sum_{i,j=1, i<j}^{n} w_{ij} y_{ij}$$

$$s.t. \quad y_{ij} - x_i - x_j \leq 0 \quad i,j = 1, ..., n, \quad i < j$$
$$y_{ij} + x_i + x_j \leq 2 \quad i,j = 1, ..., n, \quad i < j$$
$$x \in \{0,1\}^n$$

The optimal solution vector x defines a graph partition $\{V_1, V_2\}$ (if $x_i = 1$ then $v_i \in V_1$, otherwise $v_i \in V_2$) that has the maximum cut value. Let $f(x)$ denote a cost of a cut corresponding to the solution vector x.

Local search based methods require an initial solution $x \in \{0,1\}^n$ to start the chain of local improvements until the local optimum is obtained. GES provides an intelligent mechanism of generating initial solutions for local search based methods. Its metaheuristic framework proved to be extremely efficient for a variety of combinatorial problems (Pardalos, Prokopyev, Shylo, & Shylo, 2008; Shylo, Prokopyev, & Shylo, 2008).

The generation probabilities in GES are defined by some subset S of previously visited solutions (e.g., a set of local optima). These probabilities are parameterized by an ordered set of temperature values $0 \leq \mu_0 < \mu_1 < ... < \mu_K$, which bear the same function as a cooling schedule in the simulated annealing method (Aarts & Korst, 1989). The search process is organized as a repeating sequence of K temperature stages, one for each temperature value. A fixed number of initial solutions are generated at each temperature stage to be used as starting solutions for some local search based method. In case of binary decision variables, the generation procedure at temperature stage k sets jth component to 1 (or 0) with probability given by $p_j(\mu_k)(1 - p_j(\mu_k))$:

$$p_j(\mu_k) =$$
$$\left(1 + \exp\{\sum_{i=0}^{k-1} \frac{\mu_{i+1} - \mu_i}{2}(E_{ij}^0 + E_{i+1j}^0 - E_{ij}^1 - E_{i+1j}^1)\}\right)^{-1}$$

$$(1)$$

where $E_{kj}^1 \left(E_{kj}^0\right)$ is a weighted sum of objective values, that corresponds to solutions in S, such that $x_j = 1 \left(x_j = 0\right)$:

$$E_{kj}^1 =$$
$$\begin{cases} \dfrac{\sum\limits_{x \in S, x_j = 1} f(x) \exp(\mu_k f(x))}{\sum\limits_{x \in S, x_j = 1} \exp(\mu_k f(x))}, & \text{if } \exists x \in S, \text{ s.t. } x_j = 1 \\ 0, & \text{otherwise.} \end{cases}$$

$$(2)$$

These formulas are derived from an approximation of the Boltzmann distribution defined on all feasible solutions (Pardalos et al., 2008). Intuitively, they guarantee that the generated solutions are more likely to resemble the solutions in S that have high objective values.

It is worth noting that there is no need to store the whole set S in memory, since E_{kj}^1 and E_{kj}^0 can be easily updated by simple addition if the denominator and the numerator in (2) are stored separately.

In our implementation, the initial temperature μ_0 is set to zero, thus, the solutions generated at zero-stage are completely random (no bias). The rest of the temperature values are defined as: $\mu_k = \alpha^{k-1}\beta$ for $k = 1, ..., K$. The multiplier α and the initial value β have to be chosen in such a way that the probability of generating a solution x at the last temperature stage (K), such that $x_j = 1$ is approximately equal to the binary value of jth component in the best known solution:

$$\left\| \arg\max\{f(x) : x \in S\} - p(\mu_K) \right\| \approx 0$$

The same temperature vector was used for all considered benchmark problems.

The pseudo-code for the algorithm is presented in Figure 1. The algorithm generates a set of initial solutions within a temperature cycle (Figure 1, lines 8-22) that consists of K temperature stages. A temperature at kth stage is defined by a kth component of the temperature vector $\mu = [\mu_0, \mu_1 ..., \mu_K]$. The generation probabilities

are calculated using (1) and are used to construct initial solutions for the local search procedure (Figure 1, line 9). All the components of the current best solution are perturbed according to these probabilities (each independently). In our implementation, we utilize a local search procedure based on one-move operator: given a solution x, the local neighborhood consists of all solutions that differ from x by at most one component. The search method based on this neighborhood is referred to as "1-opt" local search (Figure 2). The local search procedure sequentially evaluates solutions from the neighborhood in a random order. If a solution from the neighborhood has a cost function of the same or better quality than the current solution (Figure 2, line 6), it becomes a new current solution (Figure 2, line 8). The changes to the components of the solution vector are followed by a recalculation of a so-called vector of gains $g(x)$ (Figure 2, line 9). The change of cost resulting from changing jth component of x is given by $g_j(x)$:

$$g_{j(x)} =$$
$$f(x_1, ..., x_{j-1}, 1 - x_j, x_{j+1}, ..., x_n)$$
$$- f(x_1, ..., x_{j-1}, x_j, x_{j+1}, ..., x_n)$$

Maintaining $g(x)$ throughout all the algorithmic steps allows us to accelerate the evaluation of the move costs in the local search procedure.

The locally-optimal solutions provided by the local search are used to update the set of known solutions S (Figure 1, lines 12-13) that will be used to calculate generation probabilities at the subsequent stages. In order to prevent convergence to the same solutions, we memorize a set of so-called prohibited solutions P, which contains the best solutions found during the main cycle (Figure 1, line 30). If a new solution belongs to the set of the prohibited solutions, it is excluded from further consideration (Figure 1, line 13). The set P can be quite large, thus there is a desire to uti-

Figure 1. GES with path relinking for the max-cut problem

Input: μ – vector of temperature values, K – number of temperature stages,

ngen – # of solutions generated during each stage
Function:
1: $P = \varnothing$;
2: **while** stopping criterion = FALSE **do**
3:   x = construct random solution
4:   $x^{max} = x$; $x^{best} = x$
5:   **loop**
6:     $x^{old} = x^{max}$
7:     $S = \{x^{max}\}$ (set of known solutions)
8:     **for** $k = 0$ to K **do**
9:       calculate generation probabilities $p(\mu_k)$
10:       **for** $g = 0$ to *ngen* **do**
11:         x = generate solution(x^{max}, $p(\mu_k)$)
12:         x^{loc} = 1-opt local search (x, x^{best})
13:         $S = S \cup \{x^{loc}\} \backslash P$
14:         $x^{new} = \text{argmax}\{f(x) : x \in S\}$
15:         **if** $f(x^{new}) > f(x^{max})$ **then**
16:           $x^{max} = x^{new}$
17:           **if** $f(x^{max}) > f(x^{best})$ **then**
18:             $x^{best} = x^{max}$
19:           **end if**
20:         **end if**
21:       **end for**
22:     **end for**
23:     **if** $f(x^{max}) < f(x^{best}) - H$ **then**
24:       **break**; {exit loop}
25:     **end if**
26:     **if** $f(x^{old}) \geq f(x^{max})$ **then**
27:       **break**; {exit loop}
28:     **end if**
29:   **end loop**
30:   $P = P \cup \{x^{max}\}$;
31:   **Path relinking**(P, x^{max}, S)
32: **end while**
33: **return** x^{best}

Figure 2. Local search 1-opt

Input: x – solution, gains(x) – the vector of gains
Function:
1: **repeat**
2:   Generate random permutation RP of the set {1,. . . ,n}
3:   $\Delta = 0$
4:   **for** k = 1 to n **do**
5:     j =RP[k]
6:     **if** $g_j(x) \geq 0$ **then**
7:       $\Delta = \Delta + g_j(x)$
8:       $x_j = 1 - x_j$
9:       g(x) = recalculate gains(x)
10:    **end if**
11: **end for**
12: **until** $\Delta > 0$
  13: **return** x

lize valuable information about the search space that is provided by the solutions from this set. Path relinking provides a perfect framework to achieve this goal.

The traditional implementations of the path relinking method populate the elite set with a predefined number of solutions before initiating the path relinking. In our work, the path relinking procedure is used to explore the paths that connect every new solution generated by GES to the solutions generated at the previous solution cycles (set of prohibited solutions *P)*. The solution is included in the set *P* only if the Hamming distance to other solutions in *P* is less than a predefined value d_{div} ($d_{div} = 50$). This allows us to maintain a certain level of diversity of the solutions involved in path relinking.

Usually, within the path relinking method, pairs of high quality solutions are connected with a single path, which may lead to a solution of improved quality. Our initial experiments with this scheme revealed that such improvement is probable only for initial solutions of bad quality. Since the set of prohibited solutions *P* contains

very good solutions, an application of path relinking via single path construction almost never succeeds. Instead, we suggest searching for an improvement along all the possible paths between two initial solutions. A truncated version of GES is used to provide an effective search within this restricted domain.

Given two binary solutions sol^1 and sol^2, let *J* be a subset of indices of solution components that are identical in both solutions:

$$J = \{j \in \{1,...,n\} : sol^1_j = sol^2_j\}$$

Now, there are two minor changes that need to be made to GES scheme presented in Figure 1. Firstly, the generation probabilities (Figure 1, line 9) should be fixed for all components in *J*, i.e., $p_j(\mu_k) = sol^1_j = sol^2_j$ for all temperature stages *k* and $j \in J$. Secondly, the set *J* should be excluded from the initial random permutation *RP* in the local search method (Figure 2, line 2): *RP* = *RP\J*. Let GES^{tr} denote this truncated version of the global equilibrium search.

In our implementation, the path relinking procedure is invoked after completion of the main cycle of GES (Figure 1, line 31). The steps of this procedure are outlined in Figure 3. Given the best found solution x^{max} from the main cycle, the path relinking procedure sequentially selects solutions from P (in a random order) to form an initializing/guiding solution pair. These two solutions are used to initialize the set of known solutions S to be used within GES^{tr} that was discussed above. We artificially adjust their cost functions (as used in (?) to calculate generation probabilities) to avoid early convergence (Figure 3, line 6). The choice of the maximum size of the set P is discussed in the section on computational experiments. Upon reaching this maximum size, the algorithm is restarted by deleting all the solutions from P. If the path relinking routine finds a new best solution, x^{best}, the regular implementation of GES (not GES^{tr}) is initiated with $S = \{ x^{best} \}$.

RESULTS

All computational experiments with GES were done on a personal computer with a 2.83 GHz Intel Core Quad Q9550 processors with 3.0 GB of RAM.

There are a number of benchmark instances that were suggested for testing and evaluating the efficiency of algorithms for solving the Max-Cut problem. We concentrate on two sets of problems that were extensively studied by previous works on the Max-Cut problem (Goemans & Williamson, 1995; Marti, Duarte, & Laguna, 2009; Burer, Monteiro, & Zhang, 2002; Festa, Pardalos, Resende, & Ribeiro, 2002; Palubeckis & Krivickiene, 2004):

1. 24 problems that were suggested by Helmberg and Rendl (1999): G1, G2, G3, G11 - G16, G22, G23, G24, G32 - G37, G43, G44, G45, G48, G49 and G50. These problems consist of planar, toroidal and random graphs with number of vertices from 800 to 3000. The weights of the edges belong to the set $\{-1, 0, 1\}$.

Figure 3. Path relinking

Input: x^{max} – new initial solution for path relinking, P – set of prohibited solutions, S – set of known solutions.

```
1:  Generate random permutation    RP of the set {1,...,| P| }
2:    x^new = x^max
3:   for k = 1 to| P| do
4:      i = RP[k]
5:      S̃ = x^new ∪ P[i];
```

6:      $f(x^{max}) := f(P[i]) := \sum_{x \in S} f(x)\exp(-\mu_2 f(x)) / \sum_{x \in S}\exp(-\mu_2 f(x))$

```
7:      x^max = GES^tr(S̃)
8:     if  f(x^max)≥ f(x^new) then
9:           x^new=x^max
10:     end if
11:   end for
12:   P=P∪ x^max
13:   return P
```

2. 20 problems that were considered by Burer et al. (2002): sg3dl101000 – sg3dl1010000 and sg3dl141000 – sg3dl1410000. These graphs are based on cubic lattices with 10 instances having 1000 vertices and another 10 instances having 2744 vertices. The weights of the edges belong to the set { - 1, 0,1}.

The optimal size of the elite set (the set P in our case) used by the path relinking is difficult to characterize. Our empirical experiments reveal that the large maximum size of the elite set leads to the restart distribution of the running times (Luby, Sinclair, & Zuckerman, 1993), i.e., the algorithm can be accelerated by simply removing all of the accumulated data (set P) and re-initiating its execution after a certain number of elite solutions is obtained. We conducted an extensive set of experiments in order to evaluate the best choice of the maximum size for the elite set P, which revealed that the algorithmic performance degrades after accumulating a certain number of solutions in the elite set. Figure 4 illustrates these observations, based on 300 independent runs on the problem G37. Each run was terminated as soon as the solution quality of 7688 or better was achieved, and the distribution of the running times until termination is provided for analysis. Comparing the algorithm with no restriction on the maximum elite set size (G37∞) with the algorithm that is restarted after reaching 27 solutions in the elite set (G3727), one can see that the overall performance is better in the latter case. Clearly, the algorithm without the path relinking (G37 0) is dominated by other approaches. Based on our experiments with varying sizes, the maximum size of the set P was fixed to 32 solutions and this setting was used in all consequent experiments.

Figure 4. The probability of finding the target solution (f^{target} = 7688) for the problem G37 as a function of computational time

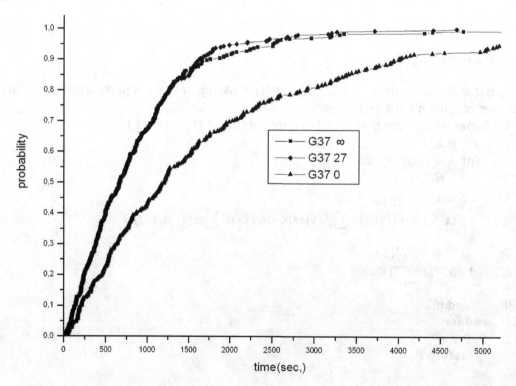

Table 1. Computational results

Problem	Size	BKS	Time (Seconds)		Average		BFS	
			GES-PR	GES	GES-PR	GES	GES-PR	GES
G1	800	11624	10.73	13.72	11624.0	11624.0	11624	11624
G2	800	11620	9.97	9.26	11620.0	11620.0	11620	11620
G3	800	11622	2.63	2.56	11622.0	11622.0	11622	11622
G11	800	564	2.43	2.44	564.0	564.0	564	564
G12	800	556	7.30	7.83	556.0	556.0	556	556
G13	800	582	1.51	1.52	582.0	582.0	582	582
G14	800	3063	707.24	509.94	3064.0	3063.6	**3064**	3064
G15	800	3050	14.33	10.56	3050.0	3050.0	3050	3050
G16	800	3052	43.10	40.48	3052.0	3052.0	3052	3052
G22	2000	13358	647.28	722.98	13358.9	13356.5	**13359**	13358
G23	2000	13329	293.36	170.95	13342.0	13342.0	**13342**	13342
G24	2000	13331	310.53	847.71	13337.0	13335.1	**13337**	13337
G32	2000	1402	66.35	87.68	1410.0	1410.0	**1410**	1410
G33	2000	1376	315.89	494.84	1382.0	1381.8	**1382**	1382
G34	2000	1372	97.50	72.89	1384.0	1384.0	**1384**	1384
G35	2000	7672	937.83	616.08	7684.8	7682.9	**7686**	7685
G36	2000	7670	861.02	943.84	7675.7	7673.9	**7677**	7675
G37	2000	7681	916.74	763.45	7688.7	7687.6	**7691**	7690
G43	1000	6660	48.69	395.53	6660.0	6660.0	6660	6660
G44	1000	6650	6.33	11.22	6650.0	6650.0	6650	6650
G45	1000	6654	146.42	744.34	6654.0	6653.5	6654	6654
G48	3000	6000	0.12	0.12	6000.0	6000.0	6000	6000
G49	3000	6000	0.16	0.16	6000.0	6000.0	6000	6000
G50	3000	5880	11.82	11.48	5880.0	5880.0	5880	5880
	Total sum:	150793	5459.28	6481.58	150841.1	150830.9	150845	150841
sg3dl101000	1000	896	77.44	128.25	896.0	896.0	896
sg3dl102000	1000	900	3.04	2.98	900.0	900.0	900
sg3dl103000	1000	892	9.80	9.73	892.0	892.0	892
sg3dl104000	1000	898	13.96	13.62	898.0	898.0	898
sg3dl105000	1000	886	130.10	106.4	886.0	886.0	886
sg3dl106000	1000	888	4.07	4.28	888.0	888.0	888
sg3dl107000	1000	900	108.68	114.96	900.0	900.0	900
sg3dl108000	1000	882	121.25	162.67	882.0	882.0	882
sg3dl109000	1000	902	36.98	25.04	902.0	902.0	902
sg3dl1010000	1000	894	6.73	8.93	894.0	894.0	894
sg3dl141000	2744	2446	643.20	714.53	2445.2	2443.6	2446

continued on following page

Table 1. Continued

Problem	Size	BKS	Time (Seconds)			Average		BFS	
			GES-PR	GES		GES-PR	GES	GES-PR	GES
sg3dl142000	2744	2458	278.61	552.15		2458.0	2457.6	2458	
sg3dl143000	2744	2442	609.80	642.61		2441.2	2439.8	2442	
sg3dl144000	2744	2450	847.39	633.33		2449.0	2447.6	2450	
sg3dl145000	2744	2446	259.69	486.88		2446.0	2446.0	2446	
sg3dl146000	2744	2450	648.79	360.03		2450.8	2450.2	**2452**	
sg3dl147000	2744	2444	604.55	614.73		2443.8	2443.8	2444	
sg3dl148000	2744	2446	617.13	587.98		2445.6	2444.8	**2448**	
sg3dl149000	2744	2424	670.98	659.87		2425.6	2425.4	**2426**	
sg3dl1410000	2744	2458	380.96	539.63		2457.0	2455.8	2458	
		Total sum: 33402	6073.15	6368.6		33400.2	33392.6	33408	

In this study, we used the same algorithmic parameters as were described by Shylo (2010). Each problem from the benchmark set was solved 10 times with a time limit set to 30 minutes. The results of these runs are presented in Table 1. The problem size and the best known solution value (BKS) in the literature (excluding the results reported by Shylo, 2010) are reported for each benchmark instance. The best found solutions (column "BFS") among all 10 runs obtained within the 30 minute interval reveal the overall superiority of the approach, which utilizes the path- relinking scheme (GES-PR) compared to GES without path relinking (see the results for G22, G35, G36, sg3dl144000, sg3dl148000 and sg3dl1410000). The average best found solutions (within the 30 minute time limit) were better for GES-PR on all benchmark problems (column "Average"). The average times (column "Time") to the best found solution for each run (average out of 10) indicate that on many problems GES-PR not only provides better solutions, but also requires less computational time.

In this paper, we investigated the potential of the path relinking methodology for the Max-Cut problem and provided its implementation within Global Equilibrium Search. The computational results on a set of standard benchmark problems revealed high potential of this approach leading to new solution records: 7686 for G35, 7691 for G37 and 2452 for sg3dl146000.

REFERENCES

Aarts, E., & Korst, J. (1989). *Simulated annealing and Boltzmann machines: A stochastic approach to combinatorial optimization and neural computing*. New York, NY: John Wiley & Sons.

Barahona, F., Grotschel, M., Junger, M., & Reinelt, G. (1988). An application of combinatorial optimization to statistical physics and circuit layout design. *Operations Research*, *36*, 493–513. doi:10.1287/opre.36.3.493

Burer, S., Monteiro, R. D. C., & Zhang, Y. (2002). Rank-two relaxation heuristics for max-cut and other binary quadratic programs. *SIAM Journal on Optimization*, *12*(2), 503–521. doi:10.1137/S1052623400382467

Chang, K. C., & Du, H. C. (1988). Layer assignment problem for three-layer routing. *IEEE Transactions on Computers*, *37*, 625–632. doi:10.1109/12.4616

Festa, P., Pardalos, P. M., Resende, M. G. C., & Ribeiro, C. C. (2002). Randomized heuristics for the max-cut problem. *Optimization Methods and Software*, *7*, 1033–1058. doi:10.1080/1055678021000090033

Glover, F., Laguna, M., & Marti, R. (2000). Fundamentals of scatter search and path relinking. *Control and Cybernetics*, *39*, 653–684.

Goemans, M. X., & Williamson, D. (1995). Improved approximation algorithms for maximum cut and satisfiability problems using semidefinite programming. *Journal of the ACM*, *42*, 1115–1145. doi:10.1145/227683.227684

Helmberg, C., & Rendl, F. (1999). A spectral bundle method for semidefinite programming. *SIAM Journal on Optimization*, *10*(3), 673–696. doi:10.1137/S1052623497328987

Kahruman, S., Kolotoglu, E., Butenko, S., & Hicks, I. V. (2007). On greedy construction heuristics for the max-cut problem. *International Journal of Computer Science Engineering*, *3*(3), 211–218.

Karp, R. (1972). Reducibility among combinatorial problems. In Miller, R., & Thatcher, J. (Eds.), *Complexity of computer computations* (pp. 85–103). New York, NY: Plenum Press.

Luby, M., Sinclair, A., & Zuckerman, D. (1993). Optimal speedup of Las Vegas algorithms. *Information Processing Letters*, *47*(4), 173–180. doi:10.1016/0020-0190(93)90029-9

Marti, R., Duarte, A., & Laguna, M. (2009). Advanced scatter search for the max-cut problem. *INFORMS Journal on Computing*, *21*(1), 26–38. doi:10.1287/ijoc.1080.0275

Palubeckis, G., & Krivickiene, V. (2004). Application of multistart tabu search to the max-cut problem. *Informaacines Technologijos Ir Valdymas*, *2*(31), 29–35.

Pardalos, P. M., Prokopyev, O. A., Shylo, O. V., & Shylo, V. P. (2008). Global equilibrium search applied to the unconstrained binary quadratic optimization problem. *Optimization Methods Software*, *23*(1), 129–140. doi:10.1080/10556780701550083

Shylo, O. V., Prokopyev, O. A., & Shylo, V. P. (2008). Solving weighted max-sat via global equilibrium search. *Operations Research Letters*, *36*(4), 434–438. doi:10.1016/j.orl.2007.11.007

Shylo, V. P., & Shylo, O. V. (2010). Solving the maxcut problem by the global equilibrium search. *Cybernetics and Systems Analysis*, *46*, 744–754. doi:10.1007/s10559-010-9256-4

This work was previously published in the International Journal of Swarm Intelligence Research, Volume 2, Issue 2, edited by Yuhui Shi, pp. 42-51, copyright 2011 by IGI Publishing (an imprint of IGI Global).

Chapter 4

Path Relinking with Multi-Start Tabu Search for the Quadratic Assignment Problem

Tabitha James
Virginia Tech, USA

Cesar Rego
University of Mississippi, USA

ABSTRACT

This paper introduces a new path relinking algorithm for the well-known quadratic assignment problem (QAP) in combinatorial optimization. The QAP has attracted considerable attention in research because of its complexity and its applicability to many domains. The algorithm presented in this study employs path relinking as a solution combination method incorporating a multistart tabu search algorithm as an improvement method. The resulting algorithm has interesting similarities and contrasts with particle swarm optimization methods. Computational testing indicates that this algorithm produces results that rival the best QAP algorithms. The authors additionally conduct an analysis disclosing how different strategies prove more or less effective depending on the landscapes of the problems to which they are applied. This analysis lays a foundation for developing more effective future QAP algorithms, both for methods based on path relinking and tabu search, and for hybrids of such methods with related processes found in particle swarm optimization.

1. INTRODUCTION

The quadratic assignment problem (QAP) is a classical NP-hard combinatorial optimization problem that has been extensively studied. In the context of facility location, the objective is to find a minimum cost assignment of facilities to loca- tions considering the flow of materials between facilities and the distance between locations. The problem may be formulated as follows:

$$\min_{p \in P} z(p) = \sum_{i=1}^{n} \sum_{j=1}^{n} f_{ij} d_{p(i)p(j)} \qquad (1)$$

DOI: 10.4018/978-1-4666-2479-5.ch004

where f is the flow matrix, d is the distance matrix, p is a permutation vector of n indexes of facilities (or locations) mapping a possible assignment of n facilities to n locations, and P is the set of all n-vector permutations. For each pair of assignments $r = p(i)$ and $s = p(j)$ in p the flow f_{ij} between the two facilities i and j is multiplied by the distance d_{rs} between the two locations r and s. The sum of these terms over all pairs gives the total cost assignment $z(p)$ for the permutation p. The objective is to find a permutation p^* in P of minimum total cost.

In addition to the facility location context, the QAP is useful in a variety of other domains, including electronics, chemistry, manufacturing, computation, data analysis, and transportation. See for example, Cela (1998) for a comprehensive discussion of these applications.

Metaheuristic approaches have been popularly applied to the QAP due to the limitations of exact methods to solve such problems within the computational boundaries of existing technology. Metaheuristic solution techniques applied to the QAP have included tabu search (Taillard, 1991; Misevicius, 2005; James, Rego, & Glover, 2009), scatter search (Cung et al., 1996), genetic algorithms (Fleurent & Ferland, 1994; Ahuja, Orlin, & Tiwari, 2000; Misevicius, 2003, 2004; Drezner, 2003, 2005), GRASP (Li, Pardalos, & Resende, 1994), path-relinking (James, Rego, & Glover, 2005), hybrid approaches of GRASP with path relinking (Oliveira, Pardalos, & Resende, 2004), iterative local search (Hussin & Stützle, 2009; Ramkumar, Ponnambalam, & Jawahar, 2009; Stützle, 2006), and several forms of particle swarm optimization (Stützle & Dorigo, 1999; Iordache, 2010).

In this study we develop a new path relinking algorithm for the QAP that combines a number of adaptive memory strategies that have shown promise in previous studies. We demonstrate highly satisfactory results for two of the more difficult well-known test sets for the QAP. In ad-

dition, competitive results are obtained against some of the best metaheuristics for the QAP.

A special aspect of our study is an analysis that identifies how different strategies prove more or less effective depending on the landscapes of the problems they are applied to, giving a foundation for future studies that may integrate these strategies within methods that are more highly responsive to the landscapes encountered. Such methods may join path relinking and tabu search, as in the present study, or may embody hybrids that combine our present framework with certain related designs derived from particle swarm optimization.

The remainder of this paper is organized as follows: Section 2 briefly reviews fundamental components of the scatter search/path relinking framework and gives a detailed description of the proposed path relinking algorithm together with observations about connections and contrasts with particle swarm optimization procedures. Section 3 presents the computational results and a comparative analysis with several of the best performing algorithms in the literature. This section also provides the analysis that identifies the performance characteristics of different strategies in relation to the problem landscapes encountered. The conclusions are presented in Section 4.

2. THE PATH-RELINKING ALGORITHM

The evolutionary path-relinking algorithm developed in the current study follows the general scatter search/path relinking (SS/PR) template described by Glover (1998). Although scatter search and path relinking methods share several principles of adaptive memory programming due to an association with tabu search, they fundamentally differ in the way parent solutions are combined to generate offspring. While scatter search operates in a vector space of solutions by generating linear combinations of solution vectors, path relinking combines solutions by generating paths in the neighborhood space between an initiating solution and one or more guiding solutions, using classical local search neighborhood structures. In general, both methods maintain a reference set of elite solutions that evolve by exploiting adaptive memory processes.

Glover suggests five primary components of scatter search and path relinking methods, as part of the SS/PR template, to both utilize and manage the reference set. These component processes are as follows:

- **Diversification Generation Method:** This method is applied to generate a set of solutions that give a reasonable representation of the entire search space for the problem. The method applied is typically dependent upon the problem type. Thus, it is tailored to generate solutions based upon some knowledge of the problem type.
- **Improvement Method:** This method applies a problem-specific heuristic with the intention of creating a better solution in terms of the objective function evaluation.
- **Reference Set Update Method:** This method is used to maintain the reference set. It is also used to build the initial reference set. This method determines which of the solutions generated by the diversification generation method and the improvement method meet the entry requirements for the reference set based upon its contribution to the diversity of the search or its solution quality.
- **Subset Generation Method:** This method creates subsets of solutions which are then combined to create new solutions which may possibly be added to the reference set. Subset of two or more solutions may be created during this procedure. This method uses information about the quality or diversity of the solutions contained in the reference set to create these subsets.

- **Structured Combination Method:** This method creates a new solution(s) from the subsets created by the subset generation method. This procedure uses information available about the characteristics of the problem as a basis for creating the new solutions. Therefore, this method is also typically customized for the particular problem type being investigated.

When properly organized, these methods form the basic structure of an SS/PR algorithm.

A salient connection exists between path relinking (PR) and particle swarm optimization (PSO), due to the construction whereby the paths of PR are guided by selected high quality solutions from the reference set. This operation is analogous to the PSO manipulation of the direction of a trajectory according to the combined influence of the "personal best experience" of a given particle (solution stream) and the "global best experience" over all particles. At the same time, there are equally salient differences between the methods. The evolving solution trajectory of a given particle in particle swarm optimization remains inseparably associated with the identity of the particle. In path relinking, by contrast, the trajectory encounters points where the search is "split off" from the initiating and guiding solutions, to spawn new focal solutions that become the source of new trajectories.

Apart from the relinking step itself, the trajectories in PR evolve separately under the control of a metaheuristic improvement process (the iterated second step of the SS/PR Template) which is often, though not invariably, provided by tabu search. Each focal solution identified at a splitting-off point becomes the starting point for additional applications of the improvement process, and the best outcome of this process is a candidate to enter the pool of solutions provided by the reference set. In this way the focal points provide new initiating and guiding solutions within the path relinking process, and hence by extension become the source of new focal solutions. In short, the operations of scatter search and path relinking contrast with those of PSO primarily by providing a more varied form of guidance to the evolving solutions, which depends on interactions with a wider variety of elite partners and is punctuated by spawning new trajectories from the focal solutions, each shaped and refined by the underlying improvement method. These connections may be exploited by creating hybrids of our present methodology with particle swarm optimization, particularly in reference to the analysis provided later concerning the relative merits of different strategies for problems exhibiting different solution landscapes.

The form of the basic structure of the SS/PR Template as manifest in our path-relinking algorithm is given in Figure 1. In what follows, we describe how the methods outlined above are implemented in our path relinking algorithm for the quadratic assignment problem (PR-QAP).

The PR-QAP algorithm begins by performing an initialization procedure to create an initial reference set. The distribution of high-quality and diverse solutions that make up the reference set is predetermined. The first step is to generate a random permutation which is then subjected to the multistart tabu search (MS-TS) procedure for possible improvement. If the goal is to produce a member of the high-quality solution set, the MS-TS is allowed to work longer. Otherwise, if the goal is to produce a solution to become a member of the diverse solution set, the operation of the MS-TS runtime is purposely shortened.

The improved permutation, once returned from the MS-TS procedure is added to the appropriate subset of the reference set. This initialization process is repeated for a number of permutations equal to the predefined reference set size. Therefore, the update to the reference set, during initialization, is simply to add the solutions to the reference set and sort the high quality solutions according to their quality measured in terms of objective function value.

The path relinking procedure is executed for a predetermined number of iterations. An iteration of the procedure begins by choosing two solutions

Figure 1. Structure of path relinking algorithm for the QAP (PR-QAP)

```
Parameters:
refSetSize (cardinality of the reference set)
maxIterations (maximum number of iterations)


Read in Instance Data
Initialization Procedure:
        Loop While i < refSetSize
                Randomly Generate Permutation
                Perform Improvement Method
                Perform Reference Set Update Method
        End Loop

Path Relinking Procedure:
        Loop While i < maxIterations
                Perform Solution Generation Method
                Perform Solution Combination Method
                Perform Improvement Method
                Perform Reference Set Update Method
                Perform Diversification Generation Method
        End Loop
```

to combine. To perform the path relinking one of the two solutions is identified as the "guiding" solution and the other solution is designated the "initiating" working solution. Each step of the path relinking process creates a new working solution by replacing assignments in the current working solution with assignments in the guiding solution. The process stops once all the assignments in the working solution match the assignments of the guiding solution. In our PR-QAP algorithm, each high quality solution in the reference set is used as a guiding solution for each of the diverse solutions.

Our path relinking method selects a number of focal solutions from among the intermediate solutions that are generated as the working solution is transformed into the guiding solution. The MS-TS improvement method is run on these focal solutions in an attempt to improve their quality. After the intermediate solutions have been improved, they are considered for inclusion in the high quality portion of the reference set.

During the first iteration of the main path relinking procedure, the diverse portion of the reference set holds solutions obtained from the initialization procedure. For subsequent iterations of the path relinking procedure, if a given coupling of a diverse solution and a high quality solutions does not result in generating a new high quality solution (by applying the MS-TS process to focal solutions on the path) that becomes added to the reference set, the diverse solution member of the combination is replaced by a diversified version of a high-quality solution which is produced by an application of the diversification generation method. In what follows, we will expand the discussion of each of the major components of the PR-QAP algorithm.

2.1. QAP Neighborhood Definition and Cost Calculations

Given a permutation, a partial cost matrix can be calculated to determine the cost of a given exchange of assignments. This partial cost can be added to the objective function value for the original permutation, when a swap is made, to reconcile z(p) without having to incur the expense of recalculating Equation 1. Specifically, let the triplet (p, r, s) define an exchange that swaps the elements r and s in a permutation p, the partial costs associated with the exchange, for symmetrical QAP instances, can be calculated by:

$$\Delta(p,r,s) = 2\sum_{k \neq r,s} (f_{sk} - f_{rk})(d_{p(s)p(k)} - d_{p(r)p(k)}) \tag{2}$$

Once an exchange (r,s) is made on the permutation p to create a new permutation t, the partial cost matrix needs to be updated. The update can be accomplished using Equation 3 for the symmetric case when u or v is not equal to r or s, in which case Equation 2 can be used.

$$\Delta(t,u,v) = \Delta(p,u,v) + 2(f_{ru} - f_{rv} + f_{sv} - f_{su}) \\ (d_{t(s)t(u)} - d_{t(s)t(v)} + d_{t(r)t(v)} - d_{t(r)t(u)}) \tag{3}$$

These cost calculations are used in MS-TS to evaluate possible exchanges and update the objective function and partial cost matrices. A more detailed description of these cost calculations and a discussion of the asymmetric case can be found in Burkard and Rendl (1984) and Taillard (1991).

2.2. Subset Generation Solution Combination Method

PR-QAP uses a simple solution combination method. Each high-quality solution in the reference set acts as the guiding solution for each diverse solution (initiating solution). Combining every high-quality solution with every diverse solution creates pairs of solutions that are then passed to the path relinking method. For each pair of solutions, we path relink between the initiating solution and the guiding solution. To illustrate, consider the solution $g(i)$ to be the guiding solution and $i(j)$ to be the initiating solution.

$g(i) = (2, 3, 1, 5, 6, 4)$

$i(j) = (3, 1, 2, 4, 6, 5)$

Path relinking considers exchanges that will transform $i(j)$ into $g(i)$. Our implementation of path relinking does this by sequentially moving through $i(j)$ and performing the transformation one element at a time. Following the example above, in position 1, $g(1)=2$. The procedure will locate the array position 2 in $i(j)$, in this case, $i(3)=2$. The cost of making the exchange $(3, 2)$ on $i(j)$ is then calculated. If the move cost is less than zero, the solution is considered for inclusion in the set of focal solutions and the swap is performed on the initiating solution. If the move cost is greater than or equal to zero, the swap is made but the solution is not added to the set of focal solutions. So in our example since this is the first exchange, if the move cost of exchange $(3,2)$ on $i(j)$ is less than zero, the solution $f(k) = (2, 1, 3, 4, 6, 5)$ would be added to the set of focal solutions.

After the first exchange, the initiating solution becomes:

$i(k) = (2, 1, 3, 4, 6, 5)$

and the next move in the sequence performs the exchange to move 3 into $i(2)$, since $g(2) = 3$. This results in the solution $f(k) = (2, 3, 1, 4, 6, 5)$ which is then considered for addition to the focal solutions. However, this solution is added only if the move cost of $(1,3)$ is negative, does not duplicate a previous move cost identified during the relinking step, and is better than the worst of

these move costs. This last condition is applied, however, only if the accumulated number of focal solutions for the current relinking process has reached its maximum allowed value.

Regardless of whether or not $f(k)$ is added to the focal solutions, the move $(1,3)$ is made on $i(j)$ and the new initiating solution becomes:

$i(j) = (2, 3, 1, 4, 6, 5)$

Since $g(3) = 1$ and now $i(3) = 1$, no move is considered and the procedure next considers $f(k) = (2, 3, 1, 5, 6, 4)$ to become a focal solution and performs the move $(4,5)$ on the initiating solution. The procedure continues in this manner until $i(j) = g(i)$. Each of the resulting focal solutions is then subjected to the improvement method.

2.3. Multistart Tabu Search Improvement Method

Tabu search is a neighborhood search technique that has demonstrated the ability to provide high quality solutions for a large variety of difficult combinatorial optimization problems, including the QAP. A key feature of tabu search is the use of adaptive memory strategies to help guide the exploration of the search space. In basic tabu search algorithms, short-term memory is most often implemented in the form of a tabu restrictions and aspiration criteria. Tabu restrictions inhibit the choice of certain moves based on considerations determined in previous iterations. A short-term memory of move attributes is generally maintained to allow for the identification of tabu moves in further iterations of the algorithm.

The number of iterations an attribute is active in a tabu restriction defines the length of the short-term memory and is called the tabu tenure. Large tabu tenures force the search to move away from previously visited regions of the solution space, thus promoting diversification, while small tabu tenure values encourage the algorithm to search more deeply in the vicinity of local optimal solutions, thus promoting intensification. Consequently, the highest degree of intensification in tabu search may be achieved when using the lowest possible tabu tenure that is sufficiently large to prevent the algorithm from cycling back to previously visited solutions.

The method also uses aspiration criteria that override the tabu status of a move if it possesses attractive qualities, such as a producing a new global best objective function value. The appropriate balance between intensification and diversification generally depends on the status of the search and the characteristics of the solution space. In order to cope with complex solution spaces, advanced tabu search algorithms make use of longer-term memory structures as fundamental components to implement adaptive learning strategies.

While intensification and diversification are both important components for an effective search, in our experience good diversification strategies are typically more complex than intensification strategies. The reason is that intensification focuses on examining regions in the vicinity of solutions that have already been visited, or on generating solutions that share characteristics of high-quality solutions previously encountered, and in either case the resulting space is much smaller space than the remaining unexplored space. Determining where to go next and how far to move away from current regions requires a means for identifying the appropriate balance between intensification and diversification at each stage of the search. Since new information is found as the search progresses, adaptive processes are necessary to effectively explore the exponentially large and complex solution spaces generally found in combinatorial optimization.

While path-relinking seeks to cover the solution space between known solutions, multistart tabu search is aimed at searching the space outside of those regions. The multistart strategy used here was suggested by James, Rego, and Glover (2009), as an improvement to the robust tabu search (RTS) method by Taillard (1991). The method carries out the basic tabu search procedure as in RTS but restarts after a defined interval by clearing the tabu list and resetting the tabu tenure and stopping criteria parameters. The pseudocode for our MS-TS approach is provided in Figure 2. As in RTS, the MS-TS algorithm uses the cost calculations

Figure 2. Pseudocode for the multistart tabu search (MS-TS)

```
Parameters:
maxFailures (maximum number of consecutive non-improving moves)
allowableFailures (maximum failures before resetting tabu parameters)

Loop while (numFailures < maxFailures)
        If is tabu but meets all aspiration criteria or is not tabu and best cost so far
                Store best exchange that meets all conditions
        End If
        Update tabu list
        Make exchange on working solution
        If strictly improving
                Update best solution
        Else
                Increment numFailures
                If (numFailures = allowableFailures)
                        Release tabu list
                        Reset tabu tenure parameters
                        Reset allowableFailures
                End If
        End If
End Loop
```

described in Section 2.1 to create an initial move cost matrix. The best move is performed and its associated tabu restrictions are created. The cost matrix is then updated.

For all subsequent iterations, tabu moves are not allowed to be made unless the aspiration criteria hold true. MS-TS adopts the RTS aspiration criteria, which subject a tabu move to three levels of aspiration. The first level requires the move to meet either one of two conditions: the move results in an improved global solution or the tabu tenure of at least one component of the swap is less than the iteration minus an aspiration value. If the exchange passes the first level, the second level determines if the tabu move is the first tabu exchange examined in the current iteration and if so, then the exchange is allowed; otherwise a third-level allows the exchange if the move cost is smaller than all of the previous move costs. Barring one of these three conditions, the aspiration criteria are unsuccessful, and the tabu status of the move remains intact.

If an improving move is not found, a counter of the number of failed attempts to obtain an improvement is increased. A limit on the number of "allowable failures" is drawn randomly from a specified range at the start of the TS. Once this limit is reached, the algorithm clears out its tabu list, modifies the range from which the tabu tenures are drawn, and draws a new value for the limit on allowable failures. Clearing the tabu list allows the algorithm to perform a restricted descent as the algorithm recreates the tabu list. The modification of the parameters alters the permissible moves of future iterations and therefore may impact the search trajectory. This multistart variant perturbs the search but maintains the same working solution. MS-TS iterates until a maximum number of failures is reached. The maximum failures condition depends on the specific subroutine of the algorithm that calls MS-TS.

2.4. Reference Set Update Method

The reference set update manages only the high quality portion of the reference set. After one of the focal solutions created during the path relinking method is improved, the reference set update method determines whether it will be added to the reference set. Duplicate solutions are not added to the high quality portion of the reference set. If the focal solution being considered for addition to the reference set is not a duplicate solution, the quality of that solution is determined. The solution is added to the reference set if it has a better objective function value than the worst solution currently in the high quality portion of the reference set. The new solution replaces the worst high quality solution.

2.5. Diversification Generation Method

After the first iteration of the main path relinking procedure, the solutions in the diverse portion of the reference set are eligible for replacement. A diverse solution is replaced if a given pairing for the path relinking procedure did not result in an update to the high quality solutions. If it is determined the diverse solution will be replaced, a solution is obtained from the high quality solutions. The diversification generation method is used to create a new solution using the high quality solution as a seed solution. Figure 3 provides the pseudocode for the diversification generation method.

The diversification generation method is designed to add controlled diversification to the algorithm. When applied at the conclusion of a path relinking step (and an unsuccessful effort to find an improved solution to add to the reference set), it modifies the diverse portion of the reference set by using one of the high quality solutions as the seed solution and creating a new diverse solution. For example, consider the following seed solution:

$ss(i) = (1, 3, 4, 2, 5, 6)$

Suppose we set the *start* = *step* = 2, hence, *j*=2. Then the first element of the new solution would become $ss(j)$ or $ss(2)$, resulting in the following permutation:

$ns(k) = (3, \_, \_, \_, \_, \_)$

The value *j* is incremented by *step* and at each iteration $ss(j)$ is copied sequentially into *ns*. The resulting permutation becomes:

$ns(k) = (3, 2, 6, \_, \_, \_)$

At this point, the procedure returns to the outer loop and *start* is decremented by 1. In our example, this sets *start* = 1. The value in $ss(1)$ is copied into the next available position in *ns*, so $ns(4) = 1$, and *j* is incremented. The resulting final permutation then becomes:

$ns(k) = (3, 2, 6, 1, 4, 5)$.

3. RESULTS AND DISCUSSION

PR-QAP was tested on a standard set of benchmark instances obtained from QAPLIB (Burkard, Karisch, & Rendl, 1997). The algorithm was written in the C programming language and run on a single 900 MHz Itanium2 processor of an SGI Altix 3700. The Altix runs the Linux operating system and the Intel C compiler was used. The parameter settings for PR-QAP are provided in Table 1. Most of the parameter settings are the same as those used in James, Rego, and Glover (2009). Those that differ, the maxFailures parameters and the range parameters that depend on maxFailures, were adjusted to provide runtimes for PR-QAP that were equivalent to the runtimes for the RTS and multistart algorithms used for comparison in Table 2, as well as to balance the maxIterations

setting of the main path relinking procedure with the length of the MS-TS runs.

Table 2 presents the computational results for PR-QAP and provides a comparison of those results to RTS and two of the best performing multistart tabu search algorithms from James, Rego, and Glover (2009). RTS provided the basis for the multistart tabu search algorithms and therefore the improvement method in PR-QAP. TTMTS is the multistart algorithm used as the improvement method for PR-QAP with its max-Failures value set to 50000*n. The DivTS multi-start method uses the same restarting techniques as TTMTS but, when restarted, additionally replaces the working solution with a diversified copy of the global best solution using the same diversification technique employed in the current study. TTMTS was chosen for use in PR-QAP because, in the restricted runs of the TS employed in PR-QAP, it was found beneficial not to perturb the working solution. However, releasing the tabu list and modifying the tabu parameters perturbs the search without introducing the harsh diversification that results from replacing the working solution. Since the diversification procedure is introduced as part of the path relinking framework, including the additional perturbation as part of the improvement method was determined to be unnecessary and in some instances counterproductive.

Three sets of QAP instances are used in the computational testing. The first are the Skorin-Kapov (sko*) instances. This set of instances has grid-based distance matrices where the distances are the Manhattan distance between points on a grid (Stützle, 2006). The second set (tai*a) consists of randomly generated points (based on a uniform distribution) from the Taillard's test set. Both sko* and tai*a instances are unstructured. Landscape analysis (Merz & Frisleben, 2000; Stutzle 2006) shows that these instances have a large number of local optima spread across the solution space sharing (almost) no similarities and

Table 1. Parameter settings for the PR-QAP

Parameter	Description	Setting	Notes
itemsInRefSet	Number of solutions kept in the reference set	8	Distribution: High Quality Solutions: 4 Diverse Solutions: 4
maxFailures1	Maximum number of failures before MS-TS is exited	$20*n$	Initialization Setting for High Quality Solutions
maxFailures2	Maximum number of failures before MS-TS is exited	$10*n$	Initialization Setting for Diverse Solutions
maxIterations	Number of iterations of the Main Path Relinking Procedure	30	
numIntermediate	Number of intermediate solutions retained by the Path Relinking Method	8	
maxFailures3	Maximum number of failures before MS-TS is exited	$10*n$	Setting for Path Relinking Method
upperTabuLimit	The upper value of the range from which to draw the limits of the tabu tenure range	$11*n/10$	The initial upper limit on the range for the tabu tenures before the first restart is $11*n/10$
lowerTabuLimit	The lower value of the range from which to draw the limits of the tabu tenure range	$1*n/10$	The initial lower limit on the range for the tabu tenures before the first restart is $9*n/10$
upperAllowF	The upper range from which to draw the allowableFailures parameter	$10*n/10$	
lowerAllowF	The lower range from which to draw the allowableFailures parameter	$5*n/10$	
aspiration	Used in first level of aspiration	$n*n*2$	
step	Step size used in diversification generation method	2 to n-1	For each seed solution, the step size iterates sequentially from 2 to n-1

being separated from the global optimum by very large distances. The last set of instances, also Taillard test instances (tai*b), was generated to appear similar to real-life problems, irregularly structured and having local optima concentrated in a small region of the feasible solution space. Landscape analysis of the largest two tai*b instances reveals that these instances have correlated local optima. These three sets of problems provide test instances from each of the major categories of the QAPLIB instances and represent some of the most difficult instances for most metaheuristic methods.

In Table 2, the average percent deviation (APD) over 10 runs is provided for each algorithm, along with the average computational times in minutes.

A 1.3 MHz Itanium processor was used to run the multistart algorithms, which is better than the processor used to run PR-QAP. Therefore, the runtimes for all of the algorithms are similar. The results presented for the PR-QAP were in many cases obtained in less time than the other algorithms even considering the disadvantage in processor speed.

The results show that PR-QAP performs exceptionally well on the sko* problems, where the method finds the best known solution (BKS) 106 out of 130 times. On 6 of the 13 sko* instances, PR-EC found the BKS on every run. On the other 7 instances the APD was good (small) and in all cases the BKS was found at least twice. PR-QAP

Table 2. Computational results for PR-QAP and comparisons to related algorithms

Problem	BKS	RTS		TTMTS		DivTS		PR-QAP	
		APD	Time	APD	Time	APD	Time	APD	Time
sko42	15812	**0.000**(10)	3.88	**0.000**	3.86	**0.000**(10)	3.98	**0.000**(10)	4.29
sko49	23386	0.038(2)	8.38	0.004	9.60	0.008(7)	9.61	**0.000**(10)	8.72
sko56	34458	0.010(4)	16.75	0.002	13.75	0.002(8)	13.16	**0.000**(10)	13.38
sko64	48498	0.005(5)	23.97	**0.000**	25.44	**0.000**(10)	22.03	**0.000**(10)	27.50
sko72	66256	0.043	37.38	0.014	35.29	**0.006**(2)	37.98	0.013(8)	39.40
sko81	90998	0.051	59.25	0.017	62.36	0.016(2)	56.36	**0.004**(8)	63.95
sko90	115534	0.062	65.60	**0.017**	99.69	0.026	89.60	**0.017**(7)	91.21
sko100a	152002	0.089	76.40	0.026	134.53	0.027	129.22	**0.010**(4)	132.01
sko100b	153890	0.056	108.80	0.011	124.84	0.008(2)	106.55	**0.000**(10)	138.48
sko100c	147862	0.031	93.84	0.008	113.95	0.006(2)	126.69	**0.000**(10)	137.11
sko100d	149576	0.055	111.97	0.016	129.23	0.027(1)	123.45	**0.015**(7)	137.53
sko100e	149150	0.041	95.80	0.007	130.14	0.009(1)	108.84	**0.000**(10)	131.98
sko100f	149036	0.066	100.28	0.021	118.90	0.023	110.28	**0.011**(2)	138.32
Average	703482	_0.042_(21)	_61.72_	_0.011_	_77.04_	_0.012_(45)	_72.13_	**_0.005_**(106)	_81.84_
tai20a	1167256	**0.000**(10)	0.24	**0.000**(10)	0.23	**0.000**(10)	0.24	**0.000**(10)	0.35
tai25a	1818146	**0.000**(10)	0.55	**0.000**(10)	0.50	**0.000**(10)	0.56	**0.000**(10)	0.68
tai30a	2422002	**0.000**(10)	1.65	**0.000**(10)	1.41	**0.000**(10)	1.31	**0.000**(10)	1.15
tai35a	3139370	0.112(5)	2.92	0.056(6)	3.16	**0.000**(10)	4.44	0.033(8)	1.92
tai40a	4938796	0.462	4.25	0.284	5.22	**0.222**(1)	5.16	0.249	2.92
tai50a	7205962	0.882	10.08	0.700	10.07	0.725	10.23	**0.566**	6.69
tai60a	13515450	0.974	24.73	0.820	25.92	0.718	25.69	**0.558**	14.29
tai80a	21059006	1.065	54.74	0.817	69.21	0.753	52.74	**0.600**	36.78
tai100a	122455319	1.071	114.55	0.846	145.26	0.825	142.06	**0.554**	80.42
Average	344355646	_0.507_(35)	_23.75_	_0.391_(36)	_29.00_	_0.360_(41)	_26.94_	**_0.285_**(38)	_16.13_
tai20b	637117113	**0.000**(10)	0.23	**0.000***(10)	0.23	**0.000**(10)	0.23	**0.000**(10)	0.23
tai25b	283315445	**0.000**(10)	0.46	**0.000***(10)	0.46	**0.000**(10)	0.46	**0.000**(10)	0.46
tai30b	637250948	**0.000**(10)	1.38	**0.000***(10)	1.28	**0.000**(10)	1.31	**0.000**(10)	1.27
tai35b	458821517	**0.000**(10)	2.20	**0.000***(10)	2.44	**0.000**(10)	2.39	**0.000**(10)	2.31
tai40b	608215054	**0.000**(10)	3.20	**0.000***(10)	3.17	**0.000**(10)	3.18	**0.000**(10)	3.18
tai50b	818415043	**0.000**(8)	11.02	**0.000***(8)	9.54	**0.000**(10)	8.82	0.132(6)	8.68
tai60b	1185996137	**0.000**(6)	17.89	**0.000***(4)	18.56	**0.000**(8)	17.08	0.133(3)	24.41
tai80b		0.008	51.99	0.013(2)	49.02	**0.006**	58.24	0.997	58.68
tai100b		**0.008**(3)	114.16	0.040(2)	107.63	0.056	118.91	0.197	145.96
Average		_0.001_(67)	_22.50_	_0.005_(66)	_21.37_	_0.006_(68)	_23.40_	_0.162_(59)	_23.59_

obtained an APD that matched or was superior to (smaller than) that of the other algorithms on all but one instance (sko72). On that one instance, only DivTS performed better than PR-QAP.

PR-QAP also performed very well on the tai*a instances, finding the BKS 38 out of 90 times. The number of best known solutions found is similar to the other algorithms in Table 2, but the APD of PR-QAP is significantly better (smaller) than that of RTS or either of the multistart tabu search variants.

The tai*b instances were more difficult for PR-QAP. While the algorithm reached the BKS on every run for the first five instances, on the larger instances the APD was higher than desired. PR-QAP did find the BKS 59 out of 90 times for this test set, even though the gap was rather high on those where it failed to find the BKS.

Since local optima distributions for sko* and tai*a show large distances between good solutions, these problems benefit from employing greater diversification. PR-QAP makes ample use of diversification by means of the diverse solutions in the reference set, and we conjecture that this accounts for the positive results for the sko* and tai*a instances. As can be seen by examining the tabu search algorithms in Table 2, the tai*b instances, which have correlated local optima, benefit from unperturbed intense searches. In fact, the best algorithm for this set of instances was RTS, with an overall APD of 0.001. This indicates that the tai*b instances are sensitive even to relatively mild search perturbations. In fact, the results for the tai*b instances present progressively worse results as more diversification is added to the search. RTS has limited diversification imposed only by the tabu list restrictions. TTMTS incorporates mild diversification by resetting the tabu parameters. DivTS makes more use of diversification by replacing the working solution and PR-QAP incorporates an additional level of diversification on top of that provided by TTMTS. For each level of diversity, the results on the tai*b instances worsen.

This analysis indicates that to solve all classes of problems well, a tradeoff between diversification and intensification needs to be made. This is a promising area for future research.

Tables 3, 4, and 5 present results on the test instances described above by both PR-QAP and some of the best performing algorithms from the literature on each test set. These comparisons are meant to provide an idea of the relative quality of PR-QAP and are not meant to be direct comparisons. Not every algorithm ran all test sets or even all instances within a set. The algorithms were all run on different platforms with different stopping conditions, so a straightforward comparison is not possible. The comparisons do provide a rough gauge of the quality of the results obtained by PR-QAP. The other algorithms in the table are as follows:

- **ACO-GA/LS:** An ant colony optimization, genetic algorithm, local search hybrid (Tseng & Liang, 2006).
- **GA/SD:** A genetic algorithm hybrid with a strict descent operator (Drezner, 2003).
- **GA-S/TS:** A genetic algorithm hybrid with a simple TS operator (Drezner, 2003).
- **GA-C/TS:** A genetic algorithm hybrid with concentric TS operator (Drezner, 2003).
- **GA/IC-TS:** A genetic algorithm hybrid with an improved concentric TS operator (Drezner, 2005).
- **ETS1, ETS2, and ETS3:** Three TS variants (Misevicius, 2005).
- **GA/TS and GA/TS/I:** Two genetic algorithm hybrids with TS (Misevicius, 2003, 2004).
- **SS-PR:** A path relinking algorithm (James, Rego, & Glover, 2005).
- **ILS1, ILS2, ILS3, and ILS4:** Four iterated local search variants (Stützle, 2006).
- **ILS5 and ILS6:** Two population-based iterated local search algorithms (Stützle, 2006).

Table 3. Comparison of PR-QAP with algorithms from the literature on the sko* instances

Problem	PR-QAP		RTS		ACO-GA/LS		GA/SD		GA-S/TS		GA-C/TS		GA-IC/TS		SS-PR		ILS1		ILS2		ILS3		ILS4		ILS5		ILS6		I-ILS6		ACO1		ACO2		ACO3	
	APD		APD		APD		APD		APD		APD		APD		APD		APD		APD		APD		APD		APD		APD		APD		APD		APD		APD	
sko42	0.000 (10)		0.000		0.000		0.014		0.001		0.000		0.000		0.004		0.269		0.010		0.010		0.161		0.022		0.000		0.000		0.076		0.015		0.104	
sko49	0.000 (10)		0.038		0.060		0.107		0.062		0.009		0.000		0.049		0.226		0.133		0.133		0.139		0.090		0.068		0.000		0.141		0.067		0.150	
sko56	0.000 (10)		0.010		0.010		0.054		0.007		0.001		0.000		0.049		0.418		0.087		0.087		0.153		0.102		0.071		0.000		0.101		0.068		0.118	
sko64	0.000 (10)		0.005		0.000		0.051		0.019		0.000		0.003		0.045		0.413		0.068		0.068		0.202		0.079		0.057		0.000		0.129		0.042		0.171	
sko72	0.013 (8)		0.043		0.020		0.112		0.056		0.014		0.001		0.104		0.383		0.134		0.134		0.294		0.139		0.085		0.000		0.277		0.109		0.243	
sko81	0.004 (8)		0.051		0.030		0.087		0.058		0.014		0.002		0.051		0.586		0.101		0.100		0.194		0.100		0.082		0.001		0.144		0.071		0.223	
sko90	0.017 (7)		0.062		0.040		0.139		0.073		0.011		0.000		0.110		0.576		0.131		0.187		0.322		0.262		0.128		0.007		0.231		0.192		0.288	
sko100a	0.010 (4)		0.089		0.020		0.114		0.070		0.018		0.001		0.092		0.358		0.115		0.161		0.257		0.191		0.109		0.006							
sko100b	0.000 (10)		0.056		0.010		0.096		0.042		0.011		0.000																0.012							
sko100c	0.000 (10)		0.031		0.000		0.075		0.045		0.003		0.000																0.007							
sko100d	0.015 (7)		0.055		0.030		0.137		0.084		0.049		0.003																0.002							
sko100e	0.000 (10)		0.041		0.000		0.071		0.028		0.002																		0.021							
sko100f	0.011 (2)		0.066		0.030		0.148		0.110		0.032																		0.037							
Average	0.005		0.042		0.019		0.093		0.050		0.013		0.001		0.063		0.404		0.097		0.110		0.215		0.123		0.075		0.007		0.157		0.081		0.185	

Table 4. Comparison of PR-QAP with algorithms from the literature on the tai*a instances

Problem	PR-QAP	RTS	ACO-GA/LS	ETS1	ETS2	ETS3	GA/TS	GA/TS/I	SS-PR	ILS1	ILS2	ILS3	ILS4	ILS5	ILS6	I-ILS6	ACO1	ACO2	ACO3
	APD	APD	BPD	APD	APD	APD	APD	APD	APD	APD	APD	APD	APD	APD	APD	APD	APD	APD	APD
tai20a	0.000(10)	0.000	0.110	0.000	0.000	0.000	0.061	0.000	0.030	0.723	0.503	0.542	0.467	0.500	0.344	0.000	0.675	0.191	0.428
tai25a	0.000(10)	0.000	0.290	0.037	0.000	0.015	0.088	0.000	0.259	1.181	0.876	0.896	0.823	0.369	0.656	0.000	1.189	0.488	1.751
tai30a	0.000(10)	0.000	0.340	0.003	0.041	0.000	0.019	0.000	0.501	1.304	0.808	0.989	1.141	0.707	0.668	0.000	1.311	0.359	1.286
tai35a	0.033(9)	0.112	0.490	0.000	0.000	0.000	0.126	0.000	0.773	1.731	1.110	1.113	1.371	1.010	0.901	0.280	1.762	0.773	1.586
tai40a	0.249	0.462	0.590	0.167	0.130	0.173	0.338	0.209	0.866	2.036	1.319	1.490	1.491	1.305	1.082	0.610	1.989	0.933	1.131
tai50a	0.566	0.882	0.850	0.322	0.354	0.388	0.567	0.424	1.082	2.127	1.496	1.491	1.968	1.574	1.211	0.820	2.800	1.236	1.900
tai60a	0.558	0.974	0.030	0.570	0.603	0.677	0.590	0.547	1.356	2.200	1.498	1.692	2.081	1.522	1.349	0.620	3.070	1.372	2.484
tai80a	0.600	1.065	0.860	0.321	0.390	0.405	0.271	0.320	1.022	1.775	1.198	1.200	1.576	1.219	1.029	0.690	2.689	1.134	2.103
tai100a	0.554	1.071	0.800	0.367	0.371	0.441	0.296	0.259	0.966										
Average	0.285	0.507	0.484	0.199	0.210	0.233	0.262	0.195	0.762	1.635	1.101	1.177	1.365	1.101	0.905	0.378	1.936	0.811	1.584

Table 5. Comparison of PR-QAP with algorithms from the literature on the tai*b instances

Problem	PR-QAP	RTS	ACO-GA/LS	ETS1	ETS2	ETS3	GA/TS	SS-PR	GA/TS/I	ILS1	ILS2	ILS3	ILS4	ILS5	ILS6	I-ILS6	ACO1	ACO2	ACO3
	APD	APD	BPD	APD	APD	APD	APD	APD	APD	APD	APD	APD	APD	APD	APD	APD	APD	APD	APD
tai20b	0.000(10)	0.000	0.000	0.000	0.000	0.000	0.000	0.000	0.000	0.045	0.000	0.045	0.000	0.000	0.000	0.000	0.091	0.000	0.000
tai25b	0.000(10)	0.000	0.000	0.000	0.000	0.000	0.007	0.000	0.000	0.000	0.000	0.007	0.000	0.000	0.000	0.000	0.000	0.000	0.000
tai30b	0.000(10)	0.000	0.000	0.000	0.000	0.000	0.000	0.000	0.000	0.000	0.000	0.093	0.000	0.000	0.000	0.000	0.000	0.000	0.000
tai35b	0.000(10)	0.000	0.000	0.000	0.019	0.000	0.059	0.037	0.000	0.131	0.049	0.081	0.000	0.000	0.000	0.000	0.026	0.051	0.000
tai40b	0.000(10)	0.000	0.000	0.000	0.000	0.000	0.000	0.000	0.000	0.000	0.000	0.204	0.000	0.000	0.000	0.000	0.000	0.402	0.000
tai50b	0.132(6)	0.000	0.000	0.000	0.003	0.000	0.002	0.062	0.000	0.203	0.185	0.282	0.028	0.042	0.033	0.000	0.192	0.172	0.002
tai60b	0.133(3)	0.000	0.000	0.000	0.001	0.003	0.000	0.042	0.000	0.029	0.059	0.645	0.023	0.005	0.000	0.000	0.048	0.005	0.005
tai80b	0.997	0.008	0.000	0.008	0.036	0.016	0.003	0.287	0.000	0.785	0.256	0.703	0.260	0.222	0.383	0.000	0.667	0.591	0.096
tai100b	0.197	0.008	0.010	0.072	0.123	0.034	0.014		0.000	0.219	0.096	0.711	0.202	0.113	0.083	0.000			
Average	0.162	0.002	0.001	0.009	0.020	0.006	0.009	0.054	0.000	0.157	0.072	0.308	0.057	0.042	0.055	0.000	0.128	0.153	0.013

- **I-ILS6:** An improved population-based iterated local search algorithm (Stützle, 2006).
- **ACO1, ACO2, and ACO3:** Three ant colony optimization variants (Stützle & Dorigo, 1999).

Table 3 presents the comparisons for the sko* instances. PR-QAP compares very favorably to the algorithms from the literature applied to this set of instances, obtaining better results than all of these algorithms with the exception of GA-IC/TS and I-ILS6. However, PR-QAP is competitive with both of these algorithms. Compared to GA-IC/TS, which is one of the best performing algorithms on this set of test instances, PR-QAP obtains matching or better solutions on 7 of the 13 instances. Compared to I-ILS6, PR-QAP obtains matching or superior solutions on 8 of the 13 instances. Both GA-IC/TS and I-ILS6 are population-based algorithms with an embedded (guided) local search. Therefore, they are similar in basic structure to the PR-QAP but one is a genetic algorithm with an embedded modified tabu search and the other employs a popular local search technique called iterated local search with use of a population. PR-QAP shows an edge over GA-C/TS, which was an earlier version of GA-IC/TS and also one of the best algorithms for the sko* instances. GA-C/TS obtains a better result for sko90, but PR-QAP ties or wins on all the other instances.

It is of interest to note some of the similarities and distinctions between the more successful population-based approaches for the sko* instances. Although all best performing GA approaches are hybrids with some variant of tabu search, GA-IC/TS extends the concentric tabu search neighborhood with more moves than the original GA-C/TS algorithm. Concentric tabu search shares some commonalities with the path-relinking concept. In concentric tabu search, series of swap moves are iteratively applied to a permutation until the distance of the working solution is maximally

different from the original solution (or an improved solution is found). In a sense, the "center" solution serves as both the solution initiating the search (the initiating solution in path-relinking terminology) and the solution being modified. The "path" the solutions are following is guided by the requirement that the solution be different from the original solution. A move can contribute a point (or two) to the distance (difference) score if the exchange moves at least one (or two) facilities to locations they did not previously occupy. Since in concentric tabu search, the reference set is open to all neighboring solutions that increase the difference from the "center" solution rather than restricted to a pre-selected subset of reference (or guiding) solutions, a larger number of intermediate solutions are available than in traditional path-relinking. In our present path relinking algorithm neighborhoods are enlarged by means of a multistart tabu search operator.

I-ILS6 is the most advanced version of the set of iterative local search (ILS) algorithms presented in Stützle (2006). The algorithm extends the traditional ILS framework with a population-based strategy. Similar to traditional scatter search and path relinking algorithms, I-ILS6 updates the population of solutions according to high-quality and diversity criteria. After ranking solutions according to their cost, a solution is inserted into the population if the distance to any of the solutions that are already members of the new population is larger than some minimum distance. Whenever the average distance between solutions in the population is considered not large enough, stronger diversification is used by performing a specified number of restarts from each solution in the population.

In order to increase both the quality and diversity of search in ILS-6, the population is updated by replacing the worst solution in the population with the best solution obtained by each diversification search. From a search strategy standpoint this mechanism resembles the type of diversification generation method commonly used in scatter search and path relinking and also considered in our PR-QAP algorithm. On the other hand, the fact that our diversification mechanism consists of structured perturbations as opposed to random perturbations establishes a fundamental difference between the two methods. A similar conceptual difference exists in the search for new diverse and improved solutions used by each of the algorithms. While I-ILS6 relies on randomization to guide the search beyond local optimality, our PR-QAP algorithm makes use of tabu search memory structures. However, as suggested in Stützle (2006) further improvements of the ILS algorithms may be achieved by using the long-term memory strategies of tabu search.

The diversity incorporated by using a population-based method combined with short runs of a tabu search work very well on the sko* test set which can be explained by landscape analysis. Population-based methods that incorporate a local search provide a tradeoff between diversification and intensification that helps move the search into new areas of the search space while still providing some intensified search in a particular area. Since the sko* test set has a relatively smooth fitness landscape with local optima scattered throughout the search space, these types of metaheuristics perform very well.

On the tai*a instances, PR-QAP obtains better results than all other algorithms with the exception of the ETS variants and the hybrid genetic algorithms. The ETS algorithms are variants of RTS with a great emphasis on diversity. On this test set, PR-QAP outperforms the ILS variants. Drezner's algorithms GA-IC/TS and GA-C/TS were not applied to this test set so comparisons cannot be made with them. However, a hybrid GA with a TS by Misevicius does report results for the tai*a instances and the PR-QAP is competitive with both versions. PR-QAP matches or surpasses the performance of GA/TS for 7 of the 9 instances, but GA/TS/I outperforms PR-QAP on 5 of the 9 instances. Other than PR-QAP, all the best

performing algorithms for the tai*a instances are due to Misevicius and place a heavy reliance on diversity. The importance of the strategic use of diversity mechanisms to a successful performance on these instances is quite apparent.

The tai*a instances have a rugged landscape (exhibiting uncorrelated local optima), and a 2-exchange local search was demonstrated to yield a lower average number of improvements on this test set than on other test sets (Merz & Frisleben, 2000). This suggests that an effort to obtain improved solutions for this set must rely on the other operators of the algorithm in order to be successful. Both of these characteristics should provide an advantage to population-based algorithms with an embedded local search. However, the improved performance of PR-QAP over I-ILS6 on this set and the strong showing of PR-QAP against one of the GA variants indicate a potential advantage of using the path relinking method. The high quality results produced by the GA hybrids appear to be a function of the extra diversity provided by the tabu searches used in these hybrids, as this problem type benefits from diversification for the same reason as the sko* instances. GA/TS and GA/TS/I did not report results for the sko* instances and neither did the ETS variants, so only limited conclusions can be drawn.

PR-QAP does not compare favorably against the other algorithms for the tai*b instances, proving competitive only with some of the ILS and ACO algorithms. However, since the basic RTS method does well on this set of instances and each additional level of diversification degrades the results, it is apparent that for this set it is important to find the correct balance between intensification and diversification. The multi-start tabu search algorithms perform better than PR-QAP because the time between restarts of the TS is longer. Allowing the TS to work longer on solutions provides good results for the tai*b instances with little effort. Further parameter testing may improve our results for the tai*b instances, but a more sophisticated implementation of the diversification and intensification tradeoff may be a more interesting area for future work.

Regarding algorithms in the same heuristic classification as PR-QAP (the scatter search/path relinking class), PR-QAP's solution quality much exceeds the path relinking algorithm (SS-PR) proposed in James, Rego, and Glover (2005). However, the runtimes are much shorter for SS-PR. SS-PR was shown to be superior to an earlier scatter search algorithm by Cung et al. (1996). The SS-PR algorithm differs in many ways from PR-QAP. The biggest distinctions are that PR-QAP uses a different tabu search improvement operator and path relinking method. SS-PR used RTS as an improvement method, whereas PR-QAP uses a multistart tabu search. The path relinking method in SS-PR attempts to sequentially transform the working solution into the guiding solution, but evaluates each move and avoids making the move if the cost is positive, thus differing substantially from the path relinking method employed in the current study. Also, in SS-PR, the diverse portion of the reference set was updated based on a difference score between a candidate permutation and the diverse set of solution. The solution combination method in SS-PR generates all pairs of solutions from the entire reference set. PR-QAP considers only pairs consisting of one high quality solution and one diverse solution. The same diversification generation method was used, but at different points in the search. The same rules were applied to update the high quality portion of the reference set.

4. CONCLUSION

The interplay between intensification and diversification of the search has long been determined crucial for metaheuristic algorithms to find effective solutions for the QAP. The size and diversity of the search landscapes arising in practical applications pose an extreme challenge for a learning algorithm to devise decision rules for search guidance. Studies have shown that local information is insufficient to form an accurate perception of the global search space. In general, relevant information appears dispersed in the solution space and needs to be properly integrated for a method to converge to a global optimum or near-optimal solution. In general, this requires adaptive processes that iteratively attempt to make effective use of current information to identify promising search directions. Although all advanced meteheuristic have in common this adaptive principle, important differences may be found in the scope and methodology employed for its implementation.

We believe that the identification of effective strategies embodied in different algorithms and methodologies is fundamental for the advancement of solution methods. By contrasting path relinking with particle swarm optimization, as instances of advanced methodologies, a number of commonalities and differences may be identified leading to approaches that can produce significantly different results depending on the complexity and topology of the search space. Similar differences may also be obtained by different algorithms of the same methodology. In this study, we show how some tabu search diversification strategies allow for the development of a more effective path-relinking algorithm for the QAP. In this instance, we attributed the success of the algorithm to the adaptive process that integrates information gathered from diverse elite solutions (previously generated by independent search trajectories and that extrapolates this information to extend the search beyond the limits of the original focal points.

We anticipate that this analysis may prove beneficial for devising improved QAP algorithms in the future, both for creating new variants that integrate path relinking with tabu search, as in our present work, and for creating hybrids of such methods with related processes derived from a particle swarm framework. The fact that our present approach rivals and in some cases surpasses the best QAP algorithms in the literature, and that we have been able to isolate features of different landscapes that make these landscapes susceptible to more effective treatment by certain strategies, lays a foundation for exploiting such information in new algorithmic designs.

REFERENCES

Ahuja, R. K., Orlin, J. B., & Tiwari, A. (2000), A descent genetic algorithm for the quadratic assignment problem. *Computers & Operations Research, 27*, 917–934. doi:10.1016/S0305-0548(99)00067-2

Burkard, R. E., Karisch, S., & Rendl, F. (1997). QAPLIB—A quadratic assignment problem library. *Journal of Global Optimization, 10*, 391–403. doi:10.1023/A:1008293323270

Burkard, R. E., & Rendl, F. (1998). A thermo-dynamically motivated simulation procedure for combinatorial optimization problems. *European Journal of Operational Research, 17*, 169–174. doi:10.1016/0377-2217(84)90231-5

Cela, E. (1998). *The quadratic assignment problem: Theory and algorithms*. Boston, MA: Kluwer Academic.

Cung, V.-D., Mautor, T., Michelon, P., & Tavares, A. (1996). Scatter search for the quadratic assignment problem. In *Proceedings of the IEEE International Conference on Evolutionary Computation* (pp. 165-169).

Drezner, Z. (2003). A new genetic algorithm for the quadratic assignment problem. *INFORMS Journal on Computing, 15*(3), 320–330. doi:10.1287/ijoc.15.3.320.16076

Drezner, Z. (2005). The extended concentric tabu for the quadratic assignment problem. *European Journal of Operational Research, 160*, 416–422. doi:10.1016/S0377-2217(03)00438-7

Fleurent, C., & Ferland, J. A. (1994). Genetic hybrids for the quadratic assignment problem. In Pardalos, P., & Wolkowicz, H. (Eds.), *Quadratic assignment and related problems (DIMACS series in discrete mathematics and theoretical computer science)* (*Vol. 16*, pp. 173–187). Providence, RI: American Mathematical Society.

Glover, F. (1998). A template for scatter search and path relinking. In J.-K. Hao, E. Lutton, E. M. A. Ronald, M. Schoenauer, & D. Snyers (Eds.), *Proceedings of the International Conference on Artificial Evolution* (LNCS 1363, pp. 3-54).

Hussin, M. S., & Stutzle, T. (2009). Hierarchical iterated local search for the quadratic assignment problem. In *Proceedings of the 6th International Workshop on Hybrid Metaheuristics* (pp. 115-129).

Iordache, S. (2010). Consultant-guided search algorithms for the quadratic assignment problem. In *Proceedings of the 7th International Conference on Hybrid Metaheuristics* (pp. 148-159).

James, T., Rego, C., & Glover, F. (2005). Sequential and parallel path-relinking algorithms for the quadratic assignment problem. *IEEE Intelligent Systems, 20*(4), 58–65. doi:10.1109/MIS.2005.74

James, T., Rego, C., & Glover, F. (2009). Multistart tabu search and diversification strategies for the quadratic assignment problem. *IEEE Transactions on Systems, Man, and Cybernetics. Part A, Systems and Humans, 39*, 579–596. doi:10.1109/TSMCA.2009.2014556

Li, Y., Pardalos, P. M., & Resende, M. G. C. (1994). A greedy randomized adaptive search procedure for the quadratic assignment problem. In Pardalos, P. M., & Wolkowicz, H. (Eds.), *Quadratic assignment and related problems (DIMACS series on discrete mathematics and theoretical computer science)* (*Vol. 16*, pp. 237–261). Providence, RI: American Mathematical Society.

Merz, P., & Freisleben, B. (2000). Fitness landscape analysis and memetic algorithms for the quadratic assignment problem. *IEEE Transactions on Evolutionary Computation, 4,* 337–352. doi:10.1109/4235.887234

Misevicius, A. (2003). Genetic algorithm hybridized with ruin and recreate procedure: Application to the quadratic assignment problem. *Knowledge-Based Systems, 16,* 261–268. doi:10.1016/S0950-7051(03)00027-3

Misevicius, A. (2004). An improved hybrid genetic algorithm: New results for the quadratic assignment problem. *Knowledge-Based Systems, 17,* 65–73. doi:10.1016/j.knosys.2004.03.001

Misevicius, A. (2005). A tabu search algorithm for the quadratic assignment problem. *Computational Optimization and Applications, 30*(1), 95–111. doi:10.1007/s10589-005-4562-x

Oliveira, C. A., Pardalos, P. M., & Resende, M. G. C. (2004). GRASP with path-relinking for the quadratic assignment problem. In C. C. Ribeiro & S. L. Martins (Eds.), *Proceedings of the Third International Conference on Experimental and Efficient Algorithms* (LNCS 3059, pp. 356-368).

Ramkumar, A. S., Ponnambalam, S. G., & Jawahar, N. (2009). A new iterated fast local search heuristic for solving QAP formulation in facility layout design. *Robotics and Computer-integrated Manufacturing, 25*(3), 620–629. doi:10.1016/j.rcim.2008.03.022

Stuzlee, T. (2006). Iterated local search for the quadratic assignment problem. *European Journal of Operational Research, 174,* 1519–1539. doi:10.1016/j.ejor.2005.01.066

Stuzle, T., & Dorigo, M. (1999). ACO algorithms for the quadratic assignment problem. In Corne, D., Dorigo, M., & Glover, F. (Eds.), *New ideas for optimization* (pp. 33–50). New York, NY: McGraw-Hill.

Taillard, E. (1991). Robust taboo search for the quadratic assignment problem. *Parallel Computing, 17,* 443–455. doi:10.1016/S0167-8191(05)80147-4

Tseng, L., & Liang, S. (2006). A hybrid metaheuristic for the quadratic assignment problem. *Computational Optimization and Applications, 34,* 85–113. doi:10.1007/s10589-005-3069-9

This work was previously published in the International Journal of Swarm Intelligence Research, Volume 2, Issue 2, edited by Yuhui Shi, pp. 52-70, copyright 2011 by IGI Publishing (an imprint of IGI Global).

Chapter 5
A Multiobjective Particle Swarm Optimizer for Constrained Optimization

Gary G. Yen
Oklahoma State University, USA

Wen-Fung Leong
Oklahoma State University, USA

ABSTRACT

Constraint handling techniques are mainly designed for evolutionary algorithms to solve constrained multiobjective optimization problems (CMOPs). Most multiojective particle swarm optimization (MOPSO) designs adopt these existing constraint handling techniques to deal with CMOPs. In the proposed constrained MOPSO, information related to particles' infeasibility and feasibility status is utilized effectively to guide the particles to search for feasible solutions and improve the quality of the optimal solution. This information is incorporated into the four main procedures of a standard MOPSO algorithm. The involved procedures include the updating of personal best archive based on the particles' Pareto ranks and their constraint violation values; the adoption of infeasible global best archives to store infeasible nondominated solutions; the adjustment of acceleration constants that depend on the personal bests' and selected global best's infeasibility and feasibility status; and the integration of personal bests' feasibility status to estimate the mutation rate in the mutation procedure. Simulation to investigate the proposed constrained MOPSO in solving the selected benchmark problems is conducted. The simulation results indicate that the proposed constrained MOPSO is highly competitive in solving most of the selected benchmark problems.

DOI: 10.4018/978-1-4666-2479-5.ch005

1. INTRODUCTION

In real world applications, most optimization problems are subject to different types of constraints. These problems are known as the constrained optimization problems (COPs) or constrained multiobjective optimization problems (CMOPs) if more than one objective function is involved. Comprehensive survey (Michalewicz & Schoenauer, 1996; Mezura-Montes & Coell Coello, 2006) shows a variety of constraint handling techniques have been developed to counter the deficiency of evolutionary algorithms (EAs), in which, their original design are unable to deal with constraints in an effective manner. These techniques are mainly targeted at EAs, particularly genetic algorithms (GAs), to solve COPs (Runarsson & Yao, 2005; Takahama & Sakai, 2006; Cai & Wang, 2006; Wang *et al*., 2007, 2008; Oyama *et al*., 2007; Tessema & Yen, 2009) and CMOPs (Fonseca & Fleming, 1998; Coello & Christiansen, 1999; Binh & Korn, 1997; Deb *et al*., 2002; Kurpati *et al*., 2002; Hingston *et al*., 2006; Jimenéz *et al*., 2002; Ray & Won, 2005; Harada *et al*., 2007; Geng *et al*., 2006; Zhang *et al*., 2006; Chafekar, Xuan & Rasheed, 2003; Woldesenbet, Tessema, & Yen, 2009). During the past few years, due to the success of particle swarm optimization (PSO) in solving many unconstrained optimization problems, research on incorporating existing constraint handling techniques in PSO for solving COPs is steadily gaining attention (Parsopoulus & Vrahatis, 2002; Zielinski & Laur, 2006; He & Wang, 2007; Pulido & Coello, 2004; Liu, Wang, & Li, 2008; Lu & Chen, 2006; Li, Li, & Yu, 2008; Liang & Suganthan, 2006; Cushman, 2007; Wei & Wang, 2006). Nevertheless, many real world problems are often multiobjective in nature. The ultimate goal is to develop multiobjective particle swarm optimization algorithms (MOPSOs) that effectively solve CMOPs. In addition to this perspective, the recent successes of MOPSOs in solving unconstrained MOPs have further motivated us to design a constrained MOPSO to solve CMOPs.

Considering a minimization problem, the general form of the CMOP with k objective functions is given as follows:

$$\text{Minimize } \mathbf{f}(\mathbf{x}) = \left[f_1(\mathbf{x}), f_2(\mathbf{x}), \ldots, f_k(\mathbf{x}) \right],$$
$$\mathbf{x} = \left[x_1, x_2, \ldots, x_n \right] \in \Re^n \tag{1}$$

subject to

$$g_j(\mathbf{x}) \leq 0, \quad j = 1, 2, \ldots, m; \tag{2a}$$

$$h_j(\mathbf{x}) = 0, \quad j = m+1, \ldots, p; \tag{2b}$$

$$x_i^{\min} \leq x_i \leq x_i^{\max}, \quad i = 1, 2, \ldots, n \tag{2c}$$

where $\mathbf{x}$ is the decision vector of n decision variables. Its upper $\left(x_i^{\max} \right)$ and lower $\left(x_i^{\min} \right)$ bounds in Equation 2c define the search space, $S \subseteq \Re^n$. $g_j(\mathbf{x})$ represents the jth inequality constraint, while $h_j(\mathbf{x})$ represents the jth equality constraint. The inequality constraints that are equal to zero, i.e., $g_j(\mathbf{x}*) = 0$, at the global optimum $(\mathbf{x}*)$ of a given problem are called active constraints. The feasible region $(F \subseteq S)$ is defined by satisfying all constraints (Equations 2a-2b). A solution in the feasible region $(\mathbf{x} \in F)$ is called a feasible solution, otherwise it is considered an infeasible solution.

A general MOPSO algorithm consists of the five key procedures: 1) particles' flight (PSO equations), 2) particles' personal best (*pbest*) updating procedure, 3) particles' global best archive (*Gbest*) maintenance method, 4) particles' global best selection scheme, and 5) mutation operation. In the proposed design, we integrated the particles' dominance relationship, and their constraint violation information to each of these key procedures.

The constraint violation information is formulated by two simple metrics that represent the particles' feasibility status individually and as a whole. The final goal is to solve the CMOPs by influencing the particles' search behavior in such that will lead them towards the feasible regions and the optimal Pareto front.

The remaining sections complete the presentation of this paper. In Section 2, a review of relevant works in this area is presented. Section 3 elaborates on the proposed constrained MOPSO (RCVMOPSO). Comparative study and pertinent discussions are given in Section 4. Finally, Section 5 provides concluding remarks of the study.

2. LITERATURE SURVEY

Publication records show majority of the novel constraint handling techniques to solve CMOPs are mainly designed for multiobjective evolutionary algorithms (MOEAs). This is partly due to their popularity and evolutionary algorithms were established earlier than other optimization algorithms such as particle swarm optimization, cultural algorithms and artificial immune systems. Given the justification, this section is dedicated to review various constraint handling techniques reported in MOEA designs.

In Fonseca's and Fleming's framework (Fonseca & Fleming, 1998), the constraint handling is incorporated within a decision making framework based on goals and priority, in which the constraints are given higher priority than the objective functions during the evolutionary process. Hence, emphasis is given to searching for feasible solutions first then to searching for global solution next.

Coello and Christiansen (1999) developed two new MOEAs based on the notion of min-max optimum to solve CMOPs. These MOEAs only optimize feasible solutions since only feasible solutions will survive to the next generation and the crossover and mutation operators are designed in

such only to produce feasible solutions. However, their algorithms may face difficulty in producing a set of feasible solutions at the initialization step and require large computational time if the feasible region is small.

Binh and Korn (1997) proposed the Multiobjective Evolutionary Strategy (MOBES). This design includes dividing the infeasible individuals into different classes according to their "nearness" to the feasible region, ranking the infeasible individuals based on the class, computing fitness values according to proportion of feasible and/ or infeasible individuals in the population, and incorporating a mechanism to maintain a set of feasible Pareto optimum solutions in every generation. Experimental results on some benchmark functions indicate MOBES is efficient in handling constraints in CMOPs.

Deb *et al.* (2002) introduced a constrained domination principle to handle constraint in their NSGA-II. An individual i is said to constrained-dominate an individual j 1) if individual i is feasible and individual j is infeasible; 2) if both individuals i and j are infeasible and individual i has smaller constraint violations; and 3) if both individuals i and j are feasible and individual i dominates individual j. All feasible individuals are ranked via usual Pareto dominance relationship while all infeasible individuals are ranked according to their amount of constraint violation. This constraint handling technique is also adopted in micorgenetic algorithm (microGA) by Coello and Pulido (2001), and another MOPSO proposed by Coello *et al.* (2004).

Kurpati *et al.* (2002) incorporated the Constraint-First-Objective-Next model into four proposed constraint handling techniques for multi-objective genetic algorithm (MOGA). In each of the first three techniques, each fitness assignment stage is based on one of the following guidelines: 1) feasible solutions are preferred over infeasible solutions; 2) the degree of constraint violation for the constraint functions should be used while handling constraints; and 3) the number of violated constraint functions should be taken into consideration while handling constraints. The fitness assignment stage in the fourth technique is based on the combination of the second and the third guidelines. The authors implemented their techniques to improve a constraint handling technique approach of CH-NA (Narayanan & Azarm, 1999). According to the experimental results, the authors concluded that their techniques surpassed CH-NA in terms of computational cost and the closeness of solutions to the true Pareto front; and also concluded that the fourth technique yielded more uniformly distributed Pareto front.

Hingston *et al.* (2006) investigated the differences between two multi-level ranking schemes for ranking the solutions (individuals). The first scheme is known as the objective-first ranking scheme in which the ranking procedure is based on objective values. The procedure is as follow: 1) solutions are first ranked via Pareto ranking scheme (Goldberg, 1989); 2) among those solutions with the same rank value, the most feasible one is considered better; and 3) for those solutions with same rank value and feasibility, the one with larger crowding distance (Deb *et al.*, 2002) is better. The second scheme is called the feasibility-first ranking scheme and the procedure is similar to objective-first ranking scheme except that the ranking is based on infeasibility function values. According to the simulation results, the authors concluded that the objective-first ranking scheme has the advantage of solving some difficult problems by allowing the infeasible solutions to remain in the search population longer and discover good solutions in the search space.

In Jimenéz *et al.*'s proposed MOEA (2002), Evolutionary Algorithm of Non-dominated Sorting with Radial Slots (ENORA), the constraint handling technique allows feasible solutions to evolve towards optimality while infeasible solutions to evolve towards feasibility using the min-max formulation. The diversity mechanism divides the decision space into a set of radial slots along with the successive populations generated. Ray

and Won (2005) also employ standard min-max formulation for constraint handling and divides the objective space into a predefined number of radial slots where the solutions will compete with members in the same slot for existence.

Harada *et al.* (2007) proposed Pareto Descent Repair (PDR) operator to repair the infeasible solution by searching for feasible solution closest to the infeasible solutions in the constraint function space. Their idea is to reduce all violated constraints simultaneously.

Geng *et al.* (2006) proposed a new constraint handling strategy to address the deficiency of Deb's constrained domination principle in NSGA-II (Deb *et al.*, 2002). In their proposal, infeasible elitists are kept to act as a bridge connecting any isolated feasible regions during the evolution process. In addition, they adopted the stochastic ranking (Runarsson & Yao, 2005) to obtain a balance in selecting between the feasible and infeasible elitists. Their idea is applied to NSGA-II and compared the performance with the original NSGA-II on six benchmark CMOPs. The proposed strategy shows significant improvement in terms of distributions and quality of the Pareto fronts on benchmark problems with disconnected feasible regions.

Two selection schemes are proposed for the hybrid of multi-objective differential evolution (MODE) and genetic algorithm (GA) with the (N+N) framework to solve CMOPs (Zhang *et al.*, 2006). The first selection scheme aims to preserve the population diversity and the current best solutions are generated by uniformly sampling the maximum objective value for each objective function in the nondominated set. For test problems with non-continuous true Pareto front, the first selection scheme may lead towards finding a portion of the Pareto optimal front. To solve the problem, the authors suggested selecting current best solutions from the current population that have the larger crowding distance and must be either feasible or infeasible with smaller constraint violation. The authors applied their schemes to a hybrid of MODE and NSGA-II with the (N+N) framework (DE-MOEA). Experiment results indicated that both schemes on DE-MOEA are superior in performance than CNSGA-II (Deb & Goel, 2001).

In Chafekar, Xuan, and Rasheed (2003), the authors proposed two algorithms to solve CMOPs. For the first algorithm, Objective Exchange Genetic Algorithm for Design Optimization (OEGADO), each single-objective GA optimizes one objective or constraint function with independent population. Since there are many objectives and constraint functions, several GAs will run concurrently. At certain generations, the solutions found by all GAs will exchange information with each other. On the contrary, for the second algorithm, Objective Switching Genetic Algorithm for Design Optimization (OSGADO), a single-objective GA optimizes several objective functions in a sequential order, in which, one objective is optimized for a certain number of fitness evaluations, then switch to the next objective to optimize for a certain number of fitness evaluations, and this continues until the fitness evaluation for the last objective is completed. The process is repeated starting from the first objective to the last objective until the maximum number of fitness evaluations is reached. Based on the experimental study, OEGADO shows better and consistent performance.

Recently, Woldesenbet, Tessema and Yen (2009) proposed an adaptive penalty function that exploits the information of the solutions to guide the solutions towards the feasible region and search for optimum solution. They proposed a modified objective function value that consists of two key components: distance measure and adaptive penalty. Then, the dominance relation of the solutions is checked using the modified objective function values. Their idea is incorporated in NSGA-II, but can be easily extended to any MOEAs. Simulation results show the superiority of their proposed algorithm in performance compared to the selected MOEAs.

From the above reviews, the constraint handling techniques build in these MOEAs can be categorized into several groups: adopt the techniques that are applied for single objective constraint optimization; make use of the original mechanism in an EA, for instance genetic operator in Coello and Christiansen, (1999), to handle constraint as well as optimization of the objective functions; develop rules or principles to emphasize the priority of the feasible and infeasible solutions; and design new mechanisms, such as min-max formulation in (Jimenéz et al., 2002) or subpopulations approach in Chafekar, Xuan, and Rasheed (2003), to evolve feasible solutions towards Pareto front while evolve the infeasible solutions towards feasibility. Based on what we learn, our proposed MOPSO design involves adopting an existing constraint handling technique and modifies the mechanism in the original PSO to simultaneously handle constraints as well as optimization of the objective functions.

3. PROPOSED APPROACH

A. Multiobjective Constraint Handling Framework

Over the past decade, various constraint handling techniques are developed to solve COPs. These techniques are initially built for EAs, particularly genetic algorithm and recently, they are adopted in PSO designs. These techniques include penalty methods (Wang et al., 2007), comparison criteria or feasibility tournament (Zielinski & Laur, 2006; He & Wang, 2007; Pulido & Coello, 2004), lexicographic order (Liu, Wang, & Li, 2008), and multiobjective constraint handling techniques (Lu & Chen, 2006; Li, Li, & Yu, 2008; Liang & Sugaanthan, 2006; Cushman, 2007), to name a few. The multiobjective constraint handling techniques, also called multiobjective optimization techniques for handling constraints, are based on multiobjective optimization concepts. The idea is to convert the constraints into one or more unconstrained objective functions and handle them via Pareto dominance relation. These techniques require neither penalty factors that need heuristic tuning nor balance the right proportion of selecting feasible and infeasible solutions in the population via selection criteria (Mezura-Montes & Coello, 2006; Cai & Wang, 2006). Due to these advantages, the proposed constrained MOPSO adopts the multiobjective optimization techniques.

Given a CMOP with k objective functions, as defined in Equation 1, the problem is transformed into an unconstrained $(k+1)$-objective optimization problem, with the p constraints ((i.e., Equations 2a and 2b) are treated as one objective. Equation 3 represents the formulation of the transformed objective functions described.

$$\text{Minimize } \mathbf{f}(\mathbf{x}) = \left[f_1(\mathbf{x}), f_2(\mathbf{x}), \dots, f_k(\mathbf{x}), cv(\mathbf{x}) \right] \tag{3}$$

where $cv(\mathbf{x})$ is the scalar constraint violation of a decision vector $\mathbf{x}$ (or particle) and it is mathematically formulated as below:

$$cv(\mathbf{x}) = \begin{cases} \dfrac{1}{p} \displaystyle\sum_{j=1}^{p} \dfrac{cv_j(\mathbf{x})}{cv_{\max}^j}, & cv_{\max}^j > 0 \\ 0, & cv_{\max}^j = 0 \end{cases} \tag{4}$$

where

$$cv_j(\mathbf{x}) = \begin{cases} \max\left(0, g_j(\mathbf{x})\right), & j = 1, \dots, m \\ \max\left(0, \left|h_j(\mathbf{x})\right| - \delta\right), & j = m+1, \dots, p \end{cases} \tag{5a}$$

$$cv_{\max}^j = \max_{\mathbf{x} \in CP} cv_j(\mathbf{x}) \tag{5b}$$

$cv_j(\mathbf{x})$ in Equation 5a represents the jth constraint violation of a decision vector $\mathbf{x}$ and the problem-dependent parameter δ is the tolerance

allowed for equality constraints, usually δ is set to 0.001 or 0.0001. If a particle or solution ($\mathbf{x}$) satisfies the jth constraints, then $cv_j(\mathbf{x})$ is set to zero, otherwise it is greater than zero. Each jth constraint violation $\left(cv_j(\mathbf{x})\right)$ is normalized by dividing it by the largest violation of the jth constraint ($cv_{\max}^j$ in Equation 5b) in the current swarm population, CP. The constraint violations are normalized to treat each constraint equally. Then the normalized constraint violations are summed together to produce, $cv(\mathbf{x})$ that lies between 0 and 1 (Venkatraman & Yen, 2005).

In solving MOPs, our final goal is to find the Pareto optimum set. Although the Pareto dominance relation is used to solve the tri-objective optimization problem in Equation 3, in this case, we only need to find the Pareto front of k functions. This is because if the set of nondominated solutions found is infeasible (i.e., $cv(\mathbf{x})>0$), it is unacceptable no matter how high quality the Pareto front of the *(k+1)* objective functions is produced. Only the set of nondominated solutions that are landed on the feasible regions (i.e., $cv(\mathbf{x})=0$) are considered potential Pareto front. Note that for the following discussion, we consider minimization for all objective functions unless specified otherwise.

B. General Framework

All of the existing constraint handling techniques involve two goals: 1) to search for feasible solutions and to guide infeasible solutions towards feasibility; and 2) to converge to the global optimal solution or Pareto front. In view of this fact, the proposed constrained MOPSO algorithm (RCV-MOPSO) encompasses the essential design elements to achieve these goals. Figure 1 presents the pseudocode of the proposed algorithm. The design elements are the key procedures (highlighted in boldface in Figure 1) and they are elaborated in the following subsections.

Figure 1. Pseudocode of RCVMOPSO

Begin
/*Initialization
Initialize swarm population and velocity
Set Maximum iterations (*tmax*)
Set iteration *t* = 0
    Update Particles' Personal Best Memory (Section 3.C)
While *t < tmax*
    Calculate Fitness and Constraint violation for all particles
    Find particles' rank values via Pareto ranking
    Update Particles' Personal Best Memory (Section 3.C)
    Calculate the Feasibility Ratio (r_t **)** (Section 3.C and Equation (7))
      Update Feasible and Infeasible Global Best Archive (Section 3.D)
      Global Best Selection (Section 3.E)
      Particle Update Mechanism (Section 3.F)
Mutation Operation (Section 3.G)
t = t + 1

    EndWhile
    Report optimal Pareto front in Feasible Global Best Archive
    End

C. Update Particles' Personal Best Memory and Feasibility Ratio

Unlike solving for MOPs, the particles' personal best updating mechanism should take into consideration of dominance and the degree of constraint violation. Recently, Li, Li, and Yu (2008) proposed two selection rules to update the particles' personal best: (Rule 1) a nondominated particle is better than dominated one; (Rule 2) a particle with lower constraint violation is better than a particle with higher constraint violation. Rule one is given higher priority. The drawback of these rules is to determine which rule should be prioritized first. If rule one is given higher priority, the progress of searching for feasible regions may slow down since personal best indirectly influence the particles' search behavior in the swarm population. On the contrary, if rule two is given higher priority, all infeasible solutions will quickly land on the feasible regions but this will indirectly degrade the diversity in the swarm population and may results in premature convergence. Hence it is important to update personal best using both rules at the same time to maintain a balance between convergence to fitter particles and search for feasible regions.

In this study, we propose the following equation to incorporate the rank value and scalar constraint violation of a particle (with decision vector $\mathbf{x}$) to update the personal best if the latest recorded personal best of a particle is in infeasible region:

$$RC\left(\mathbf{x}\right) = \left(1 - \frac{1}{rank\left(\mathbf{x}\right)}\right) + cv\left(\mathbf{x}\right) \qquad (6)$$

where $RC\left(\mathbf{x}\right)$ is the rank-constraint violation indicator of particle with decision vector $\mathbf{x}$, $rank\left(\mathbf{x}\right)$ represents the current rank value while $cv(\mathbf{x})$ refers to Equation 4. The rank values are obtained from applying the Pareto ranking (Goldberg, 1989) to the swarm population. Referring to Equation 6, the first term indicates the dominant relationship of the particles comparing the others and it is mapped between zero and one, where zero indicates non-dominated particles and any values greater than zero indicates particle is dominated in various degrees. The purpose is to search for the non-dominated solutions, regardless if the solutions are infeasible, and these solutions will possibly indirectly influence the improvement of the particles in the next iterations in terms of convergence. However, this does not guarantee that the particles will move towards the feasible regions easily since most of the time the searching is spent in the infeasible regions. So, the second term is added to Equation 6 to emphasize the current state of the particles in terms of their feasibility or the degree of infeasibility in the current swarm population. Both terms are considered equally important without any preference. Note that the range of RC is between 0 and 2, and a particle with smaller RC value indicates better solution in terms of its convergence and feasibility status. In this paper, the calculation of RC is applied to the particles in the swarm population at every iteration.

The updating procedures for particles' personal best memory, done in every iteration, are summarized below:

- If the personal best memory is empty, record all computed RC values of all particles in the current swarm population, including their corresponding positions $(pbest)$ and their scalar constraint violations $(pbest\_cv)$.

- If the personal best memory is nonempty, their recorded RC values are compared with the computed RC values of their corresponding particles in the current swarm population. Any of the current particles with smaller RC values will replace the recorded ones, including updating the corresponding RC values, $pbest$, and $pbest\_cv$. In any case if the recorded and computed RCs are the same, then one of

them is randomly chosen to update the personal best memory.

Once the updating procedure is completed, the feasibility ratio of the particles' personal bests (r_f) is updated via the following equation:

$$r_f = \frac{number\ of\ particles'\ personal\ bests\ that\ are\ feasible}{swarm\ population\ size}$$

(7)

D. Update Feasible and Infeasible Global Best Archives

Recent studies have shown the advantage of using infeasible solutions to search for global optimal solution (Geng *et al.*, 2006; Chafekar, Xuan, & Rasheed, 2003; Yang *et al.*, 2006). One purpose is to promote diversity during the search process through a balance between feasible and infeasible solutions (Cai & Wang, 2006; Wang *et al.*, 2007, 2008). Another purpose is to use the infeasible solutions as the bridge to explore isolated feasible regions in order to search for better feasible solutions and to deal with the case where the proportional feasible region is relatively smaller compared to the entire search space. Hence, we propose two fixed size global best archives: 1) The feasible global best archive stores only the best feasible solution found so far; while 2) the infeasible global best archive stores the infeasible solutions that have minimum $cv(\mathbf{x})$ found so far. The solutions in both archives serve as potential global best candidates (*Gbest)* for the particle flight update.

To maintain the archives, first the new non-dominated particles from the swarm population are found. Then, these new nondominated particles are divided into new feasible nondominated solutions and infeasible nondominated solutions. The procedures to maintain both global best archives are summarized below:

- **Maintaining Feasible Global Best Archive:** At each iteration count, new *feasible* nondominated solutions are compared with respect to any members in the archive. If new feasible solutions are not dominated by any archive members, they are accepted into the archive. Similarly, any archive members dominated by any new feasible solutions are removed from the archive. If the archive population size exceeds the allocated archive size, the dynamic crowding distance's diversity maintenance strategy (Luo *et al.*, 2008) is applied to remove the crowded members among the archive members. The idea of dynamic crowing distance is very similar to Deb's crowding distance in NSGA-II. The equation to calculate the member's dynamic crowding distance is modified to solve the flaw of Deb's crowding distance, which is the crowding distance may not accurately reflect the crowding degrees of the solutions and may end up removing the wrong members.

- **Maintaining Infeasible Global Best Archive:** Initially, if the archive is empty, then any infeasible nondominated solutions and their scalar constraint violation ($cv(\mathbf{x})$) are immediately recorded in the archive. However, if the archive is nonempty, then at each iteration count, two procedures are executed: In the first procedure, the $cv(\mathbf{x})$ of the new infeasible nondominated solutions is compared with the largest $cv(\mathbf{x})$ stored in the archive. Those new infeasible nondominated solutions with $cv(\mathbf{x})$ exceed the largest $cv(\mathbf{x})$ stored in the archive are removed. Then, in the second procedure, the remaining new infeasible nondominated solutions are compared with respect to any members in the archive. If any new solutions are not dominated by any archive members, they are accepted into the archive; and those archive members dominated by any new

solutions are removed from the archive. Similarly, the dynamic crowding distance approach (Luo *et al.*, 2008) is applied to remove any crowded members from the overflowed archive population size.

E. Global Best Selection

Once both feasible and infeasible global best archives are updated, a *Gbest* is selected either from these archives with equal probability. This provides equal probability of utilizing a set of the feasible and infeasible *Gbest*s to guide their particles. Unless one of the archives is empty, then by default all *Gbest* are selected from the remaining nonempty archive. Note that each particle selects its own *Gbest*. The procedure for a particle to select its *Gbest* in every iteration is given below:

Step 1: Two archive members from the selected Global Best Archive (Section 3.D) are randomly chosen via equal probability.

Step 2: Apply tournament selection. The dynamic crowding distance value of the two randomly chosen archive members are compared. The member with larger dynamic crowding distance value (Luo *et al.*, 2008) (i.e., less crowded area) wins the tournament and becomes the particle's *Gbest*.

The use of dynamic crowding distance values with tournament selection is a diversity preservation mechanism to encourage more exploration among the particles in the swarm population.

F. Particle Update Mechanism

In the original PSO equations, the movement of particles is influenced by their past experiences, i.e., their personal past experience (*pbest*) and successful experience attained by their peers (*Gbest*). In Lu and Chen (2006) and Cushman (2007), the PSO's velocity equation is modified to influence the particles movement towards feasibility. Lu and Chen (2006) replaced the inertial term with personal and global bests in order to restrict the velocity term so that those feasible particles (solutions) will not be moved away from the feasible regions. Cushman (2007) added a global worst term (Gworst) with a very low acceleration constant (suggested 0.0001) to nudge the particles away from the center of the least feasible solution.

In our design, the scalar constraint violation ($cv(\mathbf{x})$) and the feasibility ratio $\left(r_f\right)$ are incorporated into the velocity equation to guide the particles towards feasibility first and then influence them to search for global optimal solution. The new PSO equation and its new acceleration constants are formulated as follows:

$$v_{i,j}\left(t+1\right) =$$
$$w \times v_{i,j}\left(t\right) + c_1 \times r_1 \times \left(pbest_{i,j}\left(t\right) - x_{i,j}\left(t\right)\right)$$
$$+ c_2 \times r_2 \times \left(Gbest_j\left(t\right) - x_{i,j}\left(t\right)\right)$$

$$(8)$$

$$x_{i,j}\left(t+1\right) = x_{i,j}\left(t\right) + v_{i,j}\left(t+1\right) \qquad (9)$$

where

$$c_1 = \left(1-r_f\right) + \left(1 - pbest\_cv_i\left(t\right)\right) \qquad (10\text{a})$$

$$c_2 = r_f + \left(1 - Gbest\_cv\left(t\right)\right) \qquad (10\text{b})$$

$v_{i,j}\left(t\right)$ is the jth dimensional velocity of particle i in iteration t; $x_{i,j}\left(t\right)$ is the jth dimensional position of particle i in iteration t; $pbest_{i,j}\left(t\right)$ denotes the jth dimensional personal best position of the particle i in iteration t; $pbest\_cv_i\left(t\right)$ is the $cv(\mathbf{x})$ of the personal best of particle i in iteration t, $Gbest_j\left(t\right)$ is the jth dimensional Gbest selected from global best archive in iteration t;

$Gbest\_cv\left(t\right)$ represents the $cv(\mathbf{x})$ of the selected $Gbest\left(t\right)$ in iteration t; r_1 and r_2 are random numbers within $[0,1]$ that are regenerated every time they occur; w is the inertial weight, set to varied between 0.1 to 0.7 (Sierra & Coello, 2005) to eliminate the difficulty of fine tuning the inertial weight; and c_1 and c_2 are the acceleration constants. Please note the PSO flight equations stress the update mechanism of a particle i (so the iteration variable t and subscript i are used). On the other hand, Equations 3-5 emphasizes the $cv(\mathbf{x})$ of a particle with decision vector $\mathbf{x}$. Specifically, $pbest\_cv_i\left(t\right)$ refers to $cv(pbest(\mathbf{x}))$ in iteration t.

Adjustment of acceleration constants. In usual practice, the acceleration constants, c_1 and c_2, are fixed values and are normally set to 2. This means that both second and third terms in Equation 8 are weighted equally. If r_1 and r_2 are equal, the movement of a particle depends on both its personal past experience and the global experiences attained by the whole swarm population. Understand this concept, we proposed using the feasibility ratio of the particles' personal best (r_f), and the amount of scalar constraint violations of the *pbest* and *Gbest* to adjust the parameters c_1 and c_2 (see Equations 10a and 10b). The idea is to utilize the infeasibility information to influence a particle's movement, hopefully the particle will discover better solution. The movement depends either on its personal past experience (the second term) or the collective global experiences (the third term) or both terms. Table 1 briefly summarizes the effect of r_f, $pbest\_cv$ and $Gbest\_cv$ on the second and third terms in Equation 8. Observe Table 1, we can generally conclude that small r_f will likely influence the particles to favor on searching for feasible regions instead of optimum solution, while with large r_f, the particles are inclined to search for optimum

Table 1. Brief summary of the effects of r_f, pbest_cv, and Gbest_cv on the second and third terms in Equation 8

r_f	pbest_cv	Gbest_cv	Comments
small	small	small	$c_1 > c_2$; emphasize on the second term (Both terms will guide the particle towards feasibility)
small	small	large	$c_1 >> c_2$; highly emphasize on the second term (Second term guides the particle towards feasibility)
small	large	small	$c_1 \approx c_2$; both terms may have equal emphasis (Both terms will guide the particle towards feasibility and find better solutions)
small	large	large	$c_1 > c_2$; emphasize on the second term (Second term guides the particle towards feasibility)
large	small	small	$c_1 < c_2$; emphasize on the third term (Third term guides the particle to find better solutions)
large	small	large	$c_1 \approx c_2$; both terms may have equal emphasis (Both terms will guide the particle towards feasibility and find better solutions)
large	large	small	$c_1 << c_2$; highly emphasize on the third term (Third term guides the particle to find better solutions)
large	large	large	$c_1 < c_2$; emphasize on the third term (Third term guides the particle to find better solutions)

solution. Both *pbest_cv* and *Gbest_cv* play their role to guide the particles towards feasibility and search for better solution, but in an indirect manner.

G. Mutation Operation

In this approach, uniform and Gaussian mutation operators are applied. Uniform mutation aims to encourage exploration in the swarm population and is presented in Equation 11, while Gaussian mutation in Equation 12 promotes exploitation among the particles in the swarm population via local search characteristics.

$$x_{i,j}(t) = x_{i,j}^{\min} + r_3\left(x_{i,j}^{\max} - x_{i,j}^{\min}\right) \qquad (11)$$

$$x_{i,j}(t) = x_{i,j}(t) + \beta_i \qquad (12)$$

where $x_{i,j}(t)$ is the *j*th dimensional position of particle *i* in iteration *t*; r_3 is a random number within $[0,1]$; $x_{i,j}^{\max}$ and $x_{i,j}^{\min}$ are the *j*th dimensional upper and lower bounds of particle *i* and β_i represents a random number in which it is drawn from the Gaussian distribution, *Gaussian* $\left(0, P_m\left(x_{i,j}^U - x_{i,j}^L\right)\right)$. Parameter P_m is computed using Equations 13 and 14 (Leong & Yen, 2008; Yen & Leong, 2009).

$$lb = \frac{0.1}{n}; \quad n = \text{number of decision variables}$$

$$\tag{13}$$

$$P_m = \begin{cases} \left(0.5 - lb\right) \times \left(1 - 2 \times r_f^2 + \dfrac{lb}{0.5 - lb}\right), & 0 \le r_f \le 0.5 \\ \left(0.5 - lb\right) \times \left(2 \times \left(r_f - 1\right)^2 + \dfrac{lb}{0.5 - lb}\right), & 0.5 < r_f \le 1 \end{cases}$$

$$\tag{14}$$

The P_m parameter is adaptively determined by the feasibility ratio of the particles' personal best $\left(r_f\right)$. Figure 2 is the illustration of Equation 14. lb represents the minimum allowable P_m and is determined from Equation 13. Smaller r_f will yield larger P_m value and vise versa. If $r_f = 1$, P_m will remain to be lb. This parameter P_m serves two purposes: 1) it controls the particles' local search area by allowing larger mutation area when there are fewer feasible particles (r_f is small) to explore nearby feasible regions, and reduces the mutation area when r_f is larger to encourage

finer search for quality solutions; and 2) it represents the mutation probability, in which the mutation probability increases with r_f value decreases. The idea is to increase the chances for infeasible particles to discover potential feasible solutions or feasible particles to escape the suboptimal solutions.

After the velocity and position of each particle i in iteration t (Equations 8-10) is updated, for each jth dimensional position of particle i, $\left(x_{i,j}\left(t\right)\right)$, the procedure to implement the mutation operator are given.

Step 1: Compute Equations 13 and 14.

Step 2: Generate a random number r_4 with uniform distribution between [0,1]. If $r_4 < P_m$, go to Step 3; otherwise go to Step 4.

Step 3: Generate a random number r_5 with uniform distribution between [0,1]. If $r_5 < 0.5$ apply uniform mutation (Equation 11), otherwise Gaussian mutation (Equation 12) is applied.

Step 4: If the jth dimensional position of particle i is outside of its bounds, i.e. $x_{i,j}\left(t\right) \notin \left[x_{i,j}^{\min}, x_{i,j}^{\max}\right]$, the following rule is applied:

Figure 2. Mutation rate (P_m) versus feasibility ratio of the particles' personal best (r_f)

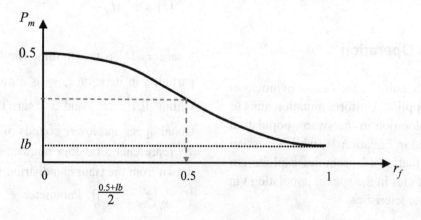

$$x_{i,j}\left(t\right) = \begin{cases} x_{i,j}\left(t\right) = x_{i,j}^{\min}, & \text{if } x_{i,j}\left(t\right) < x_{i,j}^{\min} \\ x_{i,j}\left(t\right) = x_{i,j}^{\max}, & \text{if } x_{i,j}\left(t\right) > x_{i,j}^{\max} \end{cases}$$

$$(15)$$

4. COMPARATIVE STUDY

In this section, simulation study is conducted to analyze RCVMOPSO in two aspects: 1) to evaluate and compare its performance with the selected algorithms; and 2) to find out which test problems' characteristics that our approach is having difficulty to solve.

A. Experimental Setup

Three state-of-the-art constrained MOEAs are chosen and they are NSGA-II (Deb *et al.*, 2002), Geng *et al.* (2006) (indicated by GZHW), and Woldesenbet *et al.* (2009) (indicated by WTY). All the selected algorithms are MOEAs is because no prominent constrained MOPSO designed to solve CMOPs exist. Secondly, these selected MOEAs adopted different constraint handling techniques, though their basic building blocks are based on NSGA-II. Each algorithm is set to perform 50,000 fitness evaluations. The parameter configurations for all testing algorithms are summarized in Table 2.

Eight minimization benchmark problems with different characteristics are chosen to evaluate the performance of RCVMOPSO with the selected MOEAs. Table 3 presents the summary of the main characteristics of these benchmark problems. It provides the number of objective functions and their types of constraint functions (i.e., linear inequality (LI), nonlinear inequality (NI), linear equality (LE), and nonlinear equality (NE)). The parameter **n** represents the number of decision variables, and parameter **a** represents the number of inequality constraints that are active constraints. The parameter ρ is called feasibility ratio. This ratio is determined by calculating the percentage of feasible solutions out of 1,000,000 randomly generated solutions in the entire search space (Cai & Wang, 2006). If the feasibility ratio is very small, this challenges the algorithms to

Table 2. Parameter configurations for testing algorithms

Algorithms	Parameter Settings
NSGA-II (Deb *et al.*, 2002)	Population size =100; crossover probability = 0.9; mutation probability = $1/n$; SBX crossover parameter = 20; polynomial mutation parameter = 20.
GZHW (Geng *et al.*, 2006)	Population size =100; crossover probability = 0.9; mutation probability = $1/n$; SBX crossover parameter = 20; polynomial mutation parameter = 20; comparison probability = 0.45; penalty parameters, $w_j = 1, \beta = 1$
WTY (Woldesenbet, Tessema, & Yen, 2009)	Population size =100 Test Functions CTP4, CTP8, and DTLZ9 Crossover probability = 0.9; mutation probability = $1/n$; SBX crossover parameter = 10; polynomial mutation parameter = 20. Test Functions SRN, TNK, OSY, CONSTR, and Welded Beam Crossover probability = 0.9; mutation probability = $1/n$; SBX crossover parameter = 5; polynomial mutation parameter = 5.
RCVMOPSO	Population size =100; feasible and infeasible *Gbest* archive size = 100; $\delta = 0.0001$

Table 3. Summary of main characteristics of the 8 benchmark functions

Problems	Objective Functions	n	ρ	LI	NI	LE	NE	a
SRN (Binh & Korn, 1997)	2	2	16.18%	1	1	0	0	0
TNK (Tanaka, 1995)	2	2	5.09%	0	2	0	0	1
OSY (Osyezka & Kundu, 1995)	2	6	3.25%	4	2	0	0	6
CTP4 (Deb *et al.*, 2001)	2	2	58.17%	0	1	0	0	1
CTP8 (Deb *et al.*, 2001)	2	2	17.86%	0	2	0	0	1
CONSTR (Deb, 2001)	2	2	52.52%	2	0	0	0	1
Welded Beam (Chafekar, Xuan, & Rasheed, 2003)	2	4	18.67%	1	3	0	0	0
DTLZ9 (Dev *et al.*, 2005)	3	30	10.37%	0	2	0	0	2

search for feasible solutions. In this paper, all of the algorithms use a real-number representation for decision variables. For each experiment, 50 independent runs were conducted to collect the statistical results.

B. Performance Metrics

All comparisons are based on qualitative and quantitative measures. Qualitative comparison is based on the plots of the final Pareto fronts in a given run. For quantitative comparison, two performance metrics are taken into consideration to measure the quality of algorithms with respect to dominance relations. The hypervolume indicator (S metric) (Zitzler, 1999) measures how well the algorithm converges and produces nondominated solutions that is well-distributed and well-extent along the Pareto front. The additive binary ε-indicator (Zitzler *et al.*, 2003) indicates whether a non-dominated set produced by an algorithm is better than another. In addition, Wilcoxon rank-sum test is used to measure the significant differences between the two sample sets (Conover, 1999). The null hypothesis (i.e., p-value > α) suggests that there is *no* significant differences between the two sample sets; while the alternative

hypothesis (i.e., p-value ≤ α) indicates otherwise. The symbol α represents the significant level and is set to 5%.

C. Performance Evaluation

The box plots of hypervolume indicator (I_H) values are summarized in Figure 3 and Figure 4. The algorithm with higher I_H values indicates better performance in terms of coverage and better distribution of the nondominated solutions along the Pareto front. In Figures 3 and 4, the I_H values are normalized for each test problem. So, the highest I_H value will equal one. Table 4 presents the Wilcoxon rank-sum test results of the I_H values for these algorithms. Observe the medians of the box plots in Figures 3 and 4 and the results in Table 4, RCVMOPSO yields equal and better performance than GZHW for test functions CTP8 and Welded Beam; while compare to NSGA-II, it does equal or better for test functions OSY, CTP8, and DTLZ9. RCVMOPSO yields comparable results with WTY for test functions CTP4, CTP8, and DTLZ9. By observing Figures 3 and 4, RCVMOPSO has the lowest I_H values for test functions SRN and TNK, but does not fall short in terms of performance because it has I_H values

Figure 3. Box plots of hypervolume indicator (IH values) for all test functions by algorithms 1-4 represented (in order): RCVMOPSO, NSGA-II, GZHW and WTY

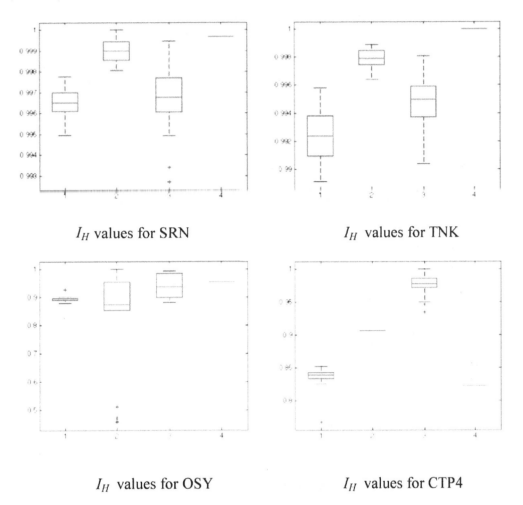

I_H values for SRN

I_H values for TNK

I_H values for OSY

I_H values for CTP4

higher than 0.99 and the difference between its I_H values compared to those achieved by the selected MOEAs are between 0.001 to 0.006. However, on test functions CTP4 and CONSTR, the proposed algorithm's performance is lacking. From the analysis, we concluded that RCVMOPSO is competitive in terms of performance for some of the test functions compared to the selected MOEAs. In addition, the y-axis in Figures 3 and 4 shows that the distributions of RCVMOPSO are consistently low for all of the test functions. This indicates its ability of producing reliable solutions for these of the benchmark functions.

Figure 5, Figure 6, and Figure 7 illustrates the results (summarized in box plots) of additive binary ε-indicator. For each test problem, there are two box plots, i.e., $I_{\varepsilon+}\left(A, B_{1-3}\right)$ and $I_{\varepsilon+}\left(B_{1-3}, A\right)$ in which RCVMOPSO is represented by A and the algorithm B_{1-3} refer to NSGA-II, GZHW, and WTY, respectively. Observed in Figures 5-7, neither RCVMOPSO and the rest of the algorithm dominate each other for test function SRN, TNK, CTP4, CTP8, and DTLZ9 since box plots show that $I_{\varepsilon+}\left(A, B_{1-3}\right) > 0$ and

Figure 4. Box plots of hypervolume indicator (IH values) for all test functions by algorithms 1-4

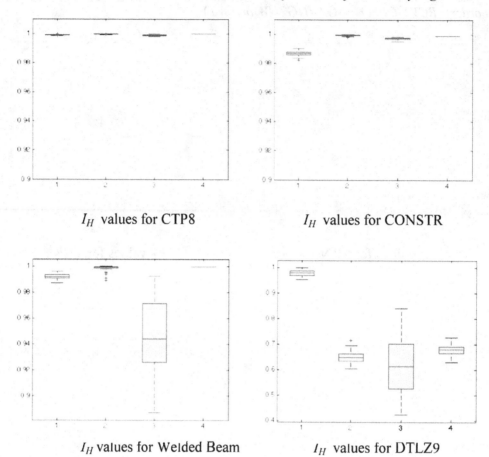

I_H values for CTP8

I_H values for CONSTR

I_H values for Welded Beam

I_H values for DTLZ9

Table 4. The distribution of IH values tested using Wilcoxon rank-sum test. The numbers in each bracket represents (z values, p-values) with respect to the alternative hypothesis (if p-value ≤ α=0.05, reject the null hypothesis) for each pair of RCVMOPSO and a selected constrained MOEAs. The distribution of RCVMOPSO is significantly different than those selected constrained MOEAs unless stated

Test Functions	I_H (RCVMOPSO) AND		
	I_H (NSGA-II)	I_H (GZHW)	I_H (WTY)
SRN	(-6.6457, 3.0E-11)	(-1.2197, >0.05) *no difference*	(-7.1040, 1.2E-12)
TNK	(-6.6458, 3.0E-11)	(-4.5314, 5.9E-06)	(-7.1040, 1.2E-12)
OSY	(2.1955, 2.8E-02)	(-4.7680, 1.86E-06)	(3.3644, 7.6E-04)
CTP4	(-6.6458, 3.0E-11)	(-6.6456, 3.0E-11)	(6.6299, 3.4E-11)
CTP8	(-6.4980, 8.1E-11)	(-0.1109,, >0.05) *no difference*	(-7.1040, 1.2E-12)
CONSTR	(-6.6459, 3.0E-11)	(-6.6456, 3.0E-11)	(-6.5846, 4.6E-11)
Welded Beam	(-5.8624, 4.6E-09)	(6.3499, 2.2E-10)	(-7.1040, 1.21E-12)
DTLZ9	(8.6138, 7.1E-18)	(8.6138, 7.1E-18)	(8.6139, 7.1E-18)

Figure 5. Box plots of additive binary epsilon indicator (Iε+ values) for all test functions (algorithm A refers to RCVMOPSO; algorithms B1-3 are referred to as NSGA-II, GZHW and WTY, respectively)

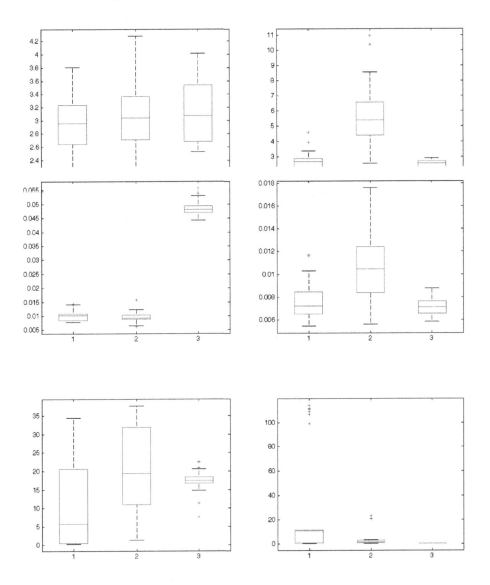

$I_{\varepsilon+}\left(B_{1-3}, A\right) > 0$. In addition, the results in Table 5 confirm this analysis and for some of the test functions, RCVMOPSO shares the same performance with GZHW and NSGA-II. Based on the mediums in the box plots and results in Figure 8, Figure 9, Figure 10, and Figure 11, RCVMOPSO weakly dominates GZHW for test function Welded Beam since the $I_{\varepsilon+}\left(A, B_{2}\right) \approx 0$ and

$I_{\varepsilon+}\left(B_{2}, A\right) > 0$. On the contrary, NSGA-II weakly dominates the proposed algorithm for test functions CTP4 and Welded Beam; this observation also applies to WTY for test functions OSY and Welded beam. In summary, in terms of dominance relationship, RCVMOPSO yields equal performance as the selected MOEAs for the 7 test functions, and obtains the best result for DTLZ9.

Figure 6. Box plots of additive binary epsilon indicator (Iε+ values) for all test functions (CONSTR, Welded Beam)

$I_{\varepsilon+}\left(A, B_{1-3}\right)$ and $I_{\varepsilon+}\left(B_{1-3}, A\right)$ for CONSTR

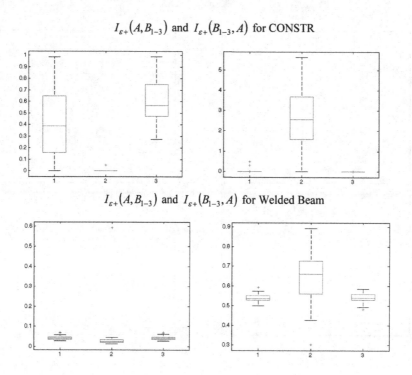

$I_{\varepsilon+}\left(A, B_{1-3}\right)$ and $I_{\varepsilon+}\left(B_{1-3}, A\right)$ for Welded Beam

Figure 7. Box plots of additive binary epsilon indicator (Iε+ values) for all test functions (OSY, CTP4)

$I_{\varepsilon+}\left(A, B_{1-3}\right)$ and $I_{\varepsilon+}\left(B_{1-3}, A\right)$ for OSY

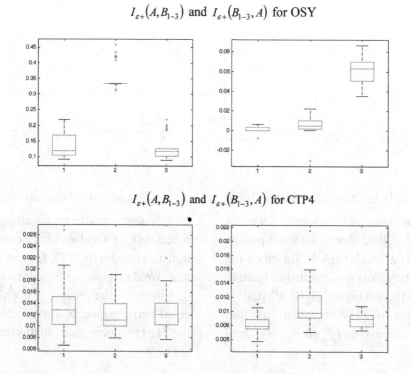

$I_{\varepsilon+}\left(A, B_{1-3}\right)$ and $I_{\varepsilon+}\left(B_{1-3}, A\right)$ for CTP4

Table 5. The distribution of $I_{\varepsilon+}$ values tested using Wilcoxon rank-sum Test. The numbers in each bracket represents (z values, p-values) with respect to the alternative hypothesis (if p-value $\leq \alpha=0.05$, reject the null hypothesis) for each pair of RCVMOPSO and a selected constrained MOEAs. RCV-MOPSO is represented by A, and algorithms B1, B2, and B3 are referred to as NSGA-II, GZHW and WTY, respectively. The distribution of RCVMOPSO is significantly difference than those selected constrained MOEAs unless stated.

Test Functions	$I_{\varepsilon+}$ (A,B1) and $I_{\varepsilon+}$ (B1,A)	$I_{\varepsilon+}$ (A,B2) and $I_{\varepsilon+}$ (B2,A)	$I_{\varepsilon+}$ (A,B3) and $I_{\varepsilon+}$ (B3,A)
SRN	(2.3138, 2.1E-01)	(-5.8916, 3.8E-09)	(4.7828, 1.7E-06)
TNK	(4.7680, 1.9E-06)	(-1.0719, >0.05) *no difference*	(6.6456, 3.0E-11)
OSY	(-1.3528,, >0.05) *no difference*	(4.9750, 6.5E-07)	(6.6456, 3.0E-11)
CTP4	(6.7223, 1.8E-11)	(6.6456, 3.0E-11)	(6.6456, 3.0E-11)
CTP8	(5.4037, 6.5E-08)	(1.7224, >0.05) *no difference*	(5.1524, 2.6E-07)
CONSTR	(6.0099, 1.9E-09)	(4.5166, 6.3E-06)	(6.2095, 5.3E-10)
Welded Beam	(6.1725, 6.7E-10)	(-6.6308, 3.3E-11)	(6.6456, 3.0E-11)
DTLZ9	(-8.6138, 7.1E-18)	(-8.4828, 2.2E-17)	(-8.6139, 7.1E-18)

Figure 8. Pareto fronts produced by the following algorithms a-d represented (in order): RCVMOPSO, NSGA-II, GZHW and WTY, respectively

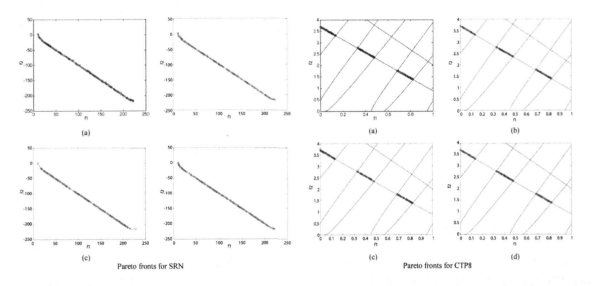

Figure 9. Pareto fronts produced by algorithms a-d (TNK, CONSTR)

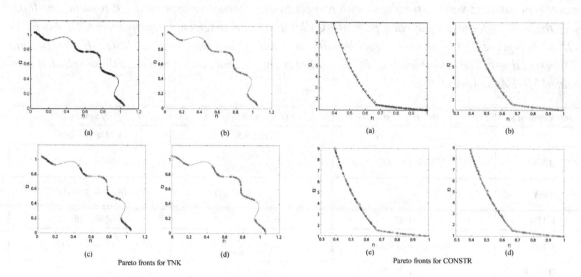

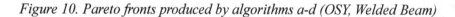

Figure 10. Pareto fronts produced by algorithms a-d (OSY, Welded Beam)

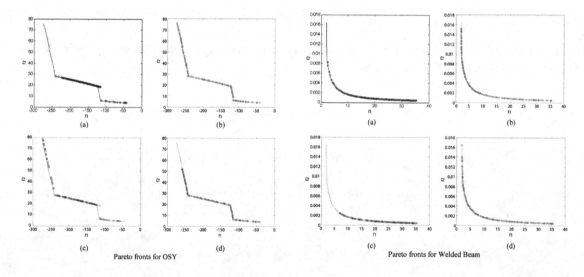

For qualitative comparison, the resulted Pareto fronts generated by all the algorithms from a single run given the same initial population are presented in Figures 8 to 11. For every test problem, four plots are presented and the labels (a)-(d) represent the following algorithms: RCVMOPSO, NSGA-II, GZHW, and WTY respectively. In this analysis, the performance is compared by the solutions' distribution and their extendibility along the true Pareto front. The observation indicates that RCVMOPSO is able to produce equal or better Pareto optimal fronts compared to the rest of the MOEAs for test functions SRN, TNK, CTP4, and CTP8. On test function DTLZ9, it produces the best Pareto optimal fronts, i.e., well-distributed and well-extended. However, for test functions OSY, CONSTR, and Welded Beam,, it achieves the worst Pareto optimal fronts. These Pareto fronts achieved by the proposed MOPSO are either incomplete (i.e., only cover part of the

Figure 11. Pareto fronts produced by algorithms a-d (CTP4, DTLZ9)

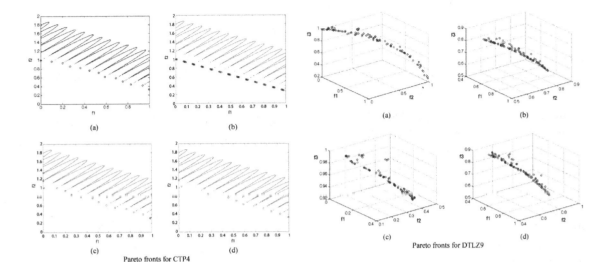

true Pareto front), such as test functions OSY, Welded Beam, and CONSTR.

Based on the results analysis given above, several conclusions are drawn:

- The additive binary ε-indicator results in Figures 5-7 and Table 5, and all the Pareto front plots in Figure 5 indicate that RCVMOPSO' performance is competitive with respect to NSGA-II, GZHW, and WTY for the eleven test functions, excluding test functions OSY, CONSTR, and Welded Beam. However, our approach's weakness is diversity maintenance. This conclusion is based on the hypervolume indicator results (i.e., I_H values) presented in Figures 3 and 4 and Table 4. The main reason lies on the basic mechanism of PSO algorithm that is designed for better convergence speed than EAs (at the cost of poor diversity), and is modeled with swarm-like characteristic.
- The strength of the proposed algorithm is solving test problems with the following profiles: Objective space with infeasible bands or feasible island (e.g., CTP8), and

continuous Pareto front with or without active constraints (e.g., SRN and DTLZ9). For test problems with multiple, isolated and disconnected Pareto front, such as CTP4, RCVMOPSO perform fairly well.
- There are certain problem characteristics that RCVMOPSO is having difficulty in solving. The true Pareto front of test problems such as OSY constitutes of several disjoint regions, in which there is at least one active constraint in each region. For test functions with the curves of the Pareto front that consists of extreme regions, such as the Welded Beam, they also present great challenge to RCVMOPSO.

5. CONCLUSION

This paper proposes a constrained MOPSO (RCV-MOPSO), to solve constrained multiobjective optimization problems. The proposed algorithm adopts a multiobjective constraint handling technique. It incorporates the following design features: 1) separate procedures to update the infeasible and feasible personal best in the personal best memory in order to guide the infeasible particles towards the feasible regions while promote search for better solutions; 2) an infeasible global best archive is adopted to make use of the infeasible nondominated solutions for searching possible isolated feasible regions or a very small feasible region while the feasible global best archive aims to guide the particles to find better solutions; 3) the adjustment of the accelerated constants in the PSO equation is based on the number of feasible personal best in the personal best archive and the scalar constraint violations of personal best and global best. The adjustment will influence the search process either to find more feasible solutions (particles) or to search for better solutions; and 4) the frequency of applying the mutation operators are based on the feasibility ratio of the particles' personal best. This feasibility ratio is exploited to encourage more exploration characteristic to search possible feasible regions when there are few feasible particles' personal best, while reduce the exploration rate when most of the particles' personal best are feasible to support convergence toward Pareto optimal front. Both uniform and Gaussian mutation operators are used to encourage a balance local and global search. A comparative study of RCVMOPSO and three state-of-the-art constrained MOEAs on 8 benchmark test functions is presented. The simulation results show the proposed MOPSO is highly competitive and able to obtain quality Pareto fronts for most of the test functions. However, after analyzing the simulated results, it indicates that RCVMOPSO has difficulty solving test functions with certain characteristics, for example, combination of Pareto fronts of several disjoint regions and multiple active constraints. Hence, in our future works we are considering to improve the diversity mechanism in the design elements and include ability to deal with active constraints.

REFERENCES

Binh, T., & Korn, U. (1997). MOBES: A multiobjective evolution strategy for constrained optimization problems. In *Proceedings of the 3rd International Conference on Genetic Algorithms*, Brno, Czech Republic (pp. 176-182).

Cai, Z., & Wang, Y. (2006). A multiobjective optimization-based evolutionary algorithm for constrained optimization. *IEEE Transactions on Evolutionary Computation*, *10*(6), 658–674. doi:10.1109/TEVC.2006.872344

Chafekar, D., Xuan, J., & Rasheed, K. (2003). Constrained multi-objective optimization using steady state genetic algorithms. In *Proceedings of the Genetic and Evolutionary Computation Conference*, Chicago, IL (pp. 813-824).

Coello, C. A., & Christiansen, A. D. (1999). MOSES: A multiobjective optimization tool for engineering design. *Engineering Optimization*, *31*, 337–368. doi:10.1080/03052159908941377

Coello, C. A., & Pulido, G. T. (2001). Multiobjective optimization using a micro-genetic algorithm. In *Proceedings of the Genetic and Evolutionary Computation Conference*, San Francisco, CA (pp. 274-282).

Coello, C. A., Pulido, G. T., & Lechuga, M. S. (2004). Handling multiple objectives with particle swarm optimization. *IEEE Transactions on Evolutionary Computation*, *8*(3), 256–279. doi:10.1109/TEVC.2004.826067

Conover, W. J. (1999). *Practical Nonparametric Statistics* (3rd ed.). New York, NY: John Wiley & Sons.

Cushman, D. L. (2007). *A particle swarm approach to constrained optimization informed by Global Worst*. University Park, PA: Pennsylvania State University.

Deb, K. (2001). *Multi-Objective Optimization Using Evolutionary Algorithms*. New York, NY: John Wiley & Sons.

Deb, K., & Goel, T. (2001). Controlled elitist non-dominated sorting genetic algorithm for better convergence. In *Proceedings of the 1st International Conference on Evolutionary Multi-Criterion Optimization*, Zurich, Switzerland (pp. 67-81).

Deb, K., Pratap, A., Agarwal, A., & Meyarivan, T. (2002). A fast and elitist multiobjective genetic algorithm: NSGA-II. *IEEE Transactions on Evolutionary Computation*, 6(2), 182–197. doi:10.1109/4235.996017

Deb, K., Pratap, A., & Meyarivan, T. (2001). Constrained test problems for multi-objective evolutionary optimization. In *Proceedings of the 1st International Conference on Evolutionary Multi-Criterion Optimization*, Zurich, Switzerland (pp. 284-298).

Deb, K., Thiele, L., Laumanns, M., & Zitzler, E. (2005). Scalable test problems for evolutionary multi-objective optimization. In Abraham, A., Jain, R., & Goldberg, R. (Eds.), *Evolutionary Multiobjective Optimization: Theoretical Advances and Applications* (pp. 105–145). Berlin, Germany: Springer. doi:10.1007/1-84628-137-7_6

Fonseca, C. M., & Fleming, P. J. (1998). Multiobjective optimization and multiple constraint handling with evolutionary algorithms, I: a unified formulation. *IEEE Transactions on Systems, Man, and Cybernetics, Part A. Cybernetics*, 28(1), 26–37.

Geng, H., Zhang, M., Huang, L., & Wang, X. (2006). Infeasible elitists and stochastic ranking selection in constrained evolutionary multiobjective optimization. In *Proceedings of the 6th International Conference on Simulated Evolution and Learning*, Hefei, China (pp. 336-344).

Goldberg, D. E. (1989). *Genetic Algorithms in Search, Optimization and Machine Learning*. Reading, MA: Addison-Wesley.

Harada, K., Sakuma, J., Ono, I., & Kobayashi, S. (2007). Constraint-handling method for multi-objective function optimization: Pareto descent repair operator. In *Proceedings of the 4th International Conference on Evolutionary Multi-Criterion Optimization*, Sendai, Japan (pp. 156-170).

He, Q., & Wang, L. (2007). A hybrid particle swarm optimization with a feasibility-based rule for constrained optimization. *Applied Mathematics and Computation*, 186, 1407–1422. doi:10.1016/j.amc.2006.07.134

Hingston, P., Barone, L., Huband, S., & While, L. (2006). Multi-level ranking for constrained multi-objective evolutionary optimization. In T. R. Runarsson (Ed.), *Parallel Problem Solving from Nature* (LNCS 4193, pp. 563-572).

Jimenéz, F., Gomez-Skarmeta, A. F., Sanchez, G., & Deb, K. (2002). An evolutionary algorithm for constrained multiobjective optimization. In *Proceedings of the Evolutionary Computation Conference*, Honolulu, HI (pp. 1133-1138).

Kurpati, A., Azarm, S., & Wu, J. (2002). Constraint handling improvements for multiobjective genetic algorithms. *Structure Multidisciplinary Optimization*, 23, 204–213. doi:10.1007/s00158-002-0178-2

Leong, W. F., & Yen, G. G. (2008). PSO-based multiobjective optimization with dynamic population size and adaptive local archives. *IEEE Transactions on Systems, Man, and Cybernetics. Part B, Cybernetics*, 38(5), 1270–1293. doi:10.1109/TSMCB.2008.925757

Li, L. D., Li, X., & Yu, X. (2008). A multi-objective constraint-handling method with PSO algorithm for constrained engineering optimization problems. In *Proceedings of the IEEE Conference on Evolutionary Computation*, Hong Kong, China (pp. 1528-1535).

Liang, J. J., & Suganthan, P. N. (2006). Dynamic multi-swarm particle swarm optimizer with a novel constraint-handling mechanism. In *Proceedings of the IEEE Conference on Evolutionary Computation*, Vancouver, BC, Canada (pp. 9-16).

Liu, Z., Wang, C., & Li, J. (2008). Solving constrained optimization via a modified genetic particle swarm optimization. In *Proceedings of the International Workshop on Knowledge Discovery and Data Mining*, Adelaide, SA, Australia (pp. 217-220).

Lu, H., & Chen, W. (2006). Dynamic-objective particle swarm optimization for constrained optimization problems. *Journal of Combinatorial Optimization, 2*(4), 409–419. doi:10.1007/s10878-006-9004-x

Luo, B., Zheng, J., Xie, J., & Wu, J. (2008). Dynamic crowding distance-a new diversity maintenance strategy for MOEAs. In *Proceedings of the 4th International Conference on Natural Computation,* Jinan, China (pp. 580-585).

Mezura-Montes, E., & Coello, C. A. (2006). *A survey of constraint-handling techniques based on evolutionary multiobjective optimization* (Tech. Rep. No. EVOCINV-04-2006). Mexico City, Mexico: Cinvestav-IPN.

Michalewicz, Z., & Schoenauer, M. (1996). Evolutionary algorithm for constrained parameter optimization problems. *Evolutionary Computation, 4*(1), 1–32. doi:10.1162/evco.1996.4.1.1

Narayanan, S., & Azarm, S. (1999). On improving multiobjective genetic algorithms for design optimization. *Structural Optimization, 18*, 146–155.

Osyezka, A., & Kundu, S. (1995). A new method to solve generalized multi-criteria optimization problems using the simple genetic algorithm. *Structural Optimization, 10*(2), 94–99. doi:10.1007/BF01743536

Oyama, A., Shimoyama, K., & Fujii, K. (2007). New constraint-handling method for multi-objective and multi-constraint evolutionary optimization. *Transactions of the Japan Society for Aeronautical and Space Sciences, 50*(167), 56–62. doi:10.2322/tjsass.50.56

Parsopoulus, K. E., & Vrahatis, M. N. (2002). Particle swarm optimization method for constrained optimization problems. In *Intelligent Technologies: Theory and Applications: New Trends in Intelligent Technologies* (pp. 214-220).

Pulido, G. T., & Coello, C. A. (2004). A constraint-handling mechanism for particle swarm optimization. In *Proceedings of the Evolutionary Computation Conference*, Portland, OR (pp. 1396-1403).

Ray, T., & Won, K. S. (2005). An evolutionary algorithm for constrained bi-objective optimization using radial slots. In *Proceedings of the 9th International Conference on Knowledge-Based Intelligent Information and Engineering Systems*, Melbourne, VIC, Australia (pp. 49-56).

Runarsson, T. P., & Yao, X. (2005). Search biases in constrained evolutionary optimization. *IEEE Transactions on Systems, Man and Cybernetics. Part C, Applications and Reviews, 35*(2), 233–243. doi:10.1109/TSMCC.2004.841906

Sierra, M. R., & Coello, C. A. (2005). Improving PSO-based multi-objective optimization using crowding, mutation and ε–dominance. In *Proceedings of the International Conference on Evolutionary Multi-Criteria Optimization*, Guanajuato, Mexico (pp. 505-519).

Takahama, T., & Sakai, S. (2006). Constrained optimization by the ε constrained differential evolution with gradient-based mutation and feasible elites. In *Proceedings of the IEEE Conference on Evolutionary Computation*, Vancouver, BC, Canada (pp. 1-8).

Tanaka, M. (1995). GA-based decision support system for multi-criteria optimization. In *Proceedings of the International Conference on Evolutionary Multi-Criteria Optimization*, Guanajuato, Mexico (pp. 1556-1561).

Tessema, B., & Yen, G. G. (2009). An adaptive penalty formulation for constrained evolutionary optimization. *IEEE Transactions on Systems, Man, and Cybernetics. Part A, Systems and Humans, 39*(3), 565–578. doi:10.1109/TSMCA.2009.2013333

Venkatraman, S., & Yen, G. G. (2005). A generic framework for constrained optimization using genetic algorithms. *IEEE Transactions on Evolutionary Computation, 9*(4), 424–435. doi:10.1109/TEVC.2005.846817

Wang, Y., Cai, Z., Guo, G., & Zhou, Y. (2007). Multiobjective optimization and hybrid evolutionary algorithm to solve constrained optimization problems. *IEEE Transactions on System, Man, and Cybernetics, Part B. Cybernetics, 37*(3), 560–575.

Wang, Y., Cai, Z., Zhou, Y., & Zeng, W. (2008). An adaptive trade-off model for constrained evolutionary optimization. *IEEE Transactions on Evolutionary Computation, 12*(1), 80–92. doi:10.1109/TEVC.2007.902851

Wei, J., & Wang, Y. (2006). A novel multi-objective PSO algorithm for constrained optimization problems. In T. D. Wang *et al.* (Eds.), *Simulated Evolution and Learning* (LNCS 4247, pp. 174-180).

Woldesenbet, Y. G., Tessema, B. G., & Yen, G. G. (2009). Constraint handling in multiobjective evolutionary optimization. *IEEE Transactions on Evolutionary Computation, 13*(2), 1–12.

Yang, B., Chen, Y., Zhao, Z., & Han, Q. (2006). A master-slave particle swarm optimization algorithm for solving constrained optimization problems. In *Proceedings of the 6th World Conference on Intelligent Control and Automation*, Dalian, China (pp. 3208-3212).

Yen, G. G., & Leong, W. F. (2009). Dynamic multiple swarms in multiobjective particle swarm optimization. *IEEE Transactions on Systems, Man, and Cybernetics. Part A, Systems and Humans, 39*(4), 890–911. doi:10.1109/TSMCA.2009.2013915

Zhang, M., Geng, H., Luo, W., Huang, L., & Wang, X. (2006). A hybrid of differential evolution and genetic algorithm for constrained multiobjective optimization problems. In *Simulated Evolution and Learning* (LNC 4247, pp. 318-327).

Zielinski, K., & Laur, R. (2006). Constrained single-objective optimization using particle swarm optimization. In *Proceedings of the IEEE Conference on Evolutionary Computation*, Vancouver, BC, Canada (pp. 443-450).

Zitzler, E. (1999). *Evolutionary Algorithms for Multiobjective Optimization: Methods and Applications*. Unpublished doctoral dissertation, Swiss Federal Institute of Technology, Zurich, Switzerland.

Zitzler, E., Thiele, L., Laumanns, M., Fonseca, C. M., & da Fonseca, V. G. (2003). Performance assessment of multiobjective optimizers: an analysis and review. *IEEE Transactions on Evolutionary Computation, 7*(2), 117–132. doi:10.1109/TEVC.2003.810758

This work was previously published in the International Journal of Swarm Intelligence Research, Volume 2, Issue 1, edited by Yuhui Shi, pp. 1-23, copyright 2011 by IGI Publishing (an imprint of IGI Global).

Chapter 6
Experimental Study on Boundary Constraint Handling in Particle Swarm Optimization:
From Population Diversity Perspective

Shi Cheng
University of Liverpool, UK

Yuhui Shi
Xi'an Jiaotong-Liverpool University, China

Quande Qin
Shenzhen University, China

ABSTRACT

Premature convergence happens in Particle Swarm Optimization (PSO) for solving both multimodal problems and unimodal problems. With an improper boundary constraints handling method, particles may get "stuck in" the boundary. Premature convergence means that an algorithm has lost its ability of exploration. Population diversity is an effective way to monitor an algorithm's ability of exploration and exploitation. Through the population diversity measurement, useful search information can be obtained. PSO with a different topology structure and a different boundary constraints handling strategy will have a different impact on particles' exploration and exploitation ability. In this paper, the phenomenon of particles gets "stuck in" the boundary in PSO is experimentally studied and reported. The authors observe the position diversity time-changing curves of PSOs with different topologies and different boundary constraints handling techniques, and analyze the impact of these setting on the algorithm's ability of exploration and exploitation. From these experimental studies, an algorithm's ability of exploration and exploitation can be observed and the search information obtained; therefore, more effective algorithms can be designed to solve problems.

DOI: 10.4018/978-1-4666-2479-5.ch006

1. INTRODUCTION

Particle Swarm Optimization (PSO) was introduced by Eberhart and Kennedy in 1995 (Eberhart & Kennedy, 1995; Kennedy & Eberhart, 1995). It is a population-based stochastic algorithm modeled on social behaviors observed in flocking birds. A particle flies through the search space with a velocity that is dynamically adjusted according to its own and its companion's historical behaviors. Each particle's position represents a solution to the problem. Particles tend to fly toward better and better search areas over the course of the search process (Eberhart & Shi, 2001).

Optimization, in general, is concerned with finding the "best available" solution(s) for a given problem. Optimization problems can be simply divided into unimodal problems and multimodal problems. As indicated by the name, a unimodal problem has only one optimum solution; on the contrary, a multimodal problem has several or numerous optimum solutions, of which many are local optimal solutions. Evolutionary optimization algorithms are generally difficult to find the global optimum solutions for multimodal problems due to the possible occurrence of the premature convergence.

Most reported optimization methods are designed to avoid premature convergence in solving multimodal problems (Blackwell & Bentley, 2002). However, premature convergence also happens in solving unimodal problems when the algorithm has an improper boundary constraint handling method. For example, even for the most simplest benchmark function—Sphere, or termed a Parabolic problem, which has a convex curve in each dimension, particles may "stick in" the boundary and the applied PSO algorithm therefore cannot find the global optimum at the end of its search process. With regards to this, premature convergence needs to be addressed in both unimodal and multimodal problems. Avoiding premature convergence is important in

problem optimization, i.e., an algorithm should have a balance between fast convergence speed and the ability of "jumping out" of local optima.

Particles fly in the search space. If particles can easily get clustered together in a short time, particles will lose their "search potential." Premature convergence means particles have a low possibility to explore new search areas. Although many methods were reported to be designed to avoid premature convergence (Chen & Montgomery, 2011), these methods did not incorporate an effective way to measure the degree of premature convergence, in other words, the measurement of particles' exploration / exploitation is still needed to be investigated. Shi and Eberhart gave several definitions on diversity measurement based on particles' positions (Shi & Eberhart, 2008, 2009). Through diversity measurements, useful exploration and / or exploitation search information can be obtained.

PSO is simple in concept and easy in implementation, however, there are still many issues that need to be considered (Kennedy, 2007). Boundary constraint handling is one of them (Xu & Rahmat-Samii, 2007). In this paper, different boundary constraints handling methods and their impacts are discussed. Position diversity will be measured and analyzed for PSO with different boundary constraints handle strategies and different topology structures.

This paper is organized as follows. Section 2 reviews the basic PSO algorithm, four different topology structures, and definitions of population diversities. Section 3 describes several boundary constraints handling techniques, which includes the classic strategy, deterministic strategy, and stochastic strategy. Experiments are conducted in Section 4 followed by analysis and discussion on the population diversity changing curves of PSOs with different boundary constraints handling methods and four kinds of topology structures. Finally, Section 6 concludes with some remarks and future research directions.

2. PARTICLE SWARM OPTIMIZATION

For the purpose of generality and clarity, m represents the number of particles and n the number of dimensions. Each particle is represented as x_{ij}, i represents the ith particle, $i = 1, \cdots, m$, and j is the jth dimension, $j = 1, \cdots, n$. The basic equations of the original PSO algorithm are as follow (Kennedy et al., 2001; Eberhart & Shi, 2007):

$$\mathbf{v}_i \leftarrow w\mathbf{v}_i + c_1 \text{rand}() \\ \times (\mathbf{p}_i - \mathbf{x}_i) + c_2 \text{Rand}() \times (\mathbf{p}_g - \mathbf{x}_i) \qquad (1)$$

$$\mathbf{x}_i \leftarrow \mathbf{x}_i + \mathbf{v}_i \qquad (2)$$

where w denotes the inertia weight and usually is less than 1, c_1 and c_2 are two positive acceleration constants, $\text{rand}()$ and $\text{Rand}()$ are two random functions to generate uniformly distributed random numbers in the range $[0, 1]$, $x_i = (x_{i1}, x_{i2}, \cdots, x_{in})$ represents the ith particle's position, $v_i = (v_{i1}, v_{i2}, \cdots, v_{in})$ represents the ith particle's velocity, v_{ij} represents the velocity of the ith particle at the jth dimension, $\mathbf{p}_i$ refers to the best position found by the ith particle, and $\mathbf{p}_g$ refers to the position found by the member in its neighborhood that has the best fitness evaluation value so far.

2.1 Topology Structure

A particle updates its position in the search space at each iteration. The velocity update in Equation 1 consists of three parts, previous velocity, cognitive part and social part. The cognitive part means that a particle learns from its own search experience, and correspondingly, the social part means that a particle can learn from other particles, or learn from the best in its neighbors in particular. Topology defines the neighborhood of a particle.

Particle swarm optimization algorithm has different kinds of topology structures, e.g., star, ring, four clusters, or Von Neumann structure. A particle in a PSO with a different structure has different number of particles in its neighborhood with a different scope. Learning from a different neighbor means that a particle follows different neighborhood (or local) best, in other words, topology structure determines the connections among particles. Although it does not relate to the particle's cognitive part directly, topology can affect the algorithm's convergence speed and the ability of avoiding premature convergence, i.e., the PSO algorithm's ability of exploration and exploitation.

A topology structure can be seen as the environment for particles (Bentley, 1999). Particles live in the environment and each particle competes to be the global / local best. If a particle is chosen to be the global or local best, its (position) information will affect other particles' positions, and this particle is considered as a leader in its neighborhood. The structure of PSO determines the environment for particles, the process of a particle competing to be a leader is like an animal struggling in its population.

In this paper, four most commonly used topology structures are considered. They are star topology, where all particles or nodes share the search information in the whole swarm; ring topology, where every particle is connected to two neighbors; four clusters topology, where four fully connected subgroups are inter-connected among themselves by linking particles; and Von Neumann structure, which is a lattice and where every particle has four neighbors that are wrapped on four sides. All are shown in Figure 1.

- **Star:** The star topology is shown in Figure 1(a). Because all particles or nodes are connected, search information is shared in a global scope, this topology is frequently termed as *global* or *all* topology. With this topology, the search information is shared

Figure 1. Four topologies used in this paper: (a) star, (b) ring, (c) four clusters, (d) Von Neumann

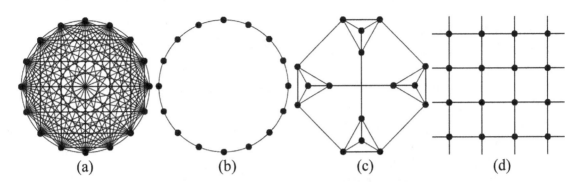

(a)   (b)   (c)   (d)

in the whole swarm, and a particle with the best fitness value will be chosen to be the "leader." Other particles will follow this particle to find optimum. This topology can be seen as a completive competition pattern. In this pattern, each particle competes with all others in the population and this requires $N - 1$ total competitions for a single-species population of N particles.

- **Ring:** The ring topology is shown in Figure 1(b). A particle is connected with two neighbors in this topology. A particle compares its fitness value with its left neighbor at first, and then the winner particle compares with the right neighbor. A particle with better fitness value in this small scope is determined by these two comparisons. This is like a small competition environment, each particle only competes with its two neighbors. This requires $2(N - 1)$ total competitions for a population of N particles.

- **Four Clusters:** The four clusters topology is shown in Figure 1(c). This topology can be seen as a species divided into four groups. Each group is a small star topology, which has a "leader" particle in this group, sharing its own search information. Besides that, each group has three link par-

ticles links to other three groups. The link particles are used to exchange search information with other three groups. For N particles, each group has $N / 4$ particles, this needs $N - 4$ competitions, plus with 12 times search information exchange. This requires $N + 8$ total competitions.

- **Von Neumann:** The Von Neumann topology is shown in Figure 1(d). This topology is also named as *Square* (Mendes et al. 2004b) or *NEWS* neighborhood (for North, East, West, and South) (Dorronsoro & Bouvry, 2011). In this topology, every particle has four neighbors that are wrapped on four sides, and the swarm is organized as a mesh. For N particles, this needs $4(N - 1)$ total competitions.

Topology determines the structure of particles' connections and the transmission of search information in the swarm. Star and ring are the two most commonly used structures. A PSO with a star structure, where all particles are connected to each other, has the smallest average distance in swarm, and on the contrary, a PSO with a local ring structure, where every particle is connected to two near particles, has the biggest average distance in swarm (Mendes, 2004; Mendes et al., 2003, 2004).

2.2 Population Diversity

An algorithm's ability of "exploration" and "exploitation" is an important factor to impact its optimization performance (Olorunda & Engelbrecht, 2008). Exploration means the ability of an optimization algorithm to explore different areas of the search space in order to have high possibility to find good optimum. Exploitation, on the other hand, means the ability for particles to concentrate the search around a promising region in order to refine a candidate solution. A good optimization algorithm should optimally balance the two conflicted objectives.

Population diversity of PSO measures the distribution of particles, and the diversity's changing curve is a way to monitor the degree of convergence / divergence of PSO search process. In other words, the status of particles, whether it is in the state of exploration or exploitation, could be obtained from this measurement. Shi and Eberhart gave several definitions on diversity measurement based on particles' positions (Shi & Eberhart, 2008, 2009). Position diversity is used to measure the distribution of particles' current positions. Cheng and Shi introduced the modified definitions of the diversity measurement based on L_1 norm (Cheng & Shi, 2011a, 2011b).

From diversity measurements, useful search information can be obtained. Position diversity measures distribution of particles' current positions. One definition of position diversity, which is based on the L_1 norm, is as follows:

$$\overline{x}_j = \frac{1}{m} \sum_{i=1}^{m} x_{ij}$$

$$D_j^p = \frac{1}{m} \sum_{i=1}^{m} |x_{ij} - \overline{x}_j|$$

$$D^p = \sum_{j=1}^{n} w_j D_j^p$$

where $\overline{x}_j$ represents the pivot of particles' position in dimension j, and D_j^p measures particles position diversity based on L_1 norm for dimension j. Then we define $\overline{\mathbf{x}} = [\overline{x}_1, \cdots, \overline{x}_j, \cdots, \overline{x}_n]$, $\overline{\mathbf{x}}$ represents the mean of particles' current positions on each dimension, and $\mathbf{D}^p = [D_1^p, \cdots, D_j^p, \cdots, D_n^p]$, which measures particles' position diversity for each dimension. D^p measures the whole swarm's population diversity.

Without lose of generality, every dimension is considered equally in this paper. Setting all $w_j = \frac{1}{n}$, then the position diversity of the whole swarm can be defined as:

$$D^p = \sum_{j=1}^{n} \frac{1}{n} D_j^p = \frac{1}{n} \sum_{j=1}^{n} D_j^p \tag{3}$$

Position diversities, which are observed based on a dimension or on the whole swarm of particles, are experimented in Section 5 of the paper.

3. BOUNDARY CONSTRAINTS HANDLING

This section presents a brief survey on the main existing methods that deal with boundary constraints in the literature. Even PSO is simple and easy in implementation, there are still some issues need to be considered (Kennedy, 2007), and boundary constraints handling is one of the issues. There are different strategies to handle a particle's position when this particle exceeds its boundary limit.

3.1. "Stuck in" the Boundary

Algorithms are generally tested on the standard benchmark functions for the purpose of comparison. These functions have an optimum in the center of solution space (Yao et al., 1999). However, for real problems, we don't know the location of an optimum, and the optimum could be at any place in the solution space. With an improper boundary constraints handling strategy, a phenomenon of particles "stuck in" the boundary will occur.

A classic boundary constraint handling strategy resets a particle at boundary in one dimension when this particle's position is exceeding the boundary in that dimension. If the fitness value of the particle at boundary is better than that of other particles, all particles in its neighborhood in this dimension will move to the boundary. If particles could not find a position with better fitness value, all particles will "stick in" the boundary at this dimension.

A particle is difficult to "jump out" of boundary even we increase the total number of fitness evaluations or the maximum number of iterations, and this phenomenon occurs more frequently for high-dimensional problems.

3.2. Classical Strategy

The conventional boundary handling methods try to keep the particles inside the feasible search space S. Search information is obtained when particles fly in the search space. However, if a particle's position exceeds the boundary limit in one dimension at one iteration, that search information will be abandoned. Instead, a new position will be reset to the particle in that dimension. The classic strategy is to set the particle at boundary when it exceeds the boundary (Zhang et al., 2004). The equation of this strategy is as follows:

$$x_{i,j,G+1} = \begin{cases} X_{\max,j} & \text{if } x_{i,j,G+1} > X_{\max,j} \\ X_{\min,j} & \text{if } x_{i,j,G+1} < X_{\min,j} \\ x_{i,j,G+1} & \text{otherwise} \end{cases} \quad (4)$$

where G is the number of the last iteration, and $G+1$ is the number of current iteration. This

strategy resets particles in a particular point—the boundary, which constrains particles to fly in the search space limited by boundary.

3.3. Deterministic Strategy

A deterministic method was reported in Zielinski et al. (2009), which resets a boundary-violating position to the middle between old position and the boundary. The equation is as follows:

$$x_{i,j,G+1} = \begin{cases} \frac{1}{2}(x_{i,j,G} + X_{\max,j}) & \text{if } x_{i,j,G+1} > X\max, j \\ \frac{1}{2}(x_{i,j,G} + X_{\min,j}) & \text{if } x_{i,j,G+1} < X_{\min,j} \\ x_{i,j,G+1} & \text{otherwise} \end{cases}$$

$$\quad (5)$$

The position in last iteration is used in this strategy. Both classic strategy and this strategy reset a particle to a deterministic position.

3.4. Stochastic Strategy

Eberhart and Shi utilized a stochastic strategy to reset the particles when particles exceed the position boundary (Eberhart & Shi, 2007).

$$x_{i,j,G+1} = \begin{cases} X_{\max,j} - (\frac{1}{2}\text{rand}()(X_{\max,j} - X_{\min,j})) & \text{if } x_{i,j,G+1} > X_{\max,j} \\ X_{\min,j} + (\frac{1}{2}\text{Rand}()(X_{\max,j} - X_{\min,j})) & \text{if } x_{i,j,G+1} < X_{\min,j} \\ x_{i,j,G+1} & \text{otherwise} \end{cases}$$

$$\quad (6)$$

where $\text{rand}()$ and $\text{Rand}()$ are two random functions to generate uniformly distributed random numbers in the range $[0, 1]$.

By this strategy, particles will be reset within the half search space when particles exceed the boundary limit. This will increases the algorithm's exploration, that is, particles have higher possibilities to explore new search areas. However, it decreases the algorithm's ability of exploitation at the same time. A particle exceeding the boundary means the global or local optimum may be close to the boundary region. An algorithm should spend more iterations in this region. With the consideration of keeping the ability of exploitation, the resetting scope should be taken into account. For most benchmark functions, particles "fly in" a symmetric search space. With regards to this

$$X_{\max,j} = \frac{1}{2}(X^{\text{top},j} - X^{\text{bottom},j}) = \frac{1}{2}X^{\text{scope},j}$$

and

$$X_{\min,j} = -X_{\max,j}$$

The equation of resetting particle into a special area is as follows:

$$x_{i,j,G+1} =$$
$$\begin{cases} X_{\max,j} \times (\text{rand}() \times c + 1 - c) & \text{if } x_{i,j,G+1} > X_{\max,j} \\ X_{\min,j} \times (\text{Rand}() \times c + 1 - c) & \text{if } x_{i,j,G+1} < X_{\min,j} \\ x_{i,j,G+1} & \text{otherwise} \end{cases}$$
$$(7)$$

where c is a parameter to control the resetting scope. When $c = 1$, this strategy is the same as the Equation 6, that is, particles reset within a half space. On the contrary, when $c = 0$, this strategy is the same as the Equation 4, i.e., it is the same as the classic strategy. The closer to 0 the c is, the more particles have a high possibility to be reset close to the boundary.

4. EXPERIMENTAL STUDY

Several performance measurements are utilized in the experiments below. The first is the best fitness value attained after a fixed number of iterations. In our case, we report the mean result found after the pre-determined maximum number of iterations. The second is the time t which indicates the times of particles stuck in the boundary. At the end of each run, we count the number of the particles, which has the best fitness value and which get stuck in boundary in at least one dimension. The number will be larger if a particle is stuck in boundary in more dimensions. All numbers will be summed after 50 runs. The summed number indicates the frequency of particles that may get stuck in boundary. Standard deviation values of the best fitness values are also utilized in this paper, which gives the solution's distribution. These values give a measurement of goodness of the algorithm.

4.1. Benchmark Test Functions

The experiments have been conducted on testing the benchmark functions listed in Table 1. Without loss of generality, five standard unimodal and five multimodal test functions are selected (Liang et al., 2006; Yao et al., 1999).

All functions are run 50 times to ensure a reasonable statistical result necessary to compare the different approaches. Every tested function's optimal point in solution space S is shifted to a randomly generated point with different value in each dimension, and $S \subseteq \mathbb{R}^n$, $\mathbb{R}^n$ is a n-dimensional Euclidean space.

4.2. Velocity Constraints

In the experiments, all benchmark functions have $V_{\min} = -V_{\max}$ which means that $V_{\min}$ has the same magnitude but opposite direction. The velocity also has a constraint to limit particle's search step:

Table 1. The benchmark functions used in our experimental study, where n is the dimension of each problem, $\mathbf{z} = (\mathbf{x} - \mathbf{o})$, $\mathbf{x} = [x_1, x_2, \cdots, x_n]$. o_i is an randomly generated number in problem's search space S, it is the same for each function at different run, but different for different function in each dimension. Global optimum $\mathbf{x}^* = \mathbf{o}$, $f_{\min}$ is the minimum value of the function, and $S \subseteq \mathbb{R}^n$.

Function	Test Function	S	$f_{\min}$
Parabolic	$f_0(\mathbf{x}) = \sum_{i=1}^{n} z_i^2 + \text{bias}_0$	$[-100, 100]^n$	-450.0
Schwefel's P2.22	$f_1(\mathbf{x}) = \sum_{i=1}^{n} |z_i| + \prod_{i=1}^{n} |z_i| + \text{bias}_1$	$[-10, 10]^n$	-330.0
Schwefel's P1.2	$f_2(\mathbf{x}) = \sum_{i=1}^{n} (\sum_{k=1}^{i} z_k)^2 + \text{bias}_2$	$[-100, 100]^n$	450.0
Step	$f_3(\mathbf{x}) = \sum_{i=1}^{n} (\lfloor z_i + 0.5 \rfloor)^2 + \text{bias}_3$	$[-100, 100]^n$	330.0
Quadric Noise	$f_4(\mathbf{x}) = \sum_{i=1}^{n} i z_i^4 + \text{random}[0,1) + \text{bias}_4$	$[-1.28, 1.28]^n$	-450.0
Griewank	$f_5(\mathbf{x}) = \dfrac{1}{4000} \sum_{i=1}^{n} z_i^2 - \prod_{i=1}^{n} \cos(\dfrac{z_i}{\sqrt{i}}) + 1 + \text{bias}_5$	$[-600, 600]^n$	120.0
Rosenbrock	$f_6(\mathbf{x}) = \sum_{i=1}^{n-1} [100(z_{i+1} - z_i^2)^2 + (z_i - 1)^2] + \text{bias}_6$	$[-10, 10]^n$	-330.0
Rastrigin	$f_7(\mathbf{x}) = \sum_{i=1}^{n} [z_i^2 - 10\cos(2\pi z_i) + 10] + \text{bias}_7$	$[-5.12, 5.12]^n$	450.0
Ackley	$f_8(\mathbf{x}) = -20 \exp\left(-0.2\sqrt{\dfrac{1}{n}\sum_{i=1}^{n} z_i^2}\right)$ $- \exp\left(\dfrac{1}{n}\sum_{i=1}^{n} \cos(2\pi z_i)\right) + 20 + e + \text{bias}_8$	$[-32, 32]^n$	180.0
Generalized Penalized	$f_9(\mathbf{x}) = \dfrac{\pi}{n}\{10\sin^2(\pi y_1) + \sum_{i=1}^{n-1}(y_i - 1)^2$ $\times [1 + 10\sin^2(\pi y_{i+1})] + (y_n - 1)^2\}$ $+ \sum_{i=1}^{n} u(z_i, 10, 100, 4) + \text{bias}_9$ $y_i = 1 + \dfrac{1}{4}(z_i + 1) \quad u(z_i, a, k, m) - \begin{cases} k(z_i - a)^m & z_i > a, \\ 0 & -a < z_i < a \\ k(-z_i - a)^m & z_i < -a \end{cases}$	$[-50, 50]^n$	330.0

if $v_{ij} > V_{max}$ then $v_{ij} = V_{max}$

else if $v_{ij} < -V_{max}$ then $v_{ij} = -V_{max}$

4.3. Parameter Setting

In all experiments, each PSO has 32 particles, and parameters are set as in the standard PSO, $w = 0.72984$, and $c_1 = c_2 = 1.496172$ (Bratton & Kennedy, 2007). Each algorithm runs 50 times.

4.4. Experimental Results

4.4.1. Observation of "Stuck In" Boundary

By applying the classic strategy of boundary handling method, the position will be reset on the boundary if the position value exceeds the boundary of the search space. Table 2 gives the experimental results of applying this strategy. Each benchmark function will be tested with dimension 25, 50, and 100 to see whether similar observation can be obtained. The maximum number of iterations will be set to be 1000, 2000, 4000 corresponding to dimension 25, 50, and 100, respectively.

From the results, we can conclude that each algorithm has different possibilities of "being stuck in" boundary when it is applied to different problems. Problem dimension does not have a significant impact on the possibility of particles "being stuck in" the boundary at least for the benchmark functions with dimensions 25, 50, and 100 that we tested. Furthermore, generally speaking, the PSO with star structure is more like to be attracted to and then to be "stuck in" the boundary, and the PSO with ring structure is less like to be "stuck in" boundary.

If particles are "stuck in" the boundary, it is difficult for them to "jump out" of the local optima even we increase the maximum number of fitness evaluations. The fitness evaluation number of each function with dimension 100 in Table 2 is $32 \times 4000 = 128\ 000$, we then increase this number to $32 \times 10000 = 320\ 000$. The experimental results are given in Table 3. From Table 3, we can see that there is no any significant improvement neither on the fitness value nor on the number of particles "stuck in" the boundary. This means that by only increasing the number of fitness evaluations cannot help particles "jump out" of boundary constraints. Some techniques should be utilized for particles to avoid converge to the boundary.

Table 4 gives the experimental results of the algorithm that ignores the boundary constraints. In Tables 4 and 5, only the PSO with star topology has the "t" column, while PSOs with other topologies do not have the "t" column because the "t" values are all zeros. For the same reason, other tables do not have the "t" column. Particles take no strategy when particles meet the boundary. Some tested functions will get good fitness value with most of the obtained solutions being out of the search space. This may be good for particles flying in a periodic search space (Zhang et al., 2004). However, most problems have strict boundary constraints which this strategy does not fit for.

4.4.2. Comparison of PSOs with Different Boundary Constraint Handling Techniques

Table 5 shows the results of PSOs with the deterministic strategy. A particle takes a middle value of the former position and the boundary limit value when the particle meets the boundary constraint. PSOs with ring, four clusters, and Von Neumann structure can obtain good fitness values by utilizing this strategy. However, "struck in" boundary will still happen for PSO with star structure for most problems. This is because particles with star structure will progressively move to boundary. With this tendency, particles will get clustered

Table 2. Results of the strategy that a particle "sticks in" boundary when it exceeds the boundary constraints. All algorithms are run for 50 times, the maximum number of iterations is 1000, 2000, and 4000 when the dimensions are 25, 50, and 100, respectively, where "mean" indicates the average of the best fitness values for each run, "times" t indicates the number of particle with the best fitness value "stuck in" the boundary at a dimension. The percentage shows the frequency of particles "stuck in" the boundary of the search space

Fun.		Star		Ring		Four Clusters		Von Neumann	
	n	Mean	Times t	Mean	t	Mean	t	Mean	t
f_0	25	4950.914	301 (24.08%)	-441.0717	2 (0.16%)	347.1880	72 (5.76%)	-64.9233	36 (2.88%)
	50	18512.65	681 (27.24%)	-391.2514	29 (1.16%)	1284.592	249 (9.96%)	467.7678	178 (7.12%)
	100	66154.79	1552 (31.04%)	**-269.469**	48 (0.96%)	7744.016	615 (12.3%)	4053.870	421 (8.42%)
f_1	25	-312.9603	159 (12.72%)	-329.9257	2 (0.16%)	-328.008	38 (3.04%)	-328.354	30 (2.4%)
	50	-265.9373	575 (23%)	-326.8749	80 (3.2%)	-314.148	242 (9.68%)	-323.725	158 (6.32%)
	100	-170.1893	1212 (24.24%)	**-299.1541**	395 (7.9%)	-254.349	791 (15.82%)	-273.921	630 (12.6%)
f_2	25	6556.133	223 (17.84%)	1418.165	55 (4.4%)	1551.690	82 (6.56%)	1151.919	68 (5.44%)
	50	59401.84	838 (33.52%)	20755.67	286 (11.44%)	18687.75	411 (16.44%)	16730.74	327 (13.08)
	100	149100.1	1614 (32.28%)	119188.2	762 (15.24%)	97555.70	1049 (20.98%)	**93162.75**	778 (15.56%)
f_3	25	6483.32	284 (22.72%)	439.7	8 (0.64%)	1105.8	86 (6.88%)	876.56	53 (4.24%)
	50	19175.24	724 (28.96%)	476.58	29 (1.16%)	2697.68	238 (9.52%)	1604.98	166 (6.64%)
	100	70026.22	1449 (28.98%)	**859.12**	36 (0.72%)	7688.02	396 (7.92%)	7021.66	311 (6.22%)
f_4	25	-446.843	245 (19.6%)	-449.9543	24 (1.92%)	-449.836	61 (4.88%)	-449.901	33 (2.64%)
	50	-386.667	696 (27.84%)	-449.8241	44 (1.76%)	-447.068	157 (6.28%)	-448.661	91 (3.64%)
	100	49.74071	1606 (32.12%)	**-448.7530**	67 (1.34%)	-418.627	359 (7.18%)	-433.289	282 (5.64%)
f_5	25	169.2253	319 (25.52%)	120.4066	7 (0.56%)	128.1231	88 (7.04%)	123.0943	36 (2.88%)
	50	308.2321	739 (29.56%)	121.6709	49 (1.96%)	141.3122	270 (10.8%)	128.9908	187 (7.48%)
	100	676.8980	1415 (28.3%)	**122.7015**	66 (1.32%)	194.1575	591 (11.82%)	156.2124	428 (8.56)

continued on following page

Table 2. Continued

Fun.	n	Star		Ring		Four Clusters		Von Neumann	
		Mean	Times t	Mean	t	Mean	t	Mean	t
f_6	25	102391.65	334 (26.72%)	-236.9387	25 (2%)	13681.40	107 (8.56%)	1472.597	76 (6.08%)
	50	1075433.7	870 (34.8%)	215.3156	118 (4.72%)	16784.12	368 (14.72)	25350.40	287 (11.48%)
	100	3500148.0	1614 (32.28%)	**2311.019**	222 (4.44%)	167064.1	712 (14.24%)	123572.6	586 (11.72%)
f_7	25	529.9848	210 (16.8%)	503.0551	103 (8.24%)	500.5270	135 (10.8%)	497.6501	129 (10.32%)
	50	730.7713	445 (17.8%)	638.3773	196 (7.84%)	635.7780	281 (11.24)	612.3373	253 (10.12%)
	100	1168.550	664 (13.28%)	968.5158	369 (7.38%)	957.5405	519 (10.38%)	**879.3672**	479 (9.58%)
f_8	25	192.2881	239 (19.12%)	181.1893	15 (1.2%)	186.4093	94 (7.52%)	184.0952	64 (5.12%)
	50	195.2231	420 (16.8%)	182.6727	69 (2.76%)	188.7666	267 (10.68%)	185.2521	183 (7.32%)
	100	199.0853	521 (10.42%)	191.6770	258 (5.16%)	191.9497	490 (9.8%)	**189.5658**	450 (9%)
f_9	25	7773207.1	250 (20%)	3567.791	15 (1.2%)	473424.72	76 (6.08%)	10931.296	54 (4.32%)
	50	163596583	749 (29.96%)	331.2763	172 (6.88%)	5365821.9	345 (13.8%)	2296129.5	291 (11.64%)
	100	1063146706	1765 (35.3%)	**5394.753**	394 (7.88%)	26421658	789 (15.78%)	6918596.1	646 (12.92%)

together at the boundary and be difficult to "jump out." Therefore, the exploration ability decreases over the iterations.

With a stochastic strategy, a particle will be reset to a random position when the particle meets the boundary. Table 6 gives the result of PSOs with the stochastic strategy, that is, a particle is reset to be within the upper half space when the particle meets the upper bound, and correspondingly, a particle is reset to be within the lower half space when the particle meets the lower bound. Compared with the classic strategy and the deterministic strategy, this strategy improves the result of PSO with the star structure, but it does not get better optimization performance for PSOs with other structures in this paper.

In Table 6, particles are reset within half space when particles meet the boundary. This increases an algorithm's the ability of exploration, and it decreases the ability of exploitation. A particle being close to the boundary may mean that the optimal area may be near the boundary, the resetting area should be restricted. Table 7 gives the result of resetting area limited to $[0.9V_{max}, V_{max}]$ when a particle meets the upper bound, and $[V_{min}, 0.9V_{min}]$ when a particle meets the lower bound. This strategy can obtain better results.

In Tables 6 and 7, the resetting area does not change during the whole search process. Intuitively, at the beginning of search process, we want a large ability of exploration and small ability of exploitation to be able to search more areas of the search space (Shi & Eberhart, 1998, 1999). Cor-

Table 3. Results of the strategy that a particle stays at boundary when it exceeds the boundary constraints. Algorithms have a large maximum number of fitness evaluations, i.e. 10000. The dimension n is 100.

Fun	Star		Ring		Four Clusters		Von Neumann	
	Mean	Times t	Mean	t	Mean	t	Mean	t
f_0	67822.60	1540 (30.8%)	-256.0704	70 (1.4%)	7843.960	604 (12.08%)	2944.748	410 (8.2%)
f_1	-176.428	1225 (24.5%)	-297.9756	475 (9.5%)	-237.3498	874 (17.48%)	-279.874	603 (12.06%)
f_2	126974.8	1675 (33.5%)	68200.22	845 (16.9%)	71934.29	1099 (21.98%)	68816.78	1002 (20.04%)
f_3	71393.22	1528 (30.56%)	931.7	43 (0.9%)	10083.18	529 (10.58%)	6138.18	371 (7.42%)
f_4	143.0742	1599 (31.98%)	-448.580	49 (0.98%)	-400.9793	425 (8.5%)	-439.6080	284 (5.68%)
f_5	723.8275	1556 (31.12%)	123.6233	106 (2.12%)	189.9494	589 (11.96%)	154.8893	454 (9.08%)
f_6	3963368.9	1881 (37.62%)	1690.535	299 (5.98%)	229710.9	810 (16.2%)	68857.72	640 (12.8%)
f_7	1201.7850	722 (14.44%)	965.6807	413 (8.26%)	971.4570	550 (11%)	912.0553	552 (11.04%)
f_8	199.5501	545 (10.9%)	193.9069	312 (6.24%)	194.2383	526 (10.52%)	190.3066	532 (10.64%)
f_9	969621012	1874 (37.48%)	73541.50	487 (9.74%)	42652667	979 (19.58%)	14202759	808 (16.16%)

respondingly, at the end of search process, the exploitation ability should be more favored to find an optimum in "good" areas. With regards to this, the resetting search space should be dynamically changed in the search process. Table 8 gives the results of the strategy that the resetting space linearly decreases in the search process.

By examining the experimental results, it is clear that different boundary constraints handling techniques have different impacts on particles' diversity changing and optimization performance. The deterministic strategy fits for PSOs with ring, four clusters and Von Neumann structure. Resetting particles randomly in a small area fits for all the four topologies utilized in this paper. Using this strategy, the PSO with star structure will have a good balance between ability of exploration and

exploitation, which get the best performance than other strategies.

5. POPULATION DIVERSITY ANALYSIS AND DISCUSSION

Without loss of generality and for the purpose of simplicity and clarity, the results for one function from five unimodal benchmark functions and one function from five multimodal functions will be displayed because others will be similar.

There are several definitions on the measurement of population diversities (Shi & Eberhart, 2008, 2009, Cheng & Shi, 2011b). The dimension-

Table 4. Results of the strategy that a particles ignores the boundary when it exceeds the boundary constraints. All algorithms are run for 50 times, where "mean" and σ indicate the average and standard deviation of the best fitness values for each run. n is 100, and maximum iteration number is 4000.

Fun	Star			Ring		Four Clusters		Von Neumann	
	Mean	σ	t	Mean	σ	Mean	σ	Mean	σ
f_0	-449.6162	1.727025	0 (0%)	-449.9999	1.20E-06	-449.9999	6.47E-09	-449.9999	8.77E-07
f_1	-327.3012	6.104924	1 (0.02%)	-329.9900	0.025155	-329.9998	0.000425	-329.9998	0.000224
f_2	35458.463	9998.671	396 (7.92%)	116972.62	23299.66	66411.144	14308.29	71154.160	14523.52
f_3	3343.06	2330.047	39 (0.78%)	334.28	3.376625	353.92	39.25701	363.56	65.76508
f_4	-449.0495	2.311998	191 (3.82%)	-449.6915	0.055767	-449.8339	0.038184	-449.8358	0.039501
f_5	120.4391	0.890941	1 (0.02%)	120.0007	0.003132	120.0176	0.056479	120.0205	0.037423
f_6	-87.33991	69.15844	216 (4.32%)	-15.65356	67.65250	-107.9635	54.60742	-92.00367	58.01067
f_7	1058.2517	125.6292	412 (8.24%)	988.66426	63.58231	945.39263	74.93225	892.9344	65.63141
f_8	199.47550	1.349835	395 (7.9%)	199.26132	3.396034	194.99493	7.570846	184.6948	5.632849
f_9	331.5831	0.911304	117 (2.34%)	336.1132	2.149815	332.4632	1.849387	332.10723	1.336155

wised population diversity based on the L_1 norm is utilized in this paper.

5.1. Position Diversity Monitoring

Figures 2 and 3 display the position diversity changing curves when PSO is applied to solve benchmark functions. Figure 2 displays the curves for the unimodal function f_0 and Figure 3 displays for multimodal function f_5. In both figures, (a) is for functions f_0 and f_5 with a classic boundary handling technique, (b) is for functions f_0 and f_5 with particles ignoring the boundary, (c) is for functions f_0 and f_5 with particles close to bound-

ary gradually, (d) is for functions f_0 and f_5 with particles resetting in half search space, (e) is for functions f_0 and f_5 with limited resetting space at a small range near boundary, (f) is for functions f_0 and f_5 with a linearly decreased resetting scope, respectively.

Figures 2 and 3 displayed the position diversity changing curves of particles with four kinds of topologies. Some conclusion can be made that PSO with star topology has the most rapid position diversity decreasing curve, and PSO with ring topology can keep its diversity in the large number of iterations, generally. PSO with four clusters and Von Neumann also keep their diver-

Table 5. Results of PSO with a deterministic boundary constraint strategy. Particles will be reset to the middle between old position and boundary when particle's position exceeds the boundary. n is 100, and iteration number is 4000.

Fun	Star			Ring		Four Clusters		Von Neumann	
	Mean	σ	t	Mean	σ	Mean	σ	Mean	σ
f_0	18125.68	12771.54	523 (10.46%)	-449.9999	3.15E-06	-409.4909	127.3536	-420.4673	155.7340
f_1	-267.2679	26.3105	368 (7.36%)	-324.0182	9.402653	-315.4557	15.36290	-324.0810	8.879355
f_2	63749.30	23677.19	11 (0.22%)	95768.66	21022.066	61791.362	17080.59	58886.36	14324.72
f_3	27628.66	14213.33	103 (2.06%)	343.04	25.91521	1378.16	1385.743	719.52	691.3372
f_4	-300.7705	173.088	0 (0%)	-449.7622	0.074653	-449.0363	1.945231	-449.3194	2.434300
f_5	271.0433	114.9603	508 (10.16%)	120.0399	0.192983	122.2650	5.086505	120.83178	1.275821
f_6	627095.6	1084062.7	657 (13.14%)	-46.8004	74.09709	360.9332	1304.484	66.08107	462.4078
f_7	1104.514	120.0267	20 (0.4%)	944.5443	70.81612	944.4611	87.02924	839.2663	68.15615
f_8	198.1596	2.591173	67 (1.34%)	183.1589	3.415466	185.4077	4.043386	183.4269	1.466134
f_9	88647933	232053019	333 (6.66%)	333.7982	1.770645	339.5574	51.57181	331.4686	1.385780

sity well in the search process, and the curves of diversity changing are smooth in most times.

The impact of different boundary constraint handling strategy on the position diversity also can be seen from these two figures. The values of position diversity changing will be very small when we utilize classic or deterministic strategies, and on the contrary, the position diversity will be kept at a "large" value when we utilize a stochastic strategy. The different position diversity changing curves indicate that particles will get clustered to a small region when we utilize a classic or deterministic strategy, and particles will be distributed in the large region when we utilize a stochastic strategy.

The changing curves of position diversity reveal the algorithm's ability of exploration and/or exploitation. The position diversity of PSO with a stochastic strategy will keep a "large" value, which indicates that with this strategy, PSO will have a good exploration ability.

5.2. Position Diversity Comparison

Different topology structures and boundary constraint handling methods will have different impacts on PSO algorithms' convergence. Figure 4 and below give some comparison among PSOs with different structures. There are four curves in each figure, which are the minimum, middle, and maximum dimensional position diversity, and

Table 6. Results of the strategy that a particle is randomly re-initialized within the half search space when the particle meets the boundary constraints. n is 100, and maximum iteration number is 4000.

Fun	Star		Ring		Four Clusters		Von Neumann	
	Mean	σ	Mean	σ	Mean	σ	Mean	σ
f_0	15106.480	5401.915	6395.5801	1164.004	6456.2857	1471.815	5777.2014	1252.942
f_1	-204.55407	27.57007	-283.72265	5.047291	-282.5310	7.374081	-286.1511	5.525085
f_2	90226.816	38529.56	128790.177	28617.91	86885.81	31845.28	89231.033	33283.20
f_3	16437.02	4735.015	7593.56	1181.772	6954.9	1147.187	6874.76	1237.944
f_4	-442.9050	5.455450	-447.7014	0.651993	-447.9193	0.610410	-448.1605	0.490777
f_5	266.77115	36.43274	186.8523	12.45620	180.9738	10.21838	178.7420	11.10882
f_6	68586.660	68055.93	16834.993	6821.930	13083.356	6063.868	12442.671	4804.749
f_7	903.1275	69.44400	928.1833	51.27520	870.4047	72.80328	823.6537	59.78453
f_8	193.9104	1.330059	190.0964	0.488740	190.1364	0.627680	189.6701	0.616846
f_9	1834.0033	8708.160	2073.1476	3587.605	489.12695	220.7106	406.0229	121.9164

position diversity as a whole. It should be noted that the dimension which has the minimum, middle, or maximum value is not fixed and may change over iterations. In other words, if the dimension i has the minimum value at iteration k, and it may be the dimension j that has the minimum value at iteration $k+1$. The figures only display position diversity's minimum, middle and maximum values at each iteration.

Figures 4 and 5 display the position diversity changing curves of a PSO with the classic boundary constraints handling method to solve unimodal function f_0 and multimodal function f_5 respectively. Four subfigures display the PSO with star, ring, four clusters, and Von Neumann topology, respectively. As can be seen from the figures, the dimensional minimum value of posi-

tion diversity is quickly getting zero for PSO with star, four clusters, and Von Neumann topology, while the dimensional minimum value of position diversity will exist during the whole search process for the PSO with ring topology.

Compared with other topologies, the position diversity of PSO with star structure can get to the smallest value at the early iteration numbers, which means particles have clustered together in a small region, and any particle generally has the smallest distance to other particles. On the contrary, the position diversity of PSO with ring structure has the largest value, which means particles are distributed in a large region, and any particle generally has the largest distance to other particles.

Table 7. Results of strategy that a particle is randomly re-initialized within a limited search space when the particle meets the boundary constraints. n is 100, and the maximum iteration number is 4000.

Fun	Star		Ring		Four Clusters		Von Neumann	
	Mean	σ	Mean	σ	Mean	σ	Mean	σ
f_0	-421.0384	106.7571	-446.7030	1.301631	-448.6723	0.544163	-448.2624	0.800959
f_1	-315.9906	14.73397	-329.2227	0.155278	-329.1543	2.610519	-329.4232	0.520195
f_2	35799.38	13401.02	99311.642	17424.32	56011.555	11425.04	56913.228	10526.66
f_3	2592.84	2381.520	351.12	6.556340	359.58	15.16123	368.96	77.62009
f_4	-449.5926	0.901977	-449.7613	0.055156	-449.8691	0.029105	-449.8604	0.034106
f_5	121.8713	3.279144	120.9374	0.090210	120.5187	0.120787	120.6400	0.102622
f_6	271.2483	757.2085	111.6548	176.7045	23.60728	144.9963	1.658537	120.5905
f_7	1059.5079	86.42771	971.4921	74.61998	930.1978	105.0998	838.0115	57.72716
f_8	197.5319	3.148760	183.0840	3.434429	182.9285	2.463089	182.3226	0.544321
f_9	331.9493	1.019762	334.1176	1.364879	332.1842	1.408311	331.2558	0.917983

Figures 6 and 7 display the position diversity curve of PSO with the strategy that a particle ignores the boundary constraints when the particle's position exceeds the limit. Figure 6 is for f_0 and Figure 7 is for f_5. Particles can keep their search "potential" with this strategy, the position diversity decreases in the whole search space, and not getting to zero at the end of each run.

Figures 8 and 9 display the position diversity changing curves of PSO with a deterministic boundary handling strategy on unimodal function f_0 and multimodal function f_5. PSO with star topology is easily "stuck in" the boundary with this strategy, and the minimum of position diversity quickly became zero in Figure 8(a) and Figure 9(a). PSO with other three topologies have

some ability to "jump out" of local optima. Figure 8(c) and Figure 9(c) display the diversity changing curves of PSO with four clusters structure. Figure 8(d) and Figure 9(d) display the diversity changing curves of PSO with Von Neumann structure. From Figure 8(c) and (d) and Figure 9(c) and (d), we can observe dramatically "up and down" changes of the position diversity curve, which may mean that as a whole, the search process is convergent but there are divergent process embedded in the convergent process.

Figures 10 and 11 display the position diversity changing curves of PSO with a stochastic boundary constraints handling technique to solve unimodal function f_0 and multimodal function f_5 respectively. By utilizing a half search space

Table 8. Results of the strategy that particles are randomly re-initialized in a linearly decreased search space when particles meet the boundary constraints. n is 100, and the maximum iteration number is 4000.

Fun	Star Mean	Star σ	Ring Mean	Ring σ	Four Clusters Mean	Four Clusters σ	Von Neumann Mean	Von Neumann σ
f_0	1702.3219	2184.3429	-408.3616	10.80574	-399.17565	53.23343	-404.6038	49.48885
f_1	-264.9917	22.439393	-327.3860	0.269110	-326.7792	2.130535	-327.5687	0.721141
f_2	53393.692	19574.620	90638.595	19706.681	59016.266	16850.516	57652.796	17353.163
f_3	5143.02	3071.211	420.66	17.44890	495.92	152.5970	484.9	180.2659
f_4	-448.64071	1.947832	-449.5890	0.082450	-449.7233	0.075943	-449.7304	0.075108
f_5	143.2678	16.39704	121.3696	0.0904944	121.4365	0.420780	121.3901	0.284098
f_6	9488.6354	18895.481	695.27241	429.34077	461.98764	413.84524	341.3105	246.16785
f_7	932.30625	74.40180	929.71921	60.000384	894.04412	61.824412	835.0238	47.61768
f_8	193.20420	2.508372	183.1691	0.417221	184.14282	1.085659	183.6688	0.974338
f_9	335.42590	1.713722	338.85667	3.039058	335.04291	1.578953	334.1127	1.2826316

resetting technique, the values of position diversities are larger than that of PSOs with other strategies, which means that particles search in a larger region, i.e., the ability of exploration can be kept with this strategy. However, the ability of exploitation will be decreased when particles are getting close to the boundary. In general a distance between any pair of particles is larger than that in PSOs with other boundary constraint handling techniques at the same iterations.

Figures 12 and 13 display the position diversity changing curves of PSO with a linearly decreased resetting space to solve unimodal function f_0 and multimodal function f_5 respectively. Four subfigures are displayed for PSO with star, ring, four clusters, and Von Neumann topology, respec-

tively. Like in other figures, the position diversities for PSO with star topology have the smallest value, and position diversities for PSO with ring topology have the largest value.

Figures 14 and 15 display the position diversity changing curves of PSO with a small resetting area to solve unimodal function f_0 and multimodal function f_5 respectively. PSO with this strategy can have a good balance between exploration and exploitation. From the figures we can see that the minimum position diversity is kept to a small value but not to zero in the whole search process. This means that particles can exploit some specific areas, and at the same time, particles will not be clustered together in this area. Particles

Figure 2. Position diversity changing curves for PSO solving parabolic function f_0 with different strategies: (a) classic, (b) cross, (c) deterministic, (d) stochastic, (e) limit, (f) linear

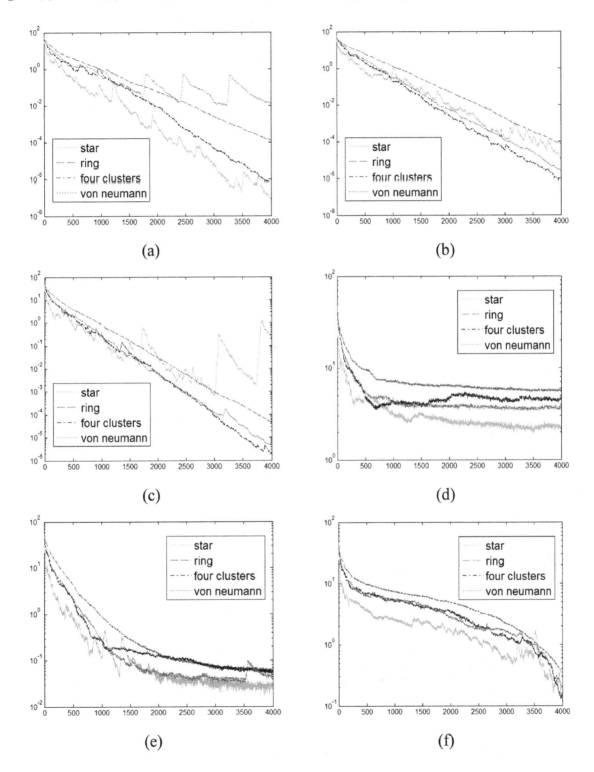

Figure 3. Position diversity changing curves for PSO solving multimodal function f_5 with different strategies: (a) classic, (b) cross, (c) deterministic, (d) stochastic, (e) limit, (f) linear

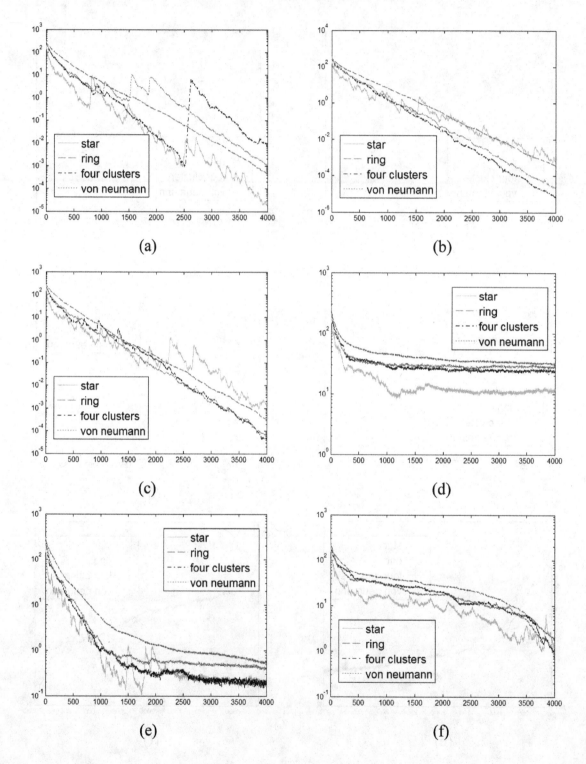

Figure 4. Comparison of PSO population diversities for solving unimodal function f_0 with classic boundary constraints handling techniques: (a) star, (b) ring, (c) four clusters, (d) Von Neumannv

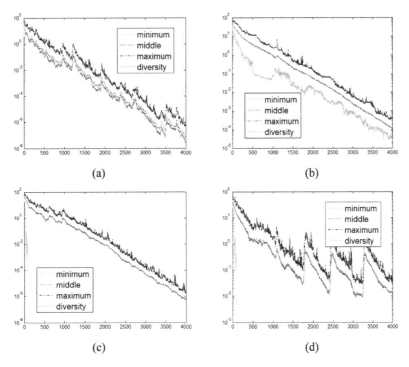

Figure 5. Comparison of PSO population diversities for solving multimodal function f_5 with classic boundary constraints handling techniques: (a) star, (b) ring, (c) four clusters, (d) Von Neumann

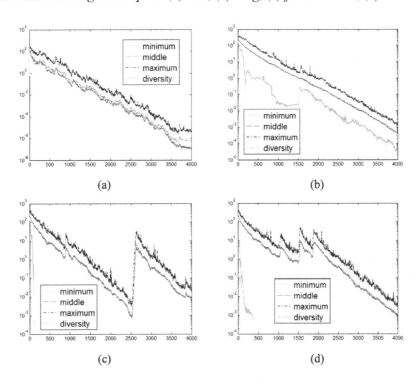

Figure 6. Comparison of PSO population diversities for solving unimodal function f_0 with exceeding boundary constraints handling techniques: (a) star, (b) ring, (c) four clusters, (d) Von Neumann

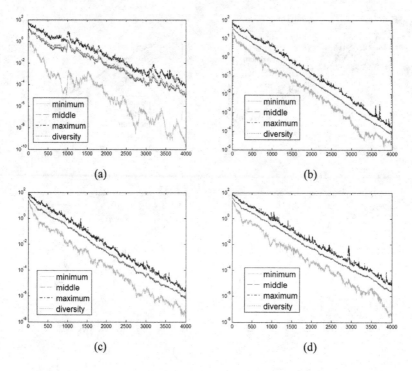

Figure 7. Comparison of PSO population diversities for solving multimodal function f_5 with exceeding boundary constraints handling techniques: (a) star, (b) ring, (c) four clusters, (d) Von Neumann

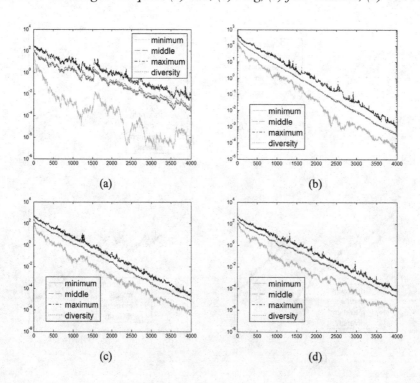

Figure 8. Comparison of PSO population diversities for solving unimodal function f_0 with deterministic boundary constraints handling techniques: (a) star, (b) ring, (c) four clusters, (d) Von Neumann

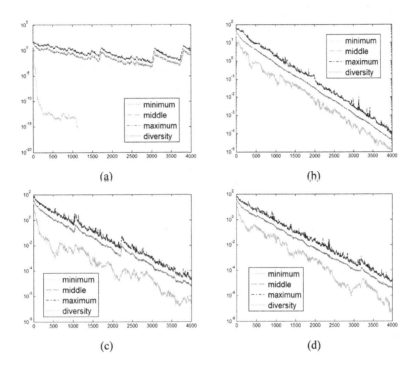

Figure 9. Comparison of PSO population diversities for solving multimodal function f_5 with deterministic boundary constraints handling techniques: (a) star, (b) ring, (c) four clusters, (d) Von Neumann

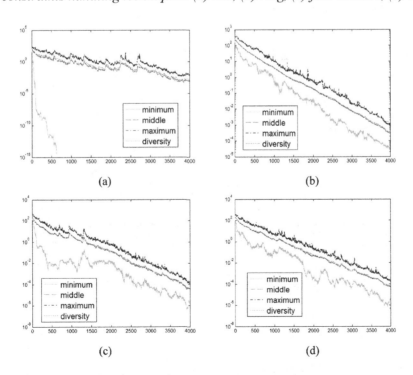

117

Figure 10. Comparison of PSO population diversities for solving unimodal function f_0 with stochastic boundary constraints handling techniques that randomly reset particles in half search space: (a) star, (b) ring, (c) four clusters, (d) Von Neumann

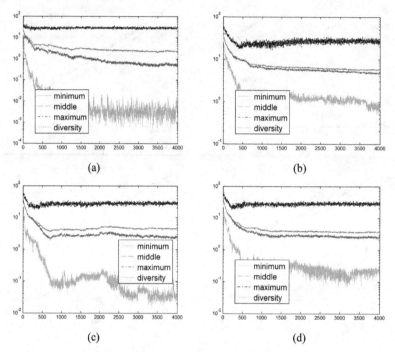

Figure 11. Comparison of PSO population diversities for solving multimodal function f_5 with stochastic boundary constraints handling techniques that randomly reset particles in half search space: (a) star, (b) ring, (c) four clusters, (d) Von Neumann

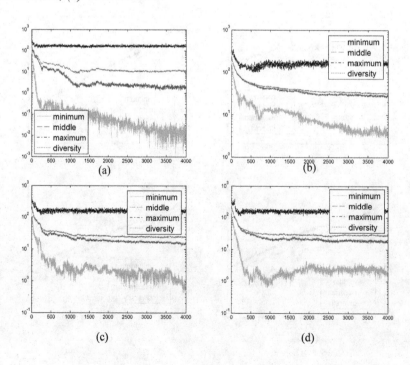

can "jump out" of the local optima with this strategy, and the experimental results also show that PSO with this strategy can get a good performance.

From Figures 4 through 15 we can see that PSO with star topology can achieve the smallest value of position diversity, and PSO with ring topology has the largest value at the same iteration. PSO with four clusters and Von Neumann nearly have the same diversity curve in our experiments. In summary, the PSO with star topology has the greatest ability to exploit the small area at the same iteration, and on contrast, the PSO with ring topology has the greatest ability to explore new search areas.

The search "potential" of particles is important to an algorithm's performance. Particles "fly" in a limited area. To ensure the performance of algorithms, not only the center of search area, but also the areas close to the boundary should be searched carefully. Some strategy should be utilized for the reason that if we take no action, particles can easily cross the boundary limit, and not return to the "limited" search area. It is a frequently used method that resets a particle's position when the particle meets the boundary. This method also has some drawbacks. Resetting a particle's position in a specific location will decrease the particle's search "potential," and the ability of exploration and exploitation will also be affected; on the other hand, resetting particles on a large area will decrease the algorithm's ability of exploitation, and particles will have difficulties to exploit the solution areas near the boundary.

Figure 12. Comparison of PSO population diversities for solving unimodal function f_0 with stochastic boundary constraints handling techniques that randomly reset particles in a small and close to boundary search space: (a) star, (b) ring, (c) four clusters, (d) Von Neumann

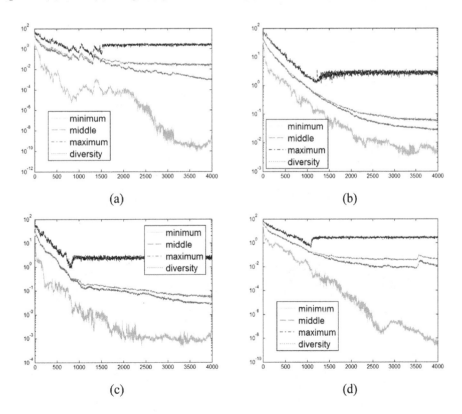

Figure 13. Comparison of PSO population diversities for solving multimodal function f_5 with stochastic boundary constraints handling techniques that randomly reset particles in a small and close to boundary search space: (a) star, (b) ring, (c) four clusters, (d) Von Neumann

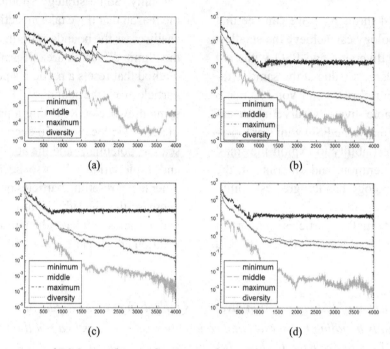

Figure 14. Comparison of PSO population diversities for solving unimodal function f_0 with stochastic boundary constraints handling techniques that randomly reset particles in a linearly decreased search space: (a) star, (b) ring, (c) four clusters, (d) Von Neumann

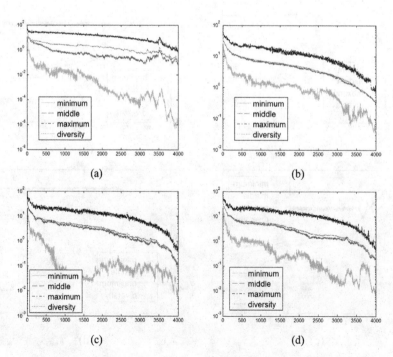

Figure 15. Comparison of PSO population diversities for solving multimodal function f_5 with stochastic boundary constraints handling techniques that randomly reset particles in a linearly decreased search space: (a) star, (b) ring, (c) four clusters, (d) Von Neumann

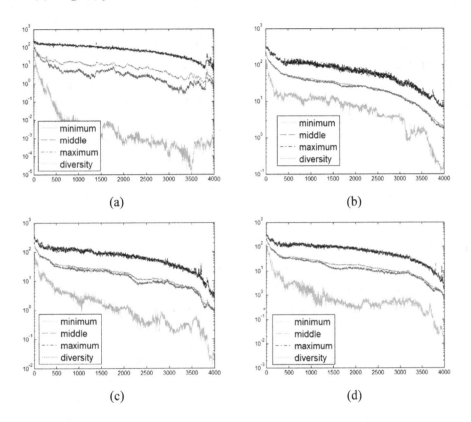

(a) (b)

(c) (d)

From experimental results of applying a deterministic strategy and three variants of stochastic strategy, we can observe that the deterministic strategy usually can obtain better optimization performance for PSO with ring, four clusters, or Von Neumann structure than PSO with other strategies at least for the ten benchmark functions and three boundary constraints handling strategies we experimented in this paper. A random re-initialization strategy fits for PSO with star, four clusters, and Von Neumann structures, and the space of re-initialization also should be considered. This conclusion is also verified on the population diversity observation.

Figures 8 and 9 display the position changing curves of PSO with deterministic strategy. It can be seen that particles in PSO with star topology are easily get clustered together. Some dimensional position diversities are quickly becoming zero, which may mean all particles stay in the same position and lose the search "potential" in these dimensions. All particles with four clusters and Von Neumann are also clustered together to the same position in some dimensions, i.e., the minimum position diversity becomes zero after several iterations.

PSO with random resetting strategy can avoid the above problem. Figures 10 through 15 displayed the position diversity curves of PSO with a stochastic strategy to handle boundary constraints. Particles can keep their position diversities with this strategy. Considering about algorithm's ability of exploitation, resetting particles in a small or decreased region can generally get better performance.

PSO with different topology will have different convergence speed. PSO with star structure has the fastest convergence speed, PSO with ring structure has the slowest speed, PSO with four clusters or Von Neumann structure is in the middle of them. Keeping particle's search "potential" and having a good balance of exploration and exploitation is important in the search process. Different boundary constraints handling strategy needs to be considered when we determine the PSO's topology because a proper strategy can give an improvement on algorithm's performance.

6. CONCLUSION

An algorithm's ability of exploration and exploitation is important in the optimization process. With good exploration ability, an algorithm can explore more areas in the search space, and find some potential regions that "good enough" solutions may exist. On the other hand, an algorithm with the ability of exploitation can finely search the potentially good regions, and find the optimum ultimately. An algorithm should have a good balance between exploration and exploitation during the search process.

In this paper, we have reviewed the different strategies to handle particles exceeding the position boundary constraint. Position diversity changing curves were utilized to study variant of algorithm's ability of the exploration and/or exploitation. The position diversity changing curves of different variant of PSO were compared. From the position diversity measurement, the impacts of different boundary constraint handing strategies on the optimization performance were studied. Boundary constraints handling can affect particles' search "potential". The classic method resets particles on the boundary when particles exceed the boundary limit, which may mislead particles to the wrong search area, and cause particles "stuck in" the boundary.

The position diversities of PSO with star, ring, four clusters, and Von Neumann topology were experimented in this paper. PSO with different topology will have different convergence. From the diversity measurement, the convergence speed and the ability of "jumping out" of local optima could be observed and/or analyzed. A deterministic boundary handling technique may improve the search results of PSO with ring, four clusters, or Von Neumann topology, but not star topology. Premature convergence still occurs in PSO with star topology. Stochastic method can avoid the premature convergence, and by resetting particles in a small or decreased region will keep PSO's ability of exploitation and therefore have a better performance.

Besides the boundary constraints handling techniques discussed in this paper, there are many other methods, such as "invisible boundaries", "damping boundaries", etc. (Huang & Mohan, 2005; Xu & Rahmat-Samii, 2007). These methods will have a different impact on the optimization performance of PSO algorithms. As the same as the boundary constraints handling methods discussed in this paper, these methods also can be analyzed by position diversity changing curves during the search process. The proper boundary constraint handling method should be considered together with the topology.

As indicated by the "no free lunch theory," there is no algorithm that is better than other one on average for all problems (Wolpert & Macready, 1997). Different variant of PSO fits for different kinds of problems. The comparison between different variants of PSOs and their population diversities should be studied when they are applied to solve different problems. The impact of parameters tuning on population diversity for solving different problems are also needed to be researched.

In addition to the position diversity, there are velocity diversity and cognitive diversity defined in PSO algorithms (Shi & Eberhart, 2008, 2009), which are unique to PSO algorithms. Experimental study on boundary constraints handling strategy based on velocity diversity and cognitive diversity should also be conducted to gain better understanding of PSO algorithms. The above are our future research work.

ACKNOWLEDGMENT

The authors' work was supported by the National Natural Science Foundation of China under grant No. 60975080, and the Suzhou Science and Technology Project under Grant No. SYJG0919.

REFERENCES

Bentley, P. J. (1999). *Evolutionary Design by Computers*. San Francisco, CA: Morgan Kaufmann.

Blackwell, T. M., & Bentley, P. (2002). Don't push me! collision-avoiding swarms. In *Proceedings of the 4th Conference on Evolutionary Computation (CEC 2002)* (pp. 1691-1696).

Bratton, D., & Kennedy, J. (2007). Defining a standard for particle swarm optimization. In *Proceedings of the 2007 IEEE Swarm Intelligence Symposium* (pp. 120-127).

Chen, S., & Montgomery, J. (2011). A simple strategy to maintain diversity and reduce crowding in particle swarm optimization. In *Proceedings of the 13th Annual Conference Companion on Genetic and Evolutionary Computation (GECCO 2011)* (pp. 811-812).

Cheng, S., & Shi, Y. (2011a). Diversity control in particle swarm optimization. In *Proceedings of the 2011 IEEE Swarm Intelligence Symposium* (pp. 110-118).

Cheng, S., & Shi, Y. (2011b). Normalized population diversity in particle swarm optimization. In *Proceedings of the 2nd International Conference on Swarm Intelligence* (LNCE 6728, pp. 38-45).

Dorronsoro, B., & Bouvry, P. (2011). Improving classical and decentralized differential evolution with new mutation operator and population topologies. *IEEE Transactions on Evolutionary Computation*, *15*(1), 67–98. doi:10.1109/TEVC.2010.2081369

Eberhart, R., & Kennedy, J. (1995). A new optimizer using particle swarm theory. In *Proceedings of the 6th International Symposium on Micro Machine and Human Science* (pp. 39-43).

Eberhart, R., & Shi, Y. (2001). Particle swarm optimization: Developments, applications and resources. In *Proceedings of the 2001 Conference on Evolutionary Computation (CEC2001)* (pp. 81-86).

Eberhart, R., & Shi, Y. (2007). *Computational Intelligence: Concepts to Implementations*. San Francisco, CA: Morgan Kaufmann.

Huang, T., & Mohan, A. (2005). A hybrid boundary condition for robust particle swarm optimization. *IEEE Antennas and Wireless Propagation Letters*, *4*, 112–117. doi:10.1109/LAWP.2005.846166

Kennedy, J. (2007). Some issues and practices for particle swarms. In *Proceedings of the 2007 IEEE Swarm Intelligence Symposium (SIS 2007)* (pp. 162-169).

Kennedy, J., & Eberhart, R. (1995). Particle swarm optimization. In *Proceedings of the IEEE International Conference on Neural Networks* (pp. 1942-1948).

Kennedy, J., Eberhart, R., & Shi, Y. (2001). *Swarm Intelligence*. San Francisco, CA: Morgan Kaufmann.

Liang, J., Qin, A., Suganthan, P., & Baskar, S. (2006). Comprehensive learning particle swarm optimizer for global optimization of multimodal functions. *IEEE Transactions on Evolutionary Computation, 10*(3), 281–295. doi:10.1109/TEVC.2005.857610

Mendes, R. (2004). *Population Topologies and Their Influence in Particle Swarm Performance.* Unpublished doctoral dissertation, University of Minho, Portugal.

Mendes, R., Kennedy, J., & Neves, J. (2003). Avoiding the pitfalls of local optima: How topologies can save the day. In *Proceedings of the 12th Conference on Intelligent Systems Application to Power Systems (ISAP 2003).* Washington, DC: IEEE Computer Society.

Mendes, R., Kennedy, J., & Neves, J. (2004). The fully informed particle warm: Simpler, maybe better. *IEEE Transactions on Evolutionary Computation, 8*(3), 204–210. doi:10.1109/TEVC.2004.826074

Olorunda, O., & Engelbrecht, A. P. (2008) Measuring exploration/exploitation in particle swarms using swarm diversity. In *Proceedings of the 2008 Conference on Evolutionary Computation(CEC 2008)* (pp. 1128-1134).

Shi, Y., & Eberhart, R. (1998). Parameter selection in particle swarm optimization. In *Evolutionary Programming VII* (LNCS 1447, pp. 591-600).

Shi, Y., & Eberhart, R. (1999). Empirical study of particle swarm optimization. In *Proceedings of the 1999 Conference on Evolutionary Computation (CEC 1999)* (pp. 1945-1950).

Shi, Y., & Eberhart, R. (2008). Population diversity of particle swarms. In *Proceedings of the 2008 Congress on Evolutionary Computation (CEC 2008).* (pp. 1063-1067)

Shi, Y., & Eberhart, R. (2009). Monitoring of particle swarm optimization. *Frontiers of Computer Science, 3*(1), 31–37. doi:10.1007/s11704-009-0008-4

Wolpert, D., & Macready, W. (1997). No free lunch theorems for optimization. *IEEE Transactions on Evolutionary Computation, 1*(1), 67–82. doi:10.1109/4235.585893

Xu, S., & Rahmat-Samii, Y. (2007). Boundary conditions in particle swarm optimization revisited. *IEEE Transactions on Antennas and Propagation, 55*(3), 760–765. doi:10.1109/TAP.2007.891562

Yao, X., Liu, Y., & Lin, G. (1999). Evolutionary programming made faster. *IEEE Transactions on Evolutionary Computation, 3*(2), 82–102. doi:10.1109/4235.771163

Zhang, W., Xie, X. F., & Bi, D. C. (2004). Handling boundary constraints for numerical optimization by particle swarm flying in periodic search space. In *Proceedings of the 2004 Conference on Evolutionary Computation (CEC 2004)* (pp. 2307-2311).

Zielinski, K., Weitkemper, P., Laur, R., & Kammeyer, K. D. (2009). Optimization of power allocation for interference cancellation with particle swarm optimization. *IEEE Transactions on Evolutionary Computation, 13*(1), 128–150. doi:10.1109/TEVC.2008.920672

This work was previously published in the International Journal of Swarm Intelligence Research, Volume 2, Issue 3, edited by Yuhui Shi, pp. 44-70, copyright 2011 by IGI Publishing (an imprint of IGI Global).

Chapter 7
Chaos-Enhanced Firefly Algorithm with Automatic Parameter Tuning

Xin-She Yang
National Physical Lab, UK

ABSTRACT

Many metaheuristic algorithms are nature-inspired, and most are population-based. Particle swarm optimization is a good example as an efficient metaheuristic algorithm. Inspired by PSO, many new algorithms have been developed in recent years. For example, firefly algorithm was inspired by the flashing behaviour of fireflies. In this paper, the author extends the standard firefly algorithm further to introduce chaos-enhanced firefly algorithm with automatic parameter tuning, which results in two more variants of FA. The author first compares the performance of these algorithms, and then uses them to solve a benchmark design problem in engineering. Results obtained by other methods will be compared and analyzed.

1. INTRODUCTION

Search for optimality in many optimization applications is a challenging task, and search efficiency is one of the most important measures for an optimization algorithm. In addition, an efficient algorithm does not necessarily guarantee the global optimality is reachable. In fact, many optimization algorithms are only efficient in finding local optima. For example, classic hill-climbing or steepest descent method is very efficient for local optimization. Global optimization typically involves objective functions which can be multimodal and highly nonlinear. Thus, it is often very challenging to find global optimality, especially for large-scale optimization problems. Recent studies suggest that metaheuristic algorithms such as particle swarm optimization are promising in solving these tough optimization problems (Kennedy & Eberhart, 1995; Kennedy et al., 2001; Shi & Eberhart, 1998; Eberhart & Shi, 2000; Yang, 2008).

DOI: 10.4018/978-1-4666-2479-5.ch007

Most metaheuristic algorithms are nature-inspired, from simulated annealing (Kirkpatrick et al., 1983) to firefly algorithm (Yang, 2008, 2010a), and from particle swarm optimization (Kennedy & Eberhart, 1995; Kennedy et al., 2001) to cuckoo search (Yang & Deb, 2010). These algorithms have been applied to almost all areas of optimization, design, scheduling and planning, data mining, machine intelligence, and many others (Gandomi et al., in press; Talbi, 2009; Yang, 2010a). On the other hand, chaotic tunneling is an important phenomenon in complex systems (Tomsovic, 1994; Podolskiy & Narmanov, 2003; Kohler et al., 1998; Delande & Zakrzewski, 2003; Shudo & Ikeda, 1998; Shudo et al., 2009). Traditional wisdom in optimization is to avoid numerical instability and chaos. Contemporary studies suggest that chaos can assist some algorithms such as genetic algorithms (Yang & Chen, 2002). For example, metaheuristic algorithms often use randomization techniques to increase the diversity of the solutions generated during search iterations (Talbi, 2009; Yang, 2010a). The most common randomization techniques are probably local random walks and Lévy flights (Gutowski, 2001; Pavlyukevich, 2007; Yang 2010b).

The key challenge for global optimization is that nonlinearity leads to multimodality, which in turns will cause problems to almost all optimization algorithms because the search process may be trapped in any local valley, and thus may cause tremendous difficulty to the search process towards global optimality. Even with most well-established stochastic search algorithms such as simulated annealing (Kirkpatrick et al., 1983), care must be taken to ensure it can escape the local modes/optimality. Premature convergence may occur in many algorithms including simulated annealing and genetic algorithms. The key ability of an efficient global search algorithm is to escape local optima, to visit all modes and to converge subsequently at the global optimality.

In this paper, we will first analyze the recently developed firefly algorithm (FA) (Yang, 2008, 2010b). Under the right conditions, FA can have chaotic behaviour, which can be used as an advantage to enhance the search efficiency, because chaos allow fireflies to sample search space more efficiently. In fact, a chaotic tunnelling feature can be observed in FA simulations when a firefly can tunnel through multimodes and jump from one mode to another modes. This enables the algorithm more versatile in escaping the local optima, and thus can guarantee to find the global optimality. Chaotic tunneling is an important phenomenon in complex systems, but this is the first time that a chaotic tunneling is observed in an optimization algorithm. Through analysis and numerical simulations, we will highlight that intrinsic chaotic characteristics in the FA can enhance the search efficiency. Then, we will introduce automatic parameter tuning to the chaotic firefly algorithm and compare its performance against a set of diverse test functions. Finally, we will apply the FA with automatic parameter tuning to solve a design benchmark whose solutions will be compared with other results in the literature.

2. FIREFLY ALGORITHM

Firefly Algorithm (FA) was developed by Yang (2008, 2010b), which was based on the flashing patterns and behaviours of fireflies. In essence, each firefly will be attracted to brighter ones, while at the same time, it explores and searches for prey randomly. In addition, the brightness of a firefly is determined by the landscape of the objective function.

The movement of a firefly i is attracted to another more attractive (brighter) firefly j is determined by

$$x_i^{t+1} = x_i^t + \beta e^{-\gamma r_{ij}^2}(x_j^t - x_i^t) + \alpha \; \varepsilon_i^t, \quad (1)$$

where α, β and γ are parameters. α controls the scale of randomization, β controls the attractiveness, while γ is a scaling factor. Here the second term is due to the attraction. The third term is randomization with α being the randomization parameter, and ε_i^t is a vector of random numbers drawn from a Gaussian distribution or other distributions such as Lévy flights. Obviously, for a given firefly, there are often many more attractive fireflies, then we can either go through all of them via a loop or use the most attractive one. For multiple modal problems, using a loop while moving toward each brighter one is usually more effective, though this will lead to a slight increase of algorithm complexity.

Here $\beta \in [0,1]$ is the attractiveness at $r=0$, and $r_{ij} =|| x_i - x_j ||_2$ is the 2-norm or Cartesian distance. For other problems such as scheduling, any measure that can effectively characterize the quantities of interest in the optimization problem can be used as the "distance" r. Furthermore, the randomization term can easily be extended to other distributions such as Lévy flights (Reynolds & Rhodes, 2009).

3. CHAOS-ENHANCED FA

In order to see the intrinsic tunneling ability, let us first carry out the convergence analysis for the firefly algorithm in a framework similar to Clerc and Kennedy's dynamical analysis (Clerc & Kennedy, 2002). For simplicity, we start from the equation for firefly motion without the randomness term:

$$x_i^{t+1} = x_i^t + \beta e^{-\gamma r_{ij}^2}(x_j^t - x_i^t) \qquad (2)$$

If we focus on a single agent, we can replace x_j^t by the global best g found so far, and we have

$$x_i^{t+1} = x_i^t + \beta e^{-\gamma r_i^2}(g - x_i^t) \qquad (3)$$

where the distance r_i can be given by the ℓ_2-norm $r_i^2 =|| g - x_i^t ||_2^2$. In an even simpler 1-D case, we can set $y_t = g - x_i^t$ and we have

$$y_{t+1} = y_t - \beta e^{-\gamma y_t^2} y_t \qquad (4)$$

We can see that γ is a scaling parameter which only affects the scales/size of the firefly movement. In fact, we can let $u_t = \sqrt{\gamma} y_t$ and we have

$$u_{t+1} = u_t [1 - \beta e^{-u_t^2}] \qquad (5)$$

These equations can be analyzed easily using the same methodology for studying the well-known logistic map

$$u_{t+1} = \lambda u_t (1 - u_t) \qquad (6)$$

The chaotic map of Equation 5 is shown in Figure 1, and the focus on the transition from periodic multiple states to chaotic behaviour is shown in the same figure.

As we can see from Figure 1, good convergence can be achieved for $\beta < 2$. There is a transition from periodic to chaos at $\beta \approx 4$. This may be surprising, as the aim of designing a metaheuristic algorithm is to try to find the optimal solution efficiently and accurately. However, chaotic behaviour is not necessarily a nuisance; in fact, we can use it to the advantage of the firefly algorithm.

It is worth pointing out that no explicit form of a random variable distribution can be found for the chaotic map of (5). However, simple chaotic characteristics from (6) can often be used as an efficient mixing technique for generating diverse solutions. Statistically, the logistic mapping (6) with $\lambda = 4$ for the initial states in (0,1) cor-

Figure 1. The chaotic map of the iteration Equation 5 in the firefly algorithm and the transition between from periodic/multiple states to chaos

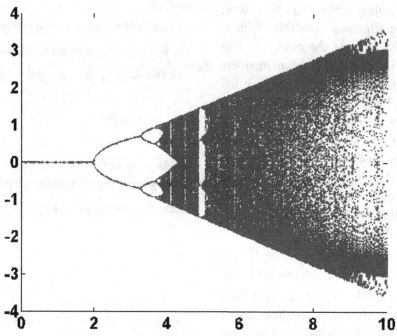

responds a beta distribution. From the algorithm implementation point of view, we can use higher attractiveness β during the early stage of iterations so that the fireflies can explore, even chaotically, the search space more effectively. As the search continues and convergence approaches, we can reduce the attractiveness β gradually, which may increase the overall efficiency of the algorithm. The simulations presented in the rest of this paper will confirm this.

4. AUTOMATIC PARAMETER TUNING

Apart from the population size n, there are three parameters in the firefly algorithm. They are α, β and γ, which control the randomness, attractiveness and modal scales, respectively. For most implementations, we can take $\beta = O(1)$, $\alpha = O(1)$ and $\gamma = O(1)$. However, randomness reduction technique is often used as iterations

continue, and this is often achieved by using an annealing-like exponential function

$$\alpha = \alpha_0 \eta^t \tag{7}$$

or

$$\alpha \leftarrow \alpha\eta \tag{8}$$

where $0 < \eta < 1$ is a cooling parameter. Typically, we can use $\alpha_0 = 1$ and $\eta = 0.9 \sim 0.99$. This equivalently introduces a cooling schedule to the firefly algorithm, as used in the traditional simulated annealing. Recently studies showed this works well (Yang, 2008). There may be better ways to tune this parameter and reduce randomness to be discussed later in this section.

It is worth pointing out that (1) is essentially a random walk biased towards the brighter fireflies. If $\beta_0 = 0$ it becomes a simple random walk.

As it is true for all metaheuristic algorithms, algorithm-dependent parameters can affect the performance of the algorithm of interest greatly, a natural question is whether we can automatically tune these parameters? If so, what is the best way to fine-tune these parameters?

For randomness reduction, it should be linked with the diversity of the current solutions. One simple way to automatically tune α is to set α as proportional to the standard deviation of the current solutions. However, for multimodal problems, this standard deviation should be calculated for each local mode among local subgroups of fireflies. For example, for two modes A and B with current best solutions x_a^* and x_b^* respectively, the population will gradually subdivide into two main subgroups with population sizes of n_1 and n_2 respectively, one around A and one around B. There are two standard deviations σ_A and σ_B which should be calculated among the solutions relative to x_a^* and x_b^* respectively. Then the overall α should be a function of σ_A and σ_B. The simplest way is to combine them by weighted average

$$\sigma = \frac{\sigma_A n_1 + \sigma_B n_2}{n_1 + n_2}, \quad n_1 + n_2 = n \tag{9}$$

As iterations continue, σ decreases in general. If we set

$$\alpha = \zeta \sigma, \quad 0 < \zeta < 1 \tag{10}$$

then α is automatically associated with the scale of the problem of interest. In practice, η may be affected by the dimensions d, so in our implementation we used $\zeta = \sqrt{d / (2d + 1)}$. The parameter γ should be linked with the scale L of the modes. A simple rule is that the change of the attractiveness term should be O(1) through the

search landscape, which provide a simple relationship $\gamma = 1 / \sqrt{L}$. Parameter β control the behavior of fireflies, however, its tuning is more subtle. From the above discussion of (5), when β is large, fireflies may experience chaotic behavior, and this can be used to enhance the search capability of the algorithm. In fact, from our intensive simulations, we have observed that fireflies can tunnel through all modes for multimodal function. This chaotic tunneling effect of the algorithm can help to search the global optimality for highly nonlinear global optimization problems.

To demonstrate this, we now first use a nonlinear multimodal function, namely, Ackley's function

$$f(x) = 20 \exp[-0.2 \sqrt{\frac{1}{d} \sum_{i=1}^{d} x_i^2}$$
$$+ \exp[\frac{1}{d} \sum_{i=1}^{d} \cos(2\pi x_i)] - (20 + e) \tag{11}$$

which has the global maximum $f_* = 0$ at $x_* = (0, 0, ..., 0)$ in the range of $-32.768 \leq x_i \leq 32.768$ where $i = 1, 2, ..., d$ and d is the number of dimensions. In the 2D case, Ackley's function is shown in Figure 2. For 25 fireflies, a snapshot at $t = 15$ of search process using the firefly algorithm is shown in Figure 3. If we ignore the randomness by setting $\alpha = 0$ and $\beta = 4$ all the time, then we can trace any one particular firefly, say, firefly number 5, its path of x-component displays a random-noise-like path. It is worth pointing out each firefly has the ability of tunneling through all modes, and distance of the tunnelling is controlled by the scaling factor γ and β.

During the iteration, if we reduce β gradually from a higher value, say, $\beta = 4$ to a lower value $\beta = 1$ by $\beta \eta^t + 1$ and also use Equation 7, the algorithm can be expected to converge more quickly. So for the same firefly 5, if we reduce β

Figure 2. Ackley's multimodal function

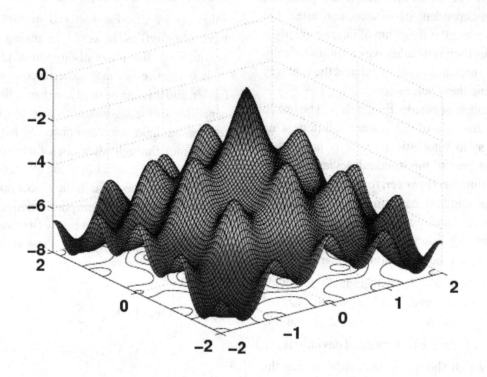

Figure 3. The snapshot of 25 fireflies during iteration t=15

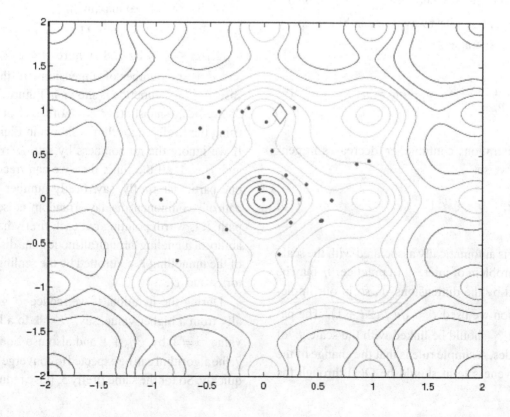

gradually, as the iteration proceeds, this path will gradually settle down and converge to a global optimal point.

Now we have three version of FA: The standard version of FA with α as a cooling schedule, a chaos-enhanced FA with β reduced gradually, and the chaotic FA in combination with automatic parameter tuning (AutoFA). In the rest of the paper, we will carry out more testing and comparison of their performance.

5. NUMERICAL EXPERIMENTS

Various test functions in the literature are designed to test the performance of optimization algorithms. Any new optimization algorithm should also be validated and tested against these benchmark functions. In our simulations, we have used the following test functions.

De Jong's first function is essentially a sphere function

$$f(x) = \sum_{i=1}^{d} x_i^2, \quad x_i \in [-5.12, 5.12] \tag{12}$$

whose global minimum $f_* = 0$ occurs at $x_* = (0,0,...,0)$. Here d is the dimension.

The generalized Rosenbrock function is given by

$$f(x) = \sum_{i=1}^{d-1} [(1-x_i)^2 + 100(x_{i+1} - x_i^2)^2] \tag{13}$$

which has a unique global minimum $f(x_*) = 0$ at $x_* = (1,1,...,1)$.

Schwefel's test function is multimodal

$$f(x) = \sum_{i=1}^{d} [-x_i \sin(\sqrt{|x_i|})], \quad -500 \le x_i \le 500 \tag{14}$$

whose global minimum $f_* = -418.9829d$ is at $x_i^* = 240.9687 (i=1,2,...,d)$.

Rastrigin's test function

$$f(x) = 10d + \sum_{i=1}^{d} [x_i^2 - 10\cos(2\pi x_i)] \tag{15}$$

has a unique global minimum $f_* = 0$ at $(0,0,...,0)$ in a hypercube $-5.12 \le x_i \le 5.12$ where $i = 1,2,...,d$.

Easom's test function has a sharp tip

$$f(x,y) = -\cos(x)\cos(y)\exp[-(x-\pi)^2 - (y-\pi)^2] \tag{16}$$

in the domain $(x,y) \in [-100,100] \times [-100,100]$. It has a global minimum of $f_* = -1$ at (π,π) in a very small region.

Rosenbrock's function

$$f(x) = \sum_{i=1}^{d-1} [(x_i - 1)^2 + 100(x_{i+1} - x_i^2)^2] \tag{17}$$

whose global minimum $f_* = 0$ occurs at $x_* = (1,1,...,1)$ in the domain $-5 \le x_i \le 5$ where $i = 1,2,...,d$. In the 2D case, it is often written as

$$f(x,y) = (x-1)^2 + 100(y-x^2)^2 \tag{18}$$

which is often referred to as the banana function.

The Michalewicz function

$$f(x) = -\sum_{i=1}^{d} \sin(x_i)[\sin(\frac{ix_i^2}{\pi})]^{2m} \tag{19}$$

where $m = 10$ and $d = 1,2,....$ The global minimum $f_* \approx -1.801$ in 2-D occurs at $(2.20319, 1.57049)$.

Griewangk's test function has many local minima

$$f(x) = \frac{1}{4000}\sum_{i=1}^{d}x_i^2 - \prod_{i=1}^{d}\cos(\frac{x_i}{\sqrt{i}}) + 1 \qquad (20)$$

but a unique global mimimum $f_* = 0$ at $(0,0,...,0)$ for all $-600 \le x_i \le 600$ where $i = 1,2,...,d$.

Yang's test function (Yang, 2010a)

$$f(x) = (\sum_{i=1}^{d}|x_i|)\exp[-\sum_{i=1}^{d}\sin(x_i^2)], \quad -2\pi \le x_i \le 2\pi \qquad (21)$$

which has a global minimum $f_* = 0$ at $(0,0,...,0)$. Rosenbrock's stochastic function was extended by Yang (2010a)

$$f(x) = \sum_{i=1}^{d-1}[\varepsilon_i(x_i - 1)^2 + 100\varepsilon_{i+1}(x_{i+1} - x_i^2)^2] \qquad (22)$$

whose global minimum $f_* = 0$ occurs at $x_* = (1,1,...,1)$ in the domain $-5 \le x_i \le 5$ where $i = 1,2,...,d$.

The functions used in Table 1 are (1) Michaelwicz (d=16), (2) Rosenrbrock (d=16), (3) De Jong (d=16), (4) Schwefel (d=8), (5) Ackley (d=16), (6) Rastrigin, (7) Easom, (8) Griewangk, (9) Yang d=16, (10) Robsenrbrock's stochastic function (d=8).

We ran the simulations for 50 times for a given accuracy of $\delta = 10^{-5}$, and the search stops when the best solution is found g_* is near the known solution x_*, that $\|x_* - g_*\| \le \delta$. We then recorded the number of iterations for finding such best solutions. In this table, the second column

Table 1. Comparison of standard, chaotic, and auto FA

Test Functions	FA	Chaotic FA (ratio)	AutoFA (ratio)
(1)	3752 ± 725	0.154 ± 0.022	0.108 ± 0.015
(2)	7792 ± 2923	0.175 ± 0.024	0.123 ± 0.017
(3)	2319 ± 337	0.069 ± 0.014	0.054 ± 0.012
(4)	7540 ± 125	0.097 ± 0.018	0.072 ± 0.014
(5)	3172 ± 723	0.071 ± 0.012	0.051 ± 0.010
(6)	11981 ± 970	0.093 ± 0.011	0.069 ± 0.009
(7)	7925 ± 1799	0.145 ± 0.027	0.127 ± 0.024
(8)	12592 ± 3715	0.112 ± 0.019	0.089 ± 0.012
(9)	7390 ± 2189	0.079 ± 0.011	0.057 ± 0.009
(10)	9125 ± 2149	0.037 ± 0.014	0.330 ± 0.049

corresponds to the average number of iterations and its standard deviation. The third column is the average ratio of the number of iterations of chaotic FA to the number of iterations for the standard FA when $\beta = 1$ (no chaos). The fourth column is the average ratio of the number of iterations of AutoFA to that of standard FA. These ratios reflect the computational effort saved. For example, if the average ratio is about 0.1, than about 90% of the computing effort is saved, that is the efficiency has been increased by a factor of about 10. We can see that the chaos-enhanced firefly algorithm indeed can improve its search efficiency significantly.

6. DESIGN OPTIMIZATION

There are many design benchmarks in the literature, however, the results are fragmental, as not all results are available and comparable. Here we select a well-known welded beam design, which has many results obtained by other methods in the literature (Ragsdell & Phillips, 1976; Cagnina et al., 2008; Gandomi et al., in press-a, in press-b). The problem typically has four design variables: the width w and length L of the welded area, the depth d and thickness h of the main beam. The objective is to minimise the overall fabrication cost, under the appropriate constraints of shear stress τ, bending stress σ, buckling load P and maximum end deflection δ.

The problem can be written as

$$\text{minimize } f(x) = \\ 1.10471w^2 L + 0.04811dh(14.0 + L) \tag{23}$$

subject to

$$g_1(x) = w - h \leq 0$$
$$g_2(x) = \delta(x) - 0.25 \leq 0$$
$$g_3(x) = \tau(x) - 13,600 \leq 0$$
$$g_4(x) = \sigma(x) - 30,000 \leq 0$$
$$g_5(x) = 0.10471w^2 + 0.04811hd(14 + L) - 5.0 \leq 0$$
$$g_6(x) = 0.125 - w \leq 0$$
$$g_7(x) = 6000 - P(x) \leq 0$$

$$\tag{24}$$

where

$$\sigma(x) = \frac{504,000}{hd^2}, \qquad Q = 6000(14 + \frac{L}{2})$$

$$D = \frac{1}{2}\sqrt{L^2 + (w + d)^2}, \quad J = \sqrt{2}\, wL[\frac{L^2}{6} + \frac{(w + d)^2}{2}]$$

$$\delta = \frac{65,856}{30,000hd^3}, \qquad \beta = \frac{QD}{J}$$

$$\alpha = \frac{6000}{\sqrt{2}wL}, \qquad \tau(x) = \sqrt{\alpha^2 + \frac{\alpha\beta L}{D} + \beta^2}$$

$$P = 0.61423 \times 10^6 \frac{dh^3}{6}(1 - \frac{d\sqrt{30/48}}{28})$$

$$\tag{25}$$

The simple limits or bounds are $0.1 \leq L, d \leq 10$ and $0.1 \leq w, h \leq 2.0$. This benchmark has been solved by many different methods, including simulated annealing (Hedar & Fukushima, 2006), genetic algorithms (Deb, 1991), particle swarm optimization (He et al., 2004; Cagnina et al., 2008), harmony search (Lee & Geem, 2004), differential evolution (Zhang et al., 2008) and firefly algorithm in this study.

It is worth pointing out that the constraints should be handled appropriately. In this case, we have used the penalty functions to incorporate the above nonlinear constraints (Yang, 2010a). Using our chaotic firefly algorithm with automatic parameter tuning, we have the following optimal solution

$$x_* = (w, L, d, h)$$
$$= (0.20573, 3.47049, 9.03662, 0.20573)$$

$$\tag{26}$$

with

$$f(x^*)_{\min} = 1.72485 \tag{27}$$

Our results are the same or better than the results obtained by other methods as summarized in Table 2.

From the above validation, comparison and benchmark design, we can see that chaotic FA with automatic parameter tuning is very efficient. Good convergence can be obtained by chaos-assisted tunnelling and automatic parameter adjustment. Effect and improvements become significant for multimodal problems.

7. CONCLUSION

Search for optimality in complex systems and global optimization problems require efficient algorithms. Metaheuristic algorithms such as particle swarm optimization and firefly algorithm are becoming very powerful. We have used a dynamical system approach to study the convergence property of the firefly algorithm and discovered its intrinsic chaotic tunneling ability. This property can be used as an advantage to enhance search efficiency of the algorithm. For multimodal optimization problems, there is a risk for any algorithm to get trapped in local optima. Chaos-assisted tunneling in the firefly algorithm makes it particular suitable for dealing with nonlinear, multimodal optimization problems. Our analysis and numerical experiments indeed demonstrated that chaotic tunneling can increase the search efficiency significantly.

An important topic for further research is to vary the scheme of automatic parameter tuning. The present study presents just one of many ways for automatic tuning of algorithm-dependent parameters. Other methods may be more appropriate and more efficient for different types of problems. In addition, more studies are highly needed to investigate whether this approach can be directly applied to other algorithms for automatic parameter tuning.

Further research can focus on the theoretical framework and extensive numerical studies on how an algorithm can be enhanced by chaotic tunneling, and thus may show insight into the working of an efficient algorithm. Such studies may help to design new generation truly intelligent optimization algorithms.

Table 2. Welded beam design

Refs	Method	w	L	d	h	cost	Number of Function Evaluations
Deb	GA	0.2489	6.1730	8.1789	0.2533	2.4331	320,080
He et al.	PSO	0.2444	6.2175	8.2915	0.2444	2.3810	30,000
Cagnina et al.	PSO	0.2057	3.4705	9.0366	0.2057	1.7248	24,000
Hedar & Fukushima	SA	0.2444	6.2158	8.2939	0.2444	2.3811	56,243
Lee & Geem	HS	0.2442	6.2231	8.2915	0.2443	2.381	110,000
Zhang et al.	DE	0.2444	6.2175	8.2915	0.2444	2.3810	24,000
This study	AutoFA	0.2057	3.4705	9.0366	0.2057	1.7248	20,000

REFERENCES

Cagnina, L. C., Esquivel, S. C., & Coello, C. A. (2008). Solving engineering optimization problems with the simple constrained particle swarm optimizer. *Informatica, 32*, 319–326.

Clerc, M., & Kennedy, J. (2002). The particle swarm - explosion, stability, and convergence in a multidimensional complex space. *IEEE Transactions on Evolutionary Computation, 6*, 58–73. doi:10.1109/4235.985692

Deb, K. (1991). Optimal design of a welded beam via genetic algorithms. *AIAA Journal, 29*(11), 2013–2015. doi:10.2514/3.10834

Delande, D., & Zakrzewski, J. (2003). Experimentally attainable example of chaotic tunneling: The hydrogen atom in parallel static electric and magnetic fields. *Physical Review A., 68*(6), 062110. doi:10.1103/PhysRevA.68.062110

Eberhart, E. C., & Shi, Y. (2000). Comparing inertia weights and constriction factors in particle swarm optimization. In *Proceedings of the Congress on Evolutionary Computation* (Vol. 1, pp. 84-88).

Gandomi, A. H., Yang, X. S., & Alavi, A. H. (in press). -a). Cuckoo search algorithm: a metaheuristic approach to solve structural optimization problems. *Engineering with Computers.*

Gandomi, A. H., Yang, X. S., & Alavi, A. H. (in press). -b). Mixed variable structural optimization using firefly algorithm. *Computers & Structures.*

Gutowski, M. (2001). *Lévy flights as an underlying mechanism for global optimization algorithms.* Retrieved from http://arxiv.org/abs/math-ph/0106003

He, S., Prempain, E., & Wu, Q. H. (2004). An improved particle swarm optimizer for mechanical design optimization problems. *Engineering Optimization, 36*(5), 585–605. doi:10.1080/0305215041 0001704854

Hedar, A. R., & Fukushima, M. (2006). Derivative-free simulated annealing method for constrained continuous global optimization. *Journal of Global Optimization, 35*(4), 521–649. doi:10.1007/s10898-005-3693-z

Kennedy, J., & Eberhart, R. C. (1995). Particle swarm optimization. In *Proceedings of the IEEE International Conference on Neural Networks* (pp. 1942-1948).

Kennedy, J., Eberhart, R. C., & Shi, Y. (2001). *Swarm intelligence.* San Francisco, CA: Morgan Kaufmann.

Kirkpatrick, S., Gellat, C. D., & Vecchi, M. P. (1983). Optimization by simulated annealing. *Science, 220*, 670–680. doi:10.1126/science.220.4598.671

Kohler, S., Utermann, R., Hagnni, R., & Dittrich, T. (1998). Coherent and incoherent chaotic tunneling near singlet-doublet crossings. *Physical Review E: Statistical Physics, Plasmas, Fluids, and Related Interdisciplinary Topics, 58*, 7219–7230. doi:10.1103/PhysRevE.58.7219

Lee, K. S., & Geem, Z. W. (2004). A new metaheuristic algorithm for continues engineering optimization: harmony search theory and practice. *Computer Methods in Applied Mechanics and Engineering, 194*, 3902–3933. doi:10.1016/j.cma.2004.09.007

Pavlyukevich, I. (2007). Lévy flights, non-local search and simulated annealing. *Journal of Computational Physics, 226*, 1830–1844. doi:10.1016/j.jcp.2007.06.008

Podolskiy, V. A., & Narmanov, E. E. (2003). Semi-classical description of chaos-assisted tunneling. *Physical Review Letters, 91*, 263601. doi:10.1103/PhysRevLett.91.263601

Ragsdell, K., & Phillips, D. (1976). Optimal design of a class of welded structures using geometric programming. *Journal of Engineering for Industry, 98*, 1021–1025. doi:10.1115/1.3438995

Reynolds, A. M., & Rhodes, C. J. (2009). The Lévy flight paradigm: random search patterns and mechanisms. *Ecology, 90*, 877–887. doi:10.1890/08-0153.1

Shi, Y., & Eberhart, R. C. (1998). A modified particle swarm optimizer. In *Proceedings of the IEEE International Conference on Evolutionary Computation* (pp. 69-73).

Shudo, A., & Ikeda, K. S. (1998). Chaotic tunneling: a remarkable manifestation of complex classical dynamics in non-integrable quantum phenomena. *Physica D. Nonlinear Phenomena, 115*, 234–292. doi:10.1016/S0167-2789(97)00239-X

Shudo, A., Ishii, Y., & Ikeda, K. S. (2009). Julia sets and chaotic tunneling: II. *Journal of Physics A. Mathematical and Theoretical, 42*, 265102. doi:10.1088/1751-8113/42/26/265102

Talbi, E.-G. (2009). *Metaheuristics: From design to implementation*. New York, NY: John Wiley & Sons.

Tomsovic, S. (1994). Chao-assisted tunneling. *Physical Review E: Statistical Physics, Plasmas, Fluids, and Related Interdisciplinary Topics, 50*, 145–162. doi:10.1103/PhysRevE.50.145

Yang, L. J., & Chen, T. L. (2002). Applications of chaos in genetic algorithms. *Communications in Theoretical Physics, 38*, 168–192.

Yang, X. S. (2008). *Nature-inspired metaheuristic algorithms*. Beckington, UK: Luniver Press.

Yang, X. S. (2010a). *Engineering optimization: An introduction with metaheuristic applications*. New York, NY: John Wiley & Sons. doi:10.1002/9780470640425

Yang, X. S. (2010b). Firefly algorithm, stochastic test functions and design optimisation. *International Journal of Bio-Inspired Computation, 2*, 78–84. doi:10.1504/IJBIC.2010.032124

Yang, X. S., & Deb, S. (2010). Engineering optimization by cuckoo search. *International Journal of Mathematical Modelling & Numerical Optimization, 1*, 330–343. doi:10.1504/IJMMNO.2010.035430

Zhang, M., Luo, W., & Wang, X. (2008). Differential evolution with dynamic stochastic selection for constrained optimization. *Information Science, 178*(15), 3043–3074. doi:10.1016/j.ins.2008.02.014

This work was previously published in the International Journal of Swarm Intelligence Research, Volume 2, Issue 4, edited by Yuhui Shi, pp. 1-11, copyright 2011 by IGI Publishing (an imprint of IGI Global).

Chapter 8

An Optimization Algorithm Based on Brainstorming Process

Yuhui Shi
Xi'an Jiaotong-Liverpool University, China

ABSTRACT

In this paper, the human brainstorming process is modeled, based on which two versions of Brain Storm Optimization (BSO) algorithm are introduced. Simulation results show that both BSO algorithms perform reasonably well on ten benchmark functions, which validates the effectiveness and usefulness of the proposed BSO algorithms. Simulation results also show that one of the BSO algorithms, BSO-II, performs better than the other BSO algorithm, BSO-I, in general. Furthermore, average inter-cluster distance D_c and inter-cluster diversity D_e are defined, which can be used to measure and monitor the distribution of cluster centroids and information entropy of the population over iterations. Simulation results illustrate that further improvement could be achieved by taking advantage of information revealed by D_c and/or D_e, which points at one direction for future research on BSO algorithms.

INTRODUCTION

Many real-world applications can be represented as optimization problems of which algorithms are required to have the capability to search for optimum. Originally, these optimization problems were mathematically represented by continuous and differentiable functions so that algorithms such as hill-climbing algorithms can be designed and/or utilized to solve them. Traditionally, these hill-climbing like algorithms are single-point based algorithms such as gradient decent

algorithms which move from the current point along the direction pointed by the negative of the gradient of the function at the current point. These hill-climbing algorithms can find solutions quickly for unimodal problems, but they have the problems of being sensitive to initial search point and being easily trapped into local optimum for nonlinear multimodal problems. Furthermore, these mathematical functions need to be continuous and differentiable, which instead greatly narrows the range of real-world problems that can be solved by hill-climbing algorithms. Recently,

DOI: 10.4018/978-1-4666-2479-5.ch008

evolutionary algorithms have been designed and utilized to solve optimization problems. Different from traditional single-point based algorithms such as hill-climbing algorithms, each evolutionary algorithm is a population-based algorithm, which consists of a set of points (population of individuals). The population of individuals is expected to have high tendency to move towards better and better solution areas iteration over iteration through cooperation and/or competition among themselves. There are a lot of evolutionary algorithms out there in the literature. The most popular evolutionary algorithms are evolutionary programming (Fogel, 1962), genetic algorithm (Holland, 1975), evolution strategy (Rechenberg, 1973), and genetic programming (Koza, 1992), which were inspired by biological evolution. In evolutionary algorithms, population of individuals survives into the next iteration. Which individual has higher probability to survive is proportional to its fitness value according to some evaluation function. The survived individuals are then updated by utilizing evolutionary operators such as crossover operator and mutation operator, *etc*. In evolutionary programming and evolution strategy, only the mutation operation is employed, while in genetic algorithms and genetic programming, both the mutation operation and crossover operation are employed. The optimization problems to be optimized by evolutionary algorithms do not need to be mathematically represented as continuous and differentiable functions, they can be represented in any form. Only requirement for representing optimization problems is that each individual can be evaluated as a value called fitness value. Therefore, evolutionary algorithms can be applied to solve more general optimization problems, especially those that are very difficult, if not impossible, for traditional hill-climbing algorithms to solve.

Recently, another kind of algorithm called swarm intelligence is attracting more and more attention from researchers. Swarm intelligence algorithms are usually nature-inspired optimization algorithms instead of evolution-inspired optimization algorithms such as evolutionary algorithms. Similar to evolutionary algorithms, a swarm intelligence algorithm is also a population-based optimization algorithm. Different from the evolutionary algorithms, each individual in a swarm intelligence algorithm represents a simple object such as ant, bird, fish, *etc*. So far, a lot of swarm intelligence algorithms have been proposed and studied. Among them are particle swarm optimization(PSO)(Eberhart & Shi, 2007; Shi & Eberhart, 1998), ant colony optimization algorithm(ACO) (Dorigo, Maniezzo, & Colorni, 1996), bacterial forging optimization algorithm(BFO)(Passino, 2010), firefly optimization algorithm (FFO) (Yang, 2008), bee colony optimization algorithm (BCO) (Tovey, 2004), artificial immune system (AIS) (de Castro & Von Zuben, 1999), fish school search optimization algorithm(FSO) (Bastos-Filho, De Lima Neto, Lins, Nascimento, & Lima, 2008), shuffled frog-leaping algorithm (SFL) (Eusuff & Lansey, 2006), intelligent water drops algorithm (IWD) (Shah-Hosseini, 2009), to just name a few.

In a swarm intelligence algorithm, an individual represents a simple object such as birds in PSO, ants in ACO, bacteria in BFO, *etc*. These simple objects cooperate and compete among themselves to have a high tendency to move toward better and better search areas. As a consequence, it is the collective behavior of all individuals that makes a swarm intelligence algorithm to be effective in problem optimization.

For example, in PSO, each particle (individual) is associated with a velocity. The velocity of each particle is dynamically updated according to its own historical best performance and its companions' historical best performance. All the particles in the PSO population fly through the solution space in the hope that particles will fly towards better and better search areas with high probability.

Mathematically, the updating process of the population of individuals over iterations can be looked as a mapping process from one population of individuals to another population of individuals from one iteration to the next iteration, which can be represented as $P_{t+1} = f(P_t)$, where P_t is the population of individuals at the iteration t, $f()$ is the mapping function. Different evolutionary algorithm or swarm intelligence algorithm has a different mapping function. Through the mapping function, we expect the population of individuals will update to better and better solutions over iterations. Therefore mapping functions should possess the property of convergence. For nonlinear and complicated problems, mapping functions more like to move population of individuals toward local minima, which may not be good enough solutions to the optimization problems to be solved. A good mapping function should have not only the capability to converge, but also the capability to diverge when it gets trapped into local minima. As for evolutionary algorithms and swarm intelligence algorithms, they should have the capability to be in convergence or divergence state accordingly. A lot of researches have been done and reported with regards to this. For example, in particle swarm optimization algorithms, diversity has been preserved to keep the algorithm to have good search capability. Different diversity measurements have been defined and monitored (Shi & Eberhart, 2008, 2009). A better designed population-based algorithm should have a good balance of convergence and divergence.

In this paper, we will introduce a new optimization algorithm that is based on the collective behavior of human beings; that is, the brainstorming process. It is natural to expect that an optimization algorithm based on human collective behavior could be a better optimization algorithm than existing swarm intelligence algorithms which are based on collective behavior of simple insects, because human beings are social animal and are the most intelligent animals in the world. The designed optimization algorithm will naturally have the capability of both convergence and divergence.

The remaining paper is organized as follows. The human brainstorming process is reviewed.

The model of a brainstorming process is proposed and discussed. Two versions of novel optimization algorithms inspired by human brainstorming process are introduced and described, followed by experiments and result discussion on benchmark functions. Finally, conclusions are given.

BRAINSTORMING PROCESS

Brainstorming has often been utilized for innovative problem solving. It can solve a lot of difficult problems which usually can't be solved by a single person. In a brainstorming process, a group of people with diverse background are gathered together to brainstorm. A facilitator will usually be involved to facilitate the brainstorming process but not directly involved in idea generation himself (or herself). The facilitator usually should have enough facilitation experience but have less knowledge about the problem to be solved so that generated ideas will have less, if not none, biases from the facilitator. The brainstorming process is used to generate many ideas as diverse as possible so that good solutions to solve the problem can be obtained from these ideas. The brainstorming process usually consists of several rounds of idea generation. In each round of idea generation, the brainstorming group is asked to come out a lot of ideas. At the end of each round of idea generation process, better ideas among them will be picked up and will serve as clues to generate ideas in the next round of idea generation process. In the brainstorming process, there is another group of persons that serve the purpose to pick up better ideas from the ideas generated in each round of idea generation process. Through the brainstorming process, hopefully great and un-expectable solution can occur from collective intelligence of human being, and the problem can usually be solved with high probability.

To help generate more diverse ideas, the Osborn's original four rules of idea generation in a brainstorming process (Osborn, 1963; Smith,

Table 1. Osborn's original rules for idea generation in a brainstorming process

Oborn's Rules	
1	Suspend judgment
2	Anything goes
3	Cross-fertilize (piggyback)
4	Go for quantity

2002) should be obeyed. The four rules are listed in the Table 1. One major role of the facilitator is to facilitate the brainstorming group to obey Osborn's four rules.

The four rules in Table 1 guide the idea generation in each round of idea generation during a brainstorming process. In order to keep the brainstorming group to be open-minded, there is no idea as good idea or bad idea, any idea is welcomed. For any idea generated during each round of idea generation process, there should be no judgment and/or criticism whether it is good idea or bad idea. Any judgment should be held back until the end of this round of idea generation process when better ideas are picked up by problem owners. This is what Rule 1, "Suspend Judgment," means. The Rule 2, "Anything Goes," means that any thought comes to your mind should be raised and recorded. Don't let any idea or thought pass by without sharing with other brainstorming group members. The Rule 3 "piggyback" says any generated idea could and should serve as a clue to inspire the brainstorming group to come out more ideas. Ideas are not independently generated. They are related. The late generated ideas are inspired and dependent on the previously generated ideas. The Rule 4 "Go for quantity" says that we focus on generating as many ideas as possible. Hopefully quality of ideas will come out of quantity of idea naturally. Without generating large quantity of ideas, it is naive to believe that good quality ideas will come out.

The purpose to generate ideas according to rules in Table 1 is to keep the brainstorming group to be open-minded as much as possible so that they will generate ideas as diverse as possible. A brainstorming process generally follows the steps listed in Table 2 (Shi, 2011).After some time of brainstorming, the brainstorming group will become tired and narrow-minded, and therefore it becomes harder to come out new diverse ideas. The operation of picking up an object in Step 6 in Table 2 serves for the purpose to help brainstorming group to diverge from previously generated ideas therefore to avoid being trapped by the previously generated ideas. Picking up several good ideas from ideas generated so far is to cause the brainstorming group to pay more attention to

Table 2. Steps in a brainstorming process

Brainstorming	
1	Get together a brainstorming group of people with as diverse background as possible
2	Generate many ideas according to the rules in Table 1
3	Have several, say 3 or 5, clients act as the owners of the problem to pick up several, say one from each owner, ideas as better ideas for solving the problem
4	Use the ideas picked up in the Step 3 with higher probability than other ideas as clues, and generate more ideas according to the rules in Table 1
5	Have the owners to pick up several better ideas generated as did in Step 3
6	Randomly pick an object and use the functions and appearance of the object as clues, generate more ideas according to the rules in Table 1
7	Have the owners to pick up several better ideas
8	Hopefully a good enough solution can be obtained by considering the ideas generated

the better ideas which the brainstorming group believes to be. The ideas picked-up works like point-attraction for the idea generation process while ideas generation works like point-expansion. Therefore, there are attraction and expansion embedded in the brainstorming process naturally.

MODELING BRAINSTORMING PROCESS

The procedure of a brainstorming process listed in Table 2 can be described by the flow chart shown in Figure 1. There are three rounds of idea generation involved in a brainstorming process in general. In each round of brainstorming process,

Figure 1. Flow chart of a brainstorming process

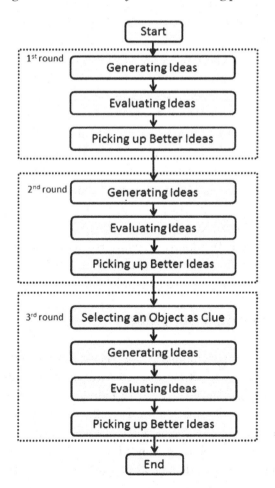

there are several steps. For example, in the first round, there are idea generations, idea evaluations, and idea picking up. The idea evaluation step serves the purpose of finding out better ideas. By idea evaluation, good ideas could be identified and picked up in the Picking up Better Ideas step, which simulates picking up good ideas by problem owners. The first round simulates Step 2 &3 in Table 2. The second round is the same as the first round which simulates Step 4 & 5 in Table 2. The third round is the same as the first two rounds except that one additional step Selecting an Object as Clue is added to simulate randomly picking up an object as clues in Step 6 in Table 2. Each step in a brainstorming process therefore can be modeled (and/or simulated) and put together as a model for the brainstorming process as shown in Figure 1, which will be further explained and modified in the following sub-sections.

Population

A solution to a problem with d variables to be optimized can be looked as a point in the d dimensional solution space. An idea can be considered as a potential solution, i.e., a point in the solution space. Therefore to find a good solution is equivalent to find a point or a solution in the solution space. A group of ideas can therefore be considered as a population of solutions or individuals in the solution space. If for every round of idea generation in the brainstorming process, a fixed number of n ideas will be generated before the problem owners pick up good ideas, then these n ideas can be considered as a population of individuals (or solutions) with population size being n in the solution space. Therefore, the human brainstorming process can be considered as generating a population of individuals iteratively three times as shown in Figure 1. One round of idea generation can be considered as one iteration of individual generations in population-based optimization algorithms such as particle swarm optimization algorithm. The difference between them is the way how new population of individuals is generated based on the current population of individuals.

Initialization

The Generating Ideas step in the very first round of idea generations can be considered as the population initialization in any population-based optimization algorithm. During the population initialization, gathering a group of people with as diverse backgrounds as possible can be considered as initializing the population of individuals randomly with uniform distribution over the dynamic range of the solution space. The whole population of individuals can be totally randomly generated or only portion of the population is randomly generated and the rest of the population of individuals will be generated by adding noise to the already randomly generated individuals. To preserve the initialized population to be diversified, usually *a priori* domain knowledge should not be utilized in the initialization process, unless when computation cost is the first priority, in which the domain knowledge should be utilized to initialize the population to find good solution quickly at the risk of premature convergence.

Clustering

Each round of idea generation generates enough ideas, but not necessary too many ideas because otherwise all the generated ideas will more like to diverge, and therefore will be far away from expected ideas which are close to expected solutions. To have diverse ideas is good to seek around all possible ideas to help find good potential solutions, but there should be a tradeoff between divergence and focus. We also need to pull the brainstorming group back to concentrate on generating ideas around some areas with high potential to speed up searching for good enough ideas. The problem owners in the brainstorming process serve this purpose. They are asked to pick good ideas from

generated ideas. Because every problem owner has different expertise and knowledge, therefore the picked ideas will be different. They represent potential good ideas that have been generated so far. Next round of idea generation should better be conducted with focus on them. Certainly, it does not exclude idea generation by piggybacking other ideas, but with small probability. One way to simulate the idea picking up by problem owners is to use clustering algorithms. All the individuals (ideas) in the population are clustered into several clusters. The number of clusters corresponds to the number of problem owners. The cluster center of each cluster corresponds to the idea(s) picked up by a problem owner. The cluster center for each cluster can be the best performed individual within this cluster. It can also be the centroid of the cluster.

One possible clustering algorithm is the k-means clustering algorithm (MacQueen, 1967), which requires to know the number of clusters k *a priori*. The number k corresponds to the number of problem owners, that is, the number of problem owners is fixed. The self-organizing feature map (Kohonen & Honkela, 2007) is another kind of clustering algorithm, in which the number of clusters is unknown before running the algorithm. The number of clusters will be determined by the algorithm itself according to the distribution of individuals in the population. Other clustering algorithms (Xu & Wunsch, 2005) such as partitioning around medoids (Theodoridis & Koutroumbas, 2006), fuzzy c-means (FCM) (Nock & Nielsen, 2006), *etc.* can also be employed.

Individual Generation

For idea generations by piggyback, it is similar to randomly select one or several existing individuals (or ideas) and generate a new individual by adding noise to the selected individual(s). The purpose of doing this is to guarantee that new individuals (ideas) are generated by piggybacking existing individuals as diverse as possible. If a new idea (individual) x_{new} is generated by piggybacking one existing idea (individual) x_{old}, it can be written as

$$x^i_{new} = x^i_{old} + \xi\left(t\right) * random(t) \qquad (1)$$

where $x_{new}{}^i$ and $x_{old}{}^i$ are the *i*th dimension of x_{new} and x_{old}, respectively; *random(t)* is a random function; *ξ(t)* is a coefficient that weights the contribution of random value to the new individual. The formula is similar to the mutation operation in evolutionary programming algorithm. The commonly utilized random function in mutation operation is the Gaussian function (Yao, Liu, & Lin, 1997). Other random functions that can be used are Cauchy function (Yao, Liu, & Lin, 1997), Levy flights (Pavlyukevich, 2007), *etc*. Compared with Gaussian function, Cauchy function has a longer tail which makes it preferable if wider areas need to be explored (Yao, Liu, & Lin, 1997).

If a new idea (individual) x_{new} is generated by piggybacking two existing ideas (individuals) x_{old1} and x_{old2}, it can be written as

$$x^i_{new} = x^i_{old} + \xi\left(t\right) * random\left(t\right) \qquad (2a)$$

$$x^i_{old} = w_1 * x^i_{old1} + w_2 * x^i_{old2} \qquad (2b)$$

where $x_{old}{}^i$ is the weighted summation of the *i*th dimension of x_{old1} and x_{old2}; w_1 and w_2 are two coefficients to weight the contribution of two existing individuals. The formula simulates generating new idea by piggybacking two existing ideas. Certainly, a new idea can also be generated by piggybacking more than two existing ideas.

No matter how many existing ideas (individuals) will be piggybacked to generate new ideas (individuals), the cluster centers will have high probability to be chosen to generate new ideas (individuals) compared with the other non-cluster-center ideas (individuals) which usually can be chosen with small probability.

The coefficient *ξ(t)* weights the contribution of randomly generated value to the new individual. Generally, large *ξ(t)* value facilitates exploration while small *ξ(t)* values facilitates exploitation. When global search capability is preferred, for example, at the beginning of search process, *ξ(t)* should give large value, while when local search capability is preferred, for example, at the end of search process, *ξ(t)* should give small value. One possible function for *ξ(t)* is

$$\xi\left(t\right) = logsig\left(\frac{\frac{T}{2} - t}{k}\right) * random(t) \qquad (3)$$

where *logsig*() is a logarithmic sigmoid transfer function, *T* is the maximum number of iterations, and *t* is the current iteration number, *k* is for changing *logsig*() function's slope, and *random*() is a random value within (*0,1*).

Disruption

After two rounds of idea generation, the mindset of the brainstorming group usually will be narrowed and therefore it becomes more difficult, if not impossible, for them to come out different ideas efficiently. To further explore whether there are potential good ideas out there somewhere, in the brainstorming process, an object will be randomly picked up, and the brainstorming group will be asked to generate new ideas which are more or less related to the functions and appearance of the object. The purpose of this is to help the brainstorming group to disrupt from their current mindset, which is usually difficult to achieve. This disruption operation can be simulated by replacing selected ideas (individuals) with randomly generated individuals. Therefore, wider areas could be explored with high probability by utilizing disruption operation.

As shown in Figure 1, there are three rounds of idea generation. The first two rounds are identical while the third round serves as the purpose of disruption with the step Selecting an Object as Clue. To further modulate the operations, this disruption operation could be distributed and shared among all three rounds of idea generation. Figure 2 shows the modified flow chart of the brainstorming process, which includes three identical rounds of idea generation. Each round of idea generation is shown in Figure 3 in which the step Selecting an Object as Clue is changed to be the step Disrupting Selected Ideas and it is put at the end of each round.

Figure 2. Flow chart of a brainstorming process

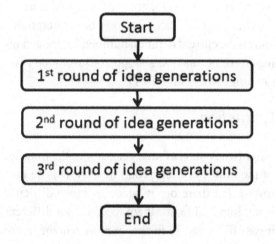

Figure 3. Flow chart of one round of idea generation

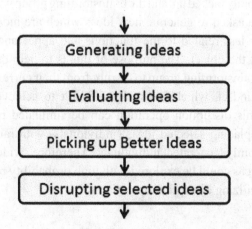

Selection

In a population-based optimization algorithm, generally speaking, if it is not because of specific requirements, the population size p is fixed and not changed during the algorithm running time. During each iteration, number of new individuals will be generated, say n $(n \geq p)$, therefore there will exist $p+n$ number of individuals, among which only p will be copied into the next iteration due to the fixed population size. Similar to other population-based algorithms, how to select p from $p+n$ individuals is critical to the optimization algorithm inspired by the brainstorming process. One simple way is that for each existing individual in the population, a new individual is generated. This pair of individuals is compared. The better one will be kept as the individual into the next iteration. Another way could be to randomly pick up p pairs of individuals from the $n+p$ individuals, and the better one of each pair will be kept into the next iteration.

To further take advantage of information embedded in each pair of individuals, crossover operations could also be applied to each pair of individuals to generate two new offspring. The best of the four will then be copied into the next iteration.

In each round of idea generation shown in Figure 3, one more step Selecting Ideas is inserted right below the step Generating Ideas. Figure 4 shows the new flow chart of each round of idea generation.

In practice, limited time will be taken for a brainstorming process; otherwise, the brainstorming group will be tired to generate new meaningful ideas efficiently. Usually as a good practice, a brainstorming process takes approximately 60 minutes. As shown in the Figure 1, there are only three rounds of idea generation in a brainstorming process. But for a model to be executed by computers, the number of rounds of idea generation can be as large as that we want. Figure 5 shows the flow chart for a brainstorming process that

Figure 4. Flow chart of one round of idea generation

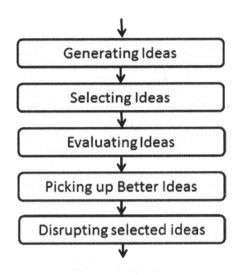

Figure 5. Flow chart of a brainstorming process

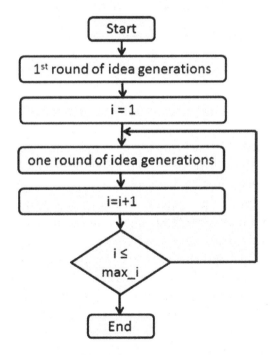

can be simulated by computers. In Figure 5, the step 1st Round of Idea Generations is the same as the step One Round of Idea Generation shown in Figure 5. The purpose to have the extra step 1st Round of Idea Generations at the beginning is to

be similar to the Initialization step in population-based algorithms. The *max_i* is the maximum number of rounds of idea generation we want to conduct. Therefore totally, *max_i* rounds of idea generation will be conducted in the brainstorming process shown in the Figure 5. By implementing this, a model or algorithm to mimic the human being brainstorming process can be built.

BRAIN STORM OPTIMIZATION ALGORITHM

According to the Figure 5, a brain storm optimization (BSO) algorithm can be designed by directly mapping the steps in the Figure 5. By some straightforward rearrangement, one possible flow chart of the BSO algorithm is shown in Figure 6. In Figure 6, there are five main operations among which three operations are unique to the BSO algorithm and the other two operations are similar to those in other evolutionary algorithms.

In the procedure of the Brain Storm Optimization (BSO) algorithm shown in the Figure 6, the first two steps are the initialization step and evaluation step which are the same as that in other swarm intelligence algorithms. In the initialization step, the population of individuals is usually uniformly and randomly initialized within the dynamic range of solution space. The population size n simulates the number of ideas generated in each round of idea generation in the brainstorming process. For the simplicity of the algorithm, the population size usually is set to be a constant number for all iterations in the BSO algorithm. In the evaluation step, each individual will be evaluated. An evaluation value (fitness) will be obtained to measure how good the individual as a potential solution to the problem to be solved. The third step is to cluster the population of individuals into several clusters. Different kind of clustering algorithms could be employed. In this paper, the k-means clustering algorithm will be used as the clustering algorithm. The disruption

Figure 6. An implementation of BSO algorithm

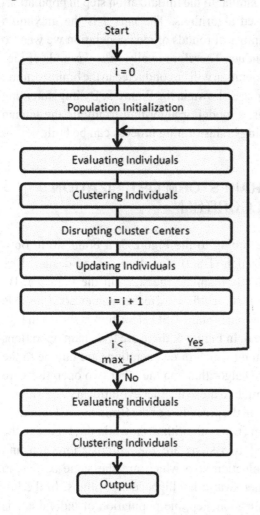

Figure 7. One implementation of updating individual operation

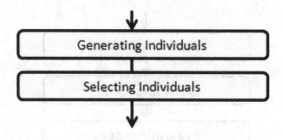

Figure 8. Another implementation of updating individual operation

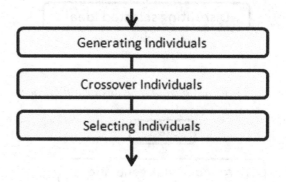

step randomly selects a cluster center and replace it with a randomly generated individual. This step will not be executed in every iteration, but will only be selected to execute with small probability.

The Updating Individuals step generally includes two sub-operations, i.e., Generating Individuals and Selecting Individuals, which is shown in Figure 7. As discussed in previous section, crossover operation could be utilized to further take advantage of existing search information. Figure 8 shows another possibility of the Updating Individuals operation which adds one additional sub-operation, i.e., crossover operation.

One implementation of the BSO algorithm was introduced in Shi (2011) and is given in Table 3 here for convenience, in which the Updating Individuals operation shown in Figure 7 is implemented. By replacing the Step 6.d in Table 3 with two sub-steps shown in Table 4, another implementation of BSO algorithm can be achieved. To distinguish the two different implementations, the first one is noted as BSO-I and the second is noted as BSO-II for the purpose of description convenience. Intuitively, the BSO algorithms should be superior to other swarm intelligence algorithms, which are inspired by collective behaviors of inferior animals, because of the highest intelligence unique to human beings.

In the BSO algorithm, the number of cluster centers is usually set to be a small number, say $m=5$, and the number of generated individuals in each iteration is usually set to be a relatively large number, say $n=100$.

Table 3. The procedure of the brainstorm optimization algorithm in Shi (2011)

Brainstorm Optimization
1. Randomly generate n potential solutions (individuals)
2. Evaluate the n individuals
3. Cluster n individuals into m clusters by k-means clustering algorithm
4. Rank individuals in each cluster and record the best individual as cluster center in each cluster
5. Randomly generate a value between 0 and 1
a) If the value is smaller than a pre-determined probability p_{5a},
i. Randomly select a cluster center
ii. Randomly generate an individual to replace the selected cluster center
b) Otherwise, do nothing
6. Generate new individuals
a) Randomly generate a value between 0 and 1
b) If the value is less than a probability p_{6b},
i. Randomly select a cluster with a probability p_{6bi}
ii. Generate a random value between 0 and 1
iii. If the value is smaller than a pre-determined probability p_{6biii}
1) Select the cluster center and add random values to it to generate new individual
iv. Otherwise randomly select an individual from this cluster and add random value to the individual to generate new individual
c) Otherwise randomly select two clusters to generate new individual
i. Generate a random value
ii. If it is less than a pre-determined probability p_{6c}, the two cluster centers are combined and then added with random values to generate new individual
iii. Otherwise, two individuals from each selected cluster are randomly selected to be combined and added with random values to generate new individual
d) The newly generated individual is compared with the existing individual with the same individual index, the better one is kept and recorded as the new individual
7. If n new individuals have been generated, go to step 8; otherwise go to step 6
8. Terminate if pre-determined maximum number of iterations has been reached; otherwise go to step 2

Table 4. Two sub-steps to replace step 6d in Table 3

6d
d. The newly generated individual crossovers with the existing individual with the same individual index to generate two more individuals (offspring)
e. The four individuals are compared, the best one is kept and recorded as the new individual

EXPERIMENTS AND DISCUSSIONS

Test Problems

To validate the brain storm optimization algorithms, ten benchmark functions listed in Table 5 are tested. Among them, the first five functions are unimodal functions and the remaining five functions are multimodal functions. They all are minimization problems with minimum zero. The third column in the Table 5 is the dynamic ranges for the ten benchmark functions, which have been used to test population-based algorithms in the literature. For each benchmark function, the tested BSO algorithm will be run 50 times to obtain reasonable statistical results.

Simulations on *k*

In Shi (2011), the BSO-I algorithm was tested on two benchmark functions, i.e., the Sphere function and the Rastrigin function. The parameters are setup as that listed in Table 6. The purpose there is to validate the usefulness and effectiveness of the proposed BSO-I algorithm. Generally speaking, the parameter *k* determines the slope of the

Table 5. Benchmark functions tested in this paper

Function	Expressions	Range
Sphere	$f_1 = \sum_{i=1}^{d} x_i^2$	$[-100, 100]^d$
Schwefel's P221	$f_2 = \max_i \{|x_i|\}$	$[-100, 100]^d$
Step	$f_3 = \sum_{i=1}^{d} (\lfloor x_i + 0.5 \rfloor)^2$	$[-100, 100]^d$
Schwefel's P222	$f_4 = \sum_{i=1}^{d} |x_i| + \prod_{i=1}^{d} |x_i|$	$[-10, 10]^d$
Quartic Noise	$f_5 = \sum_{i=1}^{d} i x_i^4 + \mathrm{random}[0,1)$	$[-1.28, 1.28]^d$
Ackely	$f_6 = -20 \exp\left(-0.2\sqrt{\dfrac{1}{d}\sum_{i=1}^{d} x_i^2}\right)$ $-\exp\left(\dfrac{1}{d}\sum_{i=1}^{d}\cos(2\pi x_i)\right) + 20 + e$	$[-32, 32]^d$
Rastrigin	$f_7 = \sum_{i=1}^{d} [x_i^2 - 10\cos(2\pi x_i) + 10]$	$[-5.12, 5.12]^d$
Roscnbrock	$f_8 = \sum_{i=1}^{d-1} [100(x_{i+1} - x_i^2)^2 + (x_i - 1)^2]$	$[-30, 30]^d$
Schwefel's P226	$f_9 = -\sum_{i=1}^{d} (x_i \sin(\sqrt{|x_i|})) + 418.9829d$	$[-500, 500]^d$
Griewank	$f_{10} = \dfrac{1}{4000}\sum_{i=1}^{d} x_i^2$ $-\prod_{i=1}^{d}\cos(\dfrac{x_i}{\sqrt{i}}) + 1$	$[-600, 600]^d$

Table 6. Set of parameters for BSO algorithm

n	m	p_{5a}	p_{6b}	p_{6biii}	p_{6c}	k	Max_iteration	μ	σ
100	5	0.2	0.8	0.4	0.5	20	2000	0	1

logsig() functions, therefore it determines the decreasing speed of the step-size $\xi(t)$ over iterations. Different k should have different impacts on the performance of BSO algorithms. In order to test the impact of k on BSO performance, we change the k value while all other parameter values are kept to be the same as that listed in Table 6. For this purpose, again only one unimodal function, Sphere function, and one multimodal function, Rastrigin function, are utilized. The dimension of the two functions is set to be 20.

Table 7 gives the simulation results. The results given in the Table 7 are mean, best, worst function values and their variance at the final iteration over *50* runs. From the Table 7, it can be observed that generally there is no single parameter k value with which the BSO algorithm can have the best performance. From the Table 7, relatively speaking, unimodal function (Sphere function) prefers a relatively small k value while multimodal function (Rastrigin function) prefers a relatively large k value. By considering the robustness of the BSO algorithm and from the results given in Table 7 itself, generally speaking, a good choice for the parameter k is *25* as a tradeoff between unimod-

al function and multimodal function. The obtained mean function values over *2000* iterations with parameter $k =25$ are shown in Figure 9. From the Figure 9, it can be observed that the BSO-I with $k =25$ can converge fast when solving the Sphere function and Rstrigin function. In all simulations, we will set the parameter k to be *25* with all other parameters are set as the same as that in Table 6.

Simulations on BSO-I Algorithm

The BSO-I algorithm is tested on the ten benchmark functions listed in Table 5 to illustrate the effectiveness and efficiency of the BSO-I algorithm instead of only two benchmark functions in Shi (2011). Each function is tested with three different dimension setting, *10, 20*, and *30*, respectively. The experimental results are given in Tables 8 and 9 for unimodal functions and multimodal functions, respectively. From the Table 8, it can be seen that good results can be achieved by BSO-I algorithm, and the results also show that the BSO-I is robust and reliable when it is applied to solve benchmark unimodal functions. From the Table 9, it can be

Table 7. Simulation results of BSO-I with different k

Function	k	Mean	Best	Worst	Variance
Sphere	10	1.20381E-11	2.55674E-86	5.27132E-10	5.61316E-21
	20	2.30827E-43	1.24079E-43	3.17853E-43	2.5931E-87
	25	9.4726E-35	5.55931E-35	1.33105E-34	3.78414E-70
	30	5.35092E-29	3.01328E-29	7.6509E-29	1.30974E-58
	40	7.70746E-22	4.18609E-22	1.10552E-21	2.74116E-44
	50	1.60782E-17	7.60191E-18	2.22015E-17	1.18045E-35
Rastrigin	10	17.11636	5.969754	29.84873	28.93288
	20	18.00875	8.954632	31.83866	20.98068
	25	17.17298	6.964713	23.879	13.24541
	30	17.15308	7.959667	29.84871	26.04389
	40	15.81984	6.964713	24.87396	17.95025
	50	16.21782	8.954632	25.8689	16.85928

Figure 9. Obtained mean minimum values vs. iterations for BSO-I with k = 25

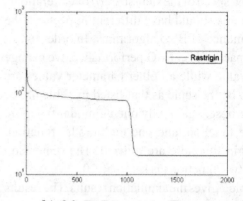

a) 20-D Sphere Function   b) 20-D Rastrigin Function

Table 8. Simulation results of BSO-I on unimodal functions

Function	Dimension	Mean	Best	Worst	Variance
	10	1.3989E-35	3.90855E-36	2.71203E-35	2.75801E-71
f_1	20	9.77845E-35	6.11475E-35	1.37856E-34	3.55418E-70
	30	2.66069E-34	1.79135E-34	3.59892E-34	2.02141E-69
	10	2.31285E-18	1.49658E-18	3.11619E-18	1.47169E-37
f_2	20	5.05671E-18	3.69394E-18	6.40744E-18	4.41064E-37
	30	0.000235	3.18538E-08	0.001718355	1.55583E-07
	10	0	0	0	0
f_3	20	0	0	0	0
	30	0	0	0	0
	10	9.28917E-18	5.51341E-18	1.21942E-17	1.81665E-36
f_4	20	3.4224E-17	2.63097E-17	4.25525E-17	1.03733E-35
	30	1.9978E-06	5.84794E-17	9.94736E-05	1.97869E-10
	10	0.000424	4.52215E-05	0.001140455	6.14016E-08
f_5	20	0.002636	0.000613	0.008465	2.8024E-06
	30	0.00835095	0.001967	0.020706	1.33183E-05

seen that good results can be obtained for function f_6, relatively good results can be obtained for functions f_7 and f_8, but not relatively good results are obtained for f_9 which is in general a difficult function to optimize, and for function f_{10}, good results can be obtained for it with dimension *20* and *30*, but not with dimension *10*, for which only relatively good results are obtained instead.

Simulation on BSO-II Algorithm

The BSO-II algorithm further exploits the search areas by generating two new offspring through utilizing crossover operation to crossover the newly generated individual with the existing individual with the same individual index. The BSO-II is applied to the ten benchmark functions

Table 9. Simulation results of BSO-I on multimodal functions

Function	Dimension	Mean	Best	Worst	Variance
f_6	10	4.44089E-15	4.44089E-15	4.44089E-15	0
	20	4.44089E-15	4.44089E-15	4.44089E-15	0
	30	5.93303E-15	4.44089E-15	7.99361E-15	3.13741E-30
f_7	10	3.502256	0	5.969754	1.949178
	20	17.75005	8.954632	26.86387	15.12629
	30	34.56484	13.92943	51.7378	51.65143
f_8	10	6.330642	2.587793	29.36235	11.77892
	20	21.60337	15.83735	87.11474	255.4539
	30	42.02786	25.91331	296.7523	2073.832
f_9	10	1350.782	454.0165	2270.172	192322.2
	20	3012.657	1598.991	4501.054	570878.2
	30	4951.779	3652.088	6771.33	563448.4
f_{10}	10	1.35123	0.497182	2.21245	0.158512
	20	0.058446	0	0.9467	0.022289
	30	0.010777	0	0.056496	0.000163

with dimensions *10, 20,* and *30,* respectively. The simulation results are given in Tables 10 and 11 for unimodal functions and multimodal functions, respectively. From the Table 10, we can observe that good results can be achieved by the BSO-II algorithm, and the results also show that the BSO-II is robust and reliable when it is applied to solve benchmark unimodal functions. From the Table 11, it can be seen that good results can be obtained for function f_6, relatively good results can be obtained for functions f_7 with dimension 30 and f_8, but not relatively good results are obtained for f_9 which is in general a difficult function to optimize, and for function f_{10}, reasonable good results can be obtained. Compared with the observation from the BSO-I algorithm, very good results (the optimum) can be obtained for f_7 with dimension *10* and *20.* For f_7 with dimension *30,* the best results over *50* runs is *0* which is the optimum of the problem, but the worst and variance over *50* runs are *3.979836* and *1.010551,* which indicates that the BSO-II

is better than the BSO-I, but it is still not robust when solving f_7 function.

To further compare the BSO-I and BSO-II algorithm, Figures 10, 11, 12, 13, 14, 15, 16, 17, 18, and 19 show curves which display the average evaluation function values over *50* runs vs. iterations for the ten benchmark functions tested. From the figures, it can be easily seen that the BSO-II algorithm performs better than the BSO-I algorithm for all the benchmark functions with all three different dimensions except the Griewank function with dimension *20* and *30.* For Griewnak function with dimension *10,* the BSO-I can't obtain very good results but the BSO-II could. Therefore, even for the Griewank function, the BSO-II could be a better choice compared with the BSO-I algorithm. For function f_9, even though still not very good results are obtained by BSO-II, but BSO-II performs much better than BSO-I does.

Table 10. Simulation results of BSO-II on unimodal functions

Function	Dimension	Mean	Best	Worst	Variance
f_1	10	4.56E-36	2.61244E-36	7.53912E-36	1.13477E-72
	20	4.54E-35	2.98742E-35	6.19235E-35	7.00667E-71
	30	1.33E-34	9.34047E-35	1.65808E-34	2.53466E-70
f_2	10	1.52E-18	1.10811E-18	1.94476E-18	3.80565E-38
	20	3.86E-18	3.23175E-18	4.44916E-18	8.94695E-38
	30	5.85E-18	4.80866E-18	6.91767E-18	2.62081E-37
f_3	10	0	0	0	0
	20	0	0	0	0
	30	0	0	0	0
f_4	10	4.76E-18	3.30555E-18	6.17314E-18	5.02845E-37
	20	2.13E-17	1.54076E-17	2.52198E-17	5.11026E-36
	30	4.49E-17	3.56463E-17	5.22311E-17	1.57E-35
f_5	10	8.85E-05	3.18035E-05	0.000256579	1.69387E-09
	20	0.000319	0.000104	0.000853	2.24337E-08
	30	0.000766	0.000176	0.001733	1.00554E-07

Table 11. Simulation results of BSO-II on multimodal functions

Function	Dimension	Mean	Best	Worst	Variance
f_6	10	4.16E-15	8.88178E-16	4.44089E-15	9.47921E-31
	20	4.44E-15	4.44089E-15	4.44089E-15	0
	30	4.44E-15	4.44089E-15	4.44089E-15	0
f_7	10	0	0	0	0
	20	0	0	0	0
	30	0.855665	0	3.979836	1.010551
f_8	10	4.558798	2.019811	9.069095	0.862945
	20	28.514436	15.49093	83.89686	604.2519
	30	34.06948	25.85653	128.9086	505.6776
f_9	10	56.23811	0.000127	236.8768	5855.616
	20	499.023	118.4386	927.8028	48176.18
	30	1128.729	335.5784	1993.748	157231
f_{10}	10	0.150697	0.022151	0.531254	0.019883
	20	0.311937	0.017241	1.519837	0.110482
	30	0.090445	0	0.568672	0.011172

Figure 10. Mean function evaluation values vs. iterations of sphere function

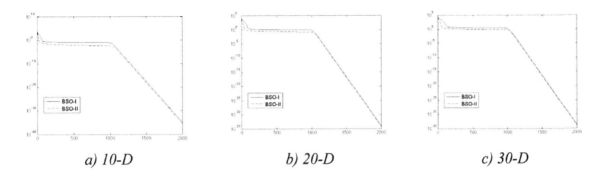

a) 10-D   *b) 20-D*   *c) 30-D*

Figure 11. Mean function evaluation values vs. iterations of Schwefel's P221

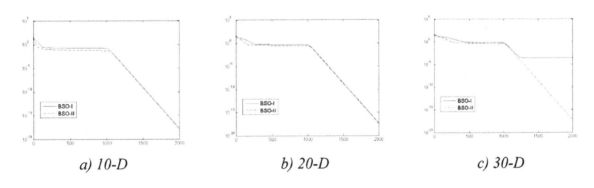

a) 10-D   *b) 20-D*   *c) 30-D*

Figure 12. Mean function evaluation values vs. iterations of step function

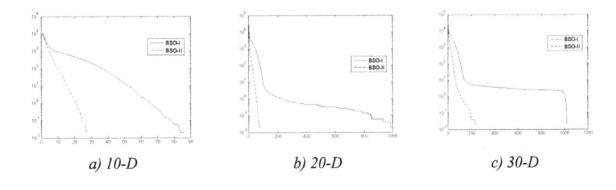

a) 10-D   *b) 20-D*   *c) 30-D*

Figure 13. Mean function evaluation values vs. iterations of Schwefel's P222

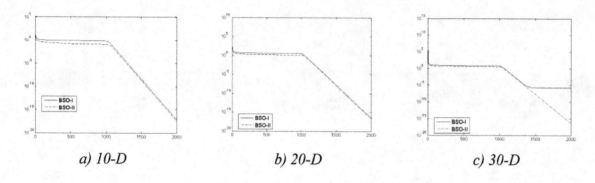

a) 10-D   *b) 20-D*   *c) 30-D*

Figure 14. Mean function evaluation values vs. iterations of quartic noise

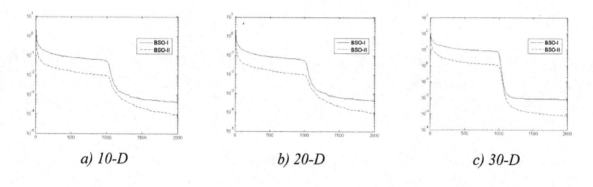

a) 10-D   *b) 20-D*   *c) 30-D*

Figure 15. Mean function evaluation values vs. iterations of Ackely function

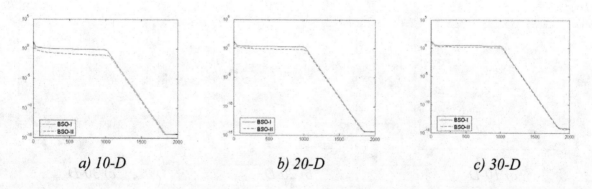

a) 10-D   *b) 20-D*   *c) 30-D*

Figure 16. Mean function evaluation values vs. iterations of Rastrigin function

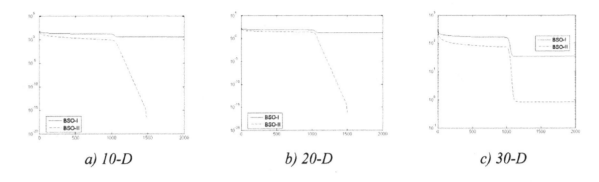

a) 10-D   *b) 20-D*   *c) 30-D*

Figure 17. Mean function evaluation values vs. iterations of Rosenbrock function

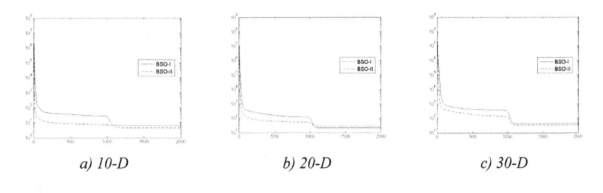

a) 10-D   *b) 20-D*   *c) 30-D*

Figure 18. Mean function evaluation values vs. iterations of Schwefel's P226

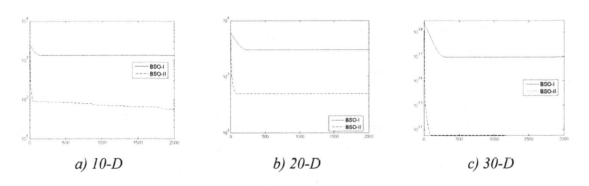

a) 10-D   *b) 20-D*   *c) 30-D*

Figure 19. Mean function evaluation values vs. iterations of Griewank function

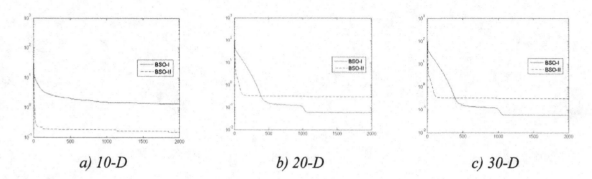

a) 10-D   b) 20-D   c) 30-D

Diversity

During each iteration, the population of individuals is clustered into m clusters. Individuals in each cluster are scattered with different distribution over iterations. To measure and monitor the distribution of individuals in each cluster, the following average intra-cluster distance is defined

$$d_c(x_i, x_j) = \left\| x_i - x_j \right\| \tag{4a}$$

$$\tilde{d}_c(x_i, x_j) = \frac{d_c(x_i, x_j)}{\left\| a - b \right\|} \tag{4b}$$

$$D_c = \frac{2}{q(q-1)} \sum_{i=1}^{q} \sum_{j=i+1}^{q} \tilde{d}(x_i, x_j) \tag{4c}$$

where q is the number of individuals in a cluster; $d(x_i, x_j)$ is the Euclidean distance between individual x_i and x_j; a and b are dynamic range; $\bar{d}$ (x_i, x_j) is the normalized Euclidean distance between individual x_i and x_j; D_c is the normalized distance for a cluster. For $m=5$, there will be 5 intra-cluster diversities. In addition to m average intra-cluster distances, there will be one average inter-cluster distance to measure and/or monitor the distribution of cluster centers. The formula for calculating average intra-cluster distance can also be utilized to calculate the average inter-

cluster distance except that here the x_i is the ith cluster center and number of individuals is m.

Over iterations, the number of individuals in each cluster will change. To measure and monitor the distribution of number of individuals in each cluster over whole population, the following inter-cluster diversity is defined

$$D_v = \sum_{i=1}^{m} \frac{(n_i - \bar{n})^2}{m}, \bar{n} = \frac{\sum_{i=1}^{m} n_i}{m} \tag{5}$$

where m is the number of clusters, n_i is the number of individuals in the ith cluster. D_v is similar to the definition of variance for distribution of number of individuals in each cluster among the population.

Another similar definition of the inter-cluster diversity can be defined as

$$D_e = -\sum_{i=1}^{m} p_i \log(p_i), \quad p_i = \frac{n_i}{n} \tag{6}$$

where m is the number of clusters, n_i is the number individuals in the ith cluster. Therefore p_i is the percentage of individuals that the ith cluster has over the population. D_e is similar to the definition of information entropy. Therefore, it can be looked as a measurement of information entropy for the population. When all the individuals are located in one cluster, the D_e has the smallest value, which is

0; when all the individuals are equally distributed into each cluster, D_e has the largest value, which is *log(m)*. If *m =5*, D_e = *log(5) = 0.699*.

Tables 12 and 13 give the results of average inter-cluster distance D_c and inter-cluster diversity D_e for ten tested benchmark functions at the end of BSO-I running. Tables 14 and 15 give the results of average inter-cluster distance D_c and inter-cluster diversity D_e for ten tested benchmark functions at the end of BSO-II running. Figures 20 through 29 show mean average inter-cluster distance over 50 runs vs. iterations for the ten benchmark functions, respectively. From both the Tables 12 through 15 and Figures 20 through 29, it could be easily observed that the average inter-cluster distance quickly decreases over iterations and gets to very small values way before reaching the prefixed maximum iteration number for both BSO algorithms, which indicates that *m* clusters move close to each other very quickly, and therefore the algorithms may lose their search capabilities quickly, may converge quickly, or may be stuck in (local) optima quickly. By double checking the

cluster centers over iterations, the same observation can be obtained. That tells us that when the situation occurs, further improvement could be achieved by randomly move away from current cluster centers and at the same time increase the step-size to a relatively large value which then will be dynamically adjusted according to the Equation 3.

The mean inter-cluster diversities of *50* runs over iterations for all benchmark functions seem to have similar behaviors except function f_9 with dimension *10* and *20*. Figures 30 and 31 display the curves of mean inter-cluster diversities over *50* runs vs. iterations for function f_1 as an example for unimodal functions and for function f_7 as an example for multimodal functions. Figure 32 displays the curves of mean inter-cluster diversities over *50* runs vs. iterations for function f_9 with dimension *20*. From Figures 30 and 31, the mean inter-cluster diversities tend to have relatively large values, which indicate that the population of individuals is generally well-uniformly divided into *m* clusters. This may be because the

Table 12. Simulation results of D_c and D_e for BSO-I on unimodal functions

F	d	D_c				D_e			
		mean	short	long	variance	mean	small	large	variance
f_1	10	3.99E-20	3.02E-20	5.45E-20	2.87E-41	0.674	0.576	0.697	0.00056
	20	7.73E-20	5.84E-20	9.83-20	7.02E-41	0.658	0.566	0.697	0.000893
	30	9.92E-20	7.47E-20	1.16E-19	1.10E-40	0.645	0.473	0.695	0.001978
f_2	10	4.6E-20	3.31E-20	5.58E-20	2.71E-41	0.671	0.583	0.695	0.000528
	20	9.11E-20	6.98E-20	1.15E-19	1.17E-40	0.653	0.579	0.693	0.000653
	30	2.2E-19	1.40E-19	3.57E-19	2.36E-39	0.624	0.488	0.694	0.002807
f_3	10	0.006908	0.005538	0.008269	2.80E-07	0.685	0.666	0.697	7.604E-05
	20	0.007145	0.005921	0.007997	1.89E-07	0.666	0.572	0.695	0.000567
	30	0.006818	0.005485	0.007595	2.15E-07	0.653	0.499	0.693	0.001402
f_4	10	4.44E-19	3.24E-19	5.95E-19	3.44E-39	0.674	0.608	0.699	0.000481
	20	8.54E-19	6.73E-19	1.12E-18	1.01E-38	0.652	0.567	0.698	0.000925
	30	1.12E-18	8.86E-19	1.55E-18	1.83E-38	0.640	0.554	0.694	0.001363
f_5	10	0.06774	0.031242	0.107543	0.000272	0.609	0.484	0.681	0.002202
	20	0.041977	0.016624	0.071656	0.000163	0.604	0.394	0.686	0.003644
	30	0.029224	0.010858	0.04638	6.94E-05	0.591	0.389	0.682	0.004305

Table 13. Simulation results of D_c and D_e for BSO-I on multimodal functions

F	d	D_c				D_e			
		mean	short	long	variance	mean	small	large	variance
f_6	10	1.01E-16	7.83E-17	1.24E-16	6.71E-35	0.677	0.617	0.698	0.00023
	20	1.01E-16	7.28E-17	1.25E-16	1.30E-34	0.642	0.560	0.695	0.001086
	30	1.14E-16	1.01E-18	2.21E-16	5.69E-33	0.613	0.384	0.692	0.003186
f_7	10	2.57E-10	1.31E-16	4.39E-10	1.16E-10	0.607	0.450	0.692	0.002966
	20	1.90E-10	4.56E-17	7.13E-10	3.82E-20	0.604	0.448	0.690	0.002892
	30	1.22E-10	1.22E-17	7.10E-10	3.49E-20	0.589	0.378	0.695	0.004818
f_8	10	1.15E-17	6.43E-19	5.77E-17	1.06E-34	0.622	0.505	0.688	0.002294
	20	2.22E-17	1.17E-18	8.01E-17	3.61E-34	0.600	0.456	0.686	0.003408
	30	2.75E-17	1.49E-18	1.81E-16	1.05E-33	0.588	0.349	0.692	0.00625
f_9	10	1.91E-09	5.68E-17	3.89E-09	7.92E-19	0.618	0.115	0.685	0.007802
	20	2.32E-09	3.22E-16	4.14E-09	8.62E-19	0.603	0.378	0.692	0.004574
	30	2.16E-09	6.82E-17	4.30E-09	1.30E-18	0.593	0.097	0.683	0.00893
f_{10}	10	1.21E-11	7.22E-19	8.07E-11	3.72E-22	0.589	0.097	0.693	0.01162
	20	5.01E-11	5.05E-18	9.57E-11	6.74E-22	0.602	0.362	0.689	0.003937
	30	5.21E-11	3.854E-16	9.28E-11	5.74E-22	0.610	0.506	0.696	0.002307

Table 14. Simulation results of D_c and D_e for BSO-II on unimodal functions

F	d	D_c				D_e			
		mean	short	long	variance	mean	small	large	variance
f_1	10	2.35E-20	1.80E-20	3.00E-20	5.86E-42	0.674	0.609	0.696	0.000435
	20	5.3E-20	4.39E-20	6.41E-20	2.37E-41	0.676	0.568	0.696	0.000443
	30	7.5E-20	6.48E-20	8.77E-20	3.51E-41	0.674	0.612	0.695	0.000363
f_2	10	3.16E-20	2.50E-20	4.16E-20	1.36E-41	0.675	0.597	0.697	0.000592
	20	7.4E-20	5.56E-20	8.36E-20	3.47E-41	0.658	0.586	0.694	0.000782
	30	1.06E-19	9.13E-20	1.22E-19	5.64E-41	0.658	0.540	0.696	0.001079
f_3	10	0.007209	0.005138	0.008104	2.81E-07	0.685	0.652	0.698	8.749E-05
	20	0.007577	0.006727	0.008262	1.37E-07	0.685	0.610	0.697	0.000214
	30	0.00797	0.007136	0.008711	1.77E-07	0.677	0.622	0.695	0.000298
f_4	10	2.51E-19	1.77E-19	3.58E-19	1.42E-39	0.667	0.546	0.697	0.000904
	20	5.58E-19	4.59E-19	8.08E-19	5.04E-39	0.658	0.509	0.699	0.001228
	30	8.14E-19	5.89E-19	1.11E-18	9.52E-39	0.662	0.567	0.696	0.001039
f_5	10	0.073914	0.052208	0.104325	0.000129	0.649	0.509	0.695	0.00143
	20	0.066032	0.044808	0.095853	0.000149	0.638	0.515	0.692	0.001513
	30	0.062562	0.041369	0.102545	0.000142	0.624	0.326	0.688	0.003219

Table 15. Simulation results of D_c and D_e for BSO-II on multimodal functions

F	d	D_c				D_e			
		mean	short	long	variance	mean	small	large	variance
f_6	10	9.83E-17	1.13E-18	1.25E-16	8.10E-34	0.684	0.616	0.698	0.00025
	20	1.17E-16	7.84E-17	1.47E-16	1.68E-34	0.655	0.570	0.693	0.000735
	30	1.02E-16	5.82E-17	1.38E-16	3.12E-34	0.597	0.419	0.691	0.00392
f_7	10	4.63E-10	3.95E-10	5.28E-10	1.12E-21	0.688	0.665	0.698	5.111E-05
	20	4.9E-10	4.10E-10	5.46E-10	8.55E-22	0.681	0.615	0.698	0.000203
	30	4.85E-10	4.03E-10	5.68E-10	8.28E-22	0.663	0.590	0.698	0.000578
f_8	10	1.93E-13	3.12E-19	9.66E-12	1.87E-24	0.589	0.411	0.687	0.004572
	20	1.52E-16	7.17E-19	6.67E-16	1.98E-32	0.599	0.434	0.683	0.003304
	30	1.38E-16	8.33E-19	6.48E-16	2.28E-32	0.585	0.468	0.668	0.002776
f_9	10	2.13E-09	0	3.22E-09	6.53E-19	0.571	0.097	0.685	0.024857
	20	3.42E-09	0	4.95E-09	1.38E-18	0.595	0.097	0.693	0.024992
	30	5.79E-09	3.21E-09	7.72E-09	9.25E-19	0.634	0.443	0.697	0.003643
f_{10}	10	3.24E-11	1.51E-19	6.07E-11	5.18E-22	0.623	0.421	0.694	0.002855
	20	5.89E-11	1.35E-18	1.04E-10	1.04E-21	0.625	0.493	0.694	0.002619
	30	8.63E-11	2.99E-20	1.24E-10	1.40E-21	0.631	0.499	0.691	0.002384

Figure 20. Mean average inter-cluster distance vs. iterations of sphere function

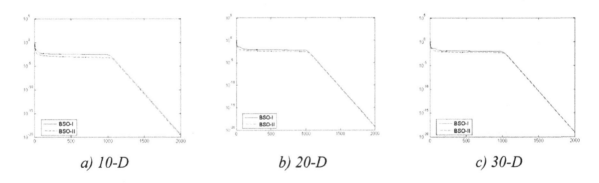

a) 10-D   *b) 20-D*   *c) 30-D*

Figure 21. Mean average inter-cluster distance vs. iterations of Schwefel's P221

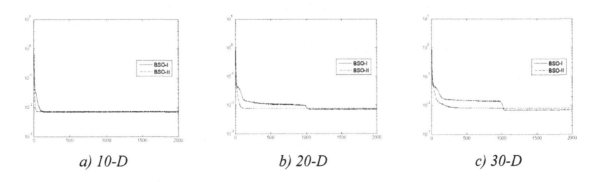

a) 10-D   *b) 20-D*   *c) 30-D*

Figure 22. Mean average inter-cluster distance vs. iterations of step function

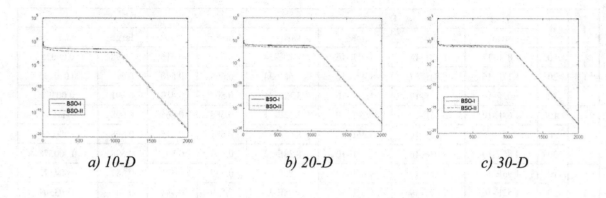

a) 10-D   b) 20-D   c) 30-D

Figure 23. Mean average inter-cluster distance vs. iterations of Schwefel's P222

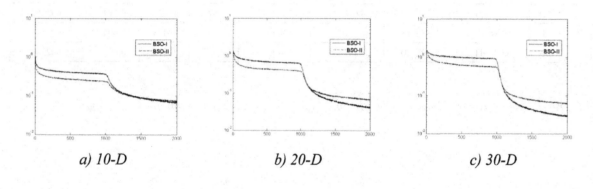

a) 10-D   b) 20-D   c) 30-D

Figure 24. mean average inter-cluster distance vs. iterations of Quartic Noise

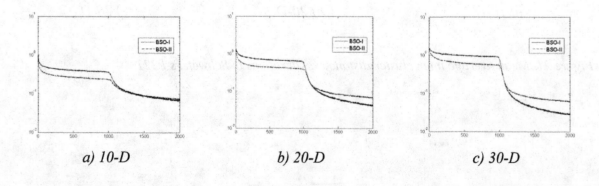

a) 10-D   b) 20-D   c) 30-D

Figure 25. Mean average inter-cluster distance vs. iterations of Ackely Function

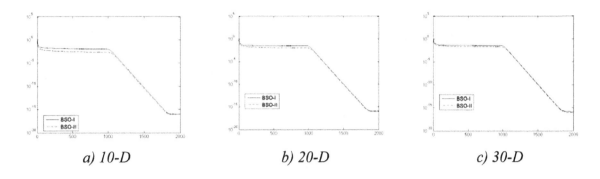

a) 10-D   *b) 20-D*   *c) 30-D*

Figure 26. mean average inter-cluster distance vs. iterations of Rastrigin Function

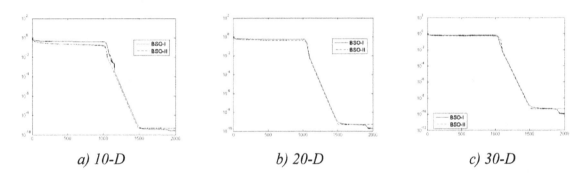

a) 10-D   *b) 20-D*   *c) 30-D*

Figure 27. Mean average inter-cluster distance vs. iterations of Rosenbrock Function

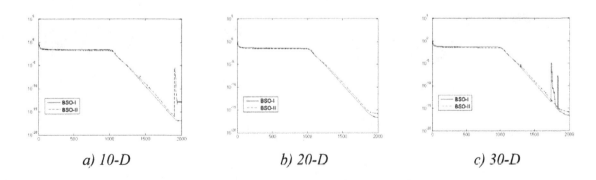

a) 10-D   *b) 20-D*   *c) 30-D*

Figure 28. Mean average inter-cluster distance vs. iterations of Schwefel's P226

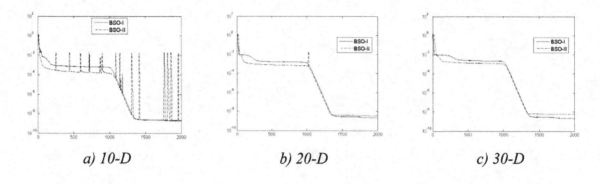

a) 10-D   b) 20-D   c) 30-D

Figure 29. Mean average inter-cluster distance vs. iterations of Griewank Function

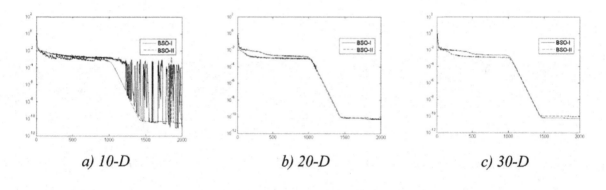

a) 10-D   b) 20-D   c) 30-D

Figure 30. Mean D_e over 50 runs vs. iterations for sphere function with dimension d = 20

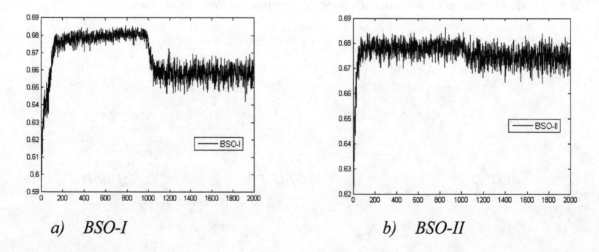

a)   BSO-I   b)   BSO-II

Figure 31. Mean D$_e$ over 50 runs vs. iterations for Rastrigin function with dimension d = 20

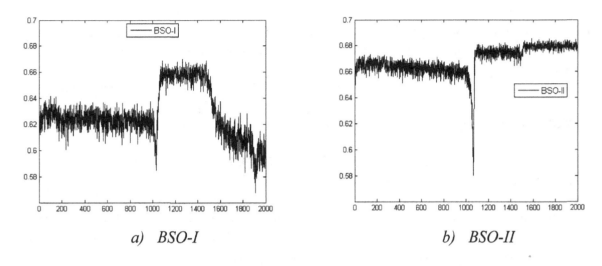

a) *BSO-I*   b) *BSO-II*

Figure 32. Mean D$_e$ over 50 runs vs. iterations for Schwefel's P226 with dimension d = 20

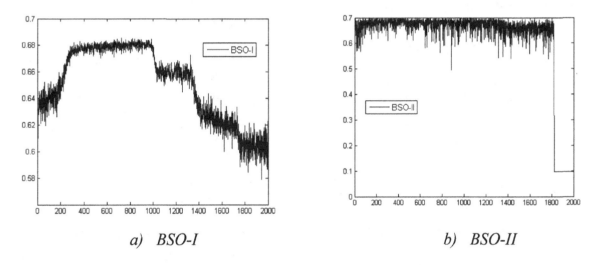

a) *BSO-I*   b) *BSO-II*

fixed number of clusters and the k-means clustering algorithm with randomly selecting k individuals as initial cluster centroid positions are used over iterations in the implementation of the BSO algorithms. If different initialization method for k-means clustering algorithm or a different clustering algorithm, especially those with unfixed number of clusters, such as the self-organizing feature map, is utilized, the mean intercluster diversity may behave quite differently. From Figure 32 and Table 15, it can be seen that

toward the end of BSO-II running for function f_9, the number of individuals in each cluster is not uniformly distributed anymore, but clustered into one cluster with other *4* clusters with only *1* individual, in which

$$D_e =$$
$$-\left(4 * \frac{1}{100} * log_{10}\left(\frac{1}{100}\right) + \frac{96}{100} * log_{10}\left(\frac{96}{100}\right)\right)$$
$$= 0.097$$

This may indicate that when the above situation occurs the portion of clustering all individuals into m clusters in the BSO algorithm may have very little, if any, contribution to the algorithm's search capability.

CONCLUSION

In this paper, we first modeled the human brainstorming process, then introduced two versions of Brain Storm Optimization algorithms It is natural to believe that BSO algorithms should be superior to the optimization algorithms inspired by collective behavior of injects such as ants, birds, *etc.* because the BSO algorithms were inspired by the human brainstorming process. The proposed BSO algorithms were implemented and tested on ten benchmark functions, of which five are unimodal functions and the other five are multimodal functions. Simulation results showed that both BSO algorithms performed reasonably well, and BSO-II performs better than BSO-I does in general. Furthermore, average inter-cluster distance D_c and inter-cluster diversity D_e were defined to measure and monitor the distribution of cluster centroids and the information entropy of the BSO population. Simulation results on D_c showed that further performance improvement for the BSO algorithms could be achieved by taking advantage of information revealed by the D_c and or D_e, which is one of future research directions.

Good optimization algorithms for solving complicated and nonlinear optimization problems should have the capability to converge in order to find better and better solutions, but at the same time, it should have the capability to diverge in order to escape from local optima which are not good enough solutions for the problem to be solved. The BSO algorithm during each iteration involves two opposite operations. One is to converge or contract by utilizing clustering methods to converge to the *m* cluster centers. Another is to diverge or expand by adding noise to generate new individuals. Depending on the amplitude of noise, different scales of areas can be searched by the BSO algorithm. Therefore, the BSO algorithms naturally include contraction and expansion operations during each iteration by design. It should be a good choice for solving complicated and nonlinear optimization problems.

ACKNOWLEDGMENT

This paper is partially supported by National Natural Science Foundation of China under Grant Number 60975080, and by the Suzhou Science and Technology Project under Grant Number SYJG0919.

REFERENCES

Bastos-Filho, C. J. A., De Lima Neto, F. B., Lins, A. J. C. C., Nascimento, A. I. S., & Lima, M. P. (2008). A novel search algorithm based on fish school behavior. In *Proceedings of the IEEE International Conference on Systems, Man and Cybernetics* (pp. 2646-2651).

de Castro, J. N., & Von Zuben, F. J. (1999). *Artificial immune systems: Part I -Basic theory and applications* (Tech. Rep. No. DCA-RT 01/99). Brazil, Campinas: School of Computing and Electrical Engineering, State University of Campinas.

Dorigo, M., Maniezzo, V., & Colorni, A. (1996). The ant system: Optimization by a colony of cooperating agents. *IEEE Transactions on Systems, Man. Cybernetics B, 26*(2), 29–41. doi:10.1109/3 477.484436doi:10.1109/3477.484436

Eberhart, R. C., & Shi, Y. (2007). *Computational intelligence, concepts to implementation* (1st ed.). San Francisco, CA: Morgan Kaufmann.

Eusuff, M., & Lansey, K. (2006). Shuffled frog-leaping algorithm: A memetic meta-heuristic for discrete optimization. *Engineering Optimization, 38*(2), 129–154. doi:10.1080/030521505003847 59doi:10.1080/03052150500384759

Fogel, L. J. (1962). Autonomous automata. *Industrial Research, 4,* 14–19.

Holland, J. H. (1975). *Adaptation in natural and artificial systems*. Ann Arbor, MI: University of Michigan Press.

Kohonen, T., & Honkela, T. (2007). Kohonen network. *Scholarpedia, 2*(1), 1568. doi:10.4249/scholarpedia.1568doi:10.4249/scholarpedia.1568

Koza, J. R. (1992). *Genetic programming: On the programming of computers by means of natural selection*. Cambridge, MA: MIT Press.

MacQueen, J. (1967). Some methods for classification and analysis of multivariate observations. In *Proceedings of the 5ᵗʰ Berkeley Symposium on Mathematical Statistics and Probability* (pp. 281-297).

Nock, R., & Nielsen, F. (2006). On weighting clustering. *IEEE Transactions on Pattern Analysis and Machine Intelligence, 28*(8), 1–13. PubMed doi:10.1109/TPAMI.2006.168doi:10.1109/TPAMI.2006.168

Osborn, A. F. (1963). *Applied imagination: Principles and procedures of creative problem solving* (3rd ed.). New York, NY: Charles Scribner's Son.

Passino, K. M. (2010). Bacterial foraging optimization. *International Journal of Swarm Intelligence Research, 1*(1), 1–16. doi:10.4018/jsir.2010010101doi:10.4018/jsir.2010010101

Pavlyukevich, I. (2007). Lévy flights, non-local search and simulated annealing. *Journal of Computational Physics, 226,* 1830–1844. doi:10.1016/j.jcp.2007.06.008doi:10.1016/j.jcp.2007.06.008

Rechenberg, I. (1973). *Evolutionsstrategie: Optimierung technischer Systeme nach Prinzipien der biologischen Evolution*. Stuttgart, Germany: Frommann-Holzboog.

Shah-Hosseini, H. (2009). The intelligent water drops algorithm: a nature-inspired swarm-based optimization algorithm. *International Journal of Bio-inspired Computation, 1*(1-2), 71–79. doi:10.1504/IJBIC.2009.022775doi:10.1504/IJBIC.2009.022775

Shi, Y. (2011, June 11-15). Brain storm optimization algorithm. In Y. Tan, Y. Shi, Y. Chai, & G. Wang (Eds.), *Proceedings of the Second International Conference on Advances in Swarm Intelligence*, Chongqing, China (LNCS 6728, pp. 303-309).

Shi, Y., & Eberhart, R. C. (1998, May 4-9). A modified particle swarm optimizer. In *Proceedings of the IEEE International Conference on Evolutionary Computation*, Anchorage, AK.

Shi, Y., & Eberhart, R. C. (2008). Population diversity of particle swarm optimization. In *Proceedings of the Congress on Evolutionary Computation*, Hong Kong, China.

Shi, Y., & Eberhart, R. C. (2009). Monitoring of particle swarm optimization. *Frontiers of Computer Science in China, 3*(1), 31–37. doi:10.1007/s11704-009-0008-4doi:10.1007/s11704-009-0008-4

Smith, R. (2002). *The 7 levels of change* (2nd ed.). Arlington, VA: Tapestry Press.

Theodoridis, S., & Koutroumbas, K. (2006). *Pattern recognition* (3rd ed.). New York, NY: Academic Press.

Tovey, C. (2004). The honey bee algorithm: A biological inspired approach to internet server optimization. *Engineering Enterprise, the Alumni Magazine for ISyE at Georgia Institute of Technology,* 13-15.

Xu, R., & Wunsch, D., II. (2005). Survey of clustering algorithms. *IEEE Transactions on Neural Networks*, *16*(3), 645–678. PubMed doi:10.1109/TNN.2005.845141doi:10.1109/TNN.2005.845141

Yang, X. (2008). *Nature-inspired metaheuristic algorithms*. Beckington, UK: Luniver Press.

Yao, X., Liu, Y., & Lin, G. (1997). Evolutionary programming made faster. *IEEE Transactions on Evolutionary Computation*, *3*, 82–102.

This work was previously published in the International Journal of Swarm Intelligence Research, Volume 2, Issue 4, edited by Yuhui Shi, pp. 35-62, copyright 2011 by IGI Publishing (an imprint of IGI Global).

Section 2
Swarm Intelligence Applications

Chapter 9
Swarm Intelligence for Non–Negative Matrix Factorization

Andreas Janecek
University of Vienna, Austria

Ying Tan
Peking University, China

ABSTRACT

The Non-negative Matrix Factorization (NMF) is a special low-rank approximation which allows for an additive parts-based and interpretable representation of the data. This article presents efforts to improve the convergence, approximation quality, and classification accuracy of NMF using five different meta-heuristics based on swarm intelligence. Several properties of the NMF objective function motivate the utilization of meta-heuristics: this function is non-convex, discontinuous, and may possess many local minima. The proposed optimization strategies are two-fold: On the one hand, a new initialization strategy for NMF is presented in order to initialize the NMF factors prior to the factorization; on the other hand, an iterative update strategy is proposed, which improves the accuracy per runtime for the multiplicative update NMF algorithm. The success of the proposed optimization strategies are shown by applying them on synthetic data and data sets coming from the areas of spam filtering/email classification, and evaluate them also in their application context. Experimental results show that both optimization strategies are able to improve NMF in terms of faster convergence, lower approximation error, and better classification accuracy. Especially the initialization strategy leads to significant reductions of the runtime per accuracy ratio for both, the NMF approximation as well as the classification results achieved with NMF.

DOI: 10.4018/978-1-4666-2479-5.ch009

1. INTRODUCTION

Low-rank approximations are utilized in several content based retrieval and data mining applications, such as text and multimedia mining, web search, etc. and achieve a more compact representation of the data with only limited loss in information. They reduce storage and runtime requirements, and also reduce redundancy and noise in the data representation while capturing the essential associations. The Non-negative Matrix Factorization (NMF) (Lee & Seung, 1999) leads to a low-rank approximation which satisfies non-negativity constraints. NMF approximates a data matrix A by $A \approx WH$, where W and H are the NMF factors. NMF requires all entries in A, W and H to be zero or positive. Contrary to other low-rank approximations such as the Singular Value Decomposition (SVD), these constraints force NMF to produce so-called "additive parts-based" representations. This is an impressive benefit of NMF, since it makes the interpretation of the NMF factors much easier than for factors containing positive and negative entries (Berry, Browne, Langville, Pauca, & Plemmons, 2007; Janecek & Gansterer, 2010; Lee & Seung, 1999).

The NMF is usually not unique if different initializations of the factors W and H are used. Moreover, there are several different NMF algorithms which all follow different strategies (e.g., mean squared error, least squares, gradient descent) and produce different results. Mathematically, the goal of NMF is to find a "good" (ideally the best) solution of an optimization problem with bound constraints in the form $\min_{x \in \Omega} f(x)$, where $f : \mathbb{R}^N \to \mathbb{R}$ is the nonlinear objective function of NMF, and Ω is the feasible region (for NMF, Ω is restricted to non-negative values). f is usually not convex, discontinuous and may possess many local minima (Stadlthanner, Lutter, Theis, Lang, Tome, Georgieva, & Puntonet, 2007). Since meta-heuristic optimization algorithms are known to be able to deal well with such difficul-

ties they seem to be a promising choice for improving the quality of NMF. Over the last decades nature-inspired meta-heuristics, including those based on swarm intelligence, have gained much popularity due to their applicability for various optimization problems. They benefit from the fact that they are able to find acceptable results within a reasonable amount of time for many complex, large and dynamic problems (Blackwell, 2007). Although they lack the ability to guarantee the optimal solution for a given problem (comparably to NMF), it has been shown that they are able to tackle various kinds of real-world optimization problems (Chiong, 2009). Meta-heuristics as well as the principles of NMF are in accordance with the *law of sufficiency* (Kennedy, Eberhart, & Shi, 2001): If a solution to a problem is good enough, fast enough and cheap enough, then it is sufficient.

In this article we present two different strategies for improving the NMF using five optimization algorithms based on swarm intelligence and evolutionary computing: Particle Swarm Optimization (PSO), Genetic Algorithms (GA), Fish School Search (FSS), Differential Evolution (DE), and Fireworks Algorithm (FWA). All algorithms are population based and can be categorized into the fields of swarm intelligence (PSO, FSS, FWA), evolutionary algorithms (GA), and a combination thereof (DE). The goal is to find a solution with smaller overall error at convergence, and/or to speed up convergence of NMF (i.e., smaller approximation error for a given number of NMF iterations) compared to identical NMF algorithms without applied optimization strategy. Another goal is to increase the classification accuracy in cases where NMF is used as dimensionality reduction method for machine learning applications. The concepts of the two optimization strategies are the following: In the first strategy, meta-heuristics are used to initialize the factors W and H in order to minimize the NMF objective function *prior* to the factorization. The second strategy aims at iteratively improving the approximation quality of NMF during the first iterations.

The proposed optimization strategies can be considered successful if they are able to improve the NMF in terms of either (i) faster convergence (i.e., better accuracy per runtime), (ii) lower final approximation error, or (iii) better classification accuracy. The optimization of different rows of W and different columns of H can be split up into several partly independent sub-tasks and can thus be executed concurrently. Since this allows for a parallel and/or distributed computation of both update strategies, we also discuss parallel implementations of the proposed optimization strategies. Experimental results show that both strategies, the initialization of NMF factors as well as an iterative update during the first iterations, are able to improve the NMF in terms of faster convergence, lower approximation error, and/or better classification accuracy.

1.1. Related Work

The work by Lee and Seung (1999) is known as a standard reference for NMF. The original Multiplicative Update (MU) algorithm introduced in this article provides a good baseline against which other algorithms, e.g., the Alternating Least Squares algorithm (Paatero & Tapper, 1994), the Gradient Descent algorithm (Lin, 2007), ALSPGRAD (Lin, 2007), quasi Newton-type NMF (Kim & Park, 2008), fastNMF and bayesNMF (Schmidt & Laurberg, 2008), etc. have to be judged. While the MU algorithm is still the fastest NMF algorithm per iteration and a good choice if a very fast and rough approximation is needed, ALSPGRAD, fastNMF and bayesNMF have shown to achieve a better approximation at convergence compared to many other NMF algorithms (Janecek, Schulze-Grotthoff et al., 2011).

NMF Initialization

Only few algorithms for non-random NMF initialization have been published. Wild, Curry, and Dougherty (2004) used spherical k-means clustering to group column vectors of A as input for W. A similar technique was used in Xue, Tong, Chen, and Chen (2008). Another clustering-based method of structured initialization designed to find spatially localized basis images can be found in Kim and Park (2008). Boutsidis and Gallopoulos (2008) used an initialization technique based on two SVD processes called non-negative double singular value decomposition (NNDSVD). Experiments indicate that this method has advantages over the centroid initialization in Wild, Curry, and Dougherty (2004) in terms of faster convergence.

NMF and Meta-Heuristics

So far, only few studies can be found that aim at combining NMF and meta-heuristics, most of them are based on Genetic Algorithms (GAs). In Stadlthanner et al. (2007), the authors have investigated the application of GAs on sparse NMF for microarray analysis, while Snásel, Platos, and Kromer (2008) have applied GAs for Boolean matrix factorization, a variant of NMF for binary data based on Boolean algebra. However, the methods presented in these studies are barely connected to the techniques presented in this article. In two preceding studies (Janecek & Tan 2011a, 2011b), we have introduced the basic concepts of the proposed update strategies.

In this article we extend our preliminary work in several ways by the following new contributions. At first, we evaluate our methods on synthetic data as well as on data sets coming from the areas of spam filtering/email classification. This allows us to evaluate the proposed methods in the application context of the applied data sets. In other words, we are now able to investigate the quality of the NMF not only in terms of approximation accuracy but also in terms of classification accuracy achieved with the approximated data sets as well as with the basic vectors of the NMF factor W. Within this evaluation process we consider two different classification settings, a static setting where NMF is computed on the complete data set (training and test data), and a dynamic setting where NMF can be applied dynamically to new data. Moreover, we present a detailed evaluation of the runtime performance of the proposed update strategies, and, finally, we are able to compare the performance of our strategies with each other using the same parameter settings, data sets, and hardware set-up.

1.2. Notation

A matrix is represented by an uppercase italic letter (A, B, Σ, ...), a vector by a lowercase bold letter ($\mathbf{u}$, $\mathbf{x}$, $\mathbf{q}_1$, ...), and a scalar by a lowercase Greek letter (λ, μ, ...). The ith row vector of a matrix D is represented as $\mathbf{d}_i^r$, and the jth column vector of D as $\mathbf{d}_j^c$. Matrix-matrix multiplications are denoted by "*", element-wise multiplications by "·", and element-wise divisions by ". / ".

1.3. Synopsis

In Section 2 we briefly review low-rank approximations and NMF algorithms. In Section 3 we summarize the swarm intelligence algorithms used in this article, and in Section 4 we present the proposed optimization strategies for NMF based on them. Moreover, we discuss different classification methods based on NMF. In Sections 5 and 6 we evaluate our methods and discuss the achieved results. Finally, in Section 7 we conclude our work and summarize ongoing and future research activities in this area.

2. LOW RANK APPROXIMATIONS

Given a data matrix $A \in \mathbb{R}^{m \times n}$ whose n columns represent instances and whose m rows contain the values of a certain feature for the instances, most low-rank approximations reduce the dimensionality by representing the original data as accurately as possible with linear combinations of the original instances and/or features. Mathematically, A is replaced with another matrix A_k with usually much smaller rank. In general, a closer approximation means a better factorization. However, it is highly likely that in some applications specific factorizations might be more desirable compared to other solutions.

The most important low-rank approximation techniques are the Singular Value Decomposition (SVD) (Berry, 1992) and the closely related Principal Component Analysis (PCA) (Jolliffe, 2002). Traditionally, the PCA uses the eigenvalue decomposition to find eigenvalues and eigenvectors of the covariance matrix $\mathrm{Cov}(A)$ of A. Then the original data matrix A can be approximated by $A_k := A Q_k$ with $Q_k = [\mathbf{q}_1, ..., \mathbf{q}_k]$ where $\mathbf{q}_1, ..., \mathbf{q}_k$ are the first k eigenvectors of $\mathrm{Cov}(A)$. The SVD decomposes A into a product of three matrices such that $A = U \Sigma V^\top$ where Σ contains the singular values along the diagonal, and U and V are the singular vectors. The reduced rank SVD to A can be found by setting all but the first k largest singular values equal to zero and using only the first k columns of U and V, such that $A_k := U_k \Sigma_k V_k^\top$. Other well-known low-rank approximation techniques comprise Factor Analysis, Independent Components Analysis, Multidimensional Scaling such as Fastmap or ISOMAP, or Locally Linear Embedding (LLE), which are all summarized in Tan, Steinbach, and Kumar (2005).

Amongst all possible rank k approximations, the approximation A_k calculated by SVD and PCA is the best approximation in the sense that $\| A - A_k \|_F$ is as small as possible (cf. Berry,

Drmac, & Jessup, 1999). In other words, SVD and PCA give the closest rank k approximation of a matrix, such that $|| A - A_k ||_F \leq || A - B_k ||_F$ where B_k is *any* matrix of rank k, and $|| . ||_F$ is the Frobenius norm, which is defined as

$$\left(\sum |a_{ij}|^2 \right)^{1/2} = || A ||_F$$

However, the main drawback of PCA and SVD refers to the interpretability of the transformed features. The resulting orthogonal matrix factors generated by the approximation usually do not allow for direct interpretations in terms of the original features because they contain positive *and* negative coefficients (Zhang, Berry, Lamb, & Samuel, 2009). In many application domains, a negative quantification of features is meaningless and the information about how much an original feature contributes in a low-rank approximation is lost. The presence of negative, meaningless components or factors may influence the entire result. This is especially important for applications where the original data matrix contains only positive entries, e.g., in text-mining applications, image classification, etc. If the factor matrices of the low-rank approximation were constrained to contain only positive or zero values, the original meaning of the data could be preserved better.

2.1. Non-Negative Matrix Factorization (NMF)

The NMF leads to special low-rank approximations which satisfy these non-negativity constraints. NMF requires that all entries in A, W and H are zero or positive. This makes the interpretation of the NMF factors much easier and enables NMF a non-subtractive combination of parts to form a whole (Lee & Seung, 1999). The NMF consists of reduced rank nonnegative factors $W \in \mathbb{R}^{m \times k}$ and $H \in \mathbb{R}^{k \times n}$ with $k \ll min\{m, n\}$ that approximate a matrix $A \in \mathbb{R}^{m \times n}$ by $A \approx WH$,

where the approximation WH has rank at most k. The nonlinear optimization problem underlying NMF can generally be stated as

$$\min_{W,H} f(W, H) = \min_{W,H} \frac{1}{2} || A - WH ||_F^2 \tag{1}$$

The Frobenius norm $|| . ||_F$ is commonly used to measure the error between the original data A and the approximation W, but other measures such as the Kullback-Leibler divergence are also possible (Lee & Seung, 2001). The error between A and WH is usually stored in a distance matrix $D = A - WH$ (cf. Figure 1). Unlike the SVD, the NMF is not unique, and convergence is not guaranteed for all NMF algorithms. If they converge, then usually to local minima only (potentially different ones for different algorithms). Nevertheless, the data compression achieved with only local minima has been shown to be of desirable quality for many data mining applications (Langville, Meyer, & Albright, 2006). Moreover, for some specific problem settings a smaller residual $D = A - WH$ (a smaller error) may not necessarily improve of the solution of the actual application (e.g., classification task) compared to a rather coarse approximation. However, as analyzed in Janecek and Gansterer (2010) a closer NMF approximation leads to qualitatively better classification results and turns out to achieve significantly more stable results.

NMF Initialization

Algorithms for computing NMF are iterative and require initialization of the factors W and H. NMF unavoidably converges to local minima, probably different ones for different initializations (cf. Boutsidis & Gallopoulos, 2008). Hence, random initialization makes the experiments unrepeatable since the solution to Equation 1 is not unique in this case. A proper non-random

Figure 1. Scheme of very coarse NMF approximation with very low rank k. Although k is significantly smaller than m and n, the typical structure of the original data matrix can be retained (note the three different groups of data objects in the left, middle, and right part of A)

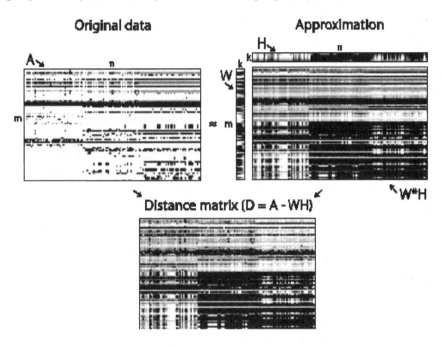

initialization can lead to faster error reduction and better overall error at convergence. Moreover, it makes the experiments repeatable. Although the benefits of good NMF initialization techniques are well known in the literature, most studies use random initialization (cf. Boutsidis & Gallopoulos, 2008). Since some initialization procedures can be rather costly in terms of runtime the trade-off between computational cost in the initialization step and the computational cost of the actual NMF algorithm need to be balanced carefully. In some situations, an expensive preprocessing step may overwhelm the cost savings in the subsequent NMF update steps.

General Structure of NMF

In the basic form of NMF (Figure 2), W and H are initialized randomly and the whole algorithm is repeated several times (*maxrepetition*). In each repetition, NMF update steps are processed until a maximum number of iterations is reached (*maxiter*). These update steps are algorithm specific and differ from one NMF variant to the other. Termination criteria: If the approximation error drops below a pre-defined threshold, or if the shift between two iterations is very small, the algorithm might stop before all iterations are processed.

Figure 2. General structure of NMF algorithms

1: given matrix $A \in \mathbb{R}^{m \times n}$ and $k \ll min\{m, n\}$:
2: **for** $rep = 1$ to *maxrepetition* **do**
3: $\quad W = \text{rand}(m, k)$;
4: $\quad (H = \text{rand}(k, n);)$
5: $\quad$ **for** $i = 1$ to *maxiter* **do**
6: $\quad\quad$ perform algorithm specific NMF update steps
7: $\quad\quad$ check termination criterion
8: $\quad$ **end for**
9: **end for**

Multiplicative Update (MU) Algorithm

To give an example of the update steps for a specific NMF algorithm we provide the update steps for the MU algorithm in Figure 3. MU is one of the two original NMF algorithms presented in Lee and Seung (1999) and still one of the fastest NMF algorithms per iteration. The update steps are based on the mean squared error objective function and consist of multiplying the current factors by a measure of the quality of the current approximation. The divisions in Figure 3 are to be performed *element-wise*. ε is used to avoid division by zero $\left(\varepsilon \approx 10^{-9} \right)$.

3. SWARM INTELLIGENCE OPTIMIZATION

Optimization techniques inspired by swarm intelligence (SI) have become increasingly popular and benefit from their robustness and flexibility (Chiong, 2009). Swarm intelligence is characterized by a decentralized design paradigm that mimics the behavior of swarms of social insects, flocks of birds, or schools of fish. Optimization techniques inspired by swarm intelligence have shown to be able to successfully deal with increasingly complex problems (Blackwell, 2007). In this article we use five different optimization algorithms. Particle Swarm Optimization (PSO) (Kennedy & Eberhart, 1995) is a classical swarm intelligence algorithm, while Fish School Search (FSS) (Bastos Filho et al., 2009) and Fireworks Algorithm (FWA) (Tan & Zhu, 2010) are two recently developed swarm intelligence methods. These three algorithms are compared to a Genetic Algorithm (GA) (Haupt & Haupt, 2005), a classical evolutionary algorithm, and Differential Evolution (DE) (Price, Storn, & Lampinen, 2005), which shares some features with swarm intelligence but can also be considered as an evolutionary algorithm. Since PSO, GA and DE

Figure 3. Update steps of the multiplicative update algorithm

$$1: \ H = H \,.* (W^{\top} A) \,./(W^{\top} W H + \varepsilon);$$
$$2: \ W = W \,.* (A H^{\top}) \,./(W H H^{\top} + \varepsilon);$$

are well known optimization techniques we will not summarize them here; instead the interested reader is referred to the references given.

Fish School Search is a recently developed swarm intelligence algorithm (Figure 4) that mimics the movements of schools of fish. The main operators are *feeding* (fish can gain/lose weight, depending on the region they swim in) and *swimming* (there are three different swimming movements).

The Fireworks Algorithm (Figure 5) is a novel swarm intelligence algorithm that is inspired by observing fireworks explosion. Two different types of explosion (search) processes are used in order to ensure diversity of resulting sparks, which are similar to particles in PSO or fish in FSS.

4. IMPROVING NMF WITH SWARM INTELLIGENCE OPTIMIZATION

Before describing our two optimization strategies for NMF based on swarm intelligence, we discuss some properties of the Frobenius norm (cf. Berry, Drmac, & Jessup, 1999). We use the Frobenius norm (Equation 1) as NMF objective function (i.e., to measure the error between A and WH) because it offers some properties that are beneficial for combining NMF and optimization algorithms. The following statements about the Frobenius norm are valid for any real matrix. However, in the following we assume that D refers to a distance matrix storing the distance (error of the approximation) between the original data and the approximation, $D = A - WH$. The

Figure 4. Pseudo code of the fish school search algorithm

1: Randomly initialize locations (x_i) of all fish, set all weights (w_i) to 1;

2: **repeat**

3:     *Swimming 1:* Compute random individual movement for each fish;

4:     *Feeding:* update weights for all fish based on new locations;

5:     *Swimming 2:* Collective instinctive movement towards overall direction;

6:     *Swimming 3:* Collective volitive movement dilation/contraction;

7: **until** termination (time, max. number of fitness evals., convergence, ...)

Figure 5. Pseudo code of the fireworks algorithm

1: Randomly initialize locations (x_i) of n fireworks;

2: **repeat**

3:     Set off n fireworks respectively at the n locations

4:     Calculate number $\hat{s}_i$ and location of sparks for each x_i

5:     Generate $\hat{m}$ specific sparks, each for a randomly selected firework

6:     Keep best location and select $n - 1$ locations for next iteration

7: **until** termination (time, max. number of fitness evals., convergence, ...)

Frobenius norm of a matrix $D \in \mathbb{R}^{m \times n}$ is defined as

$$\| D \|_F = \left(\sum_{i=1}^{min(m,n)} \sigma_i \right)^{1/2} = \left(\sum_{i=1}^{m} \sum_{j=1}^{n} | \mathbf{d}_{ij} |^2 \right)^{1/2} \qquad (2)$$

where σ_i are the singular values of D, and $\mathbf{d}_{ij}$ is the element in the ith row and j^{th} column of D. The Frobenius norm can also be computed row wise or column wise. The *row wise* calculation is

$$\| D \|_F^{RW} = \left(\sum_{i=1}^{m} | \mathbf{d}_i^r |^2 \right)^{1/2} \qquad (3)$$

where $| \mathbf{d}_i^r |$ is the norm of the ith row vector of D, i.e.,

$$| \mathbf{d}_i^r | = (\sum_{j=1}^{n} |r_j^i|^2)^{1/2}$$

and r_j^i is the jth element in row i. The *column wise* calculation is

$$\| D \|_F^{CW} = \left(\sum_{j=1}^{n} | \mathbf{d}_j^c |^2 \right)^{1/2} \qquad (4)$$

with $| \mathbf{d}_j^c |$ being the norm of the jth column vector of D, i.e.,

$$| \mathbf{d}_j^c | = (\sum_{i=1}^{m} |c_i^j|^2)^{1/2}$$

and c_i^j being the ith element in column j. Obviously, a reduction of the Frobenius norm of any row or any column of D leads to a reduction of the total Frobenius norm $\| D \|_F$.

In the following we exploit these properties of the Frobenius norm for the proposed NMF optimization strategies. While strategy 1 aims at finding heuristically optimal starting points for the NMF factors, strategy 2 aims at iteratively improving the quality of NMF during the first iterations. All meta-heuristics mentioned in Section 3 can be used within both strategies. Before discussing the optimization strategies we illustrate the basic optimization procedure for a specific row (row *l*) of *W* in Figure 6. This procedure is similar for both optimization strategies.

Parameters. Global parameters used for all optimization algorithms are upper/lower bound of the search space and the initialization, the number of particles (chromosomes, fish,...), and maximum number of fitness evaluations. Parameter settings are discussed in Sections 5. For all meta-heuristics, the problem dimension is equal to the rank k of the NMF, i.e., if, for example, k = 10, a row/column vector with 10 continuous entries is returned by the optimization algorithms.

4.1. Optimization Strategy 1: Initialization

The goal of this optimization strategy is to find heuristically optimal starting points for the rows of *W* and the columns of *H* respectively, i.e., prior to the factorization process. Figure 7 shows the pseudo code for the initialization procedure. In the beginning, *H0* needs to be initialized randomly using a non-negative lower bound (preferably 0) for the initialization. In the first loop, *W* is initialized row wise, i.e., row $\mathbf{w}_i^r$ is optimized in order to minimize the Frobenius norm of the ith row $\mathbf{d}_i^r$ of *D*, which is defined as $\mathbf{d}_i^r = \mathbf{a}_i^r - \mathbf{w}_i^r H0$. Since the optimization of any row of *W* is independent to the optimization of any other row of *W*, all $\mathbf{w}_i^r$ can be optimized concurrently. In the second loop, the columns of *H* are initialized using on the previously computed and already optimized rows of *W*, which need to be gathered beforehand (in line 7 of the

Figure 6. Illustration of the optimization process for row l of the NMF factor W. The lth row of A (a_l^r) and all columns of H0 are the input for the optimization algorithms. The output is a row-vector $\mathbf{w}_l^r$ (the lth row of W) which minimizes the norm of $\mathbf{d}_l^r$, the lth row of the distance matrix D. The norm of $\mathbf{d}_l^r$ is the fitness function for the optimization algorithms (minimization problem)

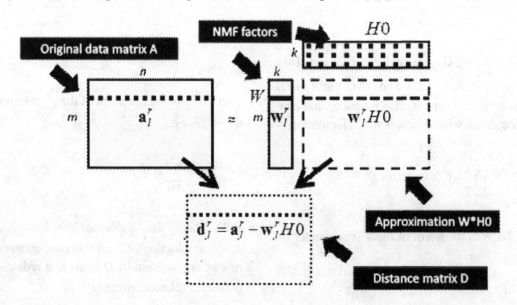

Figure 7. Pseudo code for the initialization procedure for NMF factors W and H. The two for-loops in lines 4 and 10 can be executed concurrently. SIO = swarm intelligence optimization

```
1:  Given matrix A ∈ ℝ^{m×n} and k ≪ min{m,n};
2:  H0 = rand(k,n);
3:  % Compute in parallel
4:  for i = 1 to m do
5:      Use SIO to find w_i^r that minimizes ||a_i^r − w_i^r H0||_F, (min ||.||_F of row i of D);
6:  end for;
7:  % Gather
8:  W = [w_1^r; … ; w_m^r];
9:  % Compute in parallel
10: for j = 1 to n do
11:     Use SIO to find h_j^c that minimizes ||a_j^c − W h_j^c||_F, (min ||.||_F of col j of D);
12: end for
13: % Gather
14: H = [h_1^c, … , h_n^c];
```

algorithm). H is initialized column wise, i.e., column h_j^c is optimized in order to minimize the Frobenius norm of the jth column d_j^c of D, which is defined as $d_j^c = a_j^c − W h_j^c$. The optimization of the columns of H can be performed concurrently as well.

4.2. Optimization Strategy 2: Iterative Optimization

The second optimization strategy aims at iteratively optimizing the NMF factors W and H during the first iterations of the NMF. Compared to the first strategy not all rows of W and all columns of H are optimized – instead the optimization is only performed on selected rows/columns. In order to improve the approximation as fast as possible we identify rows of D with highest norm (the approximation of this row is worse than for other rows of D) and optimize the corresponding rows of W. The same procedure is used to identify the columns of H that should be optimized. Our experiments showed that not all NMF algorithms are suited for this iterative optimization procedure. For many NMF algorithms there was no improvement with respect to the convergence or a reduction of the overall error after a fixed number of iterations. However, for the multiplicative update (MU) algorithm – which is one of the most widely used NMF algorithms – this strategy is able to improve the quality of the factorization. Hence, Figure 8 shows the pseudo code for the iterative optimization of the NMF factors during the first iterations using the update steps of the MU algorithm described in Section 2.1. As shown in Section 6, this update strategy is able to significantly reduce the approximation error per iteration for the MU algorithm. Due to the relatively high computational cost of the meta-heuristics the optimization procedure is only applied in the first m iterations and only on c selected rows/columns of the NMF factors. Similar to strategy one the optimization of all rows of W are independent from each other (identical for columns of H), which allows for a parallel implementation of the proposed method. In the following we describe the variables and functions (for updating rows of W) of Figure 8. Updating columns of H is similar to updating the rows of W.

- m : The number of iterations in which the optimization using meta-heuristics is applied

- c : The number of rows and/or columns that are optimized in the current iteration.

- Δc : The value of c is decreased by Δc in each iteration. $\Delta c = round(c_{initial} / m)$

- $[Val, IX\_W] = sort(norm(\mathbf{d}_i^r), 'descend')$: Returns the values Val and the corresponding indices (IX_W) of the norm of all row vectors $\mathbf{d}_i^r$ of D in descending order.

- $IX\_W = IX\_W(1:c)$: Returns only the first c elements of the vector IX_W

- minimize $\| \mathbf{a}_i^r - \mathbf{w}_i^r H \|_F$: See Figure 6 and optimization strategy 1

Figure 8. Pseudo code for the iterative optimization for the multiplicative update algorithm. SIO = swarm intelligence optimization.

```
1: for iter = 1 to maxiter do
2:     % perform MU specific update steps
3:     W = W · (AHᵀ)./(WHHᵀ + ε);
4:     H = H · (WᵀA)./(WᵀWH + ε);
5:     if (iter < m) then
6:         % Update rows of W ++++++++++++++++++++++++++++++++++++++++++++
7:             dᵢʳ is the iᵗʰ row vector of D = A − WH;
8:             [Val, IX_W]= sort(norm(dᵢʳ),' descend');
9:             IX_W = IX_W(1 : c);
10:            % Compute in parallel
11:            ∀i ∈ IX_W:
12:                Use SIO to find wᵢʳ that minimizes ||aᵢʳ − wᵢʳH0||_F;
13:            % Gather
14:            W = [w₁ʳ; . . . ; wₘʳ];
15:        % Update columns of H ++++++++++++++++++++++++++++++++++++++++++++
16:            dⱼᶜ is the jᵗʰ column vector of D = A − WH;
17:            [Val, IX_H] = sort(norm(dⱼᶜ),' descend');
18:            IX_H = IX_H(1 : c);
19:            % Compute in parallel
20:            ∀j ∈ IX_H:
21:                Use SIO to find hⱼᶜ that minimizes ||aⱼᶜ − Whⱼᶜ||_F;
22:            % Gather
23:            H = [h₁ᶜ, . . . , hₙᶜ];
24:            c = c − Δc;
25:    end if
26: end for
```

4.3. Using NMF for Classification Problems

As already mentioned before, we also investigate the performance of NMF when applied for classification tasks. In this article, we use two different classification methods for evaluating the classification accuracy of NMF based on the optimization strategies discussed in Sections 4.1 and 4.2. Both classification methods have shown to work well for different application areas (Janecek, 2010).

Static Classification

In the first approach we analyze the classification accuracy achieved with the basis vectors (i.e., features in W). In this setting the NMF needs to be computed on the complete dataset (training and test data) which makes this technique only applicable on test data that is already available before the approximation/classification. However, the advantage of this approach is that any freely chosen classification method can be applied on the basis features.

If the original data matrix $A \in \mathbb{R}^{m \times n}$ is an instance $\times$ feature matrix, then the NMF factor W is a $m \times k$ matrix, where every instance is described by k basis *features*, i.e., every column of W corresponds to a basis feature. Note that this setup is different to the one discussed at the beginning of Section 2. By applying a classification algorithm on the rows of W instead on the rows of A we can significantly reduce the dimension of the classification problem and thus decrease the computational cost for both, building the classification model and testing new data.

Dynamic Classification

The second approach can be applied dynamically to new data. Here the factorization of the data (NMF) and the classification process are separated from each other (i.e., the NMF is performed on labeled training data – the unlabeled test data does not have to be available at the time of performing the NMF). This approach is called *NMF-LSI* and is based on an adaptation of latent semantic indexing which is a variant of the well-known vector space model.

A vector space model (VSM) (Raghavan & Wong, 1999) is a widely used algebraic model for representing objects as vectors in a potentially very high dimensional metric vector space. The distance of a query vector $\mathbf{q}$ to all objects in a given *feature* $\times$ *instance* matrix A are usually measured in terms of the cosines of the angles between $\mathbf{q}$ and the columns of A such that

$$cos\varphi_i = \frac{e_i^\top A^\top q}{\| A e_i \|_2 \| q \|_2}$$

Latent semantic indexing (LSI) (Berry, Drmac, & Jessup, 1999) is a variant of the basic VSM that replaces the original matrix A with a low-rank approximation A_k of A. In the standard version of LSI the SVD (Section 2) is used to construct A_k and $cos\varphi_i$ can be approximated as

$$cos\varphi_i \approx \frac{e_i^\top V_k \Sigma_k U_k^\top q}{\| U_k \Sigma_k V_k^\top e_i \|_2 \| q \|_2}$$

LSI has computational advantages resulting in lower storage and computational cost, and often gives a cleaner and more efficient representation of the (latent) relationship between data elements.

In NMF-LSI, the approximation within LSI can be replaced with other approximations. Instead of using the truncated SVD $\left(A_k := U_k \Sigma_k V_k^\top \right)$, we approximate A with $A_k := W_k H_k$ (the NMF). When using NMF, the value of k must be fixed prior to the approximation. The cosine of the angle between $\mathbf{q}$ and the ith column of A can then be approximated as

$$cos\varphi_i \approx \frac{e_i^\top H_k^\top W_k^\top q}{\| W_k H_k e_i \|_2 \| q \|_2}$$

In order to save computational cost, the left term in the numerator $\left(e_i^\top H_k^\top\right)$ and the left part of the denominator $\left(\| W_k H_k e_i \|_2\right)$ can be computed a priori. In all three methods (VSM and both LSI variants) a query instance **q** is assigned to the same class as the majority of its k-closest (in terms of cosine similarity) instances in A.

5. SETUP

Software

All software is written in Matlab. We used only publicly available NMF implementations: Multiplicative Update (MU, Matlab's Statistics Toolbox since v6.2, *nnmf()*). ALS using Projected Gradient (ALSPG) (Lin, 2007), and BayesNMF and FastNMF (Schmidt & Laurberg, 2008). Matlab code for NNDSVD (Section 1.1) is also publicly available (cf. Boutsidis & Gallopoulos, 2008). Codes for PSO and DE were adapted from Pedersen (2010), and code for GA from the appendix of Haupt and Haupt (2005). For FWA we used the same implementation as in the introductory paper Tan and Zhu (2010), and FSS was self-implemented following the algorithm provided in Bastos Filho et al. (2009).

Hardware

All experiments were performed on a SUN FIRE X4600 M2 with eight AMD Opteron quad-core processors (32 cores overall) with 3.2 GHz, 2MB L3 cache, and 32GB of main memory (DDR-II 666).

Parallel Implementation

We implemented parallel variants of the optimization algorithms exploiting Matlab's parallel computing potential. Matlab's Distributed Computing Server (which requires a separate license) allows for parallelizing the optimization process over a large number (currently up to 64) of workers (threads). These workers can be nodes in multi-core computers, GPUs, or a node in a cluster of simple desktop PCs. Matlab's Parallel Computing Toolbox (which is included in the basic version of Matlab) allows running up to eight workers concurrently, but is limited to local workers, i.e., nodes on a multi-core machine or local GPUs, but no cluster support.

Parameter Setup

The dimension of the optimization problem is always identical to the rank k of the NMF (cf. Section 4). The upper/lower bound of the search space was set to the interval $[0, (4 * max(A))]$ and upper/lower bound of the initialization to $[0, max(A)]$. In order to achieve fair results which are not biased due to excessive parameter tuning we used the same parameter settings for all data sets. These parameter settings were found by running a self-written benchmark program that tested several parameter combinations on randomly generated data. For some optimization strategies (PSO, FSS and FWA) the recommended parameter settings from the literature worked fine. However, for GA and DE the parameter settings that were used in most studies in the literature did not perform very well. For GA we found that a very aggressive (high) mutation rate highly improved the results. For DE we observed a similar behavior and found that the maximum crossover probability (1) achieved the best results. For all experiments in this paper, the following parameter settings were used:

- **GA:** Mutation rate of 0.5; selection rate of 0.65
- **PSO:** (G_{best} topology) following Bratton and Kennedy (2007) $\omega = 0.8$, and $c_1 = c_2 = 2.05$
- **DE:** Crossover probability (pc) set to upper limit 1
- **FSS:** $step_{ind\_initial} = 1$, $step_{ind\_final} = 0.001$, $W_{scale} = 10$
- **FWA:** Number of sons (*sonnum*) set to 10

Data Sets

We used three different data sets to evaluate our methods. *DS-RAND* is a randomly created, fully dense 100 x 100 matrix which is used in order to provide unbiased results. To evaluate the proposed methods in a classification context we further used two data sets from the area of email classification (spam/phishing detection). Data set *DS-SPAM1* consists of 3000 e-mail messages described by 133 features, divided into three groups: spam, phishing and legitimate email. An exact description of this data set can be found in Janecek and Gansterer (2010). Data set *DS-SPAM2* is the spambase data set taken from Kjellerstrand (2011) which consists

of 1813 spam and 2788 non-spam messages. DS-SPAM1 represents a ternary classification problem; DS-SPAM2 represents a typical binary classification problem.

6. EXPERIMENTAL EVALUATION

The evaluation is split up into two parts. First we evaluate the two optimization strategies proposed in Section 4.1 and Section 4.2, then we evaluate the quality of NMF in a classification context.

6.1. Evaluation of Optimization Strategy 1

Initialization

Before evaluating the improvement of the NMF approximation quality as such, we first measure the initial error after initializing W and H *(before running the NMF algorithm)*. Figure 9 and Figure 10 show the average approximation error (i.e., Frobenius norm / fitness) per row (left) and per column (right) for data set DS-RAND.

The figures on the left side show the *average (mean)* approximation error per row after initial-

Figure 9. Left hand-side: average approximation error per row (after initializing rows of W). Right hand-side: average approximation error per column (after initializing of H). NMF rank k = 5. Legends are ordered according to approximation error (top = worst, bottom = best)

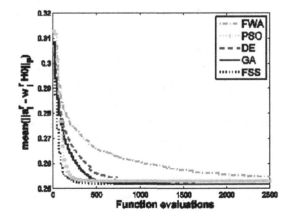
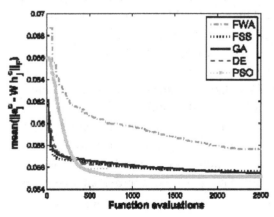

Figure 10. Similar information as for Figure 9, but for NMF rank k = 30

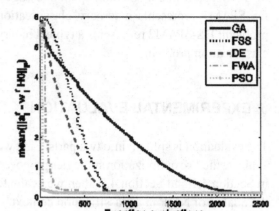
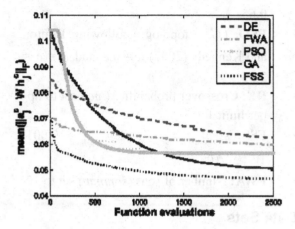

izing the rows of W (first loop in Figure 7). The figures on the right side show the average (mean) approximation error per column after initializing the columns of H (second loop in Figure 7). The legends are ordered according to the average approximation error achieved after the maximum number of function evaluations for each figure (top = worst, bottom = best). When the NMF rank k is small (Figure 9, k−5) all optimization algorithms except FWA achieve similar results. Except FWA, all optimization algorithms quickly converge to a good result. With increasing complexity (i.e., increasing rank k) FWA clearly improves its results, as shown in Figure 10. The gap between the optimization algorithms is much bigger for larger rank k. Note that GA needs more than 2000 evaluations to achieve a low approximation error for initializing the rows of W. When initializing the columns of H, PSO and GA suffer from their high approximation error during the first iterations, which is caused by the relatively sparse factor matrix W for PSO and GA. Although PSO is able to reduce the approximation error significantly during the first 500 iterations, FSS and GA achieve slightly better final results. Generally, FSS achieves the best approximation accuracy after the initialization procedure for large k. However, as shown later the initial approximation error is not necessarily an indicator for the approximation

quality of NMF or the resulting classification accuracy.

Runtime Performance

When parallelizing a sequential algorithm over p processors the speed-up indicates how much the parallel algorithm can perform specific tasks faster than the sequential algorithm. Speed-up is defined as $S_p = ET_{sequential} \, / \, ET_{parallel}$, where ET is the execution time. A linear speed-up is achieved when S_p is equal to p. Efficiency is another metric that estimates how well-utilized the processors are in solving the problem, compared to the cost of communication and synchronization. Efficiency is defined as $E_p = S_p \, / \, p$. For algorithms with linear speed-up the efficiency is 1, for algorithms with lower speed-up ratio it is between 0 and 1.

Figure 11 shows the runtime behavior for optimization strategy 1 with increasing number of Matlab workers. Runtimes are shown for the FSS optimization algorithm – however, all optimization algorithms have rather similar runtimes. Due to license limitations we only had Matlab's Parallel Computing Toolbox available which is limited to 8 workers (cf. Section 5). We measured runtimes and speed-up for up to 8 workers (average effi-

Figure 11. Runtime and speed-up measurement/estimation for DS-RAND using 1500 function evaluations per row/column for k= 5. As a reference, NNDSVD needs about 0.16 seconds for k=5. This indicates that if the number of workers is larger than 12, the proposed optimization strategy is faster than NNDSVD.

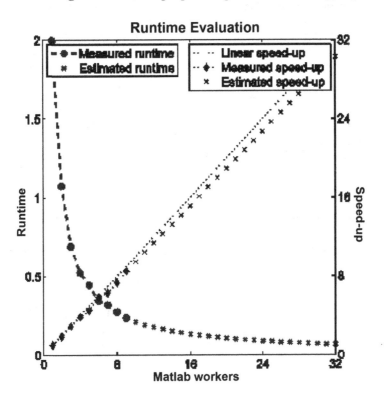

ciency of about 0.95) and estimated the behavior of speed-up and runtime for a larger number of workers (based on this efficiency). Upgrading to Matlab's Distributed Computing Server is possible without any code-changes and thus only a license issue. When using eight workers, the NNDSVD initialization (the best NMF initialization strategy from the literature, Section 1.1) is a bit faster, but estimation shows that the proposed initialization strategy is faster when 12 or more workers are used. NNDSVD is already optimized and cannot be parallelized further in its current implementation.

Approximation Quality

For evaluating the approximation results achieved by NMF using the factors *W* and *H* initialized by the optimization algorithms, we compare our results to random initialization as well as to NNDSVD. Figure 12 shows the approximation error on the *y*-axis (log scale) after a given number of NMF iterations for four NMF algorithms using different initialization methods (for DS-RAND). The initialization methods in the legend are ordered (top = worst, bottom = best). Since the MU algorithm (A) has low cost per iteration but converges slowly, the first 100 iterations are shown (for all other algorithms the first 25 iterations are shown). For MU, all initialization variants achieve a smaller approximation error than random initialization. NNDSVD shows slightly better results than PSO and FWA, but GA, DE and especially FSS are able to achieve a smaller error per iteration than NNDSVD. For ALSPG (B), the new initialization strategy achieves better results than random initialization and also achieves a better approxima-

Figure 12. Approximation error archived by different NMF algorithms using different initialization variants (k=30, after 1500 fitness evaluations)

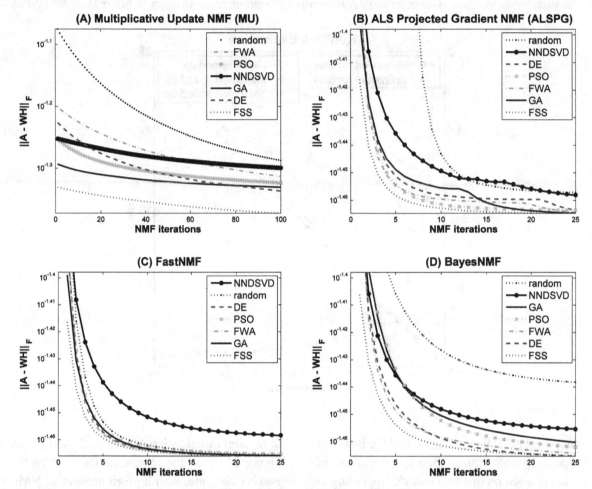

tion error than NNDSVD. This improvement is independent of the actual optimization algorithm. The same behavior can be seen for FastNMF (C) and BayesNMF (D). It has to be mentioned that FastNMF and BayesNMF were developed after the NNDSVD initialization. Surprisingly, when using FastNMF, NNDSVD achieves a lower approximation than random initialization. When comparing the different meta-heuristics, FSS achieves the best results amongst all optimization algorithms and achieves the closest approximation after 100 (MU) and 25 (ALSPG, FastNMF, BayesNMF) iterations, respectively. DE and GA follow with

a small gap since they are not as stable as FSS (i.e., they achieve good results for some, but not for all NMF algorithms.

6.2. Evaluation of Optimization Strategy 2

Figure 13 shows the convergence curves for the NMF approximation using optimization strategy 2 for different values of rank k (data set DS-RAND). Due to the relatively high computational cost of the meta-heuristics we applied our optimization procedure here only on the rows of

W, while the columns in H remained unchanged. Experiments showed that with this setting the loss in accuracy compared to optimizing both, W and H, is relatively small while the runtime can be increased significantly. m was set to 2 which indicates that the optimization is only applied in the first two iterations, and c was set to 20. As can be seen, the approximation error per iteration can be reduced when using optimization strategy 2. For small rank k (left side of Figure 13) the improvement is significant but decreases with increasing values of k (see right side of Figure

13). For larger k (larger than 10) the improvement over the basic MU is only marginal.

Runtime Performance

Figure 14 shows the reduction in runtime for different rank k when the same accuracy as for basic MU should be achieved. Runtimes are shown for a parallel implementation using 32 Matlab workers. Basic MU sets the baseline (1 = 100%), the runtimes of the optimization strategy 2 (using different optimization algorithms) are given as

Figure 13. Accuracy per Iteration when updating only the row of W, m=2, c=20. Left: k=2, right: k=5

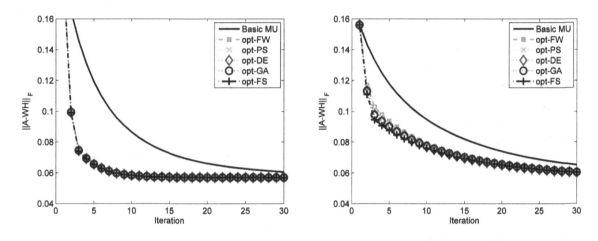

Figure 14. Proportional runtimes for achieving the same accuracy as basic MU after 30 iterations for different values of k when updating only the rows of W. (m=2, c=20)

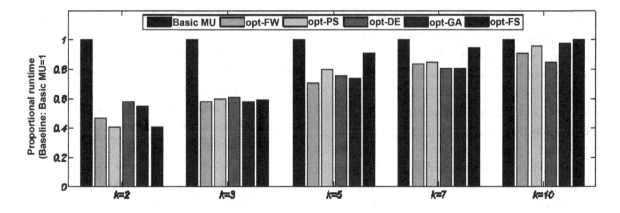

185

$t_{opt-XX} / t_{Basic\ MU}$. For example, for small rank k the runtime can often be reduced by more than 50%. With increasing rank k the runtime savings get smaller and are only marginal for $k=10$. For rank k larger than 12 the basic MU algorithm is faster than optimization strategy 2.

6.3. Evaluation of the Classification Accuracy

Since optimization strategy 1 (initialization, Sections 4.1 and 6.1) achieves a faster, closer, and more stable approximation as optimization strategy 2 (iterative update, Sections 4.2 and 6.2) we evaluate the classification accuracy for this strategy. In the following, we measure the quality of optimization strategy 1 as pre-processing step for the two classification approaches mentioned in Section 4.3. Within the static classification approach any machine learning algorithm can be used for classification, but the approximation used for reducing the dimensionality of the data set (SVD, PCA, NMF) needs to be applied on the complete data set. Contrary, the dynamic classification approach can be applied on the training data, the test data does not need to be available at the time of computing the approximation. However, this approach cannot be applied to all classification methods.

Static Classification

We used three classification algorithms from the freely available WEKA toolkit (Witten and Frank 2005) to compare the classification accuracies achieved with the NMF factor W based on different NMF initializations: A support vector machine (SVM) based on the sequential minimal optimization (SOM) algorithm using a polynomial kernel with an exponent of 1; a k-nearest neighbor (kNN) classifier; and a J4.8 decision tree based on the C4.5 decision tree algorithm. Results were achieved using a 10-fold cross-validation, i.e., by randomly partitioning the data sets into 10 subsamples and then iteratively using one 9 subsamples as training data and 1 for testing.

Table 1 shows the overall classification results achieved with data set DS-SPAM1 using three different values of rank k and the three different classification methods mentioned above. The overall classification accuracy is computed as the number of correct classified email messages divided by the total number of messages. The most-left column indicates the NMF algorithm and the second column the initialization strategy used for computing the NMF (RAND = random initialization). Note that the number of features is reduced to 30, 15 and 5, respectively, compared to 133. This reduction in the number of features significantly speeds up both, the process of building the classification model and the classification process itself. The best result for each NMF algorithm and each rank k is highlighted in bold letters. The proposed initialization strategies achieve better classification results as the state-of-the-art initialization method NNDSVD and significantly better results as random NMF initialization. Among the applied optimization algorithms there is not much difference, though FSS achieves a larger number of best results then the other algorithms. Results for J4.8 and kNN are very stable even for $k=5$ and are almost identical to the classification result achieved with all features. For SVM, the classification result tends to decrease with decreasing rank k. This behavior has been observed in another study (Janecek, Gansterer, Demel, & Ecker, 2008) where SVM has been applied on data sets from other dimensionality reduction methods (PCA). However, compared to NNDSVD and random initialization the proposed initialization methods achieve better results for all ranks of k. Comparing the different NMF algorithms it can be seen the MU achieves lower classification accuracy compared to ALSPG, FastNMF and BayesNMF.

Table 1. Classification results (static classification) for DS-SPAM1

NMF Alg	Init	J4.8 All features: 0,973			kNN(1) All features: 0,977			SVM (SMO) All features: 0,976		
		k = 30	k = 15	k = 5	k = 30	k = 15	k = 5	k = 30	k = 15	k = 5
ALSPG	DE	0,968	0,972	0,965	0,974	0,972	0,968	**0,973**	0,956	0,940
	FSS	0,961	0,972	0,967	0,971	0,972	**0,969**	**0,973**	0,954	0,939
	FWA	**0,973**	0,969	**0,970**	0,972	**0,973**	0,968	0,964	0,954	0,938
	GA	0,970	0,968	0,969	0,973	0,970	0,968	**0,973**	**0,957**	**0,947**
	PSO	0,971	0,972	0,969	**0,977**	0,971	0,968	0,972	0,954	0,937
	NNDSVD	0,963	**0,976**	0,964	0,969	0,972	0,968	0,966	0,952	0,938
	RAND	*0,943*	*0,938*	*0,935*	*0,952*	*0,940*	*0,938*	*0,948*	*0,942*	*0,913*
BAYES	DE	**0,971**	0,970	0,970	0,974	0,973	0,968	0,971	0,954	0,946
	FSS	0,966	**0,973**	**0,971**	**0,976**	0,971	0,969	**0,975**	0,953	**0,947**
	FWA	0,970	0,970	0,968	0,972	**0,974**	0,968	0,957	0,954	0,941
	GA	0,966	0,971	0,968	0,974	0,973	0,969	0,972	0,955	**0,947**
	PSO	0,968	0,967	0,969	0,970	0,971	**0,970**	0,966	**0,957**	0,937
	NNDSVD	0,968	0,972	0,968	0,970	0,973	0,969	0,966	0,952	0,947
	RAND	0,952	0,941	0,953	0,961	0,951	0,947	0,958	0,937	0,926
FAST	DE	0,966	0,969	0,969	**0,977**	0,973	0,968	0,970	0,955	0,946
	FSS	0,967	0,971	**0,970**	0,976	0,971	0,969	**0,975**	0,953	**0,947**
	FWA	**0,968**	0,970	0,969	0,971	**0,974**	0,968	0,957	0,954	0,941
	GA	0,966	0,965	0,968	0,973	0,971	0,969	0,973	0,955	**0,947**
	PSO	**0,968**	0,970	**0,970**	0,974	0,971	**0,970**	0,973	**0,956**	0,937
	NNDSVD	0,966	**0,973**	**0,970**	0,970	0,973	0,968	0,966	0,952	0,939
	RAND	0,954	0,949	0,937	0,958	0,951	0,941	0,957	0,935	0,917
MU	DE	0,955	0,952	0,965	0,966	0,959	0,968	0,962	0,953	0,940
	FSS	**0,965**	0,960	0,967	0,967	0,964	**0,969**	**0,966**	0,952	0,939
	FWA	0,949	0,956	**0,970**	0,964	0,966	0,968	0,959	**0,955**	0,938
	GA	0,954	0,961	0,969	0,966	0,966	0,968	0,961	0,944	**0,947**
	PSO	0,958	0,939	0,969	0,949	0,946	0,968	0,953	0,940	0,937
	NNDSVD	0,964	**0,967**	0,964	**0,972**	**0,973**	0,968	0,963	0,954	0,938
	RAND	0,941	0,937	0,947	0,948	0,941	0,951	0,951	0,930	0,927

Table 2 shows the static classification results achieved with data set DS-SPAM2. Results are shown for the FastNMF, which achieved the most stable results of all NMF algorithms for this data set. Again, the proposed initialization strategy again achieves better results as NNDSVD and random initialization. Compared to DS-SPAM1, the results for this data set tend to decrease with decreasing rank k. This indicates that it is important to find a good trade-off between classification accuracy and computational cost.

Table 2. Classification results (static classification) for DS-SPAM2 (FastNMF)

NMF Alg	Init	J4.8 All features: 0,921			kNN(1) All features: 0,907			SVM (SMO) All features: 0,904		
		$k = 30$	$k = 15$	$k = 5$	$k = 30$	$k = 15$	$k = 5$	$k = 30$	$k = 15$	$k = 5$
FAST	DE	0,918	0,893	0,863	**0,902**	0,880	0,821	**0,905**	0,865	0,798
	FSS	0,920	**0,920**	0,773	0,895	0,889	0,826	0,894	0,880	0,773
	FWA	0,916	0,916	0,864	0,887	**0,898**	0,797	0,893	0,885	0,757
	GA	0,918	0,914	0,865	0,889	0,896	0,827	0,896	**0,891**	0,778
	PSO	**0,921**	0,911	**0,878**	0,895	0,892	**0,850**	0,896	0,881	**0,827**
	NNDSVD	0,919	0,911	0,811	0,895	0,894	0,816	0,894	0,882	0,766
	RAND	0,907	0,908	0,813	0,885	0,886	0,803	0,887	0,864	0,752

Dynamic Classification

Table 3 shows the classification results achieved with the dynamic classification approach described in Section 4.3 for DS-SPAM1. In general, the classification accuracies achieved for data set DS-SPAM2 using the dynamic classification approach are rather similar to the results for DS-SPAM1 shown in Table 3. The baseline to which the NMF-LSI variants are compared are given by a standard LSI classification using SVD as approximation algorithm (Section 4.3). A basic vector space model achieves a classification accuracy of 0.911, while LSI achieves 0.911, 0.914 and 0.887, respectively, for rank k set to 30, 15 and 5. Similar to Table 2 (DS-SPAM2) the results are sensible with respect to the value of rank k. For very small values of k (5) the classification results generally tend to decrease. Overall, the initialization strategy based on meta-heuristics achieve much better classification accuracy as NNDSVD and random initialization, and also outperform basic LSI in many cases. The best results are again highlighted in bold letters. Especially GA and FWA achieve good classification results.

7. CONCLUSION

In this article we presented two new optimization strategies for improving the NMF using optimization algorithms based on swarm intelligence. While strategy one uses swarm intelligence algorithms to initialize the factors W and H prior to the factorization process of NMF, the second strategy aims at iteratively improving the approximation quality of NMF during the first iterations of the factorization. Overall, five different optimization algorithms were used for improving NMF: Particle Swarm Optimization (PSO), Genetic Algorithms (GA), Fish School Search (FSS), Differential Evolution (DE), and Fireworks Algorithm (FWA).

Both optimization strategies allow for efficiently computing the optimization of single rows of W and/or single columns of H in parallel. The achieved results are evaluated in terms of accuracy per runtime and per iteration, final accuracy after a given number of NMF iterations, and in terms of the classification accuracy achieved with the reduced NMF factors when being applied for machine learning applications. Especially the initialization strategy (optimization strategy 1) is able to significantly improve the approximation results of NMF compared to random initialization

Table 3. Dynamic classification using DS-SPAM1. Basic vector space model (all features): 0,911

Baseline	LSI	0,911	0,914	0,887
NMF Alg	Init	k = 30	k = 15	k = 05
ALSPG	DE	0,911	0,898	0,889
	FSS	**0,943**	0,899	0,877
	FWA	0,930	**0,914**	0,883
	GA	0,927	0,901	**0,896**
	PSO	0,918	0,889	0,885
	NNDSVD	0,914	0,911	0,840
	RAND	0,901	0,886	0,874
BAYES	DE	0,911	0,906	0,888
	FSS	0,926	0,897	0,879
	FWA	0,914	0,911	**0,891**
	GA	**0,930**	**0,916**	0,875
	PSO	0,922	0,915	0,848
	NNDSVD	0,904	0,913	0,846
	RAND	0,898	0,896	0,854
FAST	DE	0,912	0,895	0,888
	FSS	0,926	0,897	0,879
	FWA	0,913	0,912	**0,891**
	GA	**0,927**	**0,914**	0,875
	PSO	0,923	**0,914**	0,847
	NNDSVD	0,911	0,913	0,846
	RAND	0,898	0,899	0,838
MU	DE	0,893	0,897	0,834
	FSS	0,892	0,882	0,807
	FWA	**0,913**	0,882	**0,843**
	GA	0,899	0,899	0,795
	PSO	0,922	0,900	0,812
	NNDSVD	0,906	**0,908**	0,795
	RAND	0,876	0,889	0,817

and state-of-the-art methods. Among the different optimization algorithms, the recently developed fish school search algorithm achieves slightly better results than the other heuristics. The iterative strategy (optimization strategy 2) can improve one of the basic NMF algorithms (the multiplicative update strategy) for very small rank k and can thus be used if a rough and very fast approximation method is needed. Moreover, the NMF subsets achieved with optimization strategy 1 have shown to clearly improve the classification accuracy of NMF compared to state-of-the-art initialization strategies, and also achieve better results as feature subsets computed with other low-approximation techniques.

Future Work

Our investigations provide several important and interesting directions for future work. First of all, we will set the focus on developing optimization strategies that update the factor matrices W and H concurrently instead of applying an alternating update fashion where one factor is fixed and the other one is optimized. Moreover, we will apply the optimization strategies on NMF problems were sparseness constraints are enforced, i.e., the optimization strategies are enforced to compute solutions with a certain percentage of zero values. We also plan to use different NMF optimization functions (not based on the Frobenius norm) for our optimization methods and several recently developed NMF algorithms (HALS, multilayer NMF, etc.).

ACKNOWLEDGMENT

This work was supported by National Natural Science Foundation of China (NSFC), Grant No. 60875080 and No. 61170057. Andreas wants to thank the *Erasmus Mundus External Coop. Window*, Lot 14 (2009-1650/001-001-ECW).

REFERENCES

Bastos Filho, C. J. A., de Lima Neto, F. B., Lins, A. J. C. C., Nascimento, A. I. S., & Lima, M. P. (2009). Fish school search. R. Chiong (Ed.), *Nature-inspired algorithms for optimisation* (Vol. 193, pp. 261-277). Berlin, Germany: Springer-Verlag.

Berry, M. W. (1992). Large scale singular value computations. *The International Journal of Supercomputer Applications*, 6, 13–49.

Berry, M. W., Browne, M., Langville, A., Pauca, V., & Plemmons, R. (2007). Algorithms and applications for approximate nonnegative matrix factorization. *Computational Statistics & Data Analysis*, 52(1), 155–173. doi:10.1016/j.csda.2006.11.006

Berry, M. W., Drmac, Z., & Jessup, E. R. (1999). Matrices, vector spaces, and information retrieval. *SIAM Review*, 41(2), 335–362. doi:10.1137/S0036144598347035

Blackwell, T. (2007). Particle swarm optimization in dynamic environments. *Evolutionary Computation in Dynamic and Uncertain Environments*, 1, 29–49. doi:10.1007/978-3-540-49774-5_2

Boutsidis, C., & Gallopoulos, E. (2008). SVD based initialization: A head start for nonnegative matrix factorization. *Pattern Recognition*, 41(4), 1350–1362. doi:10.1016/j.patcog.2007.09.010

Bratton, D., & Kennedy, J. (2007). Defining a standard for particle swarm optimization. In *Proceedings of the IEEE Swarm Intelligence Symposium* (pp. 120-127).

Chiong, R. (2009). *Nature-inspired algorithms for optimisation*. New York, NY: Springer.

Haupt, R. L., & Haupt, S. E. (2005). *Practical genetic algorithms* (2nd ed.). New York, NY: John Wiley & Sons.

Janecek, A. (2010). *Efficient feature reduction and classification methods: Applications in drug discovery and email categorization*. Vienna, Austria: Department of Computer Science, University of Vienna.

Janecek, A., & Gansterer, W. N. (2010). Utilizing nonnegative matrix factorization for e-mail classification problems. In Berry, M. W., & Kogan, J. (Eds.), *Survey of text mining III: Application and theory* (pp. 57–80). New York, NY: John Wiley & Sons.

Janecek, A., Gansterer, W. N., Demel, M., & Ecker, G. (2008). On the relationship between feature selection and classification accuracy. *Journal of Machine Learning Research, 4*, 90–105.

Janecek, A., S. Schulze-Grotthoff, et al. (2011). libNMF - A library for nonnegative matrix factorizatrion. *Computing and Informatics, 22*.

Janecek, A., & Tan, Y. (2011a). Iterative improvement of the multiplicative update NMF algorithm using nature-inspired optimization. In *Proceedings of the 7th International Conference on Natural Computation* (pp. 1668-1672).

Janecek, A., & Tan, Y. (2011b). Using population based algorithms for initializing nonnegative matrix factorization. In Y. Tan, Y. Shi, Y. Chai, & G. Wang (Eds.), *Proceedings of the Second International Conference on Advances in Swarm Intelligence* (LNCS 6729, pp. 307-316).

Jolliffe, I. T. (2002). *Principal component analysis.* New York, NY: Springer.

Kennedy, J., & Eberhart, R. C. (1995). Particle swarm optimization. In *Proceedings of the IEEE International Conference on Neural Networks* (Vol. 4, pp. 1942-1948).

Kennedy, J., Eberhart, R. C., & Shi, Y. (2001). *Swarm intelligence.* San Francisco, CA: Morgan Kaufmann.

Kim, H., & Park, H. (2008). Nonnegative matrix factorization based on alternating nonnegativity constrained least squares and active set method. *SIAM Journal on Matrix Analysis and Applications, 30*, 713–730. doi:10.1137/07069239X

Kjellerstrand, H. (2011). *hakanks hemsida.* Retrieved from http://www.hakank.org/weka/

Langville, A. N., Meyer, C. D., & Albright, R. (2006). Initializations for the nonnegative matrix factorization. In *Proceedings of the 12th ACM International Conference on Knowledge Discovery and Data Mining.*

Lee, D. D., & Seung, H. S. (1999). Learning parts of objects by non-negative matrix factorization. *Nature, 401*(6755), 788–791. doi:10.1038/44565

Lee, D. D., & Seung, H. S. (2001). Algorithms for non-negative matrix factorization. *Advances in Neural Information Processing Systems, 13*, 556–562.

Lin, C.-J. (2007). Projected gradient methods for nonnegative matrix factorization. *Neural Computation, 19*(10), 2756–2779. doi:10.1162/neco.2007.19.10.2756

Paatero, P., & Tapper, U. (1994). Positive matrix factorization: A non-negative factor model with optimal utilization of error estimates of data values. *Environmetrics, 5*(2), 111–126. doi:10.1002/env.3170050203

Pedersen, M. E. H. (2010). *SwarmOps.* Retrieved from http://www.hvass-labs.org/projects/swarmops/cs/files/SwarmOpsCS1_0.pdf

Price, K. V., Storn, R. M., & Lampinen, J. A. (2005). *Differential evolution a practical approach to global optimization.* New York, NY: Springer.

Raghavan, V. V., & Wong, S. K. M. (1999). A critical analysis of vector space model for information retrieval. *Journal of the American Society for Information Science American Society for Information Science, 37*(5), 279–287.

Schmidt, M. N., & Laurberg, H. (2008). Non-negative matrix factorization with Gaussian process priors. *Computational Intelligence and Neuroscience, *(1): 1–10. doi:10.1155/2008/361705

Snásel, V., Platos, J., & Kromer, P. (2008). Developing genetic algorithms for Boolean matrix factorization. In *Proceedings of the DATESO International Workshop on Current Trends on Databases.*

Stadlthanner, K., Lutter, D., Theis, F. J., Lang, E. W., Tome, A. M., Georgieva, P., & Puntonet, C. G. (2007). Sparse nonnegative matrix factorization with genetic algorithms for microarray analysis. In *Proceedings of the International Joint Conference on Neural Networks* (pp. 294-299).

Tan, P.-N., Steinbach, M., & Kumar, V. (2005). *Introduction to data mining*. Reading, MA: Addison-Wesley.

Tan, Y., & Zhu, Y. (2010). Fireworks algorithm for optimization. In Y. Tan, Y. Shi, & K. C. Tan (Eds.), *Proceeding of the International Conference on Advances in Swarm Intelligence* (LNCS 6145, pp. 355-364).

Wild, S. M., Curry, J. H., & Dougherty, A. (2004). Improving non-negative matrix factorizations through structured initialization. *Pattern Recognition*, *37*(11), 2217–2232. doi:10.1016/j.patcog.2004.02.013

Witten, I. H., & Frank, E. (2005). *Data mining: Practical machine learning tools and techniques*. San Francisco, CA: Morgan Kaufmann.

Xue, Y., Tong, C. S., Chen, Y., & Chen, W. (2008). Clustering-based initialization for non-negative matrix factorization. *Applied Mathematics and Computation*, *205*(2), 525–536. doi:10.1016/j.amc.2008.05.106

Zhang, Q., & Berry, M. W., Lamb, B. T., & Samuel, T. (2009). A parallel nonnegative tensor factorization algorithm for mining global climate data. In G. Allen, J. Nabrzyski, E. Seidel, G. Dick van Albada, J. Dongarra, & P. M. A. Sloot (Eds.), *Proceedings of the 9th International Conference on Computational Science* (LNCS 5545, pp. 405-415).

This work was previously published in the International Journal of Swarm Intelligence Research, Volume 2, Issue 4, edited by Yuhui Shi, pp. 12-34, copyright 2011 by IGI Publishing (an imprint of IGI Global).

Chapter 10
How Ants Can Efficiently Solve the Generalized Watchman Route Problem

Paweł Paduch
Kielce University of Technology, Poland

Krzysztof Sapiecha
Kielce University of Technology, Poland

ABSTRACT

This paper presents a new algorithm for solving the generalized watchman problem. It is the problem of mobile robot operators that must find the shortest route for the robot to see the whole area with many obstructions. The algorithm adapts the well-known ant algorithm to the new problem. An experiment where the algorithm is applied to an area containing more than 10 obstructions is described. It proves that efficiency and accuracy of the algorithm are high.

INTRODUCTION

Problems of watching and guarding have been investigated for many years. The problem of how many static guards must be used to watch the whole art gallery built of *n* vertices (The Art Gallery Problem) was the first one. It was stated in 1973 and solved analytically in 1975 (Chvátal). Then, many different variants of the problem were formulated. Firstly, different requirements for guards, concerning their placement and behavior were taken into account. Next, new shapes of areas watched by guards were assumed. Finally,

both static and mobile guards were used. With time this has become more and more complex. Nevertheless, for polygon areas without holes analytical solutions were usually found. Detailed classification of the variants and the solutions is presented in the next section of the paper.

Watchman Route Problem (WRP) aims to find the shortest route in a polygon with holes (obstructions) such that all points of the polygon are visible from that route is the most complicated of the variants. It is NP-hard even if the holes are convex which was proved by Chin and Ntafos (1991). Therefore, it has usually been ignored.

DOI: 10.4018/978-1-4666-2479-5.ch010

Nowadays, the progress in technology of mobile robots stimulates searching for a solution of WRP.

To give people comfort and security, robots steadily replace human beings in heavy, arduous or dangerous works. In the area of security and surveillance there are many applications where mobile robots (mobots) are involved (Robotics Trends, 2010). Mobots can be used in buildings to search for bombs that were planted by terrorists. They can also be used for searching victims after disasters, guarding dangerous areas, watching buildings or mines which are likely to collapse, and in many similar situations. The shorter path mobots chose to watch the area the greater chance of survival (for both, victims and constructions). Even if human life is not in danger, shortening a path of guarding could minimize the cost of energy or time of exploration of the area.

Recently, mobots have become more and more independent. They can move from one place to another without human assistance. This depends only on data coming from mobot's camera or any device investigating environment. They may be endowed with strategies of operation or even artificial intelligence (Ali, Ghaffari, Liao, & Hall, 2006). However, when a mobot should select the shortest route between two places in an area with many different obstructions, then the task becomes much more complicated. Operators may remotely control mobots or programmers may put the route in mobot's memory. Nevertheless, the route must be found.

In the real world, areas of operation of mobots are much more complicated than simple rooms with small number of polygons. Even if obstructions could be approximated with the help of polygons, their number and configurations might be unlimited. Hence, the WRP, generalized for mobots (MRP) is a real challenge for researchers.

In the paper a new approach to solve the MRP is presented. It is based on Ant Colony Optimization (ACO) (Dorigo & Stützle, 2004). The paper is organized as follows: related work is presented, the problem is stated, adaptation of the ant algorithm for solving the problem is presented, and experimental results are discussed. The paper ends with conclusions.

RELATED WORK

Watchman Route Problem

Problems of searching and guarding have been investigated for many years. The first was The Art Gallery Problem. In 1973 Victor Klee asked Václav Chvátal how many static guards must be used to watch the whole art gallery built of n vertices. Chvátal (1975) proved that $n/3$ guards are enough. The proof was then simplified by Fisk (1978). From that time many varieties of the problem have been formulated. They are as follows:

1. **Watched Guard Problem:** Guards must see each other. Michael and Pinciu (2003) and independently Żyliński (2002) proved that $(3n-1)/7$ guards are sufficient and in some cases necessary to guard the whole polygon as well to see each other. Moreover, Żyliński proved that for spiral shape polygons only $2n/5$ it is needed and for star shape polygons $(3n-1)/7$ static guards is needed, but only if $n>=5$.

2. **Fortress Problem:** A variant of the outer guarding, where guards must see polygon from outside. It is divided into sub-problems including:
    a. **Vertex Guards:** Guards are placed on vertices of the polygon. This is easy to prove that $n/2$ guards are necessary (for example when considering a convex polygon).
    b. **Point Guards:** Guards are placed anywhere. Aggarval and O'Rourke proved in 1984 that n/3 guards are sufficient and in some cases necessary (O'Rourke, 1987).

c. **Cooperative Vertex Guards:** Guards are placed on vertices of the polygon and every guard must see at least one of the other guards. For a convex polygon minimal number of the guards is n-1.

3. **Polygon with Holes:** A gallery is built of *n* walls and *h* obstacles. This was proved by Bjorling-Sachs and Souvaine (1991) that *(n+h)/3* guards are sufficient.

4. **Rectilinear Polygon with Holes:** Every wall is rectilinear. Żyliński (2006) gave a proof that *(n+h)/4* guards are sufficient.

5. **Prison Yard Problem:** Similar to Vertex Guards but guards must watch also an interior of the polygon. Füredi and Kleitman (1994) proved that at most *n/2* guards are sufficient.

Next variants of the problem concerned mobile guards. These are as follows:

1. **Edge Guards:** A variant of The Art Gallery proposed by G. Toussaint. Every guard walks along a wall. Toussaint supposed that only *n/4* "Watching walls" are necessary, but some low *n* polygons need *(n+1)/4* (O'Rourke, 1998) (Figure 1). Bjorling-Sachs and Souvaine (1991) proved that *(n-2)/5* edge guards are necessary and sufficient to guard a monotone polygon. They also proved that *(n-2)/6* edge guards are necessary and suf-

ficient to guard rectilinear polygon (Nilsson, 1994).

2. **The Zookeeper Problem:** A guard moves inside a polygon which contains restricted areas, i.e., small sub polygons which the guard cannot enter but must approach any border of each of them. The task is to find the shortest route. First solution of this problem was presented by Chin and Ntafos (1987). They gave an algorithm with $O(n^2)$. Hersberger and Snoeyink improved the result to $O(n\log^2 n)$ and Bespamyatnikh improved it to $O(n\log n)$. However, for larger zoo there was a numerical problem. If input coordinates have L bits of precision, then the output has nL bits. Hence, the algorithm does not work well in practice (Tan, 2004).

3. **The Safari Route Problem:** Almost identical to the Zookeeper Problem but in this case guard can enter the sub polygons. Xuehou Tan and Tomio Hirata presented a dynamic programming algorithm for computing the shortest safari route in the case when a starting point on the route is known. Computational complexity of the algorithm is $O(n^3)$ (Tan & Hirata, 2003). The fastest algorithm with $O(n^2\log n)$ was presented by Dror, Efrat, Lubiw, and Mitchell (2003).

4. **Watchman Route Problem (WRP):** The task is to find the shortest route in a polygon

Figure 1. Polygon where n/4=2 edge guards (E₁ and E₂) are not sufficient

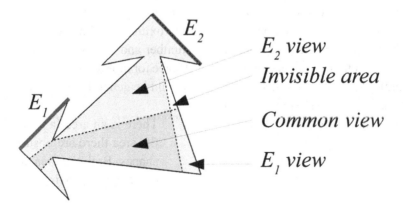

such that all points of the polygon are visible from that route. There are many variants of the problem. The basic assumption is that there is a simple polygon (without holes) and closed route which must go through the starting point. First algorithm with $O(n^4)$ solving the problem was given by Chin and Ntafos (1991). Xuehou Tan and Tomio Hirata published an algorithm with $O(n^3)$. However, the authors admitted in their later corrigendum (Tan, Hirata, & Inagaki, 1998), that previous estimation contained an error and the complexity is $O(n^4)$. An algorithm presented by Dror et al. (1998) is the best solution up till now. It is with $O(n^3 log n)$. Other variants of the problem assume rectilinear polygons, finding route with starting point or without it, finding path and not route where a guard does not need to go back to the point where he started, and finally they assume an existence of holes (obstructions). The last and the hardest problem is usually ignored because it is NP-hard even if the holes are convex as proved by Chin and Ntafos (1991). The first solution of the WRP with holes was given by Mata and Mitchell (1995). For a rectilinear polygon with n vertices and with holes, they presented a $log n$ - approximation algorithm. Its computational complexity is $O(n^9)$. Only one available solution of more general WRP was presented by Packer (2008). His approximation algorithm uses heuristics. The solution is based on computing a set of static guards, constructing routes that visit all the static guards and shortening the routes while maintaining full coverage of the polygon. The author considers also the case with multi guards where the sum of the paths should be the smallest or the length of the longest path should be the shortest.

Ant Colony Optimization

Algorithms based on Ant Colony Optimization (ACO) have got a long history. The first was the Ant System (AS) (Dorigo, 1997). Its work is very similar to the one that ants do. During the decade it was the basis for many improvements and modifications (Dorigo & Stützle, 2004). Among them are Elitist Ant System (EAS), Ant-Q founded on Q-learning and Ant Colony System (ACS) which is a direct successor to the Ant-Q. Other significant improvements of AS were introduced by Stützle and Hoos (1996) in Max-Min Ant System (MMAS) where there were upper and lower bounds of pheromone trails. One year later Bullnheimer, Hartl, and Strauß (1997) presented their rank-based AS. Approximate Nondeterministic Tree Search (ANTS) (Maniezzo, 1998), the Best-Worst Ant System (BWAS) (Cordon, Fernández de Viana, Herrera, & Moreno, 2000) and Hyper Cube Ant Colony Optimization (HC-ACO) (Blum & Dorigo, 2001) are also worth mentioning ACO algorithms. Differences between these algorithms are mainly in the strategy of leaving and evaporating pheromone.

PROBLEM STATEMENT

Presently mobots are more and more widely used for watching and guarding. In real world, areas of operation of mobots may be much more complicated than simple rooms with small number of polygons. Even if obstructions could be approximated with the help of polygons, their number and configurations might be unlimited. Hence for mobots, the Watchman Route Problem should be generalized as follows:

1.   There is an area (a room, for example). In the area there are obstructions of different shapes. Both the area and the obstructions could be approximated with the help of

polygons. Entry point and exit point for a mobot are given.

2. The mobot has cameras or sensors that allow detection of all of the obstructions around it (not blocked out).

3. The mobot watches available area at the viewpoints only.

4. The mobot starts its route from the entry point. Its goal is to watch the whole area between the obstructions (the sum of all watched areas at viewpoints is equal to the whole area Figure 2). Then it has to go to the exit point. The tour should be minimal.

5. A size of the mobot is neglected and it is assumed that the mobot may touch the limits (walls of the room, for example).

ANT ALGORITHM FOR MOBOTS

Biology has always inspired engineers. For computer programmers it has been a source of new ideas concerning algorithms. Ant Colony Optimization (ACO) is a good example. Ants were inspiration for Dorigo (1992).

Let us look closer on ants. These small insects are almost blind and have very small brains. Nevertheless they are able to find the shortest way from the ant-hill to a food. This is possible thanks to stigmergy. Stigmergy is a method of indirect cooperation inside species. It consists in changing an environment of one specimen by other specimens that influences their behavior. Ants have got a very good sense of smell. While marching every ant leaves behind smelling substance called pheromone so that other ants know which path it has chosen. When an ant-hill starts working an ant may march in any of possible directions. If an ant encounters a route of another ant it may cross the route or follow. This depends on intensity of the smell of the route. When an ant finds a food, it goes back to the ant-hill. After that the ant and other ants may go the same or other paths. Having the choice of two or more paths an ant always selects the shortest one. Over time selected paths become increasingly shorter. Ants can find the shortest path even if an obstruction appears on their way. Why? Because, the shorter the path the stronger the pheromone smell. Pheromone works as a force attracting ants. The stronger smell of the pheromone the stronger force attracting ants.

The idea of the ACO can be adopted to solve NP-hard problem of finding the shortest route for a watchman (here a mobot) in a polygon with holes. The task of a mobot is very similar to the task of an ant. Both the ant and the mobot start touring from one starting point (the ant from an ant-hill, the mobot from an entry point of the polygon), both must make decision which route should be taken, and both have a target to achieve (the ant must find a food but the mobot must visit the whole area of the polygon). Both the ant and

Figure 2. Subsequent steps of discovering the area

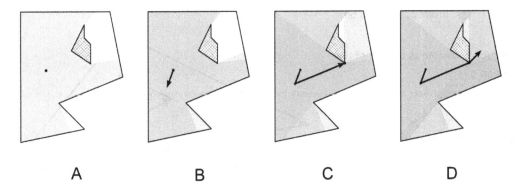

A   B   C   D

the mobot can achieve the target in many ways but they try to minimize the length of the route. Using these analogies we will simulate ants that solve the problem of mobots (that is search for the shortest route in a polygon with holes). We will call these ants "touring ants".

Preliminaries

We have made the following assumptions:

1. Investigated area is two-dimensional.
2. The area can be approximated with the help of a polygon represented with a chain of vectors arranged in counterclockwise order. Every end of the vector of the same polygon is connected with the beginning of the next vector (Figure 3). In such a case every point lying on the right from the vectors is outside the polygon. In the same way we build obstructions, but vectors lie in clockwise order. The Bézier curve could also be used for describing a closed area, but it would complicate the implementation.
3. A mobot can stop and look around (360 degree) only in viewpoints. Although the world of ants is unbounded and continual, the world of mobots is bounded and sampled.
4. A cut is a directed line segment, with two end points on a boundary of the polygon, and at last one interior point in its interior (Nilsson, 1994). Clearly, the cut divides a polygon into two disjoint (left and right) pieces (Figure 4).
5. For each reflex vertex of the polygon P two edges adjacent to the vertex are extended until the extension hits the boundary of P (Figure 4). The directions of these two extension cuts are the same as those of the edges with which they are collinear (Packer, 2008). Extension cut determines a border of the region hidden behind the reflex vertex. Extension cuts are introduced to limit the number of viewpoints that might be used by a mobot. Staying on an extension cut is enough to look around and to see the region (the region on the left side of the extension cut) without entering it. Thus viewpoints are placed only on extension cuts.
6. Visibility graph spans viewpoints lying on the extension cuts. Every viewpoint may be a node of the graph but an edge between two viewpoints exists only if they see each other (excluding nodes lying at the same extension cut). In Figure 4 only two viewpoints on each extension cut are shown. Every viewpoint has a list of viewpoints where ants can go forward from current location. Hence, ants can go from one viewpoint to another only if there is an edge in visibility graph between these viewpoints.

Figure 3. Chains of vectors defining polygons

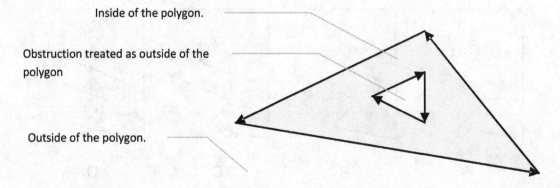

Inside of the polygon.

Obstruction treated as outside of the polygon

Outside of the polygon.

Figure 4. Vertices, cuts and visibility graph

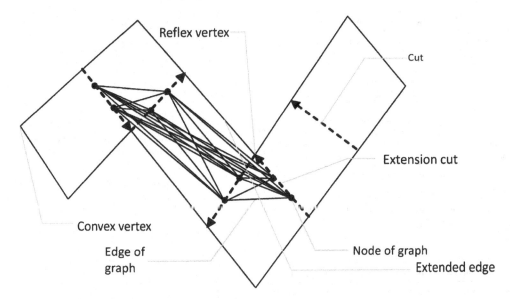

The preliminaries delimit the area of investigation and limit routes acceptable for a mobot. The mobot starts its route from the entry point belonging to polygon P and moves from one viewpoint to another along the visibility graph. In each viewpoint it looks around. What it sees is called a visibility polygon (VP) and is limited only by walls and obstructions. The mobot moves as long as every point inside polygon P is covered by a sum of the VPs of the visited viewpoints. The mobot can also find a route to the exit point. This will be discussed in future research. In order to accelerate calculations, only visible parts of the walls are considered. In consequence the mobot finishes its work when all walls are viewed entirely at least once.

How Can the Ant Model be Adapted to the Mobot Task

If ants had the task of the mobot they would start from one point and go in different directions leaving pheromones. Their route would be random but with tendency to discover new unvisited areas.

Ants would remember which parts of the area were already visited so they would know when to finish. If they visited the whole area they would come back the same route also leaving pheromones. The best ants would come back first and their pheromone path would be the strongest. The next ants would choose shorter path with probability depending upon the amount of pheromones.

Implementation

At first, extension cuts, the viewpoints and visibility graph are determined. Initially, all connections have equal amount of pheromone (Table 1). The algorithm for a single ant uses two lists of extension cuts, visited cuts list (VCL) and non-visited cuts list (NVCL). VCL is set empty and all extension cuts are included in NVCL. VP is memorized as an object built of a set of vectors surrounding visibility area from a viewpoint. The ant starts searching from the entry point. It establishes the first VP and adds the first viewpoint to the tour (Table 1, point 2). From now on the following loop is executed:

Table 1. Differences between behavior of real ants and ants in our algorithm

	Behavior of Touring Ants	Behavior of Real Ants
1	At the very beginning the amount of pheromones is equal.	There are no pheromones.
2	Every ant starts from the same entry point.	If the anthill is treated as a one point then ants also start from one point.
3	Ants move only along the visibility graph.	Ants move everywhere.
4	Ants make decisions only at the nodes.	Ants examine their route constantly.
5	A decision of which way to chose is random but depends on the amount of pheromone on an edge of the graph belonging to the current node.	The decision is also dependent on the amount of pheromone but pheromone path could lie anywhere.
6	Ants memorize a sum of VPs so that they know when the target is achieved.	Ants memorize nothing.
7	The target is achieved when the sum memorized by any of the ants is equal to the area of the polygon.	The target is achieved when an ant finds food.
8	Pheromones are left only when all ants finish.	Every ant leaves pheromone constantly.
9	The amount of pheromone depends on the quality (length) of the route or only the best ant (which found the shortest route) leaves pheromone.	Every ant leaves more or less equal amount of pheromone.
10	Pheromone evaporates iteratively, when pheromone paths were updated.	Pheromone evaporates constantly.
11	All ants begin next iteration at the same time.	All ants run independently.

1. One of the connections from the NVCL is chosen (Table 1, points 4 and 5, for details see the next subsection).

2. The viewpoint from the other side of the connection is added to the tour, and the extension cut to which this point belongs is moved from the NVCL to the VCL. A distance of the connection is added to the total length of the tour. After adding the viewpoint to the tour, the VP is summed up and checked whether the sum is equal to the area of the polygon. If so, the tour is found and the ant has visited the whole area between obstructions, so exit from the loop, otherwise go to step 3.

3. Next connection from the NVCL is chosen. If there is none then a connection to one element of the VCL is taken. This means the ant must return (then it will try to go forwards choosing different way). Repeat from step 2.

N ants (N is a big number) working in parallel find the shortest route quickly. Visual C# and .Net Remoting are used for implementing the algorithm. Computations are distributed over nodes of a multicomputer. Extra application that makes it possible to create testing boards supplements the implementation.

Choosing Subsequent Viewpoints

We adopted the well known ant optimization algorithm (Dorigo, Caro, & Gambardella, 1998) for the choosing path through the visibility graph.

Suppose that an ant reached the *i-th* viewpoint. The ant has to decide which way to go now. Choosing the next edge in visibility graph (next connection) could be random but here it is based on decision table *A*:

$$A_i = [a_{ij}(t)]_{[N_i]} \tag{1}$$

whose elements are calculated as a combination of a local amount of pheromone and a value of local heuristic information. This is done according to the following formula:

$$a_{ij} = \frac{[\tau_{ij}(t)]^\alpha [\eta_{ij}]^\beta}{\sum_{l \in N_i} [\tau_{il}(t)]^\alpha [\eta_{il}]^\beta} \; \forall j \in N_i \qquad (2)$$

where:

- $\tau_{ij}(t)$ is the amount of pheromone trail on the connection between viewpoints i and j in the *t-th* iteration.
- $\eta_{ij} = c/d_{ij}$ is a heuristic function, which is chosen to be the inverse of the distance between viewpoints i and j where c is constant.
- N_i is a set of direct adjoining viewpoints to the viewpoint i.
- α and β are parameters which control weighs of the relative importance of pheromone trail and a value of the heuristic.

The above parameters are significant for tuning the algorithm. If α is too small compared to β then the algorithm works as a greedy one minimizing a local target function. Hence, it chooses the shortest local connection. Usually a local minimum is far from the global one. If α is too big then the algorithm tends to select connections from previous routes. This narrows the range of solutions already found, and hence also to local minimum.

The probability of choosing a viewpoint $j \in N_i^k$ for the ant k which is in a position i during the *t-th* iteration of the algorithm is defined as follows:

$$p_{ij}^k(t) = \frac{a_{ij}(t)}{\sum_{l \in N_i^k} a_{il}(t)} \qquad (3)$$

where $N_i^k \subseteq N$ is a set of viewpoints in neighborhood of the viewpoint i, which the ant has still not visited. In fact, all points belong to extension cuts. These which are on the VCL, are treated as already visited. When there are no unvisited viewpoints, $N_i^k \subseteq N$ means that the whole neighborhood of the viewpoint i was considered.

When in a single iteration the best solution is found then the pheromone map is updated according to the quality of the result. All connections on the best route are updated by adding m/L of the amount of pheromone, where m is the number of ants and L is the length of the route. Except that, every connection on the whole area of the polygon fades in every iteration according to the formula $\tau_{ij} = \tau_{ij} * \rho$ where ρ defines which fraction of pheromone evaporates (from 0 - clean all, to 1 - do not evaporate at all). In addition, when next viewpoint is chosen a blur is simulated. Ants do not choose the exact viewpoint but nearest points at the same cuts with probability of 33%. This means that on average one third of the ants will choose the left point of the cut the next one third will choose the right one and the rest of the ants will be accurate (Figure 5). It reduces the chances that the algorithm will fall into a local minimum and helps to fit a better route. A draft of the algorithm is shown in Box 1.

SIMULATION EXPERIMENT

Efficiency of the algorithm depends on a few parameters. This was investigated experimentally by means of simulation. First, the question of how to use α and β for fine tuning of the algorithm was answered. Next a role of ρ was evaluated. For the experiments the following simulation parameters were assumed:

- Every cut had viewpoint at every 20 units (pixels) and additionally 3 viewpoints: in

Figure 5. Choosing neighboring points

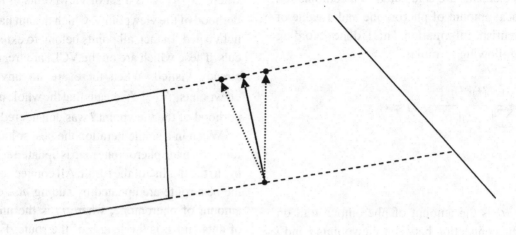

Box 1. Ant optimization algorithm

```
Determine extension cuts, the viewpoints, VPs and visibility graph.
Set initial amount of pheromone on all connections.
Set initial contents of NVCL and VCL.
FOR T iterations DO {
 FOR N ants DO {
 -Take entry point as the first viewpoint of the route.
 -Add the VP of the 1st viewpoint to the total polygon
 of visibility (TVP).
  WHILE the area of the TVP is less than the area
 of the searched polygon (P) DO {
  IF NVCL is not empty
 -Take one connection to the viewpoint
 which belongs to one of the cuts from NVCL according to the formula 3
 -Move the chosen cut from NVCL to the VCL
  ELSE
  -Take one connection to the viewpoint
 which belongs to one of the cuts from VCL according to the formula 3
  -Exchange the chosen viewpoint with the left or the right neighbor
 from the same cut, with probability of 1/3 on each side.
  -Add a viewpoint to the route
  -Add local VP of the last viewpoint to the TVP }
 IF total length of the tour is minimal, remember it.
 }
 -Update the pheromone trail by the best solution of this generation.
 -Evaporate the pheromone on all connections.
 }
```

the middle, at the very beginning and the very end of the cut.

- $c = 1$ in simple heuristic $\eta_{ij} = c/d_{ij}$ function.
- Every experiment lasted for 400 generations of ants.
- Every single generation had 640 ants.
- Entry points had coordinates 1389,909 (1st polygon) and 60,970 (2nd polygon) respectively
- The averages were calculated on the basis of 10 experiments.

Experiments were performed on a 10-node cluster based on a double core Intel Xeon, 8GB RAM, InfiniBand 10Gb.

Figure 6 shows two out of four polygons with obstructions used for experiments. Efficiency of the algorithm with parameters α and β between 0 and 4.5 (incremented by 0.5) was investigated. Most of the experiments were performed with evaporation parameter $\rho = 0.9$ (10% of pheromone evaporate every iteration).

Varying β with Constant α

When $\alpha = 0$ the influence of pheromone on ants is none and results of routing are almost random (Figure 7 for $\alpha = 0$). It is also visible that the minimal tours in each of the iterations are shorter when parameter β is high and longer when it is close to 0. But in all cases we cannot observe tendency to optimization.

When $\alpha > 0$ ants choose their route under greater influence of pheromone. Thus the subsequent generations find shorter routes. The influence of β is also visible. The greater β the earlier generation reaches minimum. This is because initial routes are shorter when β is higher.

Varying α at Constant β

Figure 8 shows the results of routing for subsequent generations of the ants, α varies at constant $\beta = 3$.

The greater parameter α the faster the minimal route is found. However, too big α can cause stuck at a local minimum. Figure 8 shows that the optimum for α is about 1 but in practice the whole range of parameter α between 1 and 4.5 gives good results (average 4975 +/- 2%).

Varying Both α and β

In all experiments the influence of parameters α and β on the best solutions after 400 iterations was examined (Figure 9).

Up to 200 iterations the influence of parameters α and β on minimal lengths of the paths is visible. After 400 iterations the averages for minimum lengths of the paths are almost the same. The curves show a saturation even for low values of α and β.

It is seen that for $\alpha = 0$ the worst results are achieved. The higher α the shorter routes may be found. It is also visible that the parameter β has a positive influence on the minimal routes.

The influence of parameters α and β on the time of calculation was also evaluated. One experiment was performed on one node of the cluster. As expected shorter times were obtained when α was high but β was low. The shortest times were about 1 hour and 15 minutes for the first polygon and about 40 minutes for the second one. The longest time was needed for $\alpha = 0$ and high value of β. It was about 2 hours and 50 minutes for the first polygon and 3 hours and 48 minutes for the second one. However, these results are only informative because useful values of α and β are in the range [0.5, 4.5]. The averages for α and β from between 0.5 and 4.5 were 1:55:38 and 1:06:23 respectively for the first and for the second polygon.

Figure 6. Example of a low space fill polygon (a) and a large space fill polygon (b) with shortest routes

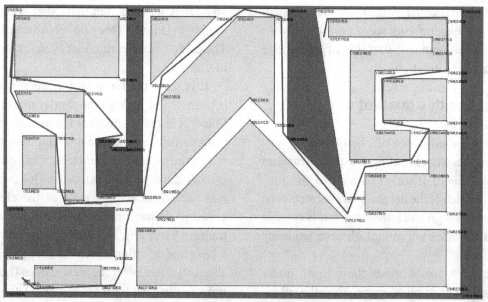

1st polygon (a)

2nd polygon (b)

Varying ρ with Constant α and β

The experiments show that ρ has an influence on speed of calculations and quality of results. Local minimum is found faster if pheromone evaporates faster, but the results are worse.

Polygon Space Fill

Figure 6 shows two polygons with substantially different space fill. The simulation parameters were the same except entry points that were different for each polygon.

Figure 7. How β works at α=0 in the first polygon

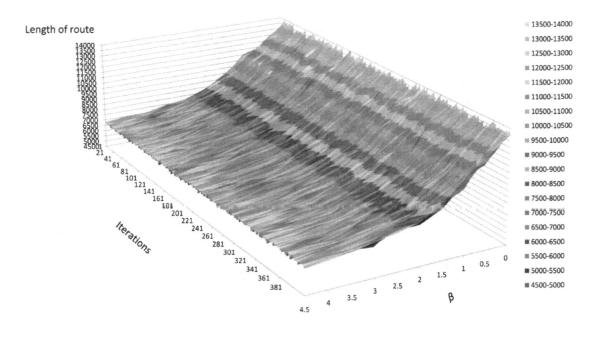

Figure 8. Influence of α at β=3 on the routes in the first polygon

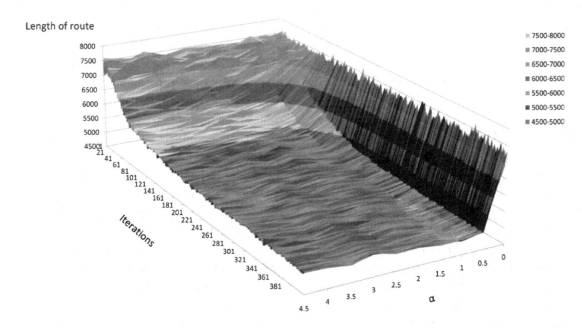

Figure 9. Average minima(α,β) after 100, 200, 300 and 400 iterations

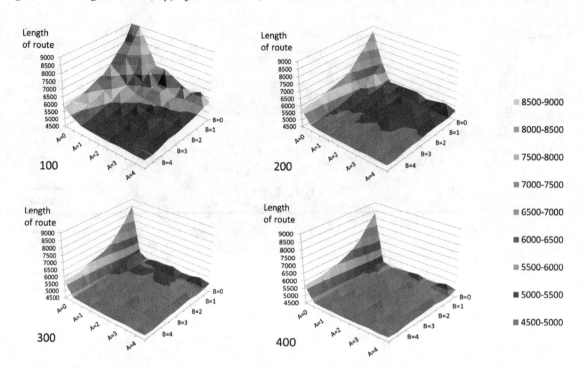

Ants with no strategy had a greater possibility of round-trip in the first polygon than in the second one. Therefore, proper selection of β was more significant for the first polygon (Figure 7) than for the second one where differences in results between $\beta = 0$ and $\beta = 4.5$ were smaller.

CONCLUSION

In the paper the generalized watchman problem is posed for a mobot. An area to be investigated by a mobot is large and complicated, containing many obstructions. In this case an analytical solution of the problem might be very difficult or even impossible (even using fragmentation of the area). Therefore, adoption of the well known ant algorithm is suggested. Analogies between the task of ants and the task of an operator of the mobot are pointed out. Finally, a mobot oriented version of the ant algorithm is formulated. It is quite simple for implementation and has very strong intuition.

Visual C# and.Net Remoting were used for the algorithm implementation.

Up to now we have performed basic series of experiments testing the influence of parameters α, β and ρ on the efficiency of the algorithm. The main goal of the experiments was to evaluate overall ability of the algorithm to find the shortest routes for a mobot in polygons with many holes. Results are optimistic because it was possible to find almost minimal tours even in polygons with more than 10 holes and the time of computations was relatively short. For all values of α and $\beta >= 0.5$, 400 iterations gave good results (Figure 9). The averages were 4855 (11% worse than the minimum, counted manually) for the first polygon and 6769 (11.6% worse than the minimum, counted manually) for the second polygon. However, there were values of parameters α and β where results were better. For example, tours found by ants at $\alpha=2$ and $\beta=4.5$ for the first polygon from Figure 6 equaled about 4727, in average. It is about 8.1% worse than the minimum, counted manually. For the second polygon from Figure 6 tours found by ants at α=1 and β=0 equaled about 6579, in average. It is about 8.3% worse than the minimum, counted manually. The best single results were 4586 (4.9% worse than the minimum) and 6398 (5.6% worse than the minimum) respectively. This is shown in Figure 6. Similar results were obtained for other experimental polygons. Summarizing, good results were achieved after 400 iterations when α>=0.5 and β>=1. Differences in lengths were very slight.

The time spent for calculation on a single node of the cluster is from about 1 to 2 hours (when α>=0.5 and β <4.5). It strongly depends on the value of parameter α (especially for its low values). Parameter β has less influence on calculation time, but it is also significant.

According to our best knowledge, it is the first approach to apply swarm intelligence to solve the generalized watchman problem. The main aim of the research was to verify if the idea of using ACO for this purpose is effective. So the simplest AS algorithm was implemented. If it gives good results, more sophisticated algorithms should work better.

The approach is promising but seems to need further research. Although the algorithm adopts one of the simplest ACO algorithms, it has already been experimentally proved to be useful and can be applied efficiently for large polygons with many holes. Moreover, it may feed new concepts on tuning the algorithm in order to increase its efficiency.

Tuning of the algorithm is neither easy nor straightforward task and requires separate and laborious research. In follow-up research we are going to examine other parameters of the algorithm and introduce some modifications, mostly in a way the pheromone is left and evaporated. We plan to introduce two stages into the algorithm. The first stage will search for proper order of cuts and the second will find the shortest route connecting all cuts found in the first stage. An evaluation of adoption of other ACO-based algorithms like ACS or MMAS will be also taken into consideration. This will supplement the knowledge about the subject.

REFERENCES

Ali, S. A., Ghaffari, M., Liao, X., & Hall, H. (2006). *Mobile robotics, moving intelligence.* Berlin, Germany: Pro Literatur Verlag.

Bjorling-Sachs, I., & Souvaine, D. (1991). *A tight bound for guarding general polygons with holes* (Tech. Rep. No. LCSR-TR-165). New Brunswick, NJ: Rutgers University.

Blum, C., & Dorigo, M. (2001). HC-ACO: The hyper-cube framework for ant colony optimization. In *Proceedings of the Metaheuristics International Conference* (pp. 399-403).

Bullnheimer, B., Hartl, R. F., & Strauß, C. (1997). A new rank based version of the ant system - a computational study. *Central European Journal for Operations Research and Economics, 7*, 25–38.

Chin, W. P., & Ntafos, S. (1987). Optimum zookeeper routes. *Congressus Numerantium, 58*, 257–266.

Chin, W. P., & Ntafos, S. (1991). Shortest watchman routes in simple polygons. *Discrete & Computational Geometry, 6*(1), 9–31. doi:10.1007/BF02574671

Chvatal, V. (1975). A combinatorial theorem in plane geometry. *Journal of Combinatorial Theory Series B, 18*, 39–41. doi:10.1016/0095-8956(75)90061-1

Cordon, O., Fernández de Viana, I., Herrera, F., & Moreno, L. (2000). A new ACO model integrating evolutionary computation concepts: The best-worst ant system. In *Proceedings of the Algorithmic Number Theory Symposium* (pp. 22-29).

Dorigo, M. (1992). *Optimization, learning and natural algorithms.* Unpublished doctoral dissertation, Politecnico di Milano, Milan, Italy.

Dorigo, M. (1997). Ant colonies for the travelling salesman problem. *Bio Systems, 43*(2), 73–81. doi:10.1016/S0303-2647(97)01708-5

Dorigo, M., Di Caro, G., & Gambardella, L. (1998). *Ant algorithms for discrete optimization.* Brussels, Belgium: Université Libre de Bruxelles.

Dorigo, M., & Stützle, T. (2004). *Ant colony optimization.* Scituate, MA: Bradford Company.

Dror, M., Efrat, A., Lubiw, A., & Mitchell, J. S. B. (2003). Touring a sequence of polygons. In *Proceedings of the 35th Annual ACM Symposium on Theory Computing* (pp. 473-482).

Fisk, S. (1978). A short proof of Chvatal's watchman theorem. *Journal of Combinatorial Theory Series B, 24,* 374. doi:10.1016/0095-8956(78)90059-X

Füredi, Z., & Kleitman, D. J. (1994). The prison yard problem. *COMBINATORICA, 14*(3), 287–300. doi:10.1007/BF01212977

Maniezzo, V. (1998). *Exact and approximate nondeterministic tree-search procedures for the quadratic assignment problem.* Bologna, Italy: Scienze Dell'informazione, Università Di Bologna.

Mata, C. S., & Mitchell, J. S. B. (1995). Approximation algorithms for geometric tour and network design problems (extended abstract). In *Proceedings of the Eleventh Annual Symposium on Computational Geometry* (pp. 360-369).

Michael, T. S., & Pinciu, V. (2003). Art gallery theorems for guarded guards. *Computational Geometry Theory and Applications, 26,* 247–258.

Nilsson, B. J. (1994). *Guarding art galleries – methods for mobile guards.* Lund, Sweden: Lund University.

O'Rourke, J. (1987). *Art gallery theorems and algorithms.* Oxford, UK: Oxford University Press.

O'Rourke, J. (1998). *Computational geometry in C (Cambridge tracts in theoretical computer science)* (2nd ed.). Cambridge, UK: Cambridge University Press.

Packer, E. (2008). Computing multiple watchman routes. In *Proceedings of the 7th International Conference on Experimental Algorithms* (pp. 114-128).

Robotics Trends. (2010). *Stories filed in security and defense.* Retrieved from http://www.roboticstrends.com/topics/security_defense_robotics

Stützle, T., & Hoos, H. (1996). *Improving the ant system: A detailed report on the max-min ant system.* Darmstadt, Germany: Technical University of Darmstadt.

Tan, X. (2004). Approximation algorithms for the watchman route and zookeeper's problems. *Discrete Applied Mathematics, 136*(2-3), 363–376. doi:10.1016/S0166-218X(03)00451-7

Tan, X., & Hirata, T. (2003). Finding shortest safari routes in simple polygons. *Information Processing Letters, 87*(4), 179–186. doi:10.1016/S0020-0190(03)00284-9

Tan, X., Hirata, T., & Inagaki, Y. (1998). Corrigendum to an incremental algorithm for constructing shortest watchman route. *International Journal of Computational Geometry & Applications, 9,* 319–323. doi:10.1142/S0218195999000212

Żyliński, P. (2002). *Some results on cooperative guards.* Gdańsk, Poland: Gdańsk University.

Żyliński, P. (2006). Orthogonal art galleries with holes: A coloring proof of Aggarwal's theorem. *Electronic Journal of Combinatorics, 13*(1).

This work was previously published in the International Journal of Swarm Intelligence Research, Volume 2, Issue 3, edited by Yuhui Shi, pp. 1-15, copyright 2011 by IGI Publishing (an imprint of IGI Global).

Chapter 11
Image Segmentation Based on Bacterial Foraging and FCM Algorithm

Hongwei Mo
Harbin Engineering University, China

Yujing Yin
Harbin Engineering University, China

ABSTRACT

This paper addresses the issue of image segmentation by clustering in the domain of image processing. The clustering algorithm taken account here is the Fuzzy C-Means which is widely adopted in this field. Bacterial Foraging Optimization Algorithm is an optimal algorithm inspired by the foraging behavior of E.coli. For the purpose to reinforce the global search capability of FCM, the Bacterial Foraging Algorithm was employed to optimize the objective criterion function which is interrelated to centroids in FCM. To evaluate the validation of the composite algorithm, cluster validation indexes were used to obtain numerical results and guide the possible best solution found by BF-FCM. Several experiments were conducted on three UCI data sets. For image segmentation, BF-FCM successfully segmented 8 typical grey scale images, and most of them obtained the desired effects. All the experiment results show that BF-FCM has better performance than that of standard FCM.

INTRODUCTION

Image segmentation is one of the central problems in computer vision and pattern recognition. It refers to the process of assigning a label to every pixel in an image such that pixels with the same label share certain visual characteristics. The result of image segmentation is a set of segments (sets of pixels) that collectively cover the entire image. Pixels in the same region are similar with respect to some characteristics or computed properties, such as color, intensity, and texture. Adjacent regions are significantly different with respect to the same characteristics. The goal of segmentation

DOI: 10.4018/978-1-4666-2479-5.ch011

is to simplify and/or change the representation of an image into something that is more meaningful and easier to analyze (Shapiro & Stockman, 2001).

There are many general-purpose approaches available for image segmentation such as threshold methods (Mardia & Hainsworth, 1988), edge-based methods (Perona & Malik, 1990), region-based methods (Hijjatoleslami & Kitter, 1998), and graph-based methods (Felzenszwalb & Huttenlocher, 2004). In contrast to the heuristic nature of these methods, one would formalize an objective criterion for evaluating a given segmentation. This would allow us to formulate the segmentation problem as an optimization problem. The objective function that one would seek to optimize is the interclass variance that is used in cluster analysis. An optimizer can lead to efficient solutions for optimal segmentation. But the objective function is usually not a monotone chain; therefore the problem is general NP-hard. Following this way, some clustering methods have been applied to solve image segmentation problems.

Clustering techniques represent the non-supervised pattern classification in groups (Jain et al., 1999). Considering the image context, the clusters correspond to some semantic meaning in the image, which is, objects. Among the many methods for data analysis through clustering and unsupervised image segmentation is: Nearest Neighbor Clustering, Fuzzy C-Means (FCM) clustering and Artificial Neural Networks for Clustering (Jain et al., 1999). Such bio and social-inspired methods try to solve the related problems using knowledge found in the way nature solves problems. Social inspired approaches intend to solve problems considering that an initial and previously defined weak solution can lead the whole population to find a better or a best so far solution.

Among them, the most successful image segmentation algorithm into homogeneous regions is fuzzy c-means algorithm (Bezdek, 1981). There are a lot of visual applications reporting the use of fuzzy c-means, e.g., in medical image analysis, soil structure analysis, satellite imagery (Felzenszwalb & Huttenlocher, 2004; Hijjatoleslami & Kitter, 1998; Mardia & Hainsworth, 1988; Perona & Malik, 1990). Many variations of approaches have been introduced over last 20 years, and image segmentation remains an open-solution problem. As global optimization techniques, evolutionary algorithms (EAs) are likely to be good tools for image segmentation task. In the past two decades, EAs have been applied to image segmentation with promising results (Andrey, 1999; Bhandarkar & Zhang, 1999; Bhanu et al., 1995; Gong et al., 2008; Koppen et al., 2003; Maulik, 2009; Melkemi et al., 2006; Veenman et al., 2003). These algorithms exploited the metaphor of natural evolution in the context of image segmentation.

The original FCM algorithm, due to its drawbacks such as poor ability of global searching and easy sticking at local optimal solution, is often improved by combining with other optimal algorithm and then used in image segmentation. Recently there has been an increase in the presence of optimization-based techniques of image segmentation. Most of them focus on searching the right center of cluster for FCM. Yang et al. (2007) proposed a FCM based on ant colony algorithm. Tian et al. (2008) applied the FCM optimized by particle swarm optimization to segment SAR images and its experimental results on the MSTAR dataset had demonstrated that the proposed method was capable of effectively segmenting SAR images and achieving better results than the improved FCM (IFCM) algorithm. Yang et al. (2008) had proposed a three-level tree model which was inspired from the ants' self-assembling behavior to make the clustering structure more adaptive for image segmentation. In order to increase the segmentation precision of brain tissues in MR images to solve some problems existing in the present genetic fuzzy clustering algorithm, Nie, et al. (2008) had proposed an improved genetic fuzzy clustering algorithm. Experiment results showed that higher segmentation accuracy was obtained using the proposed segmentation method comparing with the fast FCM algorithm and the conventional genetic fuzzy clustering algorithm. Zeng et al. (2008) directly unified GA in the magnetic resonance images (MRI) segmentation and the global optimum in MRI segmentation was obtained. Swagatam et al. (2010) had presented a modified differential evolution (DE) algorithm for clustering the pixels of an image in the gray-scale intensity space in their paper and extensive comparison results has indicated that the proposed algorithm has an edge over a few state-of-the-art algorithms for automatic multi-class image segmentation. Sowmya et al. (2011) had used a competitive neural network (CNN) and fuzzy clustering techniques to segment color images.

In this paper, we adopt Bacteria foraging optimization algorithm to search the center of cluster for FCM. The paper is organized as follows. At first, the FCM and BFOA are introduced respectively. Second, Bacteria Foraging and Fuzzy C-Means algorithm (BF-FCM) is proposed, and the validation for cluster is assessed considering the cluster validation indexes (CVIs) on three data sets from the UCI database. Third, the proposed algorithm is tested on some standard images from the USC-SIPI Image Database and the simulation results are analyzed. At last, the conclusions and some perspectives are given.

BRIEF DESCRIPTION OF FCM AND BFOA

The FCM

FCM is a kind of simple mechanical clustering method based on exploring minimum value of the objective function (Wu & Yang, 2002). The

objective function proposed by Dunn is called the clustering criterion function, namely error squares function.

Let $X = [x_1, x_2, \cdots, x_n]$ be the n dimension sample space. The criterion function is shown by Equation 1:

$$J(X; U, V) = \sum_{i=1}^{c} \sum_{k=1}^{N} (\mu_{ik})^m \left\| x_k - v_i \right\|_A^2 \qquad (1)$$

where the clustering center

$$V = [v_1, v_2, \cdots, v_c], v_i \in R^n$$

The Euclidean distance between data set x_k and clustering center v_i is

$$D_{ikA}^2 = \left\| x_k - v_i \right\|_A^2 = (x_k - v_i)^T A (x_k - v_i) \qquad (2)$$

where μ_{ik} is the membership function that the ith sample belongs to k^{th} clustering center. It is define by Equation 3

$$\mu_{ik} = \frac{1}{\displaystyle\sum_{j=1}^{c} (D_{ikA} / D_{jkA})^{2/(m-1)}} \qquad (3)$$
$$1 \leq i \leq c, 1 \leq k \leq N$$

FCM is described as follows:

Step 1: Select $e > 0$, initialize clustering centre v_0, let $g = 1$

Step 2: Calculate the fuzzy matrix U^g based on Equation 3.

Step 3: If $\exists i$ and r make $\mu_{ir}(g) = 1$ and $k \neq r$, then let $\mu_{ir}(g) = 0$

Step 4: Update the clustering center following Equation 4:

$$v_i = \frac{\sum_{k=1}^{N} \mu_{ik}^m x_k}{\sum_{k=1}^{N} \mu_{ik}^m}, 1 \le i \le c \qquad (4)$$

Step 5: If $\left\| v^{(k)} - v^{(k+1)} \right\| < e$, stop iteration, else let $g = g + 1$ and return to Step 1.

The BFOA

Passino (2002) proposed a new kind of bionic algorithm - Bacteria Foraging Optimization Algorithm (BFOA) which is based on the behavior that E. coli engulfs food in humans' intestinal tracts. In this algorithm, each individual in the colony is independent. They continuously change direction and step length to find out the local point with the most abundant food in the search space which is equivalent to the optimal solution in algorithm. Meanwhile, in order to enhance the searching accuracy, this algorithm contains replication and elimination processes to find the global optimal solution. Besides very strong global search ability, BFOA also has fine local search capability (Chu et al., 2008). The basic steps of BFOA are demonstrated as follows:

1. **Initialization:** n, S, N_C, N_S, N_{re}, N_{ed} P_{ed}, $C(i)$, $i = (1, 2, \cdots S)$ are the main parameters, where

   n: Dimension of the search space

   S: The number of bacteria in the colony

   N_C: Chemotactic steps

   N_S: Swim steps

   N_{re}: Reproductive steps

   N_{ed}: Elimination and dispersal steps

   P_{ed}: Probability of elimination

   $C(i)$: Run-length unit

2. **Elimination-Dispersal Loop:** $l = l + 1$
3. **Reproduction Loop:** $k = k + 1$

4. **Chemotaxis Loop:** $j = j + 1$
   a. For $i = 1, 2, \cdots S$, take a chemotactic step for bacterium i as follows.
   b. Compute fitness function $F(i, j, k, l)$
   c. Let $M_{last} = F(i, j, k, l)$ to save this value since we may find a better value via a swim.
   d. **Tumble:** Generate a random vector $\Delta(i) \in R^n$ with each element $\Delta m(i)$, $m = 1, 2, \cdots n$, a random number in $[-1, 1]$
   e. **Move:** Let

   $$\varphi^i(j+1, k, l) = \varphi^i(j, k, l) + C(i) \frac{\Delta(i)}{\sqrt{\Delta^T(i)\Delta(i)}} \qquad (5)$$

   which results in a step of size $C(i)$ in the direction of the tumble for bacterium i.
   f. Compute $F(i, j, k, l)$ with $\varphi^i(j+1, k, l)$
   g. Swim
      i. Let $m = 0$ (counter for swim length).
      ii. While $m < N_S$, let $m = m + 1$
      iii. If $F(i, j+1, k, l) < F_{last}$, let $F_{last} = F(i, j+1, k, l)$, then another step of size in this same direction will be taken as (5) and use the new generated $\varphi^i(j+1, k, l)$ to compute the new $F(i, j+1, k, l)$
      iv. Else let $m = N_S$
   h. Go to next bacterium $i + 1$. If $i \ne S$ go to sub-step b to process the next bacterium.
5. If $j < N_C$ go to step 3. In this case, continue chemotaxis since the life of the bacteria is not over.
6. **Reproduction:** For the given k and l, and for each $i = 1, 2, \cdots S$ let

$$F_{health}^i = \sum_{j=1}^{N_c+1} F(i, j, k, l) \qquad (6)$$

be the health of the bacteria. Sort bacteria in order of ascending values $\left(F_{health}\right)$. The S_r bacteria with the highest Fhealth values die and the other S_r bacteria with the best values split and the copies are placed at the same location as their parent.

7. If $k < N_{re}$ go to step 2. In this case the number of specified reproduction steps is not reached and start the next generation in the chemotactic loop.

8. **Elimination–Dispersal:** For $i = 1, 2, \cdots S$ with probability P_{ed}, eliminate and disperse each bacterium, which results in keeping the number of bacteria in the population constant. To do this, if a bacterium is eliminated, simply disperse one to a random location on the optimization domain. If $l < N_{ed}$ then go to step 2, otherwise ends.

In the BFOA, run-length unit is the size of the step taken in each swim or tumble. In order to use it to solve the problem of clustering, the run-length is changed to be adaptive. Here, we define $C(i)$ as follows:

$$C(i, j+1) = 0.00001 * Mlast * C(i, j) \qquad (7)$$

where i represents the ith bacterium, j the jth chemotaxis, *Mlast* the fitness value of the ith bacterium in j^{th} chemotaxis.

BF-FCM ALGORITHM

The Steps of BF-FCM

In this section, we combine BFOA and FCM to get a better clustering method called BF-FCM. We use BFOA to optimize clustering criterion function of FCM algorithm.

The clustering criterion function in FCM algorithm is taken as the fitness function $F(i, j, k, l)$ in BF-FCM. That is,

$$F(i, j, k, l) = J(X; U, V)$$
$$= \sum_{i=1}^{c} \sum_{k=1}^{N} (\mu_{ik})^m \left\| x_k - v_i \right\|_A^2 \qquad (8)$$

The steps of BF-FCM are as follows:

Step 1: According to the clustering category number c, set the bacteria number as its 10 times, which is $S = 10 * c$

Step 2: Select $e > 0$, initialize clustering center v_0 based on Equation 4, let $g = 1$

Step 3: Initialize parameters $n, S, N_C, N_S, N_{re}, N_{ed}, P_{ed}, C(i)$

Step 4: Calculate fuzzy matrix U^g according to the Equation 3.

Step 5: Compute the minimum value of the fitness function.

Step 6: If $\left\| v^{(k)} - v^{(k+1)} \right\| < e$ stop iteration, else let $g = g + 1$ and return to step 1.

Step 7: After the iteration in step 6, take the position of bacteria as the cluster centers. Then start clustering by FCM.

Step 8: When FCM finishes clustering, then BF-FCM ends.

The Effectiveness Evaluate of the BF-FCM

The experiments rely on evaluate numerical results of clustering algorithms based on FCM and BF-FCM. In order to evaluate the effectiveness of clustering, we adapt the CVIs (Chabrier et al., 2006; EL-Melegy et al., 2007; Nikhil & Bezdek, 1995) including Partition Coefficient (PC), Classification Entropy (PE), Separation index (S), Separation Coefficient (SC), Xie and Beni index (XB). BD (Better Rate) is an index that shows the better rate of CVIs obtained by BF-FCM considering the corresponding indexes by FCM. These indexes are the following:

- **Partition Coefficient (PC):** PC is used to measure the overlap between classes. It is defined by

$$PC(c) = \frac{1}{N}\sum_{i=1}^{c}\sum_{j=1}^{N}(\mu_{ij})^2 \qquad (9)$$

where μ_{ij} is the membership of data point j in category i.

- **Partition Entropy (PE):** PE measures the fuzzy degree of the category and its definition is as follows:

$$PE(c) = -\frac{1}{N}\sum_{i=1}^{c}\sum_{j=1}^{N}\mu_{ij}\log(\mu_{ij}) \qquad (10)$$

- **Separation and Compactness (SC):** What SC measures is the firmness sum between categories.

$$SC(c) = \sum_{i=1}^{c}\frac{\sum_{j=1}^{N}(\mu_{ij})^m \left\|x_j - v_i\right\|^2}{N_i\sum_{k=1}^{c}\left\|v_k - v_i\right\|^2} \qquad (11)$$

- **Separation Index (S):** On contrary to SC, the minimize distance is employs by S to classify data and it is defined by

$$S(c) = \frac{\sum_{i=1}^{c}\sum_{j=1}^{N}(\mu_{ij})^2 \left\|x_j - v_i\right\|^2}{N \min_{i,k}\left\|v_k - v_i\right\|^2} \qquad (12)$$

- **Xie and Beni Index (XB):** XB is a validation function proposed by Xie and Beni and it is defined by

$$XB(c) = \frac{\sum_{i=1}^{c}\sum_{j=1}^{N}(\mu_{ij})^m \left\|x_j - v_i\right\|^2}{N \min_{i,k}\left\|x_j - v_i\right\|^2} \qquad (13)$$

Among them, the bigger PC and S are, the better the clustering result is. While the smaller the PE, SC and XB are, the better the clustering result is. So PC and S need to be maximized, on the other hand, PE, SC and XB need to be minimized. Both FCM and BF-FCM were executed on each dataset for 100 times.

To compare the effectiveness of FCM and BF-FCM approaches, the clustering results for datasets of Iris, WISC, and Wine are given in Table 1, Table 2, and Table 3 respectively.

It is important to note that there were no heuristics for experiments with BF-FCM and the standard FCM. That means the values from Table 1 to Table 3 may be different each time after the experiment is conducted, except standard FCM, since it obtains the same results each time.

Tables 1, 2, and 3 show the quantitative results for the validity of BF-FCM. From Table 1 through Table 3, it can be seen that BF-FCM performs better than FCM considering CVIs. For data set IRIS, which contains 150 data in 3 classes (Anderson, 1935), BF-FCM outperforms FCM. PC and S of BF-FCM are bigger than those of FMC, though the minimum value and mean value of index S

Table 1. Clustering indexes of FCM and BF-FCM for Iris

CVI	FCM	BF-FCM			
	-	Min.	Mean	Max.	BD
S	0.0064	0.0017	0.0049	0.0085	16%
PC	0.7420	0.8782	0.9249	0.9802	100%
SC	0.6283	0.0411	0.1200	0.2091	100%
XB	4.0121	1.4190	3.2742	7.4386	69%
PE	0.4682	0.0403	0.1373	0.2312	100%

Table 2. Clustering indexes of FCM and BF-FCM for WISC

CVI	FCM	BF-FCM			
	-	Min.	Mean	Max.	BD
S	0.0006	0.000022	0.0016	0.0103	32%
PC	0.8751	0.9256	0.9944	1.0000	100%
SC	0.4272	0.0004	0.0315	0.2052	100%
XB	2.1816	1.6509	3.2352	13.1077	33%
PE	0.2112	0.000001	0.0106	0.1282	100%

Table 3. Clustering indexes of FCM and BF-FCM for Wine

CVI	FCM	BF-FCM			
	-	Min.	Mean	Max.	BD
S	0.0120	0.1984	12.49	305.81	100%
PC	0.5033	0.5082	0.7866	0.9776	100%
SC	1.6295	1.2556	216.53	2476.9	1%
XB	0.9725	1.2744	3.2243	9.7694	0%
PE	0.8546	0.0519	0.3790	0.8461	100%

are smaller and the BD is 16%. For index SC and index PE, all the results found by BF-FCM are smaller than that of FCM. For index XB, although the maximum value obtained by BF-FCM is bigger than that of FCM, the BF-FCM algorithm can also find smaller values, with 69% Better Rate.

The BDs are 100% for two algorithms. For index S, BF-FCM got 100% BD on only Wine dataset. The other two datasets are 16% for Iris and 32% for WISC respectively. BF-FCM got the best results on dataset Iris and WISC for SC. BDs of them are 100%, but it is only 1% for Wine. In

the case of XB, the results are extremely awful, especially for WISC and Wine. The BD indexes for Iris, WISC and Wine are 69%, 33%, 0%, respectively. In summary, BF-FCM can obtain better cluster results considering PE, PC, SC, and S for Wine, except for SC on Wine dataset,

WISC dataset contains 699 examples in 2 classes: benign and malignant (Wolberg & Mangasarian, 1990). BF-FCM (PC, SC and PE) obtained the best results since all the solutions of PC, SC and PE obtained 100% Better Rate. In the case of S and XB, BF-FCM got only 32%

and 33% Better Rate, respectively. For the third dataset, Wine contains 178 instances grouped into 3 classes (Aeberhard et al., 1992). BF-FCM obtained 100% Better Rate in considering PC, PE and S. But for XB and SC, BF-FCM got the worst results. In summary, BF-FCM can obtain better cluster based on the evaluation of CVIs,except for SC on Wine dataset.

IMAGE SEGMENTATION EXPERIMENTS

Image Segmentation Steps

The dataset used in image segmentation experiments was obtained from the USC-SIPI Image Database (http://sipi.usc.edu/database/). They are Lena, Elaine, Tank, Truck, Truck-APCs, House, Fishing Boat and Airplane. Image characteristic plays an important role in segmentation because it embodies information of the image. Pixel gray value is an important characteristic when making a distinction between target and background. The surface roughness can be used to characterize the degree of grayscale mutation between regions in image (Charalampidis & Kasparis, 2002; Yue et al., 2010). Therefore we chose pixel value and images roughness as the features of clustering.

The procedure of image segmentation of BF-FCM is described as follows:

Step 1: Selecting an image, and turn it into gray image.
Step 2: Calculate roughness according to Equation 14.
Step 3: Construct two-dimensional features data sets based on gray value and roughness.
Step 4: Initialize parameters of BA-FCM, and run it.
Step 5: Display image segmentation results after this algorithm is finished.

Initialization

The parameters of BF-FCM are given in Table 4. The number of clustering center of BF-FCM is the same as that of FCM. Amongst these parameters, e is the convergence indicator.

Experiments Results

Image segmentation approaches of current work are unsupervised, so the ground truth is used only as a final evaluation step, to quantify image segmentation results. The results are shown in Figures 1, 2, 3, 4, 5, 6, and 7.

Figure 8 shows an airplane (F-16) flying across mountains. This a little simple image for both object and background. For BF-FCM, the airplane is segmented more sufficient, but it failed to recognize the blue sky on the top right hand corner.

Results of segmentation consider each approach and all quality measures. Quantitative and qualitative image segmentation results are shown in Table 5 and Figures 1 through 8, respectively. For these images there is no ground truth (no true labels). Thus, the evaluation about how measure/

Table 4. The initialization of BF-FCM

BF-FCM		
	n	2
	c	9
	e	0.000001
	S	90
	N_C	50
Parameters	N_s	4
	N_{re}	4
	N_{ed}	2
	P_{ed}	0.25

Figure 1. The original image and the segmentation results of Lena; (a) original image for Lena; (b) Lena FCM; (c) Lena BF-FCM

(a)   (b)   (c)

Figure 2. The original image and the segmentation results of Elaine; (a) original image for Elaine; (b) Elaine FCM; (c) Elaine BF-FCM

(a)   (b)   (c)

Figure 3. The original image and the segmentation results of Tank; (a) original image for Tank; (b) Tank FCM; (c) Tank BF-FCM

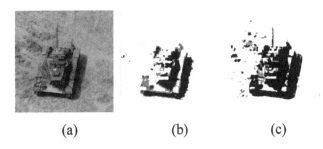

(a)   (b)   (c)

Figure 4. The original image and the segmentation results of Truck; (a) The original image for Truck; (b) Truck: FCM; (c) Truck: BF-FCM

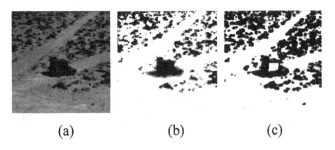

(a)   (b)   (c)

Figure 5. The original image and the segmentation results of Truck and APCs; (a) original image for Truck and APCs; (b) Truck and APCs FCM; (c) Truck and APCs BF-FCM

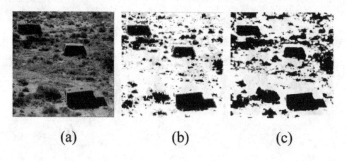

(a)   (b)   (c)

Figure 6. The original image and the segmentation results of Houser; (a) original image for House; (b) House FCM; (c) House BF_FCM

(a)   (b)   (c)

Figure 7. The original image and the segmentation results of Fishing Boat;(a) original image for Fishing Boat; (b) Fishing Boat FCM; (c) Fishing Boat BF_FCM

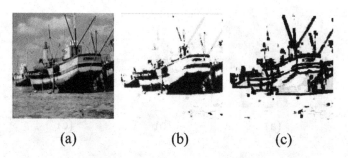

(a)   (b)   (c)

Figure 8. The original image and the segmentation results of Airplane; (a) original image for Airplane;(b) Airplane FCM; (c) Airplane BF_FCM

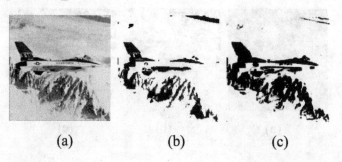

(a)   (b)   (c)

Table 5. The indexes of clustering effect evaluation of images

Image	Algorithm	S	PC	SC	XB	PE
Lena	FCM	0.0000313	0.5098	0.9832	27.2839	1.1299
	BF_FCM	0.0110000	0.8036	0.6085	2.9565	0.4206
Elaine	FCM	0.0000398	0.4820	0.9828	54.6343	1.1834
	BF-FCM	0.0175000	0.7638	1.0272	4.1596	0.5270
Tank	FCM	0.0000457	0.4777	1.1124	21.9265	1.1408
	BF-FCM	0.0100000	0.8171	0.6060	3.9722	0.4063
Truck	FCM	0.0000712	0.4521	1.6780	13.8535	1.2344
	BF-FCM	0.0111000	0.7911	0.6966	4.6567	0.4338
Truck- APCs	FCM	0.0000317	0.4268	1.3082	30.3332	1.3139
	BF-FCM	0.0189000	0.7974	1.1220	7.5732	0.4514
House	FCM	0.0000437	0.5263	1.1029	34.517	1.0916
	BF-FCM	0.0043000	0.8392	0.2870	4.7414	0.3473
Fishing Boat	FCM	0.0000353	0.4909	0.9106	24.4442	1.1362
	BF-FCM	0.0129000	0.8107	0.7913	3.3354	0.4198
Airplane	FCM	0.0000376	0.5612	0.8721	41.2151	0.9554
	BF-FCM	0.0056000	0.8486	0.3914	5.3391	0.3076

approach has the best result needs to be made through quantitative and qualitative results.

For the Lena image, both approaches have problems with regions of hat and skin, but BF-FCM got clearer boundary, and all the indexes of BF-FCM are better than those of FCM. For Elaine image, qualitative analysis shows that BF-FCM got better results in hat, face, closing and boundary. Quantitative analysis shows that all the indexes are better except SC, which is a little bigger than that of FCM. For the four military images: Tank, Truck, Truck-APCs and Airplane, although most of them are complicated with different bevels and camouflage paintings, the segmentation results of BF-FCM are better since all the indexes are better than those of FCM. For House and Fishing Boat, both of them have multi-objects and complex backgrounds. Quantitative analysis shows that BF-FCM had better results since all the indexes are better than those of FCM.

Quantitative results in Table 5 show that BF-FCM gets better results because all the indexes are better than that of FCM. On the whole, BF-FCM

indeed can make a decent improvement in image segmentation. We can see that all the clustering effect evaluation indexes are consistent with the results of the qualitative analysis.

CONCLUSION AND PERSPECTIVES

This paper proposes a hybrid algorithm, called BF-FCM, which is combined an intelligent optimization algorithm known as Bacteria Foraging with the standard FCM. It intends to make some improvements on the performance of FCM in image segmentation. This new approach aims at optimizing the cluster criterion function directly related to the cluster centers of FCM to improve the quality of clustering. Two kinds of experiments are conducted. Qualitative and quantitative results are obtained in order to evaluate the clustering effectiveness of BF-FCM. The quantitative results are obtained by calculating 5 CVIs and an additional index BD for the second experiment. All the experiments results are compared to those obtained by standard FCM and quantitative analysis shows that the BF-FCM has better performance than FCM on the datasets and images used in the paper.

Although BF-FCM can make better image segmentation, some problems still exist. The time consuming of BF-FCM will increase explosively with the increasing of number of cluster centers. For the image segmentation, it only takes gray scale images into account and adopts gray value and roughness as features for segmentation. It is necessary to testify it on color images and consider the other image characteristics, like texture, region and borders in future research.

ACKNOWLEDGMENT

This work is partially supported by the National Natural Science Foundation of China under Grant No.60973075 and the Excellent Young Teacher Foundation of Heilongjiang Province of China under Grant No.1155G18.

REFERENCES

Aeberhard, S., Coomans, D., & Vel, O. D. (1992). *Comparison of classifiers in high dimensional settings* (Tech. Rep. No. 92-02). North Queensland, Australia: James Cook University of North Queensland.

Anderson, E. (1935). The irises of the Gaspe Peninsula. *Bulletin of the American Iris Society*, *59*, 2–5.

Andrey, P. (1999). Selectionist relaxation: Genetic algorithms applied to image segmentation. *Image and Vision Computing*, *17*(3-4), 175–187. doi:10.1016/S0262-8856(98)00095-X

Bezdek, J. C. (1981). *Patten recognition with fuzzy objective function algorithm*. New York, NY: Plenum Press.

Bhandarkar, S. M., & Zhang, H. (1999). Image segmentation using evolutionary computation. *IEEE Transactions on Evolutionary Computation*, *3*(1), 1–21. doi:10.1109/4235.752917

Bhanu, L. S., & Ming, J. (1995). Adaptive image segmentation using a genetic algorithm. *IEEE Transactions on Systems, Man, and Cybernetics*, *25*(12), 1543–1567. doi:10.1109/21.478442

Chabrier, S., Emile, B., Rosenberger, C., & Laurent, H. (2006). Unsupervised performance evaluation of image segmentation. *EURASIP Journal on Applied Signal Processing*, 1–12. doi:10.1155/ASP/2006/96306

Charalampidis, D., & Kasparis, T. (2002). Wavelet-based rotational invariant roughness features for texture classification and segmentation. *IEEE Transactions on Image Processing*, *11*(8), 825–837. doi:10.1109/TIP.2002.801117

Chen, J. S., & Wei, G. (2002). A hybrid clustering algorithm incorporating fuzzy c-means into canonical genetic algorithm. *Journal of Electronics & Information Technology*, *24*(2), 102–103.

Coleman, G. B., & Andrews, H. C. (1979). Image segmentation by clustering. *Proceedings of the Institute of Electrical and Electronics Engineers*, *67*, 773–785.

Das, S., & Sila, S. (2010). Kernel-induced fuzzy clustering of image pixels with an improved differential evolution algorithm. *Information Sciences*, *180*(8), 1237–1256. doi:10.1016/j.ins.2009.11.041

El-Melegy, M., Zanaty, E. A., Abd-Elhariez, W. M., & Farag, A. (2007). On cluster validity index in fuzzy and hard clustering algorithms for image segmentation. *IEEE International Conference on Image Processing*, *6*, 5-8.

Felzenszwalb, P. F., & Huttenlocher, D. P. (2004). Efficient graph-based image segmentation. *International Journal of Computer Vision*, *59*(2), 167–181. doi:10.1023/B:VISI.0000022288.19776.77

Gong, M. G., Jiao, L. C., Bo, L. F., Wang, L., & Zhang, X. G. (2008). Image texture classification using a manifold distance based evolutionary clustering method. *Optical Engineering (Redondo Beach, Calif.)*, *47*(7), 1–10. doi:10.1117/1.2955785

Hijjatoleslami, S A , & Kitter, J (1998). Region growing: A new approach. *IEEE Transactions on Image Processing*, *7*(7), 1079–1084. doi:10.1109/83.701170

Jain, A. K., Murty, M. N., & Flynn, P. J. (1999). Data clustering: A review. *ACM Computing Surveys*, *31*(3), 264–323. doi:10.1145/331499.331504

Koppen, M., Franke, M., & Vicente-Garcia, R. (2006). Tiny GAs for image processing applications. *IEEE Computational Intelligence Magazine*, *1*(2), 17–26. doi:10.1109/MCI.2006.1626491

Liu, L. P., & Meng, Z. Q. (2004). An initial centrepoints selection method for k-means clustering. *Computer Engineering and Application*, *40*(8), 179–180.

Mardia, K. V., & Hainsworth, T. J. (1988). A spatial thresholding method for image segmentation. *IEEE Transactions on Pattern Analysis and Machine Intelligence*, *10*(6), 919–927. doi:10.1109/34.9113

Maulik, U. (2009). Medical image segmentation using genetic algorithms. *IEEE Transactions on Information Technology in Biomedicine*, *13*(2), 166–173. doi:10.1109/TITB.2008.2007301

Melkemi, K. E., Batouche, M., & Foufou, S. (2006). A multiagent system approach for image segmentation using genetic algorithms and extremal optimization heuristics. *Pattern Recognition Letters*, *27*(11), 1230–1238. doi:10.1016/j.patrec.2005.07.021

Nie, S. D., Zhang, Y. L., & Chen, Z. X. (2008). Improved genetic fuzzy clustering algorithm and its application in segmentation of MR brain images. *Chinese Journal of Biomedical Engineering*, *27*(6).

Nikhil, R. P., & Bezdek, J. C. (1995). On cluster validity for the fuzzy c-means model. *IEEE Transactions on Fuzzy Systems*, *3*(3), 370–379. doi:10.1109/91.413225

Pal, N. R., & Pal, S. K. (1993). A review on image segmentation techniques. *Pattern Recognition*, *26*(9), 1227–1294. doi:10.1016/0031-3203(93)90135-J

Passino, K. M. (2002). Biomimicry of bacterial foraging for distributed optimization and control. *Control Systems Magazine of the Institute of Electrical and Electronics Engineers*, *22*(3), 52–67. doi:10.1109/MCS.2002.1004010

Perona, P., & Malik, J. (1990). Scale-space and edge detection using anisotropic diffusion. *IEEE Transactions on Pattern Analysis and Machine Intelligence*, *12*(7), 629–639. doi:10.1109/34.56205

Shao, Y. C., & Chen, H. N. (2009). Cooperative bacterial foraging optimization. In *Proceedings of the International Conference on Future Bio-Medical Information Engineering* (pp. 486-488).

Shapiro, L. G., & Stockman, G. C. (2001). *Computer vision* (pp. 279–325). Upper Saddle River, NJ: Prentice Hall.

Sowmya, B., & Sheela Rani, B. (2011). Colour image segmentation using fuzzy clustering techniques and competitive neural network. *Applied Soft Computing, 11*(3), 3170–3178. doi:10.1016/j.asoc.2010.12.019

Tian, X. L., Jiao, L. C., & Gou, S. P. (2008). SAR image segmentation based on spatially constrained FCM optimized by particle swarm optimization. *Acta Electronica Sinica, 36*(3), 453–457.

Veenman, C. J., Reinders, M. J. T., & Backer, E. (2003). A cellular coevolutionary algorithm for image segmentation. *IEEE Transactions on Image Processing, 12*(3), 304–313. doi:10.1109/TIP.2002.806256

Wolberg, W. H., & Mangasarian, O. L. (1990). Multisurface method of pattern separation for medical diagnosis applied to breast cytology. *Proceedings of the National Academy of Sciences of the United States of America, 87*(23), 9193–9196. doi:10.1073/pnas.87.23.9193

Wu, K. L., & Yang, M. S. (2002). Alternative c-means clustering algorithms. *Pattern Recognition, 35*(10), 2267–2278. doi:10.1016/S0031-3203(01)00197-2

Yang, L. C., Zhao, L. N., & Wu, X. Q. (2007). Medical image segmentation of fuzzy C-means clustering based on the ant colony algorithm. *Journal of ShanDong University, 37*(3).

Yang, X. C., Zhao, W. D., Chen, Y. F., & Fang, X. (2008). Image segmentation with a fuzzy clustering algorithm based on ant-tree. *Signal Processing, 88*(10), 2453–2462. doi:10.1016/j.sigpro.2008.04.005

Ying, C., Shao, Z. B., Mi, H., & Wu, Q. H. (2008). An application of bacterial foraging algorithm in image compression. *Journal of ShenZhen University, 25*(2).

Yue, X. D., Miao, D. Q., & Zhong, C. M. (2010). Roughness measure approach to color image segmentation. *Acta Automatica Sinica, 36*(6), 807–816. doi:10.3724/SP.J.1004.2010.00807

Zeng, L., Wang, M. L., & Chen, H. F. (2008). Genetic fuzzy c-means clustering algorithm for magnetic resonance images segmentation. *Journal of University of Electronic Science and Technology of China, 37*(4), 627–629.

This work was previously published in the International Journal of Swarm Intelligence Research, Volume 2, Issue 3, edited by Yuhui Shi, pp. 16-29, copyright 2011 by IGI Publishing (an imprint of IGI Global).

Chapter 12
Minimum Span Frequency Assignment Based on a Multiagent Evolutionary Algorithm

Jing Liu
Xidian University, China

Weicai Zhong
Northwest A&F University, China

Jinshu Li
Xidian University, China

Li Zhang
Soochow University, China

Ruochen Liu
Xidian University, China

ABSTRACT

In frequency assignment problems (FAPs), separation of the frequencies assigned to the transmitters is necessary to avoid the interference. However, unnecessary separation causes an excess requirement of spectrum, the cost of which may be very high. Since FAPs are closely related to T-coloring problems (TCP), multiagent systems and evolutionary algorithms are combined to form a new algorithm for minimum span FAPs on the basis of the model of TCP, which is named as Multiagent Evolutionary Algorithm for Minimum Span FAPs (MAEA-MSFAPs). The objective of MAEA-MSFAPs is to minimize the frequency spectrum required for a given level of reception quality over the network. In MAEA-MSFAPs, all agents live in a latticelike environment. Making use of the designed behaviors, MAEA-MSFAPs realizes the ability of agents to sense and act on the environment in which they live. During the process of interacting with the environment and other agents, each agent increases the energy as much as possible so that MAEA-MSFAPs can find the optima. Experimental results on TCP with different sizes and Philadelphia benchmark for FAPs show that MAEA-MSFAPs have a good performance and outperform the compared methods.

DOI: 10.4018/978-1-4666-2479-5.ch012

INTRODUCTION

Wireless communication networks, which employ radio frequencies to establish communication links, have undergone a dramatic expansion over the past two decades. Since the available radio spectrum is very limited, to meet the demand of today's radio communication, this resource has to be administered and reused carefully in order to control mutual interference. Thus, given the continuing rapid growth in demand for wireless services, frequency assignment problems (FAPs) play a key role in the planning of such networks (Galinier, Gendreau, Soriano, & Bisaillon, 2005), which are concerned with the assignment of discrete channels to the transmitters of a radio network. FAPs are difficult in terms of complexity theory. Deciding whether a mobile network allows a feasible assignment is NP-complete, and the corresponding optimization problems are strongly NP-hard (Martin, 2000).

There has been a considerable research effort for solving FAPs. Valenzuela *et al.* (1998) proposed a permutation based genetic algorithm for solving minimum span FAPs (MSFAPs). Won-Young *et al.* (2006) proposed a heuristic method, namely frequency insertion strategy (FIS), which starts with a narrow enough frequency bands so as to provoke violations of constraints and then resolve the violations by inserting frequencies. Several neural network algorithms have been also proposed for FAPs. For example, Kunz (1993) used Hopfield neural network and obtained optimal solutions for some special instances of MSFAPs Idoumghar *et al.* (2009) proposed two distributed algorithms for the FAP in the field of radio broadcasting.

In FAPs, separation of the frequencies assigned to the transmitters is necessary to avoid the interference. However, unnecessary separation causes an excess requirement of spectrum, the cost of which may be very high. From this viewpoint, FAPs are closely related to T-coloring problems (TCPs) where the vertices of a graph represent the transmitters and adjacencies indicate possible interferences (Riihijärvi, Petrova, & Mähönen, 2005; Hurley & Smith, 1997; Bodlaender, Kloks, Tan, & van Leeuwen, 2000). TCPs are a generalized version of classical graph coloring problems (GCPs), which are one of the most studied NP-hard problems and can be defined informally as follows (Costa, 1993): Given an undirected graph, one wishes to color the vertices of the graph with a minimum number of colors in such a way that two colors assigned to any two adjacent vertices must be different. That is to say, they must have a minimum distance greater than zero. These classical GCPs are just a special case of TCPs. Unfortunately, due to the difficulty and complexity of TCPs, there has rather few researches on this problem. Some classical methods were proposed several years ago, such as tabu search (Dorne & Hao, 1998) and *Dsatur* (Janczewski & Kubale, 1998). Until now, there is no benchmark available for evaluating and comparing different algorithms for TCPs.

To solve TCPs, optimizing algorithms with strong searching ability are required. In our previous work, based on multiagent systems, a new numerical optimization algorithm, multiagent genetic algorithm (MAGA), has been proposed in Zhong, Liu, Xue, and Jiao (2004) to handle large-scale global numerical optimization problems. The experimental results shown that MAGA can solve numerical optimization problems with 1000 dimensions. The method was also extended to handle constraint satisfaction problems (Liu, Zhong, & Jiao, 2006) and combinatorial optimization problems (Liu, Zhong, & Jiao, 2010), which illustrated the potential of the combination of multiagent systems and evolutionary algorithms in solving complex problems. Thus, on the basis of TCPs, we extended MAGA to solve minimum span FAPs, which is labeled as MAEA-MSFAPs. In experiments, TCP with different sizes and Philadelphia benchmark for FAPs are used to validate the performance of MAEA-MSFAPs.

In the rest of this paper, the mathematical model for FAPs is described first. Next we describe MAEA-MSFAPs. We give the experimental results and the last section concludes this paper.

MATHEMATICAL MODEL FOR FAPS

We adopt the description and definition introduced by Hale (1980), which formulated FAPs in a graph-theoretical language. Given a finite set of transmitters located in a same region, the aim is to assign a frequency for each transmitter in such a way that no interference occurs. If we take each transmitter as a node, an undirected graph $G=(V, E)$ can be used to formalize this problem, where $V=\{v_1, v_2, ..., v_n\}$ represents the set of transmitters, namely nodes in the graph, and $E=\{e_{ij} \mid$ an edge between v_i and $v_j\}$ denotes the set of edges. In TCPs, the forbidden separation distance for colors assigned to adjacent vertices is no longer limited to the singleton $\{0\}$, but may be any set of positive integers. A collection of sets $T=\{T_{ij} \subset IN \mid$ for each $e_{ij} \in E\}$ is now defined to determine for each edge e_{ij} the color separations which are not allowed between the nodes v_i and v_j, where IN is the set of integers; that is, each T_{ij} is a set of unsigned integers such as $\{0, 1, 5, 8\}$, and the color constraint is (Dorne & Hao, 1998):

$$\forall e_{ij} \in \mathbf{E}, \ \left|c(v_i) - c(v_j)\right| \notin \mathbf{T}_{ij} \tag{1}$$

where the color of each vertex is coded as an integer, and $c(v_i)$ is the color assigned to vertex v_i.

The separation of colors assigned to two adjacent vertices v_i and v_j must be different from those of T_{ij}. A T-coloring of a graph is a partition of V in different color classes $C_1, C_2, ..., C_k$, so that the property (1) is satisfied for each edge of G. The *chromatic number* $\chi_T(G)$ corresponds to the minimum number of different color values used to color G. The *span* of a T-coloring is the difference between the smallest and the highest color values needed to obtain the T-coloring of G. The objective of TCPs is to determine the *minimum span $sp_T(G)$* for all the possible colorings of G (Hale, 1980).

If each $T_{ij} \in T$ is a set of consecutive integers in the form $T_{ij}=\{0, 1, 2, ..., t_{ij}-1\}$, the restricted T-coloring problem (RTCP) can be defined by changing (1) to

$$\forall e_{ij} \in \mathbf{E}, \ \left|c(v_i) - c(v_j)\right| \geq t_{ij} \tag{2}$$

where t_{ij} is a fixed positive number associated to each edge e_{ij}. It is easy to see that the classical graph coloring problem is a special case of the T-colorings problem where all $T_{ij}=\{0\}$.

In FAPs, the system must accommodate each and every customer request (or call) by assigning a frequency while satisfying the constraints imposed to avoid the radio interference among channels. Such constraints can be conveniently summarized by a symmetric matrix, called the compatibility matrix denoted by $C=[c_{ij}]$. An element in the compatibility matrix c_{ij} specifies the minimum allowed difference of the frequency spectrum assigned to an arbitrary pair of calls, when one of the pair is demanded in the ith cell and the other in the jth cell.

By defining f_{ik}, which is a non-negative integer, as the decision variable which specifies the frequency assigned to the kth call in the ith cell, the mathematical model for FAPs can be written as follows (Won-Young, Soo, Jaewwook, & Chi-Hyuck, 2006):

$$\text{Minimize } \max_{i,k} f_{ik}$$
$$\text{subject to } \left|f_{ik} - f_{jl}\right| \geq c_{ij}, \tag{3}$$
$$\text{for all } i, \ j, \ k, \ l \ (k \neq l, \text{ if } i = j)$$

The span of a FAP is the difference between the lowest and the highest frequencies used after the assignment of all the calls. The objective of MSFAPs is to find a frequency assignment that satisfies all the constraints and so that the *span* of the assignment is minimized.

The vertex v_i in RTCP has the same meaning with *call* in FAP, and t_{ij} plays the same role as c_{ij} in FAP. Both t_{ij} and c_{ij} specify the constraints. Therefore, the color $c(v_i)$ just likes the frequency f_{ik} in FAP. The difference between RTCP and FAP is that all the vertices in RTCP are different with each other. However, in FAP calls belong to cells in groups. All calls in the same cell have the same constraints. In FAP, *the degree of cell* is interpreted as the difficulty of assigning a frequency to a call in a cell (Won-Young, Soo, Jaewwook, & Chi-Hyuck, 2006). The degree of the *i*th cell, which is labeled as d_i, is defined as:

$$d_i = \left(\sum_{j=1}^{N} c_{ij} m_j \right) - c_{ii}, \quad 1 \leq i \leq N \qquad (4)$$

where N is the total number of cells and m_j is the number of calls requested in the *j*th cell. The node-degree policy is proposed by Zoellner and Beall (1977), where cells are arranged in decreasing order of their degrees.

MULTIAGENT EVOLUTIONARY ALGORITHM FOR MSFAPS

Agents for FAPs

Agents for FAPs are defined as follows.

Definition 1. An agent for FAPs, agent, represents an element in the search space, S, and each agent can be described as an integer permutation as follows:

$$\mathbf{agent} = (c_1, \ c_2, \ ..., \ c_l), \ c_i \in \mathbf{IN} \qquad (5)$$

where l is the total number of calls in all cells.

The domain for each variable is finite and discrete, thus the elements can be numbered by natural numbers. When all domains are transformed into the sets of natural numbers, the solutions of the problem present specific characteristics. So we defined the permutation agent and the solution agent. A permutation agent is represented by a permutation of 1, 2, ..., *l*, which means the order we color the vertices, while a solution agent is represented by a set of natural numbers which means the solution we colored the vertices. Each solution agent is the color result according to one permutation agent. According to Definition 1, each element in an *agent* stands for a call in a certain cell, and the number of elements in an agent is equal to the total number of calls in all cells.

Definition 2. All agents live in a latticelike environment, which is labeled as L. Each agent can only interact with the neighbors. Let the agent located at (i, j) be labeled as $L_{i,j}$, i, j=1, 2, ..., L_{size}, then the neighbors of $L_{i,j}$, namely *Neighbors*$_{i,j}$, are defined as follows:

$$\text{Neighbors}_{i,j} = \left\{ L_{i',j}, \ L_{i,j'}, \ L_{i'',j}, \ L_{i,j''} \right\} \qquad (6)$$

where

$$i' = \begin{cases} i-1 & i \neq 1 \\ L_{size} & i = 1 \end{cases}$$

$$j' = \begin{cases} j-1 & j \neq 1 \\ L_{size} & j = 1 \end{cases}$$

$$i'' = \begin{cases} i+1 & i \neq L_{size} \\ 1 & i = L_{size} \end{cases}$$

$$j'' = \begin{cases} j+1 & j \neq L_{size} \\ 1 & j = L_{size} \end{cases}$$

The agent lattice can be represented as the one in Figure 1. Each circle represents an agent, and

Figure 1. Agent lattice

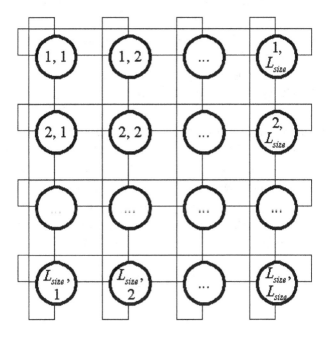

the data represent the position in the lattice. Two agents can interact with each other if and only if there is a line connecting them.

As what we are concerned about is the minimum span of FAPs, we define the energy of an agent as follows:

Definition 3. The energy of an agent is the negative value of the difference between the lowest and the highest frequency used after the assignment of all calls; that is,

$$\forall \mathbf{agent} \in S,$$
$$Energy(\mathbf{agent}) = -span(\mathrm{FAP}) \quad (7)$$

It is obvious that the energy of an agent for a TCP is equal to $-sp_T(G)$. The purpose of an agent is to maximize the energy by the behaviors it takes. As can be seen, the higher the energy is, the smaller the span is, which means the closer to the optimal solutions. Since each agent must record some information, it is represented by the following structure:

```
Agent = Record
P: P∈S;
E: The energy of the agent,
E=Energy(P);
SL: The flag for the self-learning
behavior. If SL is True, the self-
learning behavior can be performed on
the agent; otherwise, cannot;
End.
```

Behaviors of Agents

Three behaviors are designed for agents to realize their purposes, namely the competitive behavior, the self-learning behavior, and the mutation behavior.

Competitive Behavior

In this behavior, the energy of an agent is compared with those of the neighbors. The agent can survive if the energy is maximum; otherwise, it must die, and the child of the one with the maximum energy among its neighbors will take up the lattice-point.

Suppose that the competitive behavior is performed on the agent located at (i, j), which is labeled as $L_{i,j}$, and $Max_{i,j}$ is the agent with maximum energy among the neighbors of $L_{i,j}$; that is, $Max_{i,j} \in Neighbors_{i,j}$ and $\forall agent \in Neighbors_{i,j}$, $agent(E) < Max_{i,j}(E)$. If $L_{i,j}(E) < Max_{i,j}(E)$, then $Max_{i,j}$ generates a child agent, namely $Child_{i,j}$, to replace $L_{i,j}$, and the method is shown in Algorithm 1; otherwise, $L_{i,j}$ is left untouched.

In fact, $Child_{i,j}$ is generated by exchanging a small part of $Max_{i,j}$, and is equivalent to performing a local search around $Max_{i,j}$. The goal of the competitive behavior is to eliminate the agents with lower energy, and give more chances to agents which high potential.

Self-Learning Behavior

This behavior is designed by making use of local search techniques. After the self-learning behavior is performed on an agent, the probability of increasing its energy by this behavior again is very low, thus $L_{i,j}(SL)$ is set to *False* at the last step.

The goal of Algorithm 2 is to find a certain swap method for the components in the permutation to increase the energy of $L_{i,j}$. For each component, the algorithm iteratively performs a swap until the predefined iterative count, $Iteration = (N-1)/4$, is reached. Then, the algorithm goes on to deal with the next component. *Iteration* is designed to prevent the algorithm from repeating infinitely.

Algorithm 1. Competitive behavior

Input:	:$Max_{i,j}$	$Max_{i,j}(P) := \langle m_1, m_2, ..., m_N \rangle$;
	L_{size}:	The scale of the agent lattice;
	P_c:	The parameter used in the competitive behavior;
Output:	$Child_{i,j}$:	$Child_{i,j}(P) := \langle c_1, c_2, ..., c_N \rangle$;

Swap(x, y) exchanges the value of x and y. *Rand(0, 1)* is a uniform random number between 0 and 1. *Random(N, i)* is a random integer among 1, 2, ..., N and is not equal to i. Here N is the number of calls of all the cells. $P(x)$ is the position of a call x in the permutation. If x is the first element in $Child_{i,j}(P)$, $p(x):=1$; if x is the last one, $p(x):=N$. $max(x, y)$ gives the larger one between x and y, while $min(x, y)$ gives the smaller one.

```
begin
  Child_{i,j}(P):=Max_{i,j}(P);
  i:=1;
  repeat
    if (Rand(0, 1)<P_c) then
    begin
      l:=Random(N, i);
      b:=max(p(i), p(l));
      s:=min(p(i), p(l));
      if (d_b>d_s) then Swap(c_i, c_l);
    end;
    i:=i+1;
  until (i>N);
  Child_{i,j}(SL):=True;
end.
```

Algorithm 2. Self-learning behavior

Input:	$\textbf{\textit{agent}}_{best}$:	The agent with the highest energy in current generation, and $\textbf{\textit{agent}}_{best}(\textbf{\textit{P}}):=(p_1, p_2, ..., p_N)$;
Output:	$\textbf{\textit{agent}}_{learn}$:	The result after the self-learning behavior, and $\textbf{\textit{agent}}_{learn}(\textbf{\textit{P}}):=(a_1, a_2, ..., a_N)$;

```
begin
  agent_learn(P):= agent_best(P);
  repeat
    Repeat:=False;
    k:=1;
    Iteration:=1;
    while (k≤N) do
    begin
      Energy_best:=agent_best(E);
      l:=Random(N, i);
      Swap(a_i, a_l);
      Energy_learn:=agent_learn(E);
      if (Energy_best≥Energy_learn) then Swap(a_i, a_l)
      else begin Repeat:=True; k:=k+1; end;
      if (Iteration<(N-1)/4) then Iteration:=Iteration+1
      else begin Iteration:=1; k:=k+1; end;
    end;
  until (Repeat=True);
  L_{i,j}(SL):=False;
end.
```

Mutation Behavior

This behavior is similar to the mutation operator used in traditional genetic algorithms. It can enlarge the search area so as to make up the disadvantage of the other operators. We perform this behavior on 35% components of the parent generation. All agents involved in this behavior will be replaced by the children of $\textbf{\textit{agent}}_{best}$, and each child is generated by exchanging a small part of $\textbf{\textit{agent}}_{best}$ according to the mutation probability, P_m. Suppose that this behavior is performed on $L_{i,j}$, and $L_{i,j}(P)=\langle p_1, p_2, ..., p_N \rangle$. The following operation is conducted:

$$\text{If } Rand_k(0, 1) < P_m, \\ \text{then } \textbf{L}_{i,j}(P_k) = \textbf{Child}(\textbf{agent}_{best}) \tag{8}$$

where $k=1, 2, ..., N \times 0.35$. P_m is a predefined real number between 0 and 1.

Implementation of MAEA-MSFAPs

At each generation, the competitive behavior is performed on each agent first. As a result, the agents with lower energy are cleaned out from the agent lattice so that there is more space for the agents with higher energy, and then the self-learning behavior is performed according to the self-learning flag of the agent. In order to reduce the computational cost, this behavior is only performed on the best agent in the current agent lattice. Finally, the mutation behavior is performed on a part of the agents. The whole process is performed iteratively until the agent with highest energy is found or the maximum computational cost is reached. See Algorithm 3.

Algorithm 3. MAEA-MSFAPs

Input:	*Evaluation$_{max}$*:	The maximum number of evaluations for the energy;
	L_{size}:	The scale of the agent lattice;
	P_c:	The parameter used in the competitive behavior;
	P_m:	The parameter used in the mutation behavior;
Output:	A solution or an approximate solution for the MSFAPs;	

L^t represents the agent lattice in the t th generation. **agent**$_{best}^t$ is the best agent in L^0, L^1, ..., L^t, and **agent**$_{tbest}^t$ is the best agent in L^t.

begin
  for i:=1 **to** L_{size} **do**
    for j:=1 **to** L_{size} **do**
    begin
Generate a permutation randomly and assign it to $\mathbf{L}_{i,j}^0(\mathbf{P})$;
Compute $\mathbf{L}_{i,j}^0(E)$;
    $\mathbf{L}_{i,j}^0(SL) := True$;
    end;
  Evaluations:=$L_{size} \times L_{size}$;
Update **agent**$_{best}^0$;
  t:=0;
  repeat
    for i:=1 **to** L_{size} **do**
      for j:=1 **to** L_{size} **do**
      begin
if ($L_{i,j}^t$ wins in the competitive behavior) **then** $L_{i,j}^{t+1} := L_{i,j}^t$;
      else $\mathbf{L}_{i,j}^{t+1} :=$ **Child**$_{ij}$ //generated according to Algorithm 1;
Compute $\mathbf{L}_{i,j}^{t+1}(E)$;
      Evaluations:=*Evaluations*+1;
      end;
Update **agent**$_{(t+1)best}^{t+1}$;
if (**agent**$_{(t+1)best}^{t+1}(SL) = True$) **then**
Perform the self-learning behavior on **agent**$_{(t+1)best}^{t+1}$;
    for i:=1 **to** L_{size} **do**
      for j:=1 **to** L_{size} **do**
      begin
Compute $L_{i,j}^t(P)$;
Perform the mutation behavior on $L_{i,j}^t$;
      end;
Update **agent**$_{(t+1)best}^{t+1}$;
if (**agent**$_{(t+1)best}^{t+1}(E) <$ **agent**$_{best}^t(E)$) **then**
begin
    agent$_{best}^{t+1} :=$ **agent**$_{best}^t$;
    agent$_{worst}^{t+1} :=$ **agent**$_{best}^t$ // **agent**$_{worst}^{t+1}$ is the agent with the lowest energy in L^{t+1};
end
  else agent$_{best}^{t+1} :=$ **agent**$_{(t+1)best}^t$;
  t:=t+1;
  until (*Evaluations* $\geq$ *Evaluation$_{max}$*);
end.

Table 1. The instances of TCPs used in the experiments

Instances	N	d	E
30.1.*Tcol*	30	0.1	43
30.5.*Tcol*	30	0.5	217
30.9.*Tcol*	30	0.9	391
100.1.*Tcol*	100	0.1	495
100.5.*Tcol*	100	0.5	2475
100.9.*Tcol*	100	0.9	4455
300.1.*Tcol*	300	0.1	4485
300.5.*Tcol*	300	0.5	22425
300.9.*Tcol*	300	0.9	40365
500.1.*Tcol*	500	0.1	12475
500.5.*Tcol*	500	0.5	62375
500.9.*Tcol*	500	0.9	112275
1000.1.*Tcol*	1000	0.1	49950
1000.5.*Tcol*	1000	0.5	249750
1000.9.*Tcol*	1000	0.9	449550

EXPERIMENTAL STUDY

Experiments on T-Coloring Problems

As no benchmark is available for TCPs, we follow the method referred in Riihijärvi, Petrova, and Mähönen (2005) to develop a random instance generator for restricted T-colorings. In this generator, each instance is defined by three parameters: (a) N: the number of vertices; (b) $d \in [0, 1]$: the edge density; (c) *Sep*: the largest color separation.

To generate such an instance, we first build a graph of N vertices with $d(N(N-1))/2$ edges uniformly distributed on these vertices. Then, a uniform random value from [1, *Sep*] is assigned to each edge. Thus, we build 15 random instances of restricted T-coloring denoted by *N.d.Tcol* with the following possible values: $N \in \{30, 100, 300, 500, 1000\}$, $d \in \{0.1, 0.5, 0.9\}$, *Sep*=5 (Table 1). In this table, E stands for the number of edges of different graphs. All these instances can be divided into five suites according to the different number of vertices.

Table 2 shows the experimental results of MAEA-MSFAPs on the instances in Table 1, and makes a comparison with the classical algorithm

Dsatur (Janczewski & Kubale, 1998). We used two criteria to evaluate the algorithm: sp_{best} and sp_{ave}, which respectively stand for the minimum span we could find and the average value of the minimum span we found. The smaller the estimate value is, the better the solution is. The experimental results in Table 2 show that our method outperforms *Dsatur* on all instances.

Experiments on Minimum Span Frequency Assignment Problems

Philadelphia benchmark is the most widely used problem set for evaluating algorithms for FAPs, which was introduced by Anderson (1973). This benchmark consists of nine problems, and the instances are characterized by 21 hexagons denoting the cells of a cellular phone practice to model wireless phone network around Philadelphia (see Figure 2). For the 21 cells, a demand c_v is given. Figure 3 shows the demand for the original instance P1. Table 3 contains the demand vectors of all instances. In the basic model, interference of cells is characterized by a co-channel reuse distance d. No interference occurs if and only if the centers of two cells have mutual distance

Table 2. Comparation between MAEA-MSFAPs and Dsatur on TCPs

Instances	Dsatur		MAEA-MSFAPs	
	sp_{best}	sp_{ave}	sp_{best}	sp_{ave}
30.1.*Tcol*	9	9.0	8	8.0
30.5.*Tcol*	23	25.2	19	19.0
30.9.*Tcol*	40	44.9	34	35.6
100.1.*Tcol*	23	23.0	17	17.8
100.5.*Tcol*	63	66.1	58	59.0
100.9.*Tcol*	124	125.0	112	114.1
300.1.*Tcol*	40	43.8	35	35.6
300.5.*Tcol*	159	161.3	156	157.8
300.9.*Tcol*	304	318.9	292	294.5
500.1.*Tcol*	61	62.5	55	56.6
500.5.*Tcol*	240	247.5	231	232.3
500.9.*Tcol*	483	493.1	473	474.1
1000.1.*Tcol*	104	105.1	92	93.7
1000.5.*Tcol*	436	441.4	426	430.3
1000.9.*Tcol*	896	904.2	879	886.7

Figure 2. Network structure of Philadelphia instances

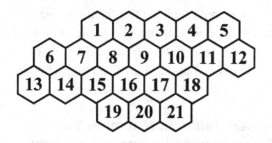

Figure 3. Demand of instance P1

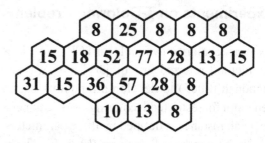

higher than or equal to *d*. In the case that the mutual distance is less than *d* (normalized by the radius of cells), it is not allowed to assign the same frequency to both calls. This pure co-channel case is generalized by replacing the reuse distance *d* by a series of non-increasing values d^0, d^1, ..., d^k. For instance P1, the values d^0, d^1, ..., d^5 are $2\sqrt{3}$, $\sqrt{3}$, 1, 1, 1, 0. Therefore, frequency assigned to the same site should be separated by at least 1 other frequency, whereas frequencies assigned to the second and third "call" of cells should still differ. For other Philadelphia instances, the reuse distances are given in Table 4.

A lot of research has been devoted to find lower and upper bounds on the required number of frequencies for Philadelphia instances, and Table 5 summarizes the best results reported so far. The shaded cells represent the optimum values. In this subsection, the performance of MAEA-MSFAPs is tested on the Philadelphia instances, and Table 6 shows the performance of MAEA-MSFAPs over 50 independent runs and the comparison with a new heuristic method presented in Won-Young, Soo, Jaewwook, and Chi-Hyuckm (2006), namely frequency insertion strategy (FIS). The termination criterion of MAEA-MSFAPs is set as follows: stop when optimal solutions are found or 100 generations are conducted. L_{size}, P_c,

Table 3. Call demand of Philadelphia instances

	Demand Vector
P1	(8, 25, 8, 8, 8, 15, 18, 52, 77, 28, 13, 15, 31, 15, 36, 57, 28, 8, 10, 13, 8)
P2	(8, 25, 8, 8, 8, 15, 18, 52, 77, 28, 13, 15, 31, 15, 36, 57, 28, 8, 10, 13, 8)
P3	(5, 5, 5, 8, 12, 25, 30, 25, 30, 40, 40, 45, 20, 30, 25, 15, 15, 30, 20, 20, 25)
P4	(5, 5, 5, 8, 12, 25, 30, 25, 30, 40, 40, 45, 20, 30, 25, 15, 15, 30, 20, 20, 25)
P5	(20, 20, 20, 20, 20, 20, 20, 20, 20, 20, 20, 20, 20, 20, 20, 20, 20, 20, 20, 20, 20)
P6	(20, 20, 20, 20, 20, 20, 20, 20, 20, 20, 20, 20, 20, 20, 20, 20, 20, 20, 20, 20, 20)
P7	(16, 50, 16, 16, 16, 30, 36, 104, 154, 56, 26, 30, 62, 30, 72, 114, 56, 16, 20, 26, 16)
P8	(8, 25, 8, 8, 8, 15, 18, 52, 77, 28, 13, 15, 31, 15, 36, 57, 28, 8, 10, 13, 8)
P9	(32, 100, 32, 32, 32, 60, 72, 208, 308, 112, 52, 60, 124, 60, 144, 228, 112, 32, 40, 52, 32)

Table 4. Frequency interference constraints of Philadelphia instances

Instances	Reuse Distances
P1, P3, P5, P7, P9	$\left(2\sqrt{3},\ \sqrt{3},\ 1,\ 1,\ 1,\ 0\right)$
P2, P4, P6	$\left(\sqrt{7},\ \sqrt{3},\ 1,\ 1,\ 1,\ 0\right)$
P8	$\left(2\sqrt{3},\ 2,\ 1,\ 1,\ 1,\ 0\right)$

Table 5. Results reported so far on Philadelphia instances

	Lower Bounds					Known Optimum	Upper Bounds					
	Janssen & Kilakos (1999)	Hurley et al. (1997)	Sung & Wong (1997)	Hellebrandt & Heller (2000)	Avenali et al. (2002)		Hurley et al. (1997)	Valenzuela et al. (1998)	Hurley et al. (1997)	Allen et al. 1999	Matsui & Tokoro (2001)	Avenali et al. (2002)
P1	426	426	426	-	426	426	428	426	426	-	426	426
P2	426	426	426	-	426	426	438	426	426	-	426	426
P3	-	257	252	-	257	257	260	258	257	-	257	275
P4	252	252	252	-	252	252	259	253	252	-	252	253
P5	-	239	177	-	239	239	239	239	-	-	239	239
P6	177	178	177	179	177	179	200	198	-	179	179	183
P7	-	855	855	-	855	855	858	856	855	-	855	855
P8	-	524	427	-	523	524	546	527	-	-	524	524
P9	-	1713	1713	-	1713	1713	1724	-	1713	-	-	1713

Table 6. Comparison between FIS and MAEA-MSFAPs

Instances	FIS	MAEA-MSFAPs		Optimal
	sp_{best}	sp_{best}	sp_{ave}	Solutions
P1	426	426	426.00	426
P2	426	426	426.00	426
P3	298	261	265.00	257
P4	263	252	254.03	252
P5	268	240	241.15	239
P6	222	194	199.00	179
P7	855	855	855.00	855
P8	538	524	525.65	524
P9	1713	1713	1713.00	1713

and P_m are respectively set to 15, 0.5 and 0.4. The results in Table 6 show that our algorithm yields much better solutions than FIS in all the nine cases, and finds optimal solutions for six out of nine instances.

CONCLUSION

In this paper, multiagent systems and evolutionary algorithms are integrated to form a new algorithm to solve minimum span frequency assignment problems. Based on the characteristic and encoding method of MSFAPs, we designed agent, agent environment, and agent behaviors. In experiments, our approach obtains a good performance on 15 T-coloring problems which various parameters and the famous Philadelphia instances. Compared with the classical algorithm *Dsatur* and FIS, the experimental results show that MAEA-MSFAPs is a competitive algorithm in solving large-scale T-coloring problems and MSFAPs. The combination of multiagent systems and EAs is of high potential in solving complex and ill-defined problems, and can be applied as an attempt to other similar problems, such as timetable problem, job assignment problem.

ACKNOWLEDGMENT

This work was supported by the National Natural Science Foundations of China under Grants 60872135, 60803098, and 60970067, the National Research Foundation for the Doctoral Program of Higher Education of China under Grant 20070701022, and the Provincial Natural Science Foundation of Shaanxi of China under Grant 2010JM8030.

REFERENCES

Allen, S. M., Hurley, S., Smith, D. H., & Thiel, S. U. (1999). Using lower bounds in minimum span frequency assignment. *Meta-Heuristics: Advances and Trends in Local Search Paradigms for Optimization*, 191-204.

Anderson, L. G. (1973). A simulation study of some dynamic channel assignment algorithm in a high capacity mobile telecommunication system. *IEEE Transactions on Communications, 21*, 1294–1301. doi:10.1109/TCOM.1973.1091583

Avenali, A., Mannino, M., & Sassano, A. (2002). Minimizing the span of d-walks to compute optimum frequency assignments. *Mathematical Programming, 91*(2), 357–374. doi:10.1007/s101070100247

Bodlaender, H. L. Kloks, Tan, R. B., & van Leeuwen, J. (2000). λ-coloring of graphs. In H. Reichel & S. Tison (Eds.), *Proceedings of the 17ᵗʰ Annual Symposium on Theoretical Aspects of Computer Science* (LNCS 1770, pp. 395-406).

Costa, D. (1993). On the use of some known methods for T-colorings of graphs. *Annals of Operations Research, 41*, 343–358. doi:10.1007/BF02023000

Dorne, R., & Hao, J.-K. (1998). Tabu search for graph coloring, t-colorings and set t-colorings. *Meta-heuristics Theory and Applications, 98*, 33–47.

Galinier, P., Gendreau, M., Soriano, P., & Bisaillon, S. (2005). Solving the frequency assignment problem with polarization by local search and Tabu. *OR, 3*(1), 59–78.

Hale, W. K. (1980). Frequency assignment: Theory and applications. *Proceedings of the IEEE, 68*(12), 1497–1514. doi:10.1109/PROC.1980.11899

Hellebrandt, M., & Heller, H. (2000). A new heuristic method for frequency assignment. *Number TD, 003.*

Hurley, S., & Smith, D. H. (1997). Bounds for the frequency assignment problem. *Discrete Mathematics,* (167-168): 571–582.

Hurley, S., Smith, D. H., & Thiel, S. U. (1997). A system for discrete channel frequency assignment. *Radio Science, 32*, 1921–1939. doi:10.1029/97RS01866

Idoumghar, L., & Schott, R. (2009). Two distributed algorithms for the frequency assignment problem in the field of radio broadcasting. *IEEE Transactions on Broadcasting, 55*(2), 223–229. doi:10.1109/TBC.2008.2012023

Janczewski, R., & Kubale, M. (1998). The T-DSATUR algorithm: An interesting generalization of the DSATUR algorithm. In *Proceedings of the International Conference on Advanced Computer Systems* (pp. 288-292).

Janssen, J., & Kilakos, K. (1999). An optimal solution to the "Philadelphia" channel assignment problem. *IEEE Transactions on Vehicular Technology, 48*(3), 1012–1014. doi:10.1109/25.765037

Kunz, D. (1993). Channel assignment for cellular radio networks. *IEEE Transactions on Vehicular Technology, 42*, 647–656. doi:10.1109/25.260746

Liu, J., Zhong, W., & Jiao, L. (2006). A multiagent evolutionary algorithm for constraint satisfaction problems. *IEEE Transactions on Systems, Man, and Cybernetics B, 36*(1), 54–73. doi:10.1109/TSMCB.2005.852980

Liu, J., Zhong, W., & Jiao, L. (2010). A multiagent evolutionary algorithm for combinatorial optimization problems. *IEEE Transactions on Systems, Man, and Cybernetics B, 40*(1), 229–240. doi:10.1109/TSMCB.2009.2025775

Martin, G. (2000). Frequency assignment in mobile phone systems. *Foundations of Software Technology Computer Science, 1974*, 81–86.

Matsui, S., & Tokoro, K. (2001). Improving the performance of a genetic algorithm for minimum span frequency assignment problem with an adaptive mutation rate and a new initialization method. In *Proceedings of the Conference on Genetic and Evolutionary Computation* (pp. 1359-1366).

Riihijärvi, J., Petrova, M., & Mähönen, P. (2005). Frequency allocation for WLANs using graph coloring techniques. In *Proceedings of the Second Annual Conference on Wireless On-demand Network System and Services* (pp. 216-222).

Sung, C. W., & Wong, W. S. (1997). Sequential packing algorithm for channel assignment under cochannel and adjacent channel interference constraint. *IEEE Transactions on Vehicular Technology, 46,* 676–685. doi:10.1109/25.618193

Valenzuela, C., Hurley, S., & Smith, D. H. (1998). A permutation based genetic algorithm for minimum span frequency assignment. In A. E. Eiben, T. Bäck, M. Schoenauer, & H.-P. Schwefel (Eds.), *Proceedings of the 5th International Conference on Parallel Problem Solving from Nature* (LNCS 1498, pp. 907-916).

Won-Young, S., Soo, Y. C., Jaewwook, L., & Chi-Hyuck, J. (2006). Frequency insertion strategy for channel assignment problem. *Wireless Networks, 12*(1), 45–52. doi:10.1007/s11276-006-6149-6

Zhong, W., Liu, J., Xue, M., & Jiao, L. (2004). A multiagent genetic algorithm for global numerical optimization. *IEEE Transactions on Systems. Man and Cybernetics B, 34*(2), 1128–1141. doi:10.1109/TSMCB.2003.821456

Zoellner, J. A., & Beall, C. L. (1977). A breakthrough in spectrum conserving frequency assignment technology. *IEEE Transactions on Electromagnetic Compatibility, 19*(3), 313–319. doi:10.1109/TEMC.1977.303601

This work was previously published in the International Journal of Swarm Intelligence Research, Volume 2, Issue 3, edited by Yuhui Shi, pp. 30-43, copyright 2011 by IGI Publishing (an imprint of IGI Global).

Chapter 13
Design of Robust Approach for Failure Detection in Dynamic Control Systems

Gomaa Zaki El-Far
Menoufia University, Egypt

ABSTRACT

This paper presents a robust instrument fault detection (IFD) scheme based on modified immune mechanism based evolutionary algorithm (MIMEA) that determines on line the optimal control actions, detects faults quickly in the control process, and reconfigures the controller structure. To ensure the capability of the proposed MIMEA, repeating cycles of crossover, mutation, and clonally selection are included through the sampling time. This increases the ability of the proposed algorithm to reach the global optimum performance and optimize the controller parameters through a few generations. A fault diagnosis logic system is created based on the proposed algorithm, nonlinear decision functions, and its derivatives with respect to time. Threshold limits are implied to improve the system dynamics and sensitivity of the IFD scheme to the faults. The proposed algorithm is able to reconfigure the control law safely in all the situations. The presented false alarm rates are also clearly indicated. To illustrate the performance of the proposed MIMEA, it is applied successfully to tune and optimize the controller parameters of the nonlinear nuclear power reactor such that a robust behavior is obtained. Simulation results show the effectiveness of the proposed IFD scheme based MIMEA in detecting and isolating the dynamic system faults.

INTRODUCTION

The application of modern control theories plays an important role for the improvement of the dynamic performance and safety of nuclear reactors (Subramaniam & Rajakumar, 1995). The model equations of the nuclear reactor are nonlinear. Conventional PI controllers may require several tuning adjustments to get satisfactory performance. Nonlinear control strategy is a must for the control of nuclear reactors. Input-output linearizing controller for a nuclear reactor is designed

DOI: 10.4018/978-1-4666-2479-5.ch013

which shows that the performance of the closed loop system is good. However, it has not evaluated the robustness of both system parameters perturbations and component failure detection (Guimara & Lapa, 2004, 2005). The operation of any industrial plant is based on the readings of a set of sensors. The ability to identify the state of operation, or the events that are occurring, from the time evolution of these readings is essential for the satisfactory execution of the appropriate control actions. In supervisory control, detection and diagnosis of faults, adaptive control, process quality control, recovery from operational deviations, and determining the correct mapping from process trends to overcome some problems of operational conditions are the pivotal task of (Roverso, 2000).

Control systems are becoming more and more powerful and sophisticated. Reliability, availability, and safety are primary goals in the operation of the process systems (Odgaard & Thøgersen, 2010). The aim is to develop a fast and reliable control system that could detect undesirable changes in the process (referred to as "faults") and isolate the impact of faults has been attracting much attention of researchers. Various methods for fault detection and control of process systems have been studied and developed over recent years (Staroswiecki, 2005; Zhang & Jiang, 2003; Ducard & Geering, 2008; Li & Parker, 2007) but there are relatively few successful developments of controller systems that can deal with faults in stochastic hybrid sense where faults are modeled as multiple-model set with variable structure and use of a stochastic model predictive control algorithm. Faults are difficult to foresee and prevent. Traditionally, faults were handled by describing the result behavior of the system and were grouped into a hierarchical structure of fault model (Li & Parker, 2007). This approach is still used for some fields in practice. When a failure occurs, the system behavior changes and should be described by a different mode from the one that corresponds to the normal mode. A more appropriate mathematical model for such a system is the so-called stochastic hybrid approach. It differs from the conventional hierarchical structure in that its state may jump as well as it may vary continuously. Apart from the applications to problems involving failures, hybrid systems have found some success in such areas as target tracking and control that involve possible structure changes (Zhang & Campillo, 2005). For detecting the faults, a critical assumption, in the simulation test runs, which is the availability of the system component models under different input excitations. Such models may not be available for the necessary input conditions in an operating system (Sarkar & Yasar, 2008; Gupta & Ray, 2008).

Artificial immune systems constitute intelligent methodologies that can be used to churn out effective solutions to real world problems. Inspired by the natural immune system, an artificial immune system banks on concepts derived from theoretical immunology and observed immune functions to solve a problem. The body's defense mechanism can be divided into two sub-systems: (i) the innate immune system, and (ii) the adaptive immune system. The former is available for immediate combat while the latter produces antibodies depending on the invading agent. The skin and the lining of the body cavities that are open to the outside world provide the initial protective barrier. A virus or bacteria (generically known as a germ) may invade the human body and reproduce. The germ's presence produces some side effects, like fever, inflammation, etc. Some bacteria on the contrary are benign. In immune system terminology, the invading agent is called the antigen while the defending agent is termed the antibody (Wang & Hirsbrunner, 2003). The vertebrate immune system is a rich source of theories and acts as an inspiration for computer-based solutions over the last few years there has been an increasing interest in the area of artificial immune system. Artificial immune systems uses ideas gleaned from immunology in order to develop systems capable of performing tasks in various engineering applications. Although artificial immune systems have demonstrated great values, few applications are reported in remote sensing. Therefore, in this paper, our aim is to modify an artificial immune approach as new tool of information analysis for controlling the dynamic system behavior.

In the case of unstable dynamic systems, the failure of one sensor can be catastrophic if the control system has not some degree of redundancy, physical or analytical. Due to this characteristic, it is very important to these systems to have a redundant control system with the ability to identify sensor failures as quickly as possible and then to reconfigure the control law from the failed control law to an alternative control law. Although many systems achieve fault tolerance by using hardware redundancy, there are several problems associated with hardware redundancy. Some of these problems are extra cost, additional space and weight, and extra software. Besides this, it has been noticed that redundant sensor tend to have similar life expectancies, so, it is likely that when one of a set of sensors fails, the other will be failing very soon too (Oliva, 1998). In view of these problems, it is much better to use the proposed IFD scheme which is based on MIMEA algorithm to detect and isolate the fault tolerant systems. So, The main objective of this paper is to develop and validate an important methodology for IFD scheme based on the proposed MIMEA of pertinent data observers and analytically design logic functions for detecting and isolate the impact of faults occurred in the dynamic systems.

In this paper, a robust IFD scheme based on the MIMEA algorithm is proposed. The MIMEA is an optimal searching algorithm that is suitable for the problem of finding an optimal solution in controlling the behavior of dynamic systems and has a better capability of learning from its experience. To ensure the capability of the proposed MIMEA algorithm in designing the fault diagnosis logic system, repeating cycles of crossover, mutation and clonally selection are included through the sampling time. This will increase the

ability of the proposed algorithm to reach the global optimum performance and optimize the controller parameters through a few numbers of generations and overcome the drawbacks of the traditional immune mechanism-based evolutionary algorithm (IMEA). A fault diagnosis logic system has been created based on the proposed algorithm, nonlinear decision functions and its derivatives with respect to time. These decision nonlinear functions which are designed based on the state feedback observer are used to evaluate the decision logic system. Also, the gain parameters of the state feedback observer are determined and adjusted by the proposed MIMEA algorithm. Several simulations are run to assess the system performance, and a study about the robustness of the system with respect to system parameters uncertainties and noisy data is also performed. It is found that the system is able to reconfigure the control law safely in all the situations and the false alarm rates are also quickly indicated. Threshold values will be used for the purpose of reducing false alarm rate caused by parameters uncertainties and noisy data. To illustrate the performance of the proposed IFD scheme, the MIMEA algorithm is applied successfully to tune and optimize the controller parameters of the nonlinear nuclear power reactor. Simulation results show its strong ability for real applications to detect faults in dynamic control systems. The outline of this paper is as follows. In the next section, problem formulation is discussed. Proposed modified hybrid immune algorithm is then given. Adaptive state feedback observer controller based on MIMEA algorithm is presented. The design of robust IFD scheme is given, as well as the simulation results.

PROBLEM FORMULATION

The nuclear power plant dual-purpose research reactor (DPRR) is described in (Nassef, 2005; Atary, 1971). In the DPRR, the thermal power of 200 MW is generated in the fuel rods of the reactor.

The model equations are given here for easy reference (Nassef, 2005; Atary, 1971):

$$\dot{x}_1(t) = (u(t) - \frac{1.4325}{\sqrt{abs(x_3(t)) + 109.2}} x_3(t) -$$

$$a_1(t)x_5(t) - a_2(t)x_6(t)) + (5.5556 + .111x_1(t))$$
$$-(7.9 - .00126t)x_1(t) + .075x_2(t)$$

$$\tag{1}$$

$$\dot{x}_2(t) = (7.9 - .00126t)x_1(t) - .075x_2(t) \tag{2}$$

$$\dot{x}_3(t) =$$
$$0.3342x_1(t) - 0.1342x_3(t) + 0.0134x_4(t)$$

$$\tag{3}$$

$$\dot{x}_4(t) =$$
$$9.281x_3(t) - 13.75x_4(t) + 12.82x_5(t)$$

$$\tag{4}$$

$$\dot{x}_5(t) = 1.301x_4(t) - 1.323x_5(t)$$
$$+ 0.0446x_6(t) - 2.09x_5(t)(t - 5)$$

$$\tag{5}$$

$$\dot{x}_6(t) =$$
$$0.0023x_1(t) + 0.00044x_5(t) - 0.00087x_6(t)$$

$$\tag{6}$$

where

$$a_1(t) = \frac{17.72}{x_6(t) + 1092.0}$$

and

$$a_2(t) = \frac{1001.18}{x_6(t) + 546.0}$$

In these equations:

- $x_1(t)$ is the change in thermal energy.
- $x_2(t)$ is the change in delayed neutron density.
- $x_3(t)$ is the change in average fuel element temperature.
- $x_4(t)$ is the change in average clad temperature.
- $x_5(t)$ is the change in average coolant temperature.
- $x_6(t)$ is the change in average moderator temperature.
- $u(t)$ is the control input signal to magnetic jack mechanism.

The control system was designed based on this model output $y(t)$ ($y(t)=x_1(t)$) with the objective to track a reference signal $y_r(t)$ and regulation of the remaining states. So the control system will require six observers to work adequately that are the observers for $x_1(t)$, $x_2(t)$, $x_3(t)$, $x_4(t)$, $x_5(t)$ and $x_6(t)$. Certainly, if one of these observers fails, the nuclear reactor power system will become unstable. In view of these facts it is very important to determine the extent of the loss in the control effectiveness by designing decision logic functions. These decision logic functions are designed based on the proposed MIMEA algorithm and state feedback observer so that an on-line automatic reconfigurable controller can be synthesized and the corresponding closed-loop system can keep asymptotically stable under any actuator faults.

PROPOSED MODIFIED HYBRID IMMUNE ALGORITHM

Immune Mechanism Based Evolutionary Algorithm (IMEA)

Evolution algorithm is similar to genetic algorithm (GA) except the following difference. This difference is the special genetic operators which are demonstrated in the following. Let $r \in [0,1]$ is a random number (uniform distribution), $t = 0, 1, ...,$ G. G is the maximum generation number, s_f and s_d are two chromosomes selected for the operation. Let $k \in \{1, 2, ..., m\}$ is the position of an element in the chromosome. $l_k^{s_f}$ and $u_k^{s_f}$ are the lower and upper bounds respectively on the parameter encoded by the element k.

The IMEA approach consists of five steps (Wang & Hirsbrunner, 2003):

1. Initialization of the population randomly in the problem space.

2. **Crossover with Special Operators:** For crossover operations, the chromosomes are selected in pairs (s_f, s_d). s_f^t and s_d^t are obtained from crossing after the kth positions. The resulting offspring are:

$$s_f^{t+1} = \left(f_1, ..., f_k, d_{k+1}, ..., d_m \right) \qquad (7)$$

$$s_d^{t+1} = \left(d_1, ..., d_k, f_{k+1}, ..., f_m \right) \qquad (8)$$

where k is selected as $\{2,..,m-1\}$ and f_i and d_i are the elements of the chromosomes.

3. **Mutation with Special Operators:** A random selection of an element $v_k, k \in \{1, 2..., m\}$ is replaced by v_k^1. v_k^1 is a random number in the range of $[l_k^{s_v^t}, u_k^{s_v^t}]$. The resulting chromosome is given as:

$$s_v^{t+1} = \left(v_1, ..., v_k', ..., v_m \right) \qquad (9)$$

4. **Clonally Selection:** This operation is composed of two main steps which are:

    a. **Updating of the Memory Cells Set:** The memory set is composed of L_d individuals (in fact, it is also a special population). In the current population, $\phi (\phi << z)$ individuals with the stron-

gest vitality are selected to replace the ϕ individuals in the memory set that are the most weak. Here, the word of vitality is a concept similar to the ordinarily said *fitness*. For an example, as the problem of finding the maximum value of a function, the real value of an individual can be just regarded as the vitality of itself.

    b. **Selection Based on Density:** Compose the current population and the memory set to a temporary population, and calculates every individual's fitness as follows:

$$Fitness(i) = vitality(i)$$
$$+ \zeta \frac{vitality(i)}{MaxVitality} vitality(i)$$
$$+ \delta(1 - Ds)\left(1 + \text{sgn}(\vartheta - Ds)\frac{vitality(i)}{MaxVitality} \right) vitality(i) \qquad (10)$$

where δ and ζ are two adjustable parameters in $[0:1]$. Also, ϑ is a threshold value in $[0:1]$ that is used for determining if an individual's vitality is strong or not. *MaxVitality* means the maximal vitality value of the current population. Sgn $(\cdot)$ is the symbol function and Ds suggests the density of the individuals with stronger vitality that can be calculated as follows:

$$Ds = \frac{\sum_i (\vartheta . MaxVitality \le vitality(i) \le MaxVitality)}{z + L_d} \qquad (11)$$

where z is the population size, L_d is a special population stored in memory initialized from L_d best individuals in the population, and ϕ are the strongest individuals in the population that are replaced the weakest individuals in L_d at every generation. So $\phi < L_d < z$, $i.e(\phi << z)$.

5. If the stop criterion is not satisfied, return to step 2.

It necessary to point out that before the stop criterion is satisfied, any individual is immature no matter how high its fitness has got, and the individuals are regarded as premature if their density has exceeded a special value (i.e., the threshold ϑ shown as above). To some extent, the function of immunity is mainly used for controlling the existence of this kind of population.

Basic Features of the IMEA

The immune system is able to automatically produce some corresponding antibodies aiming to a certain foreign antigen. With combining to these antigens, the antibodies will destroy them through a series of reactions, and simultaneously, there are also some reactions of stimulus and/or restraint among the antibodies. Especially, these reactions, on the other hand, are helpful for generating more mature antibodies; on the other hand, they are based on the density of the antibodies, in which there are two outstanding features: 1) The diversity of a certain kind of antibodies, which suggests that the immune mechanism ensures all the variety of antibodies existing in the organism at any time, and 2) The density controls the property of reactions, i.e., stimulus or restrain. That means the higher density of the antibodies, the more possibility of restraint; on the contrary, the lower density, the more possibility of stimulus, which makes the antibodies have some capabilities of adapting their around environment. The main features of these phenomena are used to design a corresponding operation in order to improve the algorithm's adaptive ability. Especially in this paper, the word of antigen is corresponded to the problem to be dealt with, and antibody is supposed to be a possible answer/solution to this problem. The calculation on an individual's vitality can be understood as the process of an antibody bending to the antigen.

From the viewpoint of function, IMEA is an optimal algorithm that mainly applies the principles of evolution found in nature to the problem of finding an optimal solution, and usually, the problem needs to be encoded in a series of strings that are manipulated by the algorithm. This algorithm for optimization is quite different from classical optimization methods, because, (i) a solution is randomly (but not absolutely so) produced while the operation in the classical methods is deterministic, and (ii) once a time there are lots of solutions produced that compose a population while in the classical method only a single best solution is operated.

Hybrid IMEA with Simplex Method

The traditional IMEA suffers from some drawbacks. These drawbacks include premature convergence of the IMEA to the true values and slow capability of learning from its experience. To increase the search ability of the IMEA algorithm and improve its convergence rate, a combination between IMEA and a local search technique called simplex method is carried out which result into a hybrid architecture. The simplex method is applied to the top N chromosomes in the population to produce N children. The remaining $(z-N)$ chromosomes are generated by using the IMEA algorithm to the reproduction scheme (i.e., selection, crossover, and mutation) where z is the population size. The simplex method is defined by a number of points equal to one more than the number of dimension of the search space. For an optimization problem involving N variables, the simplex method searches for an optimal solution by evaluating a set of $N + 1$ points (i.e., points forming a simplex) which are denoted as $h_1, h_2, ..., h_{N+1}$. The method continually forms new simples by replacing the worst point in the simplex, denoted as $h_w^{'}$, with a new point h_r generated by reflecting h_w over the centroid $\bar{h}$ of the remaining points as (Nassef, 2005):

$$h_r = \bar{h} + (\bar{h} - h_w) \qquad (12)$$

where

$$\bar{h} = \frac{h_1 + h_2 + ... + h_{w-1} + h_{w+1} + ... + h_{N+1}}{N} \qquad (13)$$

The new simples are then defined by h_1, h_2, ..., h_{w-1}, h_{w+1}, ..., h_{N+1}, h_r. This cycle of evaluation and reflection iterates until the step size i.e., $(h_r - h_w)$ becomes less than a predetermined value or simplex circles around an optimum value.

Modified Hybrid Immune Mechanism Based Evolutionary Algorithm (MIMEA)

In order to complete the modifications of the IMEA algorithm which is hybridized with the simplex method in the above section, repeating cycles of crossover, mutation and clonally selection are included to the algorithm through the sampling time to ensure its global optimum behavior and improve its convergence characteristics. This will increase the ability of the proposed algorithm to optimize the controller parameters through a few numbers of generations and thus overcomes the drawbacks of the traditional IMEA approach. It is seen that the sampling period depends on the time required to perform the inner repeating cycles. So, the sampling period must be equal to the time required for performing the inner repeating cycles. Practically, fast computers have the ability of performing such operations effectively during the sampling time and easily keep the stability of performance satisfied. The proposed MIMEA

Figure 1. Proposed MIMEA algorithm

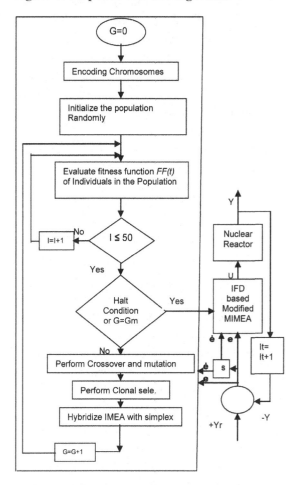

algorithm is used effectively in the following sections to detect the failed observers and designing the fault diagnosis logic system. The detailed steps of this algorithm are shown in Figure 1.

Suppose that the candidate controller is the proportional-derivative (PI) form, and the MIMEA is used to pick the proportional (K_p), the integral (K_i) and the feedback (K_f) gains. The procedure of the proposed MIMEA of Figure 1 can be summarized in the following steps:

1. Choose the algorithm initial parameters such as population size z, crossover probability P_c, mutation probability P_m and initial Clonally selection and iteration k.

2. Initialize the algorithm population C_i, $i = 1, 2,..., z$ for the proportional (K_p) and the integral (K_i) and the feedback K_f parameters.

3. Collect $y_r(t)$ and $y(t)$.

4. Loop the generations (inner repeated cycles) from $G=1$ to G_m, where G_m the maximum number of generations permissible for the system sampling time.

5. Generate $u(t)$, for each population member C_i, $i = 1, 2,..., z$ using the PI control law as:

$$u(t) = k_p e(t) + k_i \int e(t)\, dt\,) - k_f^T \hat{x}(t)$$

where $e(t) = y_r(t) - y_o(t)$.

6. Compute the fitness function $FF(t)$ of Equation 21 to each element of the population C_i, $i = 1, 2,..., z$. The fitness function must capture such dynamical changes so that it can evolve a new set of controllers parameters K_p, K_i and K_f for the new conditions.

7. If the halt condition ($G=G_m$) is achieved (optimal solution is obtained) then extract the optimum controller parameters K_p, K_i and K_f, go to step 10.

8. If the optimal solution does not satisfy, use the following MIMEA operators to improve the information in the population, selection, crossover, mutation and clonally selection and then hybridize IMEA with simplex method.

9 $G=G+1$.

10. If $k=k_m$, k_m is the maximum number of iterations, *Go to 12*.

11. $k=k+1$, *Go to step 2*.

12. *End*.

The proposed hybridized MIMEA algorithm has the following advantages:

- It has fast convergence to the true values.
- It is easy for construction and implementation in practical applications.
- It has a better capability for fast learning from its experiences.

- The proposed IFD approach which is based on the MIMEA scheme is used for detecting and isolating the dynamic control system faults effectively.

ADAPTIVE STATE FEEDBACK OBSERVER CONTROLLER BASED ON MIMEA

The state feedback technique requires the feedback of all states variables. Therefore, it becomes necessary that all the state variables must be available for feedback. However, some state variables may be immeasurable and may not be available for feedback. Then, it is very necessary to estimate such immeasurable state variables by using the state feedback observers based on the proposed MIMEA algorithm. Figure 2 shows the adaptive state feedback observer based on MIMEA algorithm. The state equations of the time varying nonlinear nuclear power reactor mentioned in the above section, can be rewritten in a more compact form as:

$$\dot{x}(t) = f(t, x(t)) + g(t, x(t))\, u(t) \tag{14}$$

$$y(t) = c^T x(t) \tag{15}$$

where the vector-valued functions $f(t,x)$ and $g(t,x)$ may be nonlinear functions; $x(t) = [x_1,..., x_6]^T$, $u(t)$ and $y(t)$ denote the state vector, control input and output variables respectively. The vector c is defined as: $c = [1\ 0\ 0\ 0\ 0\ 0]^T$.

The state feedback observer equations can be defined by:

$$\hat{\dot{x}}(t) = f\left(t, \hat{x}(t)\right) + g\left(t, \hat{x}(t)\right)u\left(t\right) + G\left(y\left(t\right) - y_0\left(t\right)\right) \tag{16}$$

$$y_o(t) = c_o^T \hat{x}(t) \tag{17}$$

where $\hat{x}$ (nx1) are the estimated states of the adaptive state feedback observer, G is the observer gain parameters (nx1), $y(t)$ is the system output, $y_o(t)$ is the observer output and C_o is (nx1) output vector. The control signal $u(t)$ is computed as:

$$u(t) = k_p e(t) + k_i \int e(t)\, dt\ ) - k_f^T\ \hat{x}(t) \qquad (18)$$

and

$$e(t) = y_r(t) - y_o(t) \qquad (19)$$

where $e(t)$ is the error between $y_r(t)$ and $y_o(t)$, $y_r(t)$ is the desired reference signal and n is the total number of observations.

Define the objective function (J) as:

$$J(t) = \sum_{t=1}^{n} e(t)^2 \qquad (20)$$

J must be minimized such that the fitness function FF maximizes the MIMEA algorithm. So, the fitness function FF is defined as:

$$FF(t) = 1/(1 + J) \qquad (21)$$

The feedback vector $K_f(nx1)$, observer gain vector $G(nx1)$, the proportion parameter K_p and the integral parameter K_i are determined on-line by using the proposed. MIMEA algorithm, and hence the state feedback observer design, is then completed.

DESIGN OF ROBUST IFD SCHEME

Nonlinear Decision Functions

It is now necessary to build nonlinear decision functions that will allow the detection of failed observers and then to reconfigure the control law. Six reduced order observers are designed for the system, namely, the observers no.1 to no. 6 are designed by considering:

Figure 2. Adaptive state observer controller based on MIMEA

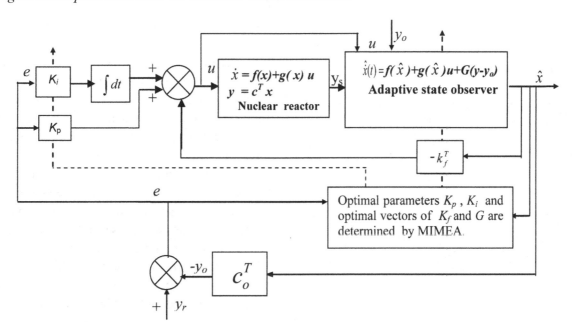

$$y_1\left(t\right) = x_1\left(t\right), \quad y_2\left(t\right) = \hat{x}_2\left(t\right)$$
$$y_3\left(t\right) = x_3\left(t\right), \quad y_4\left(t\right) = x_4\left(t\right) \qquad (22)$$
$$y_5\left(t\right) = x_5\left(t\right), \quad y_6\left(t\right) = x_6\left(t\right)$$

The inputs to observer no. 1 will be $y_1(t)$ and $u(t)$ and its outputs will be $\hat{x}_2(t)$, $\hat{x}_3(t)$, $\hat{x}_4(t)$, $\hat{x}_5(t)$ and $\hat{x}_6(t)$. It is then possible to build the following functions:

$$f_2\left(t\right) = \left| y_2\left(t\right) - \hat{x}_2\left(t\right) \right| \qquad (23)$$

$$f_3\left(t\right) = \left| y_3\left(t\right) - \hat{x}_3\left(t\right) \right| \qquad (24)$$

$$f_4\left(t\right) = \left| y_4\left(t\right) - \hat{x}_4\left(t\right) \right| \qquad (25)$$

$$f_5\left(t\right) = \left| y_5\left(t\right) - \hat{x}_5\left(t\right) \right| \qquad (26)$$

$$f_6\left(t\right) = \left| y_6\left(t\right) - \hat{x}_6\left(t\right) \right| \qquad (27)$$

$$\varepsilon_1(t) = f_2(t) \cdot f_3(t) \cdot f_4(t) \cdot f_5(t) \cdot f_6(t) \qquad (28)$$

The inputs to observer no. 2 will be $y_2(t)$ and $u(t)$ and its outputs will be $\hat{x}_1(t)$, $\hat{x}_3(t)$, $\hat{x}_4(t)$, $\hat{x}_5(t)$ and $\hat{x}_6(t)$. It is then possible to build the following functions:

$$f_1\left(t\right) = \left| y_1\left(t\right) - \hat{x}_1\left(t\right) \right| \qquad (29)$$

$$f_3\left(t\right) = \left| y_3\left(t\right) - \hat{x}_3\left(t\right) \right| \qquad (30)$$

$$f_4\left(t\right) = \left| y_4\left(t\right) - \hat{x}_4\left(t\right) \right| \qquad (31)$$

$$f_5\left(t\right) = \left| y_5\left(t\right) - \hat{x}_5\left(t\right) \right| \qquad (32)$$

$$f_6\left(t\right) = \left| y_6\left(t\right) - \hat{x}_6\left(t\right) \right| \qquad (33)$$

$$\varepsilon_2(t) = f_1(t).f_3(t).f_4(t).f_5(t).f_6(t) \qquad (34)$$

Similarly, for observers 3 to 6, the decision functions are defined as:

$$\varepsilon_3(t) = f_1(t).f_2(t).f_4(t).f_5(t).f_6(t) \qquad (35)$$

$$\varepsilon_4(t) = f_1(t).f_2(t).f_3(t).f_5(t).f_6(t) \qquad (36)$$

$$\varepsilon_5(t) = f_1(t).f_2(t).f_3(t).f_4(t).f_6(t) \qquad (37)$$

$$\varepsilon_6(t) = f_1(t).f_2(t).f_3(t).f_4(t).f_5(t) \qquad (38)$$

The functions $\varepsilon_1(t)$ to $\varepsilon_6(t)$ will be used as decision functions together with their derivatives ($\dot{\varepsilon}_1(t)$ to $\dot{\varepsilon}_6(t)$) to ensure the capability of the proposed IFD scheme of detecting the faults effectively. For simplicity, as shown in Figure 3, $\gamma_1(t)$, $\gamma_2(t)$, $\gamma_3(t)$, $\gamma_4(t)$, $\gamma_5(t)$ and $\gamma_6(t)$ are denoted to the outputs of the observer no.1 to the observer no. 6 respectively.

Decision Logic System

Based on the nonlinear functions given by Equations 28, 34, 35, 36, 37 and 38, it is possible to build a decision logic system. If, for example the observer of the change in thermal energy ($x_1(t)$) fails, the functions $f_2(t)$, $f_3(t)$, $f_4(t)$, $f_5(t)$ and $f_6(t)$ will grow very quickly and so $\varepsilon_1(t)$ will grow much faster than $f_2(t), f_3(t), f_4(t), f_5(t)$ and $f_6(t)$. This shows that the change in thermal energy observer has failed. It is necessary to find an appropriate threshold value for the function $\varepsilon_1(t)$. To find an appropriate threshold value for $\varepsilon_1(t)$ is not an easy task, since the nuclear reactor parameters can have some values not so close from those used in the observers design, there are several failure modes and the nuclear reactor can perform several kinds of tasks. To ensure the capability of the proposed IFD scheme of detecting the system faults effectively, $\dot{\varepsilon}(t)$ must be included in the decision logic system design. So it is not only necessary to find an appropriate threshold value for $\varepsilon_1(t)$ but also for $\dot{\varepsilon}_1(t)$. These threshold values can be adjusted by simulation. In a similar way it is also necessary to find appropriate threshold values for the functions $\varepsilon_2(t)$, $\dot{\varepsilon}_2(t)$, $\varepsilon_3(t)$, $\dot{\varepsilon}_3(t)$, $\varepsilon_4(t)$, $\dot{\varepsilon}_4(t)$, $\varepsilon_5(t)$, $\dot{\varepsilon}_5(t)$, $\varepsilon_6(t)$ and $\dot{\varepsilon}_6(t)$, what can be done by the simulations. The procedure to find these threshold values is an iterative one, starting with simulations for the nuclear reactor with the nominal parameters and for a step input in $y_r(t)$, and then going for the cases where there are some non nominal parameters.

Figure 3 shows the IFD diagram implementation. From the performed simulations, it was noticed that the system which is working with the threshold values of $\varepsilon_1(t)$, $\dot{\varepsilon}_1(t)$, $\varepsilon_2(t)$, $\dot{\varepsilon}_2(t)$, $\varepsilon_3(t)$, $\dot{\varepsilon}_3(t)$, $\varepsilon_4(t)$, $\dot{\varepsilon}_4(t)$, $\varepsilon_5(t)$, $\dot{\varepsilon}_5(t)$, $\varepsilon_6(t)$ and $\dot{\varepsilon}_6(t)$ shows a very good performance for the proposed IFD scheme to detect the faults quickly. Certainly if the threshold values for $\varepsilon(t)$ and $\dot{\varepsilon}(t)$ were reached,

a failure must be occurred. The performed work used the following decision logic:

- If $\varepsilon_1(t) > \varepsilon_{1lim}(t)$ and $\dot{\varepsilon}_1(t) > \dot{\varepsilon}_{1lim}(t)$, it was considered that the change in the thermal energy $(x_1(t))$ observer has failed.
- If $\varepsilon_2(t) > \varepsilon_{2lim}(t)$ and $\dot{\varepsilon}_2(t) > \dot{\varepsilon}_{2lim}(t)$, it was considered that the change in the delayed neutron density $(x_2(t))$ observer has failed.
- If $\varepsilon_3(t) > \varepsilon_{3lim}(t)$ and $\dot{\varepsilon}_3(t) > \dot{\varepsilon}_{3lim}(t)$, it was considered that the change in the average fuel temperature $(x_3(t))$ observer has failed.
- If $\varepsilon_4(t) > \varepsilon_{4lim}(t)$ and $\dot{\varepsilon}_4(t) > \dot{\varepsilon}_{4lim}(t)$, it was considered that the change in the average clad temperature $(x_4(t))$ observer has failed.
- If $\varepsilon_5(t) > \varepsilon_{5lim}(t)$ and $\dot{\varepsilon}_5(t) > \dot{\varepsilon}_{5lim}(t)$, it was considered that the change in the average coolant temperature $(x_5(t))$ observer has failed.
- If $\varepsilon_6(t) > \varepsilon_{6lim}(t)$ and $\dot{\varepsilon}_6(t) > \dot{\varepsilon}_{6lim}(t)$, it was considered that the change in the average

Figure 3. IFD diagram implementation

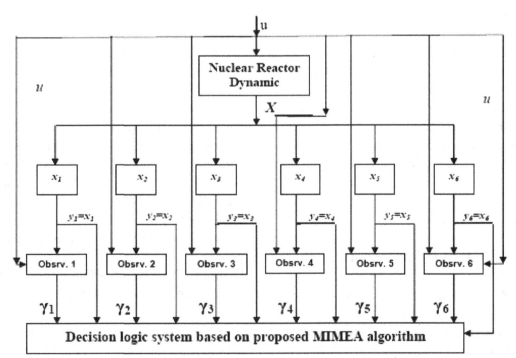

moderator temperature $(x_6(t))$ observer has failed.

$\varepsilon_{1lim}(t)$, $\varepsilon_{2lim}(t)$, $\varepsilon_{3lim}(t)$, $\varepsilon_{4lim}(t)$, $\varepsilon_{5lim}(t)$ and $\varepsilon_{6lim}(t)$ are the threshold limits for $\varepsilon_1(t)$, $\varepsilon_2(t)$, $\varepsilon_3(t)$, $\varepsilon_4(t)$, $\varepsilon_5(t)$, and $\varepsilon_6(t)$ respectively. Also, $\dot{\varepsilon}_{1lim}(t)$, $\dot{\varepsilon}_{2lim}(t)$, $\dot{\varepsilon}_{3lim}(t)$, $\dot{\varepsilon}_{4lim}(t)$, $\dot{\varepsilon}_{5lim}(t)$ and $\dot{\varepsilon}_{6lim}(t)$ are the threshold limits for $\dot{\varepsilon}_1(t)$, $\dot{\varepsilon}_2(t)$, $\dot{\varepsilon}_3(t)$, $\dot{\varepsilon}_4(t)$, $\dot{\varepsilon}_5(t)$ and $\dot{\varepsilon}_6(t)$ respectively.

SIMULATION RESULTS

Identification of Controller Parameters

For the proposed IFD scheme based on state feedback observer, the chromosome consists of 14 parameters $[k_{f1}\ k_{f2}\ k_{f3}\ k_{f4}\ k_{f5}\ k_{f6}\ k_p\ k_i\ g_1\ g_2\ g_3\ g_4\ g_5\ g_6]$. These parameters are identified and optimized by the proposed MIMEA algorithm. Where the coefficients of k_{f1} to k_{f6} are the state feedback parameters, k_p and k_i are the proportion and the integral parameters and g_1 to g_6 are the gain parameters of the state feedback observer. Real-code is used for coding the population chromosomes. The clonally selection is used. The crossover operator with probability of 0.8, the mutation operator with probability of 0.1 and the immunity operator with probability of 0.2 are used. Also, for hybridization 0.1 from the population size is chosen i.e. only simplex local search method alters these strings without genetic operators. The used Values of z, δ, ϑ and ζ are 50, 0.1, 0.2 and 0.5 respectively. The following cases are carried out.

Case 1: Without IFD Scheme

Figure 4 shows state variables of the open loop system. The tracking of the system output power $y(k)=x_1(k)$ to the desired performance $y_r(k)$ is given in Figure 5. The control signal, the tracking error,

the estimated state feedback controller parameters (k_{f1} to k_{f6}), the estimated controller parameters k_p and k_i and the estimated gain parameters of the state feedback observer (g_1 to g_6) are given in Figure 6, Figure 7, Figure 8, Figure 9, and Figure 10, respectively. From the obtained results of the proposed controller structure based on the MIMEA algorithm it is seen that, the actual output of the non-linear time varying nuclear power plant tracks the desired performance closely in some sense and the tracking error converge rapidly to zero. Also, the controller parameters converge to its desired values.

Case 2: Proposed IFD Scheme

In this case, to make a fault in the system, suddenly changes in the parameters $a_1(t)$ and $a_2(t)$ (by amount of 40%) are carried out as shown in Figure 11 and Figure 12 respectively. Figure 13 shows the tracking of $y(k)$ to the desired performance $y_r(k)$ while the tracking error and control signal are given in Figure 14 and Figure 15 respectively. It is seen that a robust behavior of the proposed IFD scheme is obtained. Figure 16 and Figure 17 show the decision functions behavior of $\varepsilon_1(t)$ and $\varepsilon_3(t)$ for detecting the faults. Also, the derivative of the decision functions behavior of $\dot{\varepsilon}_1(t)$ and $\dot{\varepsilon}_6(t)$ are shown in Figure 18 and Figure 19 respectively. From the obtained results of the proposed IFD scheme based on the MIMEA algorithm it is seen that, the actual output of the non-linear time varying nuclear power plant tracks the desired performance closely in some sense and the tracking error converge rapidly to zero. Also, the dynamic system faults based on the decision functions are detected and isolated quickly.

Case 3: Proposed IFD Scheme with Data Contaminated with Noise

This case shows the effectiveness of the proposed IFD scheme when data is noisy contaminated. Figure 20 shows the additive noise signal to the

Figure 4. Open loop system behavior

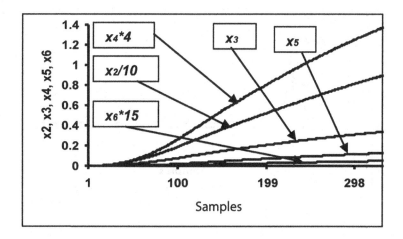

Figure 5. Tracking to the desired performance without IFD

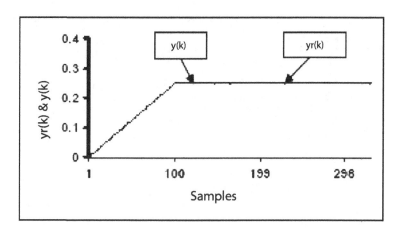

Figure 6. Control signal

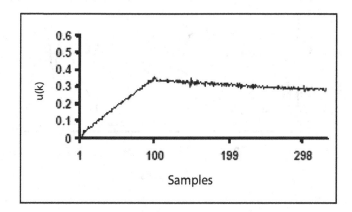

Figure 7. Tracking error

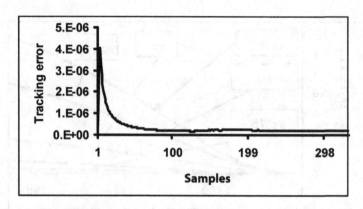

Figure 8. State feedback controller parameters K_f

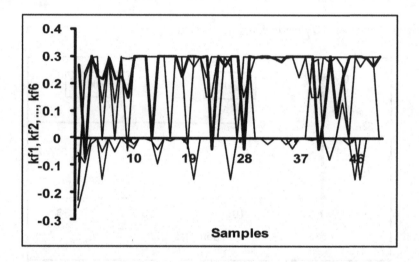

Figure 9. Controller parameters k_p and k_i

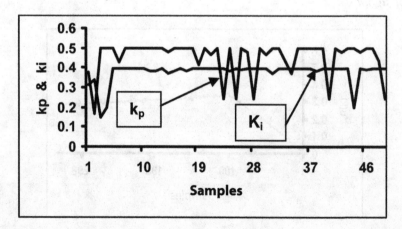

Figure 10. Gain parameters G(t) of the observer

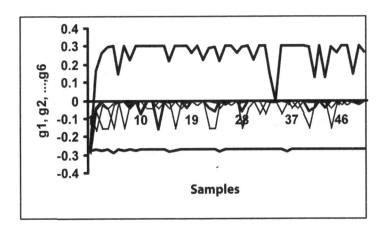

Figure 11. Sudden change in the parameter $a_1(t)$

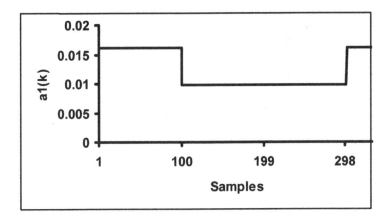

Figure 12. Sudden change in the parameter $a_2(t)$

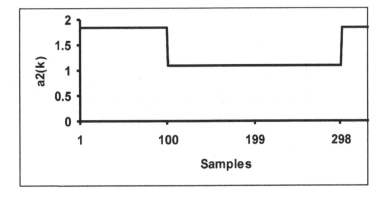

Figure 13. Tracking to the desired performance (IFD)

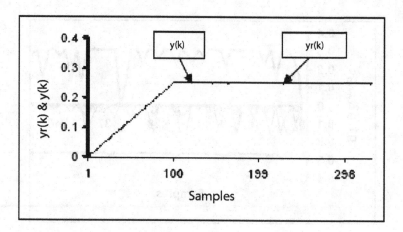

Figure 14. Tracking error (IFD)

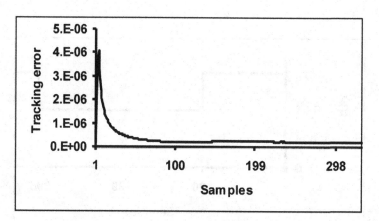

Figure 15. Control signal (IFD)

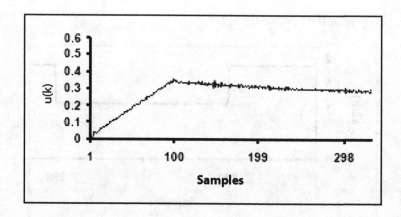

Figure 16. Design of the decision function ε_1(IFD)

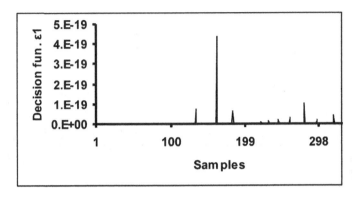

Figure 17. Design of the decision function ε_3 (IFD)

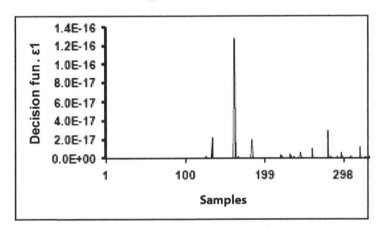

Figure 18. Design of the decision function $\acute{\varepsilon}_1$ (IFD)

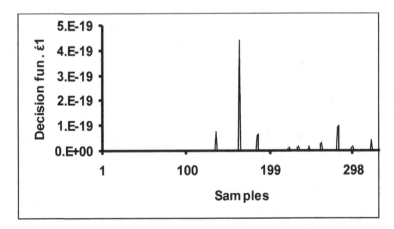

Figure 19. Design of the decision function $\dot{\varepsilon}_6$ (IFD)

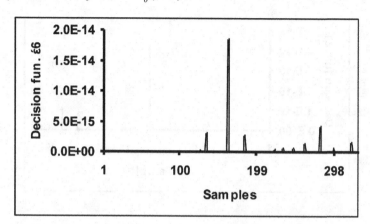

control system while Figure 21 shows the tracking of *y(k)* to the desired performance *y$_r$(k)*. Figure 22 shows the control signal for this case. Figure 23, Figure 24, and Figure 25 show the decision functions behavior of *ε$_4$(t)*, *ε$_5$(t)* and, *ε̇$_5$(t)* respectively. It is seen that, the actual output of the non-linear time varying nuclear power plant tracks the desired performance closely in some sense in the presence of data contaminated with noise and system faults and the tracking error converge rapidly to zero. Also, the dynamic system faults based on the decision functions are detected and isolated quickly. A comparison between the traditional IMEA method and the proposed MIMEA algorithm is given in Figure 26. From Figure 26, the proposed MIMEA algorithm converges rapidly to true values than that of the traditional IMEA and the tracking error associated with MIMEA is asymptotically approached to zero faster than that of traditional IMEA. This comparison ensures the robust behavior of the proposed IFD scheme based on the MIMEA algorithm. Finally, a design of the optimal number of the repeating cycles is shown in Figure 27. This optimal number is based on achieving least mean square errors between the tracking output and the reference signal. From Figure 27, it is seen that the optimum number of the repeating cycles is equal to 12 cycles. It is seen that the sampling period depends on the time

required to perform the inner repeating cycles. So, the sampling period must be equal to the time required for performing the inner repeating cycles. Practically, fast computers have the ability of performing such operations effectively during the sampling time and easily keep the stability of performance satisfied.

From the obtained results, a robust behavior of the proposed IFD scheme based on MIMEA algorithm in detecting and isolating system faults quickly is satisfied and a superior performance is achieved.

Obtaining the Threshold Values

To get the first approximation for the threshold values for *ε$_1$(t)*, *ε$_2$(t)*, *ε$_3$(t)*, *ε$_4$(t)*, *ε$_5$(t)*, and *ε$_6$(t)*, several simulations were performed for the nuclear reactor power plant with a step input in *y$_r$(k)* and change some of the nuclear reactor power plant parameters (by amount of 40%) to allow uncertainties in the parameters. Some simulations studies were also made for the nuclear reactor suffering a failure in each observer. After this first attempt, the threshold values for *ε$_1$(t)*, *ε$_2$(t)*, *ε$_3$(t)*, *ε$_4$(t)*, *ε$_5$(t)*, and *ε$_6$(t)* are taken as 4.42E-19, 5.45E-18, 1.29E-16, 2.21E-15, 3.0E-13 and 1.87E-14 respectively. Also, for this study, the threshold values of *ε̇$_1$(t)* to *ε̇$_6$(t)* are taken the same threshold values of *ε$_1$(t)*

Figure 20. Additive noise signal

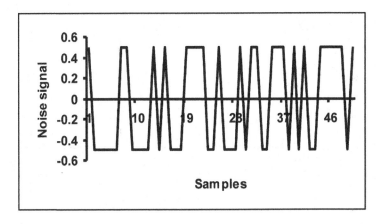

Figure 21. Trackig to the desired performance (IFD+noise)

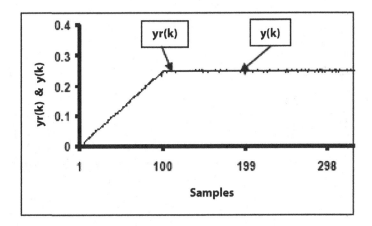

Figure 22. Control signal (IFD+noise)

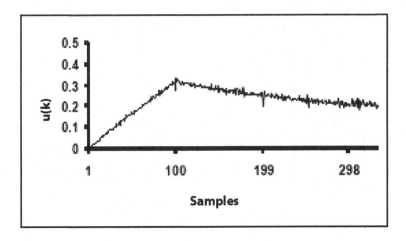

Figure 23. Design of decision fun. ε_4 (IFD+noise)

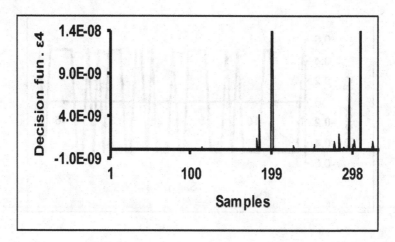

Figure 24. Design of decision fun. ε_5 (IFD+noise

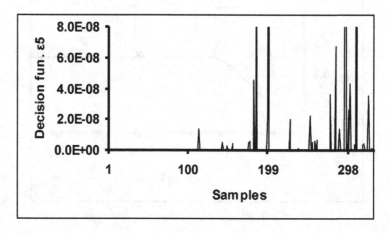

Figure 25. Design of decision fun. $\acute{\varepsilon}_5$ (IFD+noise)

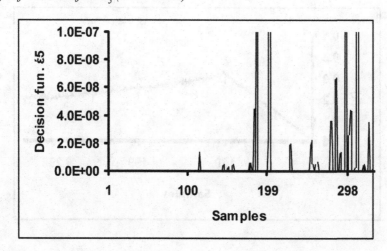

Figure 26. Comparison between IMEA and MIMEA

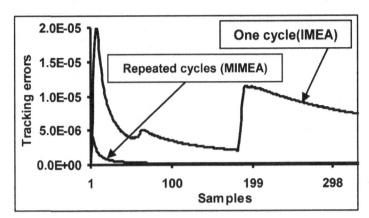

Figure 27. Design the optimal no. of the repeating cycles

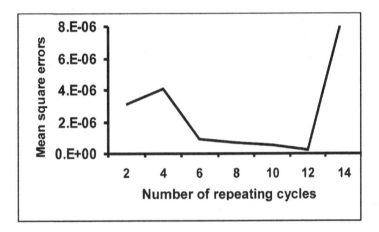

to $\varepsilon_6(t)$ respectively. These threshold values for both $\dot{\varepsilon}(t)$ and $\varepsilon(t)$ are used as limit values to give the false alarms when faults take place.

Robustness Study for the System

A robustness study for uncertainties in the system parameters was performed to assess the false alarm rate of the system, and so to find a new decision logic. The parameters which are considered in the study are $a_1(t)$ and $a_2(t)$. Several simulations were performed with uncertainties in these parameters, and with working of the IFD system. It is necessary to note that the uncertainties used for the parameters $a_1(t)$ and $a_2(t)$ (changes of system

parameters $a_1(t)$ and $a_2(t)$) equal to 40% from its maximum values. In spite of existence of the uncertainties in system parameters, additive noise signal and time variation of system parameters, the system performance will be much better and has superior tracking to the desired reference signal. This is clearly indicated in the figures of Figure 5, Figure 13 and Figure 21.

CONCLUSION

This paper presented a robust IFD scheme based on MIMEA algorithm that can determine on line the optimal control actions, detect the faults quickly in the control process, and reconfigure the controller structure. To ensure the capability of the proposed MIMEA algorithm in designing the fault diagnosis logic system, repeating cycles of crossover, mutation and clonally selection are included through the sampling time. This will increase the ability of the proposed algorithm to optimize the controller parameters through a few numbers of generations and overcome the drawbacks of the traditional IMEA approach. A fault diagnosis logic system has been created based on the proposed algorithm, nonlinear decision functions and its derivatives with respect to time. These decision nonlinear functions which are designed based on the state feedback observer are used to evaluate the decision logic system. Also, the gain parameters of the state feedback observer are determined and adjusted by the proposed MIMEA algorithm. When a fault is detected by the proposed fault diagnosis IFD scheme, the reconfigurable controller parameters are adjusted and optimized adaptively. Several simulations were run to assess the system performance, and a study about the robustness of the system with respect to system parameters uncertainties and noisy data was also performed. Threshold limits are proposed to improve the system dynamics and the sensitivity of the IFD scheme to the faults. It was found that the system is able to reconfigure the control law safely in all the situations and the false alarm rates were also quickly indicated. To illustrate the performance of the proposed IFD scheme, the MIMEA algorithm is applied successfully to tune and optimize the controller parameters of the nonlinear nuclear power reactor. Comparisons between the proposed algorithm and traditional IMEA are carried out. Simulation results show the strong ability of the proposed IFD scheme for real applications to detect the dynamic system faults.

ACKNOWLEDGMENT

The author would like to thank Prof. Dr. Yuhui Shi, the editor-in-chief and anonymous reviewers for their constructive comments and suggestions which help to improve the quality of this article highly.

REFERENCES

Atary, J. (1971). *Modeling and optimization of a nuclear power plant.* Unpublished doctoral dissertation, University of Cambridge, UK.

Ducard, G., & Geering, H. (2008). Efficient nonlinear actuator fault detection and isolation system for unmanned aerial vehicles. *Journal of Guidance, Control, and Dynamics, 31*(1), 225–244. doi:10.2514/1.31693

Guimara, A., & Lapa, C. (2004). Fuzzy inference system for evaluating and improving nuclear power plant operating performance. *Annals of Nuclear Energy, 31,* 311–322. doi:10.1016/S0306-4549(03)00224-X

Guimara, A., & Lapa, C. (2005). *Fuzzy inference to risk assessment on nuclear engineering systems introduction.* Rio de Janeiro, Brazil: Institute de Engenharia Nuclear.

Gupta, S., Ray, A., Sarkar, S., & Yasar, M. (2008). *Fault detection and isolation in aircraft gas turbine engines. Part 1: Underlying concept.* University Park, PA: Department of Mechanical Engineering, The Pennsylvania State University.

Li, X., & Parker, L. (2007). Sensor analysis for fault detection in tightly-coupled multi-robot team tasks. In *Proceedings of the IEEE International Conference on Robotics and Automation,* Rome, Italy.

Nassef, M. (2005). *Genetic algorithm and its application in control systems.* Unpublished doctoral dissertation, Menoufia University, Eygpt.

Odgaard, P., Thøgersen, P., & Stoustrup, J. (2010, September). Fault isolation in parallel coupled wind turbine converters. In *Proceedings of the 2010 IEEE Multiconference on Systems and Control*, Yokohama, Japan (pp. 1069-1072).

Oliva, A. (1998). Sensor fault detection and analytical redundancy satellite launcher flight control system. *SBA Controle & Automação, 9*(3), 156–164.

Roverso, D. (2000). *Soft computing tools for transient classification.* Oxford, UK: Elsevier Science.

Sarkar, S., Yasar, M., Gupta, S., Ray, A., & Mukherjee, K. (2008). *Fault detection and isolation in aircraft gas turbine engines. Part 2: validation on a simulation test bed.* University Park, PA: Department of Mechanical Engineering, The Pennsylvania State University.

Staroswiecki, M. (2005). *Fault tolerant control: The pseudo-inverse method revisited.* Lille, France: Ecole Polytechnique Universitaire de Lille.

Subramaniam, M., Rajakumar, A., & Chidambaram, M. (1995). Nonlinear control of nuclear reactors. *Control Theory and Advanced Technology, 10*(4), 1531–1540.

Wang, L., & Hirsbrunner, B. (2003, December 8-12). An evolutionary algorithm with population immunity and its application on autonomous robot control. In *Proceedings of the IEEE Conference on Evolutionary Computation,* Canberra, Australia (pp. 1-8).

Zhang, Q., Campillo, F., Cerou, F., & Legland, F. (2005, December 12-15). Nonlinear system fault detection and isolation based on bootstrap particle filters. In *Proceedings of the 44th IEEE Conference on Decision and Control and the European Control Conference,* Seville, Spain (pp. 3821-3826).

Zhang, Y., & Jiang, J. (2003). Fault tolerant control system design with explicit consideration of performance degradation. *IEEE Transactions on Aerospace and Electronic Systems, 39*(3), 838–848. doi:10.1109/TAES.2003.1238740

This work was previously published in the International Journal of Swarm Intelligence Research, Volume 2, Issue 1, edited by Yuhui Shi, pp. 24-44, copyright 2011 by IGI Publishing (an imprint of IGI Global).

Chapter 14
Effects of Multi–Robot Team Formations on Distributed Area Coverage

Prithviraj Dasgupta
University of Nebraska at Omaha, USA

Taylor Whipple
University of Nebraska at Omaha, USA

Ke Cheng
University of Nebraska at Omaha, USA

ABSTRACT

This paper examines the problem of distributed coverage of an initially unknown environment using a multi-robot system. Specifically, focus is on a coverage technique for coordinating teams of multiple mobile robots that are deployed and maintained in a certain formation while covering the environment. The technique is analyzed theoretically and experimentally to verify its operation and performance within the Webots robot simulator, as well as on physical robots. Experimental results show that the described coverage technique with robot teams moving in formation can perform comparably with a technique where the robots move individually while covering the environment. The authors also quantify the effect of various parameters of the system, such as the size of the robot teams, the presence of localization, and wheel slip noise, as well as environment related features like the size of the environment and the presence of obstacles and walls on the performance of the area coverage operation.

DOI: 10.4018/978-1-4666-2479-5.ch014

INTRODUCTION

Robotic exploration of an unknown environment using a multi-robot system is an important topic within robotics that is relevant in several applications of robotic systems. These applications include automated reconnaissance and surveillance operations, automated inspection of engineering structures, and even domestic applications such as automated lawn mowing and vacuum cleaning. An integral part of robotic exploration is to enable robots to cover an initially unknown environment using a distributed terrain or area coverage algorithm. The coverage algorithm should ensure that every portion of the environment is covered by the coverage sensor or tool of at least one robot. Simultaneously, to ensure that the coverage is efficient, the coverage algorithm should prevent robots from repeatedly covering the same regions that have already been covered by themselves or by other robots. In most of the current multi-robot area coverage techniques, each robot performs and coordinates its motion individually. While individual coverage has shown promising results in many domains, there are a significant number of scenarios for multi-robot exploration such as extra-terrestrial exploration, robotic demining, unmanned search and rescue, etc., where the system can perform more efficiently if multiple robots with different types of sensors or redundant arrays of sensors can remain together as single or multiple cohesive teams (Cassinis, 2000; Chien *et al.*, 2005; De Mot, 2005). For example, in the domain of robotic demining (Bloch, Milisavljevc, & Acheroy, 2007), where autonomous robots are used to detect buried landmines, the incidence of false positive readings from underground landmines can be significantly reduced if robots with different types of sensors such as ground penetrating radar (GPR), IR (infra-red) sensors and metal detectors are able to simultaneously analyze the signals from potential landmines. In such a scenario, it would benefit if robots, each provided with one of these sensors, are able to

explore the environment while maneuvering themselves together as a team. Multi-robot formation control techniques provide a suitable mechanism to build teams of robots that maintain and dynamically reconfigure their formation, while avoiding obstacles along their path (Mastellone, Stipanovic, Graunke, Intlekofer, & Spong, 2008; Olfati Saber, 2006; Smith, Egerstedt, & Howard, 2009). However, these techniques are not principally concerned with issues related to area coverage and coverage efficiency. To address this deficit, in this paper, we investigate whether multi-robot formation control techniques and multi-robot area coverage techniques can be integrated effectively to improve the efficiency of the area coverage operation in an unknown environment by maintaining teams of multiple robots.

Recently, miniature robots that have a small footprint size are being used for applications such as automated exploration of engineering structures (Rutishauser, Corell, & Martinoli, 2009; Tache *et al.*, 2009). Similarly, unmanned aerial vehicles (UAVs) and micro-helicopters that have memory and computation capabilities comparable to these mini-robots are being widely used in several domains such as aerial reconnaissance for homeland security, search and rescue following natural disasters, monitoring forest fires, wildlife monitoring, etc. (Anderson *et al.*, 2008). Mini-robots are attractive because they are relatively inexpensive to field and a swarm of several mini-robots can be fielded at a cost comparable to fielding one or a few large robots. A multi-robot system that consists of several mini-robots also improves the robustness of the system. However, coordinating the actions of mini-robots to make them work cooperatively (e.g., move in formation) in a distributed manner becomes a challenging problem. We have approached this problem using a flocking-based technique (Gokce & Sahin, 2009; Balch & Arkin, 1998) to control the movement of robots so that they can move in formation. We have theoretically analyzed our team-formation techniques and identified certain conditions under which team formation improves the efficiency of distributed area coverage. We have also verified our techniques through extensive experiments on the Webots robotic simulation platform as well as using physical robots within an indoor environment. Our analytical and experimental results show that our team-based coverage techniques for distributed area coverage can perform comparably with other coverage strategies where the robots are coordinated individually. We also show that various parameters of the system such as the size of the robot teams, the presence of localization and wheel slip noise[1], as well as environment-related features like the size of the environment and the presence of obstacles and walls significantly affect the performance of the area coverage operation.

RELATED WORK

Much of the formation control research with multi-robot teams (Bahceci, Soysal, & Sahin, 2003; Gokce & Sahin, 2009; Olfati Saber, 2006; Sahin & Zergeroglu, 2008; Turgut, Celikkanat, Gokce, & Sahin, 2008) has been based on Reynolds' model for the mobility of flocks (Reynolds, 1987). Reynolds prescribes three fundamental operations for each team member to realize flocking - separation, alignment and cohesion. In the flocking model, each robot in a robot team adapts its motion and position based on the current position and heading of other team members such as a team leader or an immediate neighbor(s). This allows the robot team to remain in formation while moving as well as adapt its formation while avoiding obstacles. Following Reynolds' model, Chen and Luh (1994) and Wang (1989) describe mechanisms for robot-team motion while maintaining specific formations where individual robots determine their motion strategies from the movement of a team leader or neighbor(s). In Balch and Arkin (1998), the authors describe three reactive behavior-based strategies for robot teams to move in formation, viz., unit-center-referenced,

neighbor-referenced, or leader-referenced. In contrast to these approaches, Fredslund and Mataric (2002) describe techniques for robot team formation without using global knowledge such as robot locations, or the positions/headings of other robots, while using little communication between robots. Smith, Egerstedt, and Howard (2009) have used a combination of graph theory and control theory-based techniques to effect multi-robot formations However, in most of these approaches, the main objective is to achieve and maintain a certain formation and not to ensure the efficiency of tasks, like area coverage, being performed by the robots. Complementary to these approaches Spears, Kerr, and Spears (2006) have used physics-based approaches to form and navigate multi-robot teams.

Distributed coverage of an unknown environment using a multi-robot system has been an active area of research for over a decade and excellent overviews of this area are given in (Choset, 2001; Stachniss, Mozos, & Burgard, 2008). Subsequently, several techniques for multi-robot coverage such as using Boustrophedon decomposition (Rekleitis, New, Rankin, & Choset, 2008), using occupancy grid maps (Burgard, Moors, Fox, Simmons, & Thrun, 2005), using probabilistic Bayesian models of the coverage map, information gain-based heuristics and graph segmentation techniques (Wurm, Stachniss, & Burgard, 2008), ant-based coverage algorithms (Koenig, Szymanski, & Liu, 2001; Wagner, Altshuler, Yanovski, & Bruckstein, 2008) have also been proposed. Tzanov (2006) provides techniques that can be used by a group of robots to cover an initially unknown environment using either a frontier expansion method when the robots have perfect localization, or, using depth first traversal proceeding along triangulations of the environment when the robots localize themselves only with respect to each other. Recently, several techniques have been proposed where robots incrementally build a map of the environment, using a graph traversal technique (Gabriely & Rimon, 2001) and store the map either within the memory of each robot (Cheng & Dasgupta, 2007; Kaminka, Schechter, & Sadov, 2008; Rutishauser, Correll, & Martinoli, 2009) or at a central location that can be accessed by all robots (Koenig, Szymanski, & Liu, 2001). However, these researchers principally focus on controlling robots individually and designing different coordination strategies between them so that the robots can cover the environment while reducing repeated coverage among the regions covered by different robots. In contrast, our work focuses on achieving area coverage while coordinating teams of robots in a distributed manner instead of coordinating each robot's movements individually

MULTI-ROBOT DISTRIBUTED AREA COVERAGE

We consider a scenario where R mobile robots are deployed into an initially unknown two-dimensional environment. Without loss of generality, we assume that the environment is a square with each side of length D. The obstacles in the environment are assumed to be convex and the locations of these obstacles are not known initially by the robots. Let O be the area within the environment that is inaccessible to the robots because those areas are either occupied by obstacles or too tight for a single robot to fit into. The area of the environment to be covered by robots is given by D^2-O sq. units. Each robot is equipped with a square coverage tool with a width $d \ll D$. We define the duration of a single timestep as the time required by a robot to travel a distance equal to the length of its own footprint measured in the direction of its motion. Let a_r^t denote the action performed by a robot $r \in R$ during a timestep t that results in the robot's motion. Let c_r^t denote the corresponding area covered by robot r's coverage tool because of its motion during the timestep t. The objective of the distributed area coverage problem is to find

a sequence of actions for each robot that ensures the following criteria:

1. **Maximum Coverage Criterion:** The area of the environment covered by the coverage tool of at least one robot is maximized, i.e., $max\{\cup_{r \in R} \cup_{t=1...T} c_r^t\} \cap \{D^2 - O\}$.
2. **Minimum Overlap Criterion:** The overlap between the regions covered by different robots is minimized, i.e., $min \cap_{r \in R} \cap_{t=1...T} c_r^t$. This criterion ensures that the system performs efficiently and robots do not expend time and energy to revisit regions that have already been covered by other robots.
3. **Distributed Behavior Criterion:** Each robot should determine its actions autonomously, in a completely distributed manner, so that the system can be scalable and robust.

Each robot in our system is a two-wheeled robot equipped with forward-facing distance sensors to avoid obstacles and is capable of wireless communication. Each robot is also provided with a local positioning system (a GPS node in the simulator or an overhead camera-based positioning system in the physical experiments) to determine its position in the environment.

Team Representation

We have defined a robot team as a set of robots (>=2) that are able to navigate within an environment while avoiding obstacles and while preserving the team's shape and configuration. The essential parameters related to a robot team are described as follows:

- **Team Leader:** Our robot team formation technique is inspired by the leader-referenced motion described in Reynolds' flocking model (Reynolds, 1987). In the leader referenced motion, one robot in a team of robots is selected as the leader. The leader robot guides the motion of the rest of the robots in the team by communicating its direction of movement to all other team members. A robot that is not the team leader is called a follower robot.

- **Team Position Identifiers:** To interact with the follower robots in a team, each leader robot assigns a local position identifier to each robot within the team. The leader robot's position identifier is 0, robots to the left of the leader robot are assigned odd integer identifiers starting from 1, while robots to the right of the leader robot are assigned even integer identifiers starting from 2.

- **Team Shape:** To enable efficient movement of a team, the number of follower robots that are located on either side of a leader robot in a team are equally balanced. The angular separation between the two sets of followers robots, denoted by $u \in [0,\pi]$, denotes the shape of the team, where u is measured in radians. When $u = 0$, the team is organized into a vertical line-shape, when $u = \pi$, the team is organized into a horizontal line-shape, and when $0 \leq u \leq \pi$, we get a V-shape formation in the team, as shown in Figure 1.

Figure 1. A robot team showing the position identifiers of each robot. The angular separation in the team is u, the separation between adjacent robots is d_{sep} and α is the heading of the team

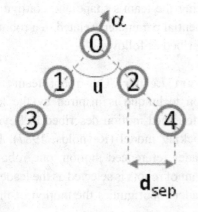

- **Team Configuration:** To maintain the shape of the team while in motion, each robot has to ensure that its relative position within the team does not change when the team moves. To achieve this, every pair of robots in the team maintains a separation of d_{sep} units between each other.

Single-Team Flocking

In our single-team flocking technique, the leader robot communicates the direction it is moving as the prescribed direction of motion for each follower robot in the team. Each follower robot then attempts to move in the prescribed direction. If any follower robot fails to move in this direction, it stops and communicates to the leader robot that its motion failed. Depending on the position of the follower robot in the team and its attempted direction of motion, the team leader then selects a new direction of motion that would possibly allow the affected follower robot to avoid the obstruction in its path. The team leader then broadcasts this newly selected direction as the prescribed direction for the next time step to all the follower robots in the team. In some scenarios, due to communication noise, a follower robot might fail to receive the communication containing the prescribed direction of motion from the leader robot. Then the follower robot just continues to move in the same direction it moved during its previous time step. The pseudo-code algorithm used by a team of robots in the leader-referenced motion strategy is described in Figure 2.

Formation Maintenance

When a team of robots moves in formation, the wheel slip noise and encoder readings can cause one or more of the team members to lose their desired positions which destroys the configuration in the team. To address this problem, a leader robot uses a dynamic formation maintenance protocol to ensure that each follower robot retains its position

Figure 2. Algorithm used by a robot to realize the leader-referenced formation control

```
function LeaderReferencedMotion
    ac^{t-1} ← action(movement direction) performed during
            last time step t − 1;
    if (I am not the leader)
        Ac_{leader} ← movement direction received from leader;
        if (Ac_{leader} ≠ NULL)
            ac^t ← Ac_{leader};
        else ac^t ← ac^{t-1}
        execute ac^t;
        if (ac^t fails due to obstacle)
            STOP;
        sendMessage (MotionFailed, local id in team, leader);
    else // I am the leader
        ac^t ← ac^{t-1}
        execute ac^t;
        if (ac^t fails due to obstacle)
            STOP;
        broadcastMessage (selectNewLeader);
        if (received MotionFailed message from follower robot)
            newAction ← An new direction of motion that will
                allow the follower robot to avoid the obstacle
                in the next step
            ac^t ← newAction;
            broadcastMessage(nextAction, ac^t);
```

in the team. In this protocol, the team leader first calculates the desired positions (DP_i) of every follower robot i relative to its own position and sends it to follower robot i. Each follower robot i compares its desired position DP_i with its actual position AP_i. A follower robot i adjusts its speed (move faster or slower) proportionally to $\|AP_i - DP_i\|$ so that it can reach its desired position and maintain the configuration of the team. The calculation of DP_i for follower robot i is given below. In these formulae, the actual position AP_i is represented by (x_{AP_i}, y_{AP_i}), the desired position DP_i is represented by (x_{DP_i}, y_{DP_i}), α is the direction of motion of the team, u is the angular separation in the team, d_{sep} is the linear separation between adjacent robots and i is the local identifier of a follower robot in a team:

Case 1: $0 \leq a < \pi$

$$x_{DP_i} = \begin{cases} x_{AP_i} = -\dfrac{i}{2} \times d_{sep} \times \cos(\alpha - \dfrac{u}{2}) & \text{if } i \text{ is odd} \\ x_{AP_i} = +\dfrac{i}{2} \times d_{sep} \times \cos(\alpha - \dfrac{u}{2}) & \text{if } i \text{ is even} \end{cases}$$

$$y_{DP_i} = y_{AP_i} - \dfrac{i}{2} \times d_{sep} \times \sin(\alpha - \dfrac{u}{2})$$

Case 2: $\pi < a \leq 2\pi$

$$x_{DP_i} = \begin{cases} x_{AP_i} + \dfrac{i}{2} \times d_{sep} \times \cos(\alpha - \dfrac{u}{2}) & \text{if } i \text{ is odd} \\ x_{AP_i} - \dfrac{i}{2} \times d_{sep} \times \cos(\alpha - \dfrac{u}{2}) & \text{if } i \text{ is even} \end{cases}$$

$$y_{DP_i} = y_{AP_i} + \frac{i}{2} \times d_{sep} \times \sin\left(\alpha - \frac{u}{2}\right)$$

Team Reconfiguration

A leader robot that encounters an obstacle ahead of it will fail to move in its direction of motion. In such a scenario, the team leader stops and communicates to the follower robots to stop moving. Then, the leader robot selects a new leader. If the obstacle is encountered by the old leader using its forward-facing distance sensors on its righthand (lefthand) side going clockwise from current heading, then the follower robot that is farthest from the leader on its lefthand (righthand) side is selected as the new leader. If the old leader robot approaches the obstacle orthogonally resulting in comparable readings on both pairs of the forward-facing (left and right) distance sensors, then one of the two follower robots that is farthest from the old leader robot and has the lowest identifier is selected to become the new leader. Sometimes a team of robots may end up in a tight space such as concave shape where two walls of an obstacle converge. Such scenarios are difficult for reformation because the team is surrounded by obstacles on both its left and right sides. To handle such

scenarios, when the leader robot encounters an obstacle the entire team stops and all the robots in the team back up a certain distance by reversing the direction of rotation of their wheels but not changing their heading. The team attempts to reform only after backing up a fixed distance after none of the robots in the team pick up an obstacle on their IR proximity sensors.

A scenario illustrating team reconfiguration is shown in Figure 3. One of the principal objectives of the team reconfiguration is to enable rapid reconfiguration of the team when the leader encounters an obstacle. To enable this, the follower robots between and including the new and old leader robots do not change their relative position in the team while reconfiguring (Figure 3(b)). The old leader then calculates the relative positions of the remaining follower robots in the new team so that the sum of the distances traveled by these robots to get into their desired positions under the new team leader is minimized (Figure 3(c)). It then communicates these desired positions to the respective follower robots. The new leader robot also selects a new heading for itself and the team based on a Braitenberg controller that uses the perceived location of the obstacle on the old leader robot's sensor and calculates an appropri-

Figure 3. (a) The leader robot (id=0) in a team of five robots encounters an obstacle, (b) A new leader is selected (id=3); robots (id=2, 4) are the robots that have to move the minimum distance to get into the new formation, (c) New robot id-s are assigned and the new leader robot selects its heading from randomly between $-\alpha\pm\beta$

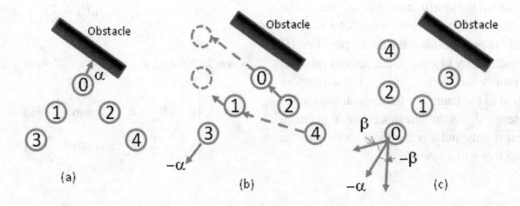

ate turning angle to ensure that the team turns away from the obstacle and does not encounter it again after forming a new team The new leader robot adds a certain amount of random noise to the new direction calculated by the Braitenberg controller - if α is the turning angle calculated, it selects a value in the range of $\alpha \pm \beta$, where $\beta \in U$ [0, 10] degrees.

In certain scenarios, the obstacles encountered by the robot team might have a complex shape. This can result in the desired positions of one or more the follower robots being unreachable or being occupied by an obstacle and the robots might have to re-attempt several times, perhaps unsuccessfully to get into the desired configuration. To avoid repeated looping by the follower robots to get into their desired position and thereby reduce the stoppage time of the team following reconfiguration, the new leader and the follower robots do not wait to get into their new positions before start to move as a new team. Instead, as soon as the new leader robot reaches its desired position, it starts to move in its new direction. If the path of the follower robots to their desired positions while reconfiguring is occluded or occupied by an obstacle, the robots attempt to avoid the obstacle by turning away from the obstacle using the perceived location of the obstacle from their IR distance sensors, moving a random distance away from the obstacle, and reattempting to resume its desired motion as the team. The new leader robot adjusts its speed to give the follower robots that have not yet reached their desired positions more time to catch up with the rest of the team. After starting to move in its new direction, the new leader updates and communicates the desired positions of the follower robots so that they can move directly towards their new position and retain the formation of the new team. Finally, if the new leader is unable to reach its desired position after repeated tries, it aborts the movement and attempts to go in a direction in which it does not perceive any obstacles. It moves for a random distance in this new direction and tries to reform the team from its new position.

Single-Team Coverage Technique

After a team of multiple robots is assimilated using the technique described above, the next step is to enable the team to cover the environment using a coverage technique. The coverage technique for a robot team is implemented by the team's leader robot. Each robot in the team, including the leader robot records the coordinates of the locations it has covered over the last H time steps within a data structure called its coverage history. Each follower robot communicates this coverage information at intervals of H time steps to the leader robot. The finite size H of the coverage information recorded makes the coverage technique amenable to implementation within on-board memory limitations of robots. To combine the coverage information of the team, the leader robot uses a node counting technique (Koenig, Szymanski & Liu, 2001). In the node-counting technique, the leader robot uses a data structure called a coverage map that contains the locations or coordinates visited by itself and the follower robots. Each location is associated with a real number that is initialized to zero. Every time a location appears in the coverage history of the leader robot or one of the follower robots, the number associated with the location is incremented. This results in the formation of a landscape within the leader robot's coverage map. Locations associated with large number or a 'high altitude' on this landscape indicate regions that have been covered multiple times, while regions with a smaller number or zero associated with them denote infrequently visited and unvisited regions respectively. To navigate the team, the leader robot selects a direction that will take it towards the lowest (least covered) point on this coverage landscape. A detailed description of the coverage technique used by the team leader to navigate a single team is given in (Cheng &

Dasgupta, 2007). When the leader robot of a team has to change because the team encountered an obstacle, the old leader robot communicates its coverage history to the new leader robot so that it can continue efficient coverage without re-covering regions already covered by the team in its previous configuration.

Multi-Team Distributed Coverage Technique

The single-team coverage technique described above provides a mechanism for multiple robots to move together as a single team. However, when team sizes are large (for example, greater than 10 robots per team), it becomes challenging for the robots to maintain the configuration of the follower robots in the team because of frequent reformations of the team to avoid obstacles, and the motion and communication noise in the follower robots. To prevent the formation of large teams, we limit the maximum allowable size of a team to T_{max} robots. We then use multiple teams to perform the coverage operation in the environment.

These multiple teams of robots need to be co-ordinated appropriately, in a distributed manner, to ensure that each team covers the environment efficiently while reducing the overlap of regions previously covered by that and other teams. We have used a potential field-based navigation strat-egy that also uses the recent coverage history of the teams' leader robots to enable multiple teams navigate themselves and perform coverage of the environment. In this strategy, each leader robot of a team has a virtual potential field of radius χ_r around it. When the leader robots of two teams get within the communication range χ_r of each other the leader robots of the teams exchange their current coverage maps, including the maps received from their respective follower robots, with each other. They then fuse each other's coverage information using the node counting technique described in the previous section. Finally, each team leader selects the region that closest to its team that has been least visited, and adjusts its heading to move towards that region. The pseudo-code of the algorithm for implementing the multi-team coverage technique is shown in Figure 4.

Figure 4. Algorithm used by a leader robot to disperse from other teams in the multi-team coverage technique

```
function PotentialFieldNavigation
    if (I am the leader)
        if (there is another leader robot within radius χr)
            Receive location, heading and coverage map
                from the leader robot of the other team
            Select a new direction to move that has
                the least overlap with the coverage history
                of my team and that obtained from the other team
            Perform team reconfiguration
        else
            Use single-team coverage technique to navigate
                until an obstacle is encountered
```

ANALYSIS

In this section, we investigate analytically whether area coverage using multiple robots organized as a team is more efficient than an area coverage technique that uses the same number of robots that are not configured into teams and perform coverage individually. We refer to this latter scenario as coverage with individually coordinated robots. Using the notation introduced in the section title "Multi-Robot Distributed Area Coverage," we consider a square environment where D is the length of a side of a square, O is the area within the environment occupied by obstacles and $d \ll D$ is the width of the coverage tool of a robot. We let D_{free} denote the area of the free space in the environment that needs to be covered by the robots, i.e., $D_{free} = D^2 - O$. As mentioned before, the values of D, O and D_{free} are unknown to each robot. To simplify our analysis, we consider that covering the surface of an environment with a coverage tool of width d is analogous to painting stripes in a two dimensional space with a "brush" of width d. The actual length of each such stripe depends on the number of obstacles and the number of robots in the environment. For our analysis, we let $\bar{l}$ denote the average length of a stripe.

Proposition 1: Coverage using a single robot. With a single robot performing the coverage of the environment, there is no guarantee of the robot covering previous uncovered terrain after it has made $4\bar{l}/d - 1$ stripes.

Proof. We consider that the single robot travels in a straight line until it encounters a wall or an obstacle. It then turns away from the wall at an angle determined by the Braitenberg controller from the sensor data of its proximity sensors. Using this technique, when the robot starts the i-th stripe, it has already encountered $(i-1)$ walls or obstacles. This means that there are $(i-1)$ points along the boundaries of the environment or on the obstacles within the environment that have been encountered by the robot. The i-th stripe partitions this set of $(i-1)$ points into two disjoint subsets, one subset lying to the left (or counter-clockwise) from the endpoint of the i-th stripe, and the other subset lying to the right (or clockwise) from the endpoint of the i-th stripe. We denote these two subsets of points on either side of the i-th stripe as CCW_i and CW_i respectively. Let $| CW_i | = p_k$, and, consequently, $| CCW_i | = (i-1)-p_k$. Now, if the $(i+1)$-th stripe is made to the left of the i-th stripe, then the $(i+1)$-th stripe will intersect the points in CCW_i. The expected number of intersects the $(i+1)$-th stripe will have is given by: $E(intersects^{i+1}) = | p_k | \times 2 - E(\text{stripes in } CCW_i)$. Now, because the angle at which a robot turns is distributed uniformly over $[0, \pi]$, we can assume that the robot has an equal probability of 0.5 of making the $(i+1)$-th stripe to the left or to the right of the i-th stripe. This gives us $| p_k | = [i/2]$. Also, the uniform distribution of the turning angle implies that the average number of stripes made by the robot in each of the sets CW_i and CCW_i are equal. Therefore, we can write $E(\text{stripes in } CCW_i) = [i/2]$. Therefore, $E(intersects^{i+1}) = [i/2] \times 2 - [i/2] = [i/2]$. Then, the expected number of intersects between the i-th stripe and previous stripes is given by $[1/2] + [2/2]+[3/2]+....[i/2] = [1/2] \times [(i(i+1))/2] = [(i(i+1))/4]$ Because each stripe is of width d, every time two stripes intersect there is an overlap of d^2 square units. Correspondingly, the area overlap between the i-th stripe and previous stripes is given by: $d^2 \times [(i(i+1))/4]$. In general, if the average stripe length is $\bar{l}$, then the area of the new region covered till the i-th stripe by the single robot is given by:

$$R^i_{new,SR} = (i \times l \times d) - \left(d^2 \times \frac{i(i+1)}{4}\right) \qquad (1)$$

In Equation 1, the first term on the r.h.s. indicates the area of the region covered until the i-th stripe while the second term indicates the area of the region over which there was repeated coverage until the i-th stripe. The value of i after which the second term exceeds the first indicates the number of stripes after which a single robot performs more repeated coverage than covering new region. To find the duration in number of stripes (denoted by $\hat{1}_{SR}$) we differentiate the expression in Equation 1 w. r. t. i and set the differential equal to zero. This gives us

$$\hat{1}_{SR} = \frac{4l}{d} - 1.$$

Proposition 2: Multi-robot non-flocking coverage. When multiple memoryless robots are coordinated individually to perform distributed coverage in an unknown environment, increasing the number of robots by a factor R results in a speedup that is less than R.

Proof. Consider R robots, each with a coverage tool of width d. As before, let $-l$ denote the average length of a stripe if there was a single robot in the environment. The robots use the navigation strategy described in the previous section to cover the environment. For this multi-robot scenario, let i_{enc} denote the frequency with which any two robots encounter each other and let $-l_{frac}$ denote the average length of the incomplete stripe for each robot at that point. The proof follows in a manner similar to the proof of Proposition 1. In the multi-robot case, when a robot does not encounter another robot it makes a stripe of average length $-l$. Since the frequency of encountering another robot is $[1/(i_{enc})]$, therefore, out of i stripes, there are $1 - [1/(i_{enc})]$ stripes of length $-l$. The new area covered by these stripes can be obtained by substituting i with $i \times (1 - [1/(i_{enc})])$ in Equation 1. For, the remaining $[i/(i_{enc})]$ stripes, a robot encounters another robot after doing an incomplete stripe of average length l_{frac} and moves away from the robot, thereby starting a new stripe.

Combining these $i \times (1 - [1/(i_{enc})])$ complete and $[i/(i_{enc})]$ incomplete stripes, we can get $R_{new,MR}^{i}$, the amount of new area covered till the i-th stripe in the multi-robot case as:

$$R_{new,MR}^{i} = (i[\frac{i}{i_{enc}}]) \times l \times d \times R$$

$$- \frac{(i - [\frac{i}{i_{enc}}])(i - [\frac{i}{i_{enc}}] + 1)}{4} \times d^2 R$$

$$+ [\frac{i}{i_{enc}}] \times l_{frac} \times d \times R$$

$$- \frac{([\frac{i}{i_{enc}}])([\frac{i}{i_{enc}}] + 1)}{4} \times i_{enc} \times d^2 R \qquad (2)$$

The stripe $\hat{i}_{MR}$ in the multi-robot case after which a robot covers more previously covered region than new region can be obtained by differentiating the expression in Equation 2 w. r. t. i and setting the differential equal to zero. This gives:

$$\hat{i}_{MR} = \frac{4(1 - \frac{1}{i_{enc}})l + 4\frac{-l_{frac}}{i_{enc}} - (2 - \frac{1}{i_{enc}})d}{2d((1 - \frac{1}{i_{enc}})^2 + \frac{1}{i_{enc}})} \qquad (3)$$

Comparing the values of the time measured in number of stripes after which a robot covers more previously covered region than previously uncovered region for the single and multi-robot cases, we can get an estimate of the speedup between these two settings. The speedup is given by the following expression:

$$speedup_{MR-SR} = \frac{\hat{i}_{MR}}{R \times \hat{i}_{SR}}$$

$$= \frac{1}{R} \times \left[\frac{(1 - \frac{1}{i_{enc}}) + \frac{\frac{4l_{frac}}{i_{enc}} - d}{4l - d}}{2((1 - \frac{1}{i_{enc}})^2 + \frac{1}{i_{enc}})} \right] \qquad (4)$$

Since, the average stripe length $\bar{l}$ is greater than the d ($\bar{l} > d$), and $i_{enc} >= 1$, the factor within square brackets in the above expression is <1. Consequently, we get sub-linear speedup by increasing the number of robots by a factor of R.

The result of sublinear speedup obtained above can be attributed to the fact that when the number of robots is increased, although they are able to cover more region in less time, the repeated coverage done by the robots over regions previously covered by other robots also increases.

Proposition 3: Multi-robot, multi-team flocking-based coverage. When multiple robots are organized to form teams to perform distributed coverage in an unknown environment, the coverage improves by a factor proportional to the size of each team τ.

Proof. Let us suppose that R robots are organized to form teams of size τ. This yields R / τ teams. The footprint of each team is then $d \times \tau$. This setting is similar to the multi-robot case analyzed in proposition 2, with the following changes - each 'unit' of coverage is not a single robot but a team of τ robots with a footprint of $d \times \tau$, the number of teams is R / τ and the teams encounter each other after every $\tau \times i_{enc}$ stripes, where i_{enc} is number of stripes after which two robots encounter each other in the individually coordinated multi-robot case. The values of the new region covered till the i-th stripe, $R^i_{new,team}$ and the stripe after which a robot covers more

previously covered region than previously uncovered region $\hat{i}_{team}$ can be obtained from the corresponding values in the multi-robot case given in Proposition 2 as shown:

$$R^i_{new,team} = (i - [\frac{i}{\tau \times i_{enc}}]) \times l \times d \times \tau \times \frac{R}{\tau}$$

$$- \frac{(i - [\frac{i}{\tau \times i_{enc}}])(i - [\frac{i}{\tau \times i_{enc}}] + 1)}{4} \times (d\tau)^2 \times \frac{R}{\tau}$$

$$+ [\frac{i}{\tau \times i_{enc}}] \times l_{frac} \times d \times \tau \times \frac{R}{\tau}$$

$$- \frac{([\frac{i}{\tau \times i_{enc}}])([\frac{i}{\tau \times i_{enc}}] + 1)}{4} \times \tau \times i_{enc} (d \times \tau)^2 \frac{R}{\tau}$$

(5)

and

$$\hat{i}_{team} = \frac{4(1 - \frac{1}{\tau \times i_{enc}})l + \frac{4l_{frac}}{\tau \times i_{enc}} - (2 - \frac{1}{\tau \times i_{enc}}) \times \tau \times d}{\tau \times 2d[(1 - \frac{1}{\tau \times i_{enc}})^2 + \frac{1}{\tau \times i_{enc}}]}$$

(6)

Figure 5(a) and (b) show the improvement in coverage for different team sizes with 20 and 48 robots in the environment for different team sizes. We observe that as the team size increases but the total number of robots in the environment remains fixed, the robots are able to cover more previously uncovered region. The second derivative of $R^i_{new,team}$ from Equation 5 is proportional to

$$2\tau(1 - \frac{1}{\tau \times i_{enc}})^2 - \frac{2}{i_{enc}}$$

Although our analyses presented in this section provide insights into the behavior of our system there are several characteristics of the system such as the effect of the frequency with which teams

Figure 5. Area of new region covered by robots for different team sizes. (a) with 20 robots in the environment, (b) with 48 robots in the environment

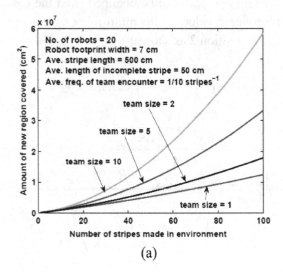
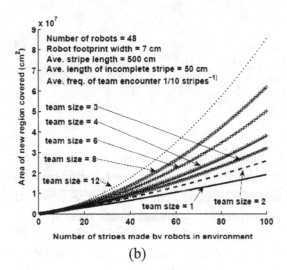

| (a) | (b) |

encounter each other on the performance of the system, the effect of team reformation delays due to physical characteristics that were not mathematically modeled such as the localization error and wheel slip noise, the effect of dynamic change in team configurations due to obstacles encountered by the teams, etc.., which are not directly amenable to theoretical analysis. To understand the behavior of our system further, we provide several empirical analyses of the performance of our system under different values of system parameters and different environment and operational constraints in the following section.

EXPERIMENTAL RESULTS

We have evaluated our team-based, multi-robot flocking and area coverage techniques through extensive experiments using simulated robots as well as on physical e-puck robots. An e-puck robot has a diameter of 7 cm and a memory capacity of 144 KB including RAM and Flash memory. Each wheel is 4.1 cm in diameter and is capable of a maximum speed of about 12cm/s. We have used the following sensors that are available on the e-puck

robot: (1) Eight infra-red distance sensors measuring ambient light and proximity of obstacles in a range of 4 cm, and, (2) Bluetooth capability for wireless communication. Each e-puck robot is also provided with a local positioning system (a GPS node in the simulator or an overhead camera-based positioning system in the physical experiments) to determine its position in the environment within a 2-D coordinate system. A photograph of the e-puck robot is shown in Figure 6(a). For all our simulations, the inter-robot separation between a pair of follower robots in a team is set to 20 cm. For multi-team coverage, the radius for the potential field-based navigation (χ_r) is set to 1.1 m.

Simulations in Webots

The first objective of our experiments is to understand the behavior of a multi-robot system using the coverage techniques described in this paper, and, to quantify the performance of those techniques while varying the different system and environment related parameters. To achieve this objective we have used extensive multi-robot simulations that allows us to analyze the

Figure 6. (a) An actual e-puck robot (photo courtesy of http://www.e-puck.org) (b) The model of the e-puck robot in the Webots simulator used for our simulations

(a)

(b)

robots' coverage performance within different experimental settings. We have used the Webots simulation platform (Michel, 2004) for our experiments under this category. Webots is a powerful robotic simulation platform that allows realistic modeling of robots and environments including the parameters of different sensors on robots and the physics of the environment. Each robot in our simulated system is modeled as an e-puck robot with accurate models of the features and characteristics of the physical e-puck robot, as shown in Figure 6(b).

We have used four metrics to evaluate the performance of our multi-robot team-based area coverage techniques which are given below:

1. The percentage of the area of an environment covered during 2 hours of real time.
2. The percentage of time spent in reformations by a multi-robot team. This metric measures the direct overhead in terms of time of team-based coverage vs. covering the environment individually.
3. The competitive ratio (CR) of the distributed coverage compared to an optimal offline coverage technique. To calculate the competitive ratio(CR), we first calculate the

amount of redundancy or repeated coverage of the environment given by:

$$WR = \sum_i i \times \text{Area of the region visited } i \text{ times}$$

The competitive ratio (CR) is given by:

$$CR = \frac{\text{Free area of the environment}}{WR}$$

A higher value of CR (near 1) indicates near-optimal coverage while smaller values of CR (approaching 0) indicate increased repeated coverage of the same region by multiple robots that degrades the performance of the system.

4. The number of obstacles (including walls) encountered by the leader and follower robots in a team. This metric measures the overhead of having larger sized teams because larger (wider) teams encounter obstacles more frequently than smaller ones.

For evaluating the efficacy of team-based coverage, we have compared each of the results obtained using multi-robot teams with an identical scenario where the same number of robots cover the environment individually without forming teams. Each scenario was allowed to run for a duration of 2 hours of real time and results were averaged over 10 runs for each scenario. We have divided our experiments into four categories to verify the performance of area coverage while using different configurations of robot teams, and to understand the effect of different types of environments and noise on the performance of the system.

Effect of Varying Number of Robots and Robot Team Size

In our first set of experiments we quantify the effect of changing the number of robots, number of teams and the team sizes of the robots covering the environment on the performance of our metrics. Our simulation and physical robot experiments are done with different numbers of robot teams, where the size of each team is either 1 robot (individual), 3 robots, 5 robots, 7 robots or 9 robots[2].

With these sizes for each robot team, we tested our algorithms with three different population sizes of robots within the environment 15, 27 and 48 robots. These population sizes ensure that the robots can be divided into the desired size for each team (3, 5, 7 or 9 robots) while approximately doubling the total number of robots in the environment from one population size to the next. The numbers of different sized teams for each population size are shown in the first column of Table 1. The circled multiplicand (e.g., ⑤) denotes the number of robots in a team, while the multiplier denotes the number of teams. Using this convention, the notation 3× ⑤ denotes 3 teams with 5 robots in each team. The last configuration within each set denoted by *number of robots* × ① considers robots moving individually without forming teams and provides a comparison along the different metrics between forming and not forming teams while using the same number of robots. The results of varying the number of robots, number of teams and the sizes of the teams on the metrics used for our experiments are shown in Table 1. We observe that the percentage of environment covered by the robots

Table 1. Effect of changing number of robots, number of teams and team sizes with 15, 27 and 48 robots on the different metrics used in our experiments. All results shown are for the office environment shown in Figure 7(c)

No. of Robots and Their Configurations	Average Team Size	% of Env. Covered		% of Time Spent in Reformations		CR
		Mean	Std. Dev.	Mean	Std. Dev.	
15 robots						
{3 x ⑤}	5	76.59	4.29	70.82	6.95	0.30
{1 x ③, 1 x ⑤, 1 x ⑦}	5	76.13	5.49	66.14	4.85	0.31
{5 x ③}	3	82.95	1.97	59.36	2.28	0.29
{15 x ①}	1	89.13	0.83	39.65	1.36	0.26
27 robots						
{3 x ⑨}	9	76.91	5.70	78.23	3.05	0.27
{1 x ③, 2 x ⑤, 2 x ⑦}	5.4	87.18	2.26	70.82	3.10	0.22
{4 x ③, 2 x ⑤}	3.85	90.21	1.06	64.90	2.15	0.20
{27 x ①}	1	93.60	0.15	43.09	1.27	0.16
48 robots						
{4 x ⑤, 4 x ⑨}	6	91.95	1.92	71.46	1.72	0.22
{6 x ③, 6 x ⑤}	4	93.56	0.62	68.83	2.63	0.22
{16 x ③}	3	94.45	0.39	63.13	1.61	0.21
{48 x ①}	1	94.48	0.12	40.71	1.03	0.19

increases with the number of robots - ranging from an average value of 81.2% with 15 robots to 86.98% with 27 robots and finally to 93.61% with 48 robots. However, the increase in the amount area covered is sublinear in the number of robots because with more robots, robot teams encounter each other more often and spend more time in reformations to avoid colliding with each other. Further analysis of the values in Table 1 shows that with 15 robots in the environment, when the average team size changes from 5 to 3 robots, the coverage improves by

$$\frac{82.95 - 76.13}{76.13} \times 100 = 8.96\%$$

With 27 robots, when the average team size drops from 9 to 3.85 robots, the improvement in coverage becomes

$$\frac{90.21 - 76.91}{76.91} \times 100 = 17.29\%$$

Finally, the improvement in coverage from a team size of 6 to a team size of 3 robots is

$$\frac{94.45 - 91.95}{91.95} \times 100 = 2.72\%$$

These numbers indicate the smaller team sizes are able to achieve better coverage. To further validate this hypothesis, we performed a regression analysis between the average team size and the percentage of environment covered from the data reported in Table 1. The correlation coefficient for different numbers of robots in the environment are shown in Table 2. We observe that a strong inverse correlation exists between the average size of the robot teams and the percentage of environment covered. Overall, the results of the percentage of environment covered for different robot teams sizes indicate that smaller team

Table 2. Table showing the correlation coefficient between the average size of robot team and the percentage of environment covered for a different numbers of robots in the environment

No. of Robots in Env.	Correl (team size, % of env. covered)
15	−0.999
27	−0.977
48	−0.914

sizes are able to achieve better coverage. This is in contrast to the result from Proposition 3 that the coverage performance is proportional to the robot team size. The anomaly in the analytical and experimental results can be explained by the fact that the analytical model does assumes 'instantaneous' reformation when the team leader encounters an obstacle. On the other hand, the experiments include physical characteristics of the setting such as localization errors, wheel slip noise and follower robots encountering obstacles. All of these characteristics force the team to reform and these additional reformation times degrade the coverage performance of larger robot teams.

The better performance of smaller robot teams due to rapid reformation times can also be explained by analyzing the percentage of time spent in reformations column of Table 1. We observe that smaller teams with a size of 3 robots spend about 60% of their total time of operation in reformations. This value increases to as much as 78.23% for a team size of 9 robots. To further validate the correlation between team size and time spent in reformations, we performed a linear regression test between the team size as the independent variable and the percentage of time spent in reformations as the independent variable, from the data reported in Table 1. The correlation coefficient between the team size and the percentage of time spent in reformations is 0.92, the slope of the linear curve is 5.06 and its y-coefficient is 41.49 - confirming our hypothesis that team size affects the time spent in reformations by a team. The larger reformation times for larger robot teams follows intuitively too because when a larger team encounters an obstacle, more robots have to get into new positions before the team can regain formation and start moving in a new direction. When robots move individually, the reformation times are the lowest because a single robot only has to turn itself to avoid an obstacle without worrying about getting all follower robots into correct positions to regain team formation after avoiding an obstacle.

Among the experimental results reported in Table 1, individually moving robots also appear to achieve better or comparable coverage than robots that move together as a team, irrespective of the team size. The inferior coverage performance of larger teams together with longer reformation times leads us to the question - are larger teams always worse for team-based area coverage? The answer to this question can be inferred from the results in the competitive ratio (CR) column of Table 1. The competitive ratio expresses the efficiency of the coverage performed by the robots by incorporating the amount of repeated, and hence, unnecessary coverage of previously covered regions done by the robots. The repeated coverage happens in our system because leader robots refresh their coverage histories after H steps. We observe that although robots that move individually are able to cover a marginally higher percentage of the total environment than team-based robots, the competitive ratio of robots that move individually is lower than that of robots moving in teams. This indicates that robots that move individually sacrifice a significant amount of the advantage of their lower reformation times by performing repeated coverage of previously covered regions. The lower competitive ratio for area coverage by the individually moving robots can be attributed to the fact that individual coordination between robots requires each robot to exchange and fuse coverage information from more robots,

more frequently. In contrast, with team-based coverage only leader robots aggregate the team's coverage information and exchange it with each other. This results in more efficient information exchange and judicious decision making by robot teams to avoid repeated coverage of previously covered regions.

Effect of Different Environments

For our next set of experiments we vary the environment in which the robots operate and observe the effect on the performance of the system. We consider three different environments with different geometric features and different numbers of obstacles in the environment as shown in Figure 7. The results of this experiment for different team sizes while using 27 robots are shown in Figure 8(a)-(d). We observe that for the square environment with no obstacles, the percentage of the environment covered by the robots shown in Figure 8(a) and the competitive ratio shown in Figure 8(c) are not significantly affected by changing the team size. This is substantiated by the high correlation coefficient of 0.97 and 0.98 respectively, but a very small slope of the linear best-fit curve, 0.23 and 0.003 respectively, for these cases obtained by a linear regression analysis of the data. These results are in contrast to the analytical results mentioned in Proposition 3 which state that the area of the previously uncovered region increases proportionally with the robot team size. However, the mathematical model of the robots did not account for physical characteristics such as the localization error and wheel slip noise, which cause the performance of the area coverage to get adversely affected in the experimental results. For the more complex environments of the corridor and the office, the robot team size adversely affects the percentage of the area of the environment that gets covered as shown in Figure 8(a). This relationship between the average team size and coverage performance

Figure 7. The three different types of environment used in our experiments. (a) 4×4 m square environment with no obstacles, (b) corridor environment consisting of two diamond shaped regions, joined by a corridor 8 m long and 1 m wide, (c) 4 m ×2 m office occupied by furniture

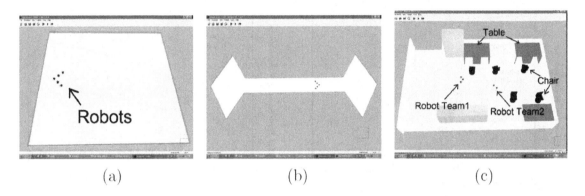

(a)   (b)   (c)

is confirmed by the high negative value of the correlation coefficient −0.89 and −0.97 respectively, coupled with a considerable slope of the linear best-fit curve at −1.35 and −2.11 respectively, as shown in Figure 8(a). The decrease in coverage can be attributed to the longer reformation times of larger teams as shown in Figure 8(b). Larger robot teams spend longer times to reconfigure after encountering an obstacle, and therefore, have lesser time to perform coverage of the environment. The competitive ratio of the robots in the corridor and office environments increases marginally with larger sized robot teams as shown by the positive slope of the linear best-fit curve of 0.02 and 0.01 respectively in Figure 8(c). But this improvement comes at the expense of lower coverage in the environment. Finally, Figure 8(d) shows the number of obstacles encountered by the leader and follower robots in robot teams for different team sizes. We observe in this graph that as the team size gets larger, follower robots evidently encounter more obstacles because of the larger physical width of the team. This further aggravates the reformation time for larger teams as evidenced in Figure 8(b), and reduces the coverage efficiency for large sized teams in environments with a considerable number of obstacles like the corridor and office environments.

Effect of Noise on the System

In our final set of experiments we quantify the effect of noise on the coverage performance of the robots. We consider two sources of noise: a) wheel slip noise that depends on the friction between the robot's wheels and floor of the environment, and, b) localization noise that is introduced due to the local positioning mechanism used by the robots in our system.

For determining the wheel slip noise, we performed 5 sets of trials by moving a physical e-puck robot from a fixed start location to a target location. Each trial set consisted of 10 individual runs and in each trial set, the robot was moved through a distance of 3.85 m at different angles (0, 30, 45, 60 and 90 degrees) relative to the local coordinate system in the environment. For each trial, we measured the difference in distance between the actual location reached by the robot and its target location. The error due to wheel slip noise, obtained by averaging the results of these trials, was calculated as 0.1339 in the x-axis and 0.1261 in the y-axis of the environment's coordinate system. We averaged these two values to set a wheel slip noise of 0.13 for each simulated e-puck robot inside Webots. The effects of the wheel slip noise of the coverage metrics is shown

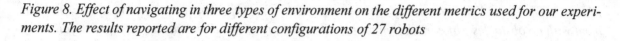

Figure 8. Effect of navigating in three types of environment on the different metrics used for our experiments. The results reported are for different configurations of 27 robots

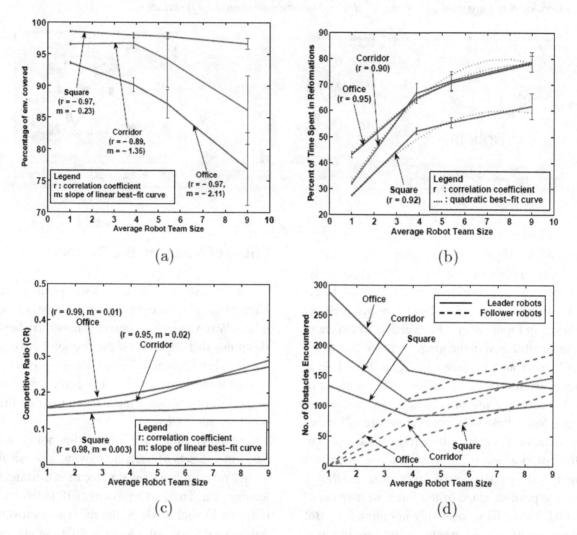

in Figure 9(a)-(d) with different configurations of 15 robots moving in the three environments shown in Figure 7. We observe that the effect of the wheel slip noise on the different metrics used for our experiments is nominal in the case of the square and the office environments. However, the wheel slip noise results in a more pronounced effect on these metrics when the robots move in the corridor environment. Specifically, for the configurations {3× ⑤} and {1× ③, 1× ⑤, 1× ⑦} in the corridor environment, we observe that the

wheel sleep noise adversely affects the coverage performance, the competitive ratio and the number of obstacles encountered by follower robots. The reason for this behavior can be understood by analyzing the effect of wheel slip noise and the space of the corridor. The wheel slip noise we observed on the physical robots causes each wheel to turn at a different speed than was set by the wheel encoders, due to friction with the floor's surface. This causes the robots to drift intermittently from their planned paths instead of

Figure 9. Effect of incorporating wheel slip noise within the three types of environments considered on the different metrics used for our experiments. The results reported are for different configurations of 15 robots

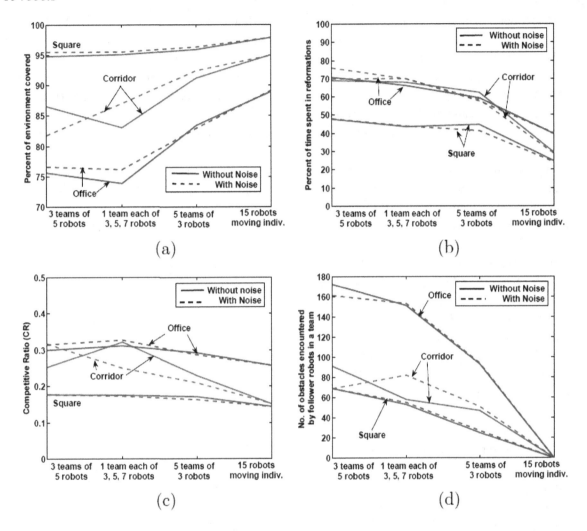

moving in a straight line. In the corridor, that is 1 m wide, the wheel slip noise causes the robots, especially the follower robots, to drift from their planned path through the corridor and encounter the walls of the narrow corridor. This results in the higher number of obstacles encountered by the follower robots with the $\{1\times \text{③}, 1\times \text{⑤}, 1\times \text{⑦}\}$ configuration in the corridor environment as shown in Figure 9(d).

We further performed 2-way and 1-way ANOVA (analysis of variance) tests at 95% con-

fidence interval to validate our conclusions for each of the data sets shown in Figure 9(a)-(d). The results show that when considered together with the team size variable (in column 2 of Table 4), slip noise does not have a significant effect on the first three metrics - percentage of environment covered by the robots, percentage of time spent in reformations, and competitive ratio. However, for the last metric, number of obstacles encountered by follower robots, the wheel slip noise does make a significant impact. The marginal impact of the wheel slip noise is in accordance with the results shown in Figure 9(a)-(c), where the graphs for the metrics with and without slip noise are almost identical. To further analyze our results we also performed 1-way ANOVA tests with the variables team size and wheel slip noise respectively. As noted previously in this section, we once again observe from the significance results that the team size variable affects the performance of the first three metrics. The wheel slip noise is a significant variable only for the percentage of environment covered and the number of obstacles encountered by follower robots metrics. These results can be explained by the fact that when the follower robots are closer to walls of obstacles, especially for the narrow channel connecting the two rooms in the corridor environment, the wheel slip noise causes the robots to deviate from their desired locations within the team and encounter the walls more often. Without wheel slip noise added to their motion, the robots deviate from their positions less frequently, and, therefore, they encounter obstacles less frequently. More obstacles should result in more reformation time. However, the percentage of reformation times shown in Figure 9(b) is not affected significantly by the wheel slip noise. An increased number of obstacles encountered, but unchanged number of reformations indicate that robot teams are able to avoid obstacles encountered by followers without reforming. In other words, teams are able to continue coverage despite follower robots encountering obstacles. This behavior in turn translates to a slight improvement in the amount of coverage achieved by the robots, while considering wheel slip noise, as shown in Figure 9(a).

Localization noise in our system is caused mainly by the image processing algorithm that processes the video stream of the robots' movement captured by the overhead camera overlooking the experiment arena and calculates each robot's coordinates in the local coordinate system. For calculating the localization noise, we used

five physical e-puck robots and tracked their paths over a distance of 3.85 m for 5 trials. Each robot was fitted with uniquely colored marker on its top that showed its heading relative to the local coordinate system. The error in the location and heading of the different robots is shown in Table 3. We added these noise values to the "accurate" GPS readings provided by Webots (using the GPSNode class) to simulate the effect of localization noise in our simulations. The results are reported in Table 5 for a team of 5 robots moving in the square environment with and without localization noise added to its coordinates. We observe that localization noise marginally affects the coverage and competitive ratio metrics. To validate this observation, we performed the Kruksal-Wallis analysis of variance test to deter-

Table 3. Localization error due to image processing errors for five experiments

Parameter	The epuck with a red hat		
	X (cm)	Y (cm)	Θ (Degrees)
Mean Error	0.25	0.088	-3.49
Standard Deviation	0.33	0.15	2.38
	The epuck with a blue hat		
Mean Error	0.68	0.62	3.05
Standard Deviation	0.15	0.148	0.3
	The epuck with a green hat		
Mean Error	-0.07	-0.18	-1.43
Standard Deviation	0.12	0.147	5.72
	The epuck with a pink hat		
Mean Error	-0.02	-0.089	4.85
Standard Deviation	0.19	0.14	1.75
	The epuck with a purple hat		
Mean Error	-0.29	-0.398	5.69
Standard Deviation	0.18	0.137	2.17

Table 4. Analysis of variance of the results with slip noise for different metrics used in our experiments shown in Figure 9(a)-(d). The significance level α is set to α=0.05 (95% confidence intervals). The abbreviation "sig." stands for significant

Metric	Sig. Value with 2-Way ANOVA (team size * slip noise)	Sig. Value with 1-Way ANOVA (team size)	Sig. Value with 1-Way ANOVA (slip noise)
% of env. covered	0.974 (not sig.)	0 (sig.)	0.05 (sig.)
% of time in reform	0.992 (not sig.)	0 (sig.)	0.974 (not sig.)
CR	0.956 (not sig.)	0 (sig.)	0.969 (not sig.)
No. of obst. (followers)	0.05 (sig.)	0.679 (not sig.)	0.05 (sig.)

Table 5. Effect of localization noise on the different metrics used for our experiments. The results are reported for navigating a team of 5 robots in the square environment

Environment	% of Env. Covered		% of Time Spent in Reformations		CR
	Mean	Std. Dev.	Mean	Std. Dev.	
1 team of 5 robots WITHOUT localization noise					
Square	75.13	3.90	26.56	4.56	0.43
Corridor	70.57	5.67	45.23	4.66	0.46
Office	45.42	7.35	62.09	7.77	0.79
1 team of 5 robots WITH localization noise					
Square	78.56	3.64	38.33	4.78	0.44
Corridor	59.81	10.52	60.42	10.31	0.60
Office	43.44	8.82	67.19	9.86	0.82

mine if localization noise had a significant effect on the metrics used in our experiments. The results of the tests are reported in Table 6. For each of the metrics, the p-value of the data set is found to be greater than the confidence level α=0.05, indicating that the medians of the distributions with and without localization noise are identical at 95% confidence interval. This implies that the localization noise only has a marginal effect on percentage of the environment covered, the time spent in reformations and the competitive ratio.

Table 6. Different metrics and corresponding p-values from Kruksal-Wallis Test on the data with and without localization noise reported in Table 5

Metric	p-value
% of env. covered	0.873
% of time in reform	0.513
CR	0.513

Experiments on E-Puck Robots

To test the performance of our team-based coverage algorithm on physical e-puck robots, we performed coverage within a 2.31×2.31 m^2 environment using 3 e-puck robots that moved together as a team. We compared the metrics obtained from this scenario with a scenario where the robots are coordinated to move individually.

The environment either had no obstacles, or had 10% of its area covered by obstacles. Each scenario was run for 60 minutes and five runs were conducted for each scenario. A snapshot of the 3 e-puck robots within the image processing software's user interface and a photograph of the robots within our experiment arena is shown in Figure 10. A video of a simulation run from the e-puck robot experiments is available at http://

Figure 10. (a) Screen shot of three e-pucks within our experiment arena in the image processing software's user console (b) photo of three e-pucks in a V-shape formation within the experiment arena

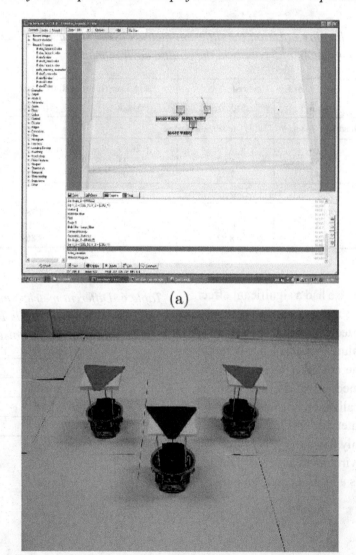

(a)

(b)

www.youtube.com/watch?v=jmyhURYq5Uc. We observed that in the individually coordinated case robots obtain 7% to 20% more coverage than the team-based coverage at the different running times. Due to the localization error and wheel slip noise, the robot team needs to reform its shape approximately every 2 minutes, and spends about 35-40 seconds to get the team reconfigured. This results in about 2/3 of its total runtime being spent by the robot team to perform coverage while the remaining 1/3 is spent in reconfigurations (Table 7). However, we observed that when robots are individually coordinated, they encounter 10 times more obstacles than the team-based coverage. The team based coverage performs especially better than the individually coordinated strategy when the robots are at a corner. The individual robot gets "stuck" for some time oscillating between the two walls of the corner, while the robot team, because of its wider coverage swath, can navigate out of the corner more efficiently.

CONCLUSION AND FUTURE WORK

In this paper, we have described a technique for multi-team flocking for distributed area coverage. We have shown that with many small sized teams, team-based coverage performs comparably with coverage when the robots are individually coordinated. Our techniques hold promise in scenarios where a suite of robots have to maneuver themselves as a cohesive team to provide an array of sensors located on the different robots of the team or to provide redundancy in the sensor measurements. We are currently enhancing the team-based coverage techniques to record and compress local coverage maps within the memory of each robot so that they can reduce redundant coverage. We are also investigating techniques to improve the basic formation control mechanisms described in this paper so that robot teams can dynamically adapt their formation as well as move across teams depending on their performance.

Table 7. Experimental results showing the different metrics for coverage with 3 e-puck robots

Percentage of Coverage (%)				
	15 min.	**30 min.**	**45 min.**	**60 min.**
Ind. no obs.	20.1	32.5	48.3	53.4
Team, no obs.	13.4	18.6	29.6	42.9
Ind. 10% obs.	20.39	33.17	49.6	55.7
Team, 10% obs.	16.44	21.78	30.67	45.33
No. of Times Obstacle Encountered				
Ind., no obs.	16	44	69	99
Team, no obs.	2	5	7	8
Ind., 10% obs.	21	46	78	107
Team, 10% obs.	2	6	7	10
Avg. Reformation Time				
Team, no obs.	34.7	39.15	39.33	38.08
Team, 10% obs.	33.94	37.13	36.57	37.55

ACKNOWLEDGMENT

The research reported in this paper has been supported as part of the COMRADES project, sponsored by the U.S. Office of Naval Research, grant no. N000140911174.

We are grateful to Prof. Lotfollah Najjar of the Information Systems and Quantitative Analysis Department, University of Nebraska, Omaha for his help with statistical analysis of our test results.

A preliminary version of this paper appeared as a conference paper: Cheng, K., Wang, Y., & Dasgupta, P. (2009). Distributed Area Coverage using Robot Flocks. World Congress on Nature and Biology Inspired Computing (NABIC) (pp. 678-683).

REFERENCES

Anderson, D., Carter, S., Hazzard, M., Josey, T., Pearson, J., Scoggins, J., & Soltmann, L. (2008). *Open Source Autonomous Miniature Unmanned Aerial Vehicles (OSAM-UAV) Team's System Design & Development for the 2009 AUVSI Student UAS Competition.* Retrieved March 15, 2010, from http://www.navair.navy.mil/pma263/seafarers/journal/journal2008/AUVSI08-NCSU.pdf

Bahceci, E., Soysal, O., & Sahin, E. (2003). *Review: Pattern formation and adaptation in multi-robot systems* (Tech. Rep. No. CMU-RI-TR-03-43). Pittsburgh, PA: Carnegie Mellon University.

Balch, T., & Arkin, R. (1998). Behavior-based formation control of multi-robot teams. *IEEE Transactions on Robotics and Automation, 14*(6), 926–939. doi:10.1109/70.736776

Bloch, I., Milisavljevc, N., & Acheroy, M. (2007). Multisensor Data Fusion for Spaceborne and Airborne Reduction of Mine Suspected Areas. *International Journal of Advanced Robotic Systems, 4*(2), 173–186.

Burgard, W., Moors, M., Fox, D., Simmons, R., & Thrun, S. (2005). Collaborative multi-robot exploration. *IEEE Transactions on Robotics, 21*(3), 376–386. doi:10.1109/TRO.2004.839232

Cassinis, R. (2000). *Multiple single sensor robots rather than a single multi-sensor platforms: a reasonable alternative.* Paper presented at International Conference on Explosives and Drug Detection Techniques.

Chen, Q., & Luh, J. (1994). Coordination and control of a group of small mobile robots. In *Proceedings of the International Conference on Robotics and Automation* (pp. 2315-2320).

Cheng, K., & Dasgupta, P. (2007). Dynamic Area Coverage using Faulty Multi-agent Swarms. In *Proceedings of the IEEE/WIC/ACM International Conference on Intelligent Agent Technology* (pp. 17-24).

Chien, S., Sherwood, R., Tran, D., Cichy, B., Rabideau, G., & Castano, R. (2005). Using Autonomy Flight Software to Improve Science Return on Earth Observing One. *Journal of Aerospace Computing, Information, and Communication, 2,* 196–216. doi:10.2514/1.12923

Choset, H. (2001). Coverage for robotics: A survey of recent results. *Annals of Mathematics and Artificial Intelligence, 31,* 113–126. doi:10.1023/A:1016639210559

De Mot, J. (2005). *Optimal Agent Cooperation with Local Information.* Unpublished doctoral dissertation, Massachusetts Institute of Technology.

Dudenhoefer, D., & Jones, M. (2000). A formation behavior for large-scale micro-robot force. In *Proceedings of the 32nd Winter Simulation Conference* (pp. 972-982).

Fredslund, J., & Mataric, M. (2002). A general algorithm for robot formations using local sensing and minimal communication. *IEEE Transactions on Robotics and Automation*, *18*(5), 837–846. doi:10.1109/TRA.2002.803458

Gabriely, Y., & Rimon, E. (2001). Spanning-tree based coverage of continuous areas by a mobile robot. *Annals of Mathematics and Artificial Intelligence*, *31*(1-4), 77–98. doi:10.1023/A:1016610507833

Gokce, F., & Sahin, E. (2009). To flock or not to flock: the pros and cons of flocking in long-range migration of mobile robot swarms. In *Proceedings of the 8th International Conference on Autonomous Agents and MultiAgent Systems (AAMAS)* (pp. 65-72).

Kaminka, G., Schechter, R., & Sadov, V. (2008). Using Sensor Morphology for Multirobot Formations. *IEEE Transactions on Robotics*, *24*(2), 271–282. doi:10.1109/TRO.2008.918054

Koenig, S., Szymanski, B., & Liu, Y. (2001). Efficient and Inefficient Ant Coverage Methods. *Annals of Mathematics and Artificial Intelligence*, *31*(1-4), 41–76. doi:10.1023/A:1016665115585

Mastellone, S., Stipanovic, D., Graunke, C., Intlekofer, K., & Spong, M. (2008). Formation Control and Collision Avoidance for Multi-agent Nonholonomic Systems: Theory and Experiments. *The International Journal of Robotics Research*, *27*(1), 107–126. doi:10.1177/0278364907084441

Michel, O. (2004). Webots: Professional Mobile Robot Simulation. *International Journal of Advanced Robotic Systems*, *1*(1), 39–42.

Olfati Saber, R. (2006). Flocking for Multi-Agent Dynamic Systems: Algorithms and Theory. *IEEE Transactions on Automatic Control*, *51*(3), 401–420. doi:10.1109/TAC.2005.864190

Rekleitis, I., New, A., Rankin, E., & Choset, H. (2008). Efficient Boustrophedon Multi-Robot Coverage: an algorithmic approach. *Annals of Mathematics and Artificial Intelligence*, *52*(2-4), 109–142. doi:10.1007/s10472-009-9120-2

Reynolds, C. (1987). Flocks, herds and schools: A distributed behavioral model. *Computer Graphics*, *21*(4), 25–34. doi:10.1145/37402.37406

Rutishauser, S., Correll, N., & Martinoli, A. (2009). Collaborative Coverage using a Swarm of Networked Miniature Robots. *Robotics and Autonomous Systems*, *57*(5), 517–525. doi:10.1016/j.robot.2008.10.023

Sahin, T., & Zergeroglu, E. (2008). Mobile Dynamically Reformable Formations for Efficient Flocking Behavior in Complex Environments. In *Proceedings of the IEEE International Conference on Robotics and Automation* (pp. 1910-1915).

Smith, B., Egerstedt, M., & Howard, A. (2009). Automatic Generation of Persistent Formations for Multi-Agent Networks Under Range Constraints. *Mobile Networks and Applications Journal*, *14*, 322–335. doi:10.1007/s11036-009-0153-x

Spears, D., Kerr, W., & Spears, W. (2006). Physics-based Robot Swarms for Coverage Problems. *International Journal of Intelligent Control and Systems*, *11*(3), 124–140.

Stachniss, C., Mozos, O., & Burgard, W. (2008). Efficient exploration of unknown indoor environments using a team of mobile robots. *Annals of Mathematics and Artificial Intelligence*, *52*(2-4), 205–227. doi:10.1007/s10472-009-9123-z

Tache, F., Fischer, W., Caprari, G., Siegwart, R., Moser, R., & Mondada, F. (2009). Magnebike: A magnetic wheeled robot with high mobility for inspecting complex-shaped structures. *Journal of Field Robotics, 26*(5), 431–452. doi:10.1002/rob.20296

Turgut, A., Celikkanat, H., Gokce, F., & Sahin, E. (2008). Self-organized flocking with a mobile robot swarm. In *Proceedings of the International Conference on Autonomous Agents and MultiAgent Systems* (pp. 39-46).

Tzanov, V. (2006). *Distributed Area Search with a Team of Robots*. Unpublished master's thesis, Massachusetts Institute of Technology.

Wagner, I., Altshuler, Y., Yanovski, V., & Bruckstein, A. (2008). Cooperative Cleaners: A Study in Ant Robotics. *The International Journal of Robotics Research, 27*, 127–151. doi:10.1177/0278364907085789

Wang, P. (1989). Navigation Strategies for Multiple Autonomous Mobile Robots. In *Proceedings of the IEEE/RSJ International Workshop on Intelligent Robots & Systems* (pp. 486-493).

Wurm, K., Stachniss, C., & Burgard, W. (2008). Coordinated multi-robot exploration using a segmentation of the environment. In *Proceedings of the IEEE/RSJ International Conference on Intelligent Robots and Systems* (pp. 1160-1165).

ENDNOTES

[1] Wheel slip noise is the error in the wheel's encoder readings caused by the slippage of the wheels on the floor.

[2] Controlling teams larger than 9 robots is difficult with the current hardware capabilities including Bluetooth communication available on the robots.

This work was previously published in the International Journal of Swarm Intelligence Research, Volume 2, Issue 1, edited by Yuhui Shi, pp. 45-70, copyright 2011 by IGI Publishing (an imprint of IGI Global).

Compilation of References

Aarts, E., & Korst, J. (1989). *Simulated annealing and Boltzmann machines: A stochastic approach to combinatorial optimization and neural computing.* New York, NY: John Wiley & Sons.

Adolphson, D., & Hu, T. C. (1973). Optimal linear ordering. *SIAM Journal on Applied Mathematics, 25*(3), 403–423. doi:10.1137/0125042

Aeberhard, S., Coomans, D., & Vel, O. D. (1992). *Comparison of classifiers in high dimensional settings* (Tech. Rep. No. 92-02). North Queensland, Australia: James Cook University of North Queensland.

Ahuja, R. K., Orlin, J. B., & Tiwari, A. (2000). A descent genetic algorithm for the quadratic assignment problem. *Computers & Operations Research, 27*, 917–934. doi:10.1016/S0305-0548(99)00067-2

Ali, S. A., Ghaffari, M., Liao, X., & Hall, H. (2006). *Mobile robotics, moving intelligence.* Berlin, Germany: Pro Literatur Verlag.

Allen, S. M., Hurley, S., Smith, D. H., & Thiel, S. U. (1999). Using lower bounds in minimum span frequency assignment. *Meta-Heuristics: Advances and Trends in Local Search Paradigms for Optimization,* 191-204.

Anderson, D., Carter, S., Hazzard, M., Josey, T., Pearson, J., Scoggins, J., & Soltmann, L. (2008). *Open Source Autonomous Miniature Unmanned Aerial Vehicles (OSAM-UAV) Team's System Design & Development for the 2009 AUVSI Student UAS Competition.* Retrieved March 15, 2010, from http://www.navair.navy.mil/pma263/seafarers/journal/journal2008/AUVSI08-NCSU.pdf

Anderson, E. (1935). The irises of the Gaspe Peninsula. *Bulletin of the American Iris Society, 59*, 2–5.

Anderson, L. G. (1973). A simulation study of some dynamic channel assignment algorithm in a high capacity mobile telecommunication system. *IEEE Transactions on Communications, 21*, 1294–1301. doi:10.1109/TCOM.1973.1091583

Andrey, P. (1999). Selectionist relaxation: Genetic algorithms applied to image segmentation. *Image and Vision Computing, 17*(3-4), 175–187. doi:10.1016/S0262-8856(98)00095-X

Angeline, P. J. (1999). Using selection to improve particle swarm optimization. In *Proceedings of the IEEE International Joint Conference on Neural Networks* (pp. 84-89).

Atary, J. (1971). *Modeling and optimization of a nuclear power plant.* Unpublished doctoral dissertation, University of Cambridge, UK.

Audet, C., & Dennis, J. E. (2003). Analysis of generalized pattern searches. *SIAM Journal on Optimization, 13*, 889–903. doi:10.1137/S1052623400378742

Avenali, A., Mannino, M., & Sassano, A. (2002). Minimizing the span of d-walks to compute optimum frequency assignments. *Mathematical Programming, 91*(2), 357–374. doi:10.1007/s101070100247

Bahceci, E., Soysal, O., & Sahin, E. (2003). *Review: Pattern formation and adaptation in multi-robot systems* (Tech. Rep. No. CMU-RI-TR-03-43). Pittsburgh, PA: Carnegie Mellon University.

Balch, T., & Arkin, R. (1998). Behavior-based formation control of multi-robot teams. *IEEE Transactions on Robotics and Automation, 14*(6), 926–939. doi:10.1109/70.736776

Barahona, F., Grotschel, M., Junger, M., & Reinelt, G. (1988). An application of combinatorial optimization to statistical physics and circuit layout design. *Operations Research*, *36*, 493–513. doi:10.1287/opre.36.3.493

Bastos Filho, C. J. A., de Lima Neto, F. B., Lins, A. J. C. C., Nascimento, A. I. S., & Lima, M. P. (2009). Fish school search. R. Chiong (Ed.), *Nature-inspired algorithms for optimisation* (Vol. 193, pp. 261-277). Berlin, Germany: Springer-Verlag.

Bastos-Filho, C. J. A., De Lima Neto, F. B., Lins, A. J. C. C., Nascimento, A. I. S., & Lima, M. P. (2008). A novel search algorithm based on fish school behavior. In *Proceedings of the IEEE International Conference on Systems, Man and Cybernetics* (pp. 2646-2651).

Bentley, P. J. (1999). *Evolutionary Design by Computers*. San Francisco, CA: Morgan Kaufmann.

Berry, M. W. (1992). Large scale singular value computations. *The International Journal of Supercomputer Applications*, *6*, 13–49.

Berry, M. W., Browne, M., Langville, A., Pauca, V., & Plemmons, R. (2007). Algorithms and applications for approximate nonnegative matrix factorization. *Computational Statistics & Data Analysis*, *52*(1), 155–173. doi:10.1016/j.csda.2006.11.006

Berry, M. W., Drmac, Z., & Jessup, E. R. (1999). Matrices, vector spaces, and information retrieval. *SIAM Review*, *41*(2), 335–362. doi:10.1137/S0036144598347035

Bezdek, J. C. (1981). *Patten recognition with fuzzy objective function algorithm*. New York, NY: Plenum Press.

Bhandarkar, S. M., & Zhang, H. (1999). Image segmentation using evolutionary computation. *IEEE Transactions on Evolutionary Computation*, *3*(1), 1–21. doi:10.1109/4235.752917

Bhanu, L. S., & Ming, J. (1995). Adaptive image segmentation using a genetic algorithm. *IEEE Transactions on Systems, Man, and Cybernetics*, *25*(12), 1543–1567. doi:10.1109/21.478442

Binh, T., & Korn, U. (1997). MOBES: A multiobjective evolution strategy for constrained optimization problems. In *Proceedings of the 3rd International Conference on Genetic Algorithms*, Brno, Czech Republic (pp. 176-182).

Bjorling-Sachs, I., & Souvaine, D. (1991). *A tight bound for guarding general polygons with holes* (Tech. Rep. No. LCSR-TR-165). New Brunswick, NJ: Rutgers University.

Blackwell, T. M., & Bentley, P. (2002). Don't push me! collision-avoiding swarms. In *Proceedings of the 4th Conference on Evolutionary Computation (CEC 2002)* (pp. 1691-1696).

Blackwell, T. (2007). Particle swarm optimization in dynamic environments. *Evolutionary Computation in Dynamic and Uncertain Environments*, *1*, 29–49. doi:10.1007/978-3-540-49774-5_2

Bloch, I., Milisavljevc, N., & Acheroy, M. (2007). Multi-sensor Data Fusion for Spaceborne and Airborne Reduction of Mine Suspected Areas. *International Journal of Advanced Robotic Systems*, *4*(2), 173–186.

Blum, C., & Dorigo, M. (2001). HC-ACO: The hyper-cube framework for ant colony optimization. In *Proceedings of the Metaheuristics International Conference* (pp. 399-403).

Bodlaender, H. L. Kloks, Tan, R. B., & van Leeuwen, J. (2000). λ-coloring of graphs. In H. Reichel & S. Tison (Eds.), *Proceedings of the 17th Annual Symposium on Theoretical Aspects of Computer Science* (LNCS 1770, pp. 395-406).

Boutsidis, C., & Gallopoulos, E. (2008). SVD based initialization: A head start for nonnegative matrix factorization. *Pattern Recognition*, *41*(4), 1350–1362. doi:10.1016/j.patcog.2007.09.010

Bratton, D., & Kennedy, J. (2007). Defining a standard for particle swarm optimization. In *Proceedings of the 2007 IEEE Swarm Intelligence Symposium* (pp. 120-127).

Bullnheimer, B., Hartl, R. F., & Strauß, C. (1997). A new rank based version of the ant system - a computational study. *Central European Journal for Operations Research and Economics*, *7*, 25–38.

Burer, S., Monteiro, R. D. C., & Zhang, Y. (2002). Rank-two relaxation heuristics for max-cut and other binary quadratic programs. *SIAM Journal on Optimization*, *12*(2), 503–521. doi:10.1137/S1052623400382467

Burgard, W., Moors, M., Fox, D., Simmons, R., & Thrun, S. (2005). Collaborative multi-robot exploration. *IEEE Transactions on Robotics, 21*(3), 376–386. doi:10.1109/TRO.2004.839232

Burkard, R. E., Karisch, S., & Rendl, F. (1997). QAPLIB—A quadratic assignment problem library. *Journal of Global Optimization, 10*, 391–403. doi:10.1023/A:1008293323270

Burkard, R. E., & Rendl, F. (1998). A thermodynamically motivated simulation procedure for combinatorial optimization problems. *European Journal of Operational Research, 17*, 169–174. doi:10.1016/0377-2217(84)90231-5

Cagnina, L. C., Esquivel, S. C., & Coello, C. A. (2008). Solving engineering optimization problems with the simple constrained particle swarm optimizer. *Informatica, 32*, 319–326.

Cai, Z., & Wang, Y. (2006). A multiobjective optimization-based evolutionary algorithm for constrained optimization. *IEEE Transactions on Evolutionary Computation, 10*(6), 658–674. doi:10.1109/TEVC.2006.872344

Campos, V., Glover, F., Laguna, M., & Martí, R. (2001). An experimental evaluation of a scatter search for the linear ordering problem. *Journal of Global Optimization, 21*(4), 397–414. doi:10.1023/A:1012793906010

Cassinis, R. (2000). *Multiple single sensor robots rather than a single multi-sensor platforms: a reasonable alternative*. Paper presented at International Conference on Explosives and Drug Detection Techniques.

Cela, E. (1998). *The quadratic assignment problem: Theory and algorithms*. Boston, MA: Kluwer Academic.

Chabrier, S., Emile, B., Rosenberger, C., & Laurent, H. (2006). Unsupervised performance evaluation of image segmentation. *EURASIP Journal on Applied Signal Processing*, 1–12. doi:10.1155/ASP/2006/96306

Chafekar, D., Xuan, J., & Rasheed, K. (2003). Constrained multi-objective optimization using steady state genetic algorithms. In *Proceedings of the Genetic and Evolutionary Computation Conference*, Chicago, IL (pp. 813-824).

Chang, K. C., & Du, H. C. (1988). Layer assignment problem for three-layer routing. *IEEE Transactions on Computers, 37*, 625–632. doi:10.1109/12.4616

Charalampidis, D., & Kasparis, T. (2002). Wavelet-based rotational invariant roughness features for texture classification and segmentation. *IEEE Transactions on Image Processing, 11*(8), 825–837. doi:10.1109/TIP.2002.801117

Chelouah, R., & Siarry, P. (2000). Tabu search applied to global optimization. *European Journal of Operational Research, 123*, 256–270. doi:10.1016/S0377-2217(99)00255-6

Chelouah, R., & Siarry, P. (2005). A hybrid method combining continuous tabu search and Nelder–Mead simplex algorithms for the global optimization of multiminima functions. *European Journal of Operational Research, 161*, 636–654. doi:10.1016/j.ejor.2003.08.053

Chen, Q., & Luh, J. (1994). Coordination and control of a group of small mobile robots. In *Proceedings of the International Conference on Robotics and Automation* (pp. 2315-2320).

Chen, S., & Montgomery, J. (2011). A simple strategy to maintain diversity and reduce crowding in particle swarm optimization. In *Proceedings of the 13th Annual Conference Companion on Genetic and Evolutionary Computation (GECCO 2011)* (pp. 811-812).

Cheng, K., & Dasgupta, P. (2007). Dynamic Area Coverage using Faulty Multi-agent Swarms. In *Proceedings of the IEEE/WIC/ACM International Conference on Intelligent Agent Technology* (pp. 17-24).

Cheng, S., & Shi, Y. (2011). Diversity control in particle swarm optimization. In *Proceedings of the 2011 IEEE Swarm Intelligence Symposium* (pp. 110-118).

Cheng, S., & Shi, Y. (2011). Normalized population diversity in particle swarm optimization. In *Proceedings of the 2nd International Conference on Swarm Intelligence* (LNCE 6728, pp. 38-45).

Chen, J. S., & Wei, G. (2002). A hybrid clustering algorithm incorporating fuzzy c-means into canonical genetic algorithm. *Journal of Electronics & Information Technology, 24*(2), 102–103.

Chien, S., Sherwood, R., Tran, D., Cichy, B., Rabideau, G., & Castano, R. (2005). Using Autonomy Flight Software to Improve Science Return on Earth Observing One. *Journal of Aerospace Computing, Information, and Communication, 2*, 196–216. doi:10.2514/1.12923

Chin, W. P., & Ntafos, S. (1987). Optimum zoo-keeper routes. *Congressus Numerantium, 58*, 257–266.

Chin, W. P., & Ntafos, S. (1991). Shortest watchman routes in simple polygons. *Discrete & Computational Geometry, 6*(1), 9–31. doi:10.1007/BF02574671

Chiong, R. (2009). *Nature-inspired algorithms for optimisation*. New York, NY: Springer.

Choset, H. (2001). Coverage for robotics: A survey of recent results. *Annals of Mathematics and Artificial Intelligence, 31*, 113–126. doi:10.1023/A:1016639210559

Chvatal, V. (1975). A combinatorial theorem in plane geometry. *Journal of Combinatorial Theory Series B, 18*, 39–41. doi:10.1016/0095-8956(75)90061-1

Clerc, M. (2008). *Particle swarm programs*. Retrieved from http://www.particleswarm.info/Programs.html

Clerc, M., & Kennedy, J. (2002). The particle swarm - explosion, stability, and convergence in a multidimensional complex space. *IEEE Transactions on Evolutionary Computation, 6*, 58–73. doi:10.1109/4235.985692

Coello, C. A., & Pulido, G. T. (2001). Multiobjective optimization using a micro-genetic algorithm. In *Proceedings of the Genetic and Evolutionary Computation Conference*, San Francisco, CA (pp. 274-282).

Coello, C. A., & Christiansen, A. D. (1999). MOSES: A multiobjective optimization tool for engineering design. *Engineering Optimization, 31*, 337–368. doi:10.1080/03052159908941377

Coello, C. A., Pulido, G. T., & Lechuga, M. S. (2004). Handling multiple objectives with particle swarm optimization. *IEEE Transactions on Evolutionary Computation, 8*(3), 256–279. doi:10.1109/TEVC.2004.826067

Coleman, G. B., & Andrews, H. C. (1979). Image segmentation by clustering. *Proceedings of the Institute of Electrical and Electronics Engineers, 67*, 773–785.

Conover, W. J. (1999). *Practical Nonparametric Statistics* (3rd ed.). New York, NY: John Wiley & Sons.

Cordon, O., Fernández de Viana, I., Herrera, F., & Moreno, L. (2000). A new ACO model integrating evolutionary computation concepts: The best-worst ant system. In *Proceedings of the Algorithmic Number Theory Symposium* (pp. 22-29).

Costa, D. (1993). On the use of some known methods for T-colorings of graphs. *Annals of Operations Research, 41*, 343–358. doi:10.1007/BF02023000

Cung, V.-D., Mautor, T., Michelon, P., & Tavares, A. (1996). Scatter search for the quadratic assignment problem. In *Proceedings of the IEEE International Conference on Evolutionary Computation* (pp. 165-169).

Cushman, D. L. (2007). *A particle swarm approach to constrained optimization informed by Global Worst*. University Park, PA: Pennsylvania State University.

Das, S., & Sila, S. (2010). Kernel-induced fuzzy clustering of image pixels with an improved differential evolution algorithm. *Information Sciences, 180*(8), 1237–1256. doi:10.1016/j.ins.2009.11.041

de Castro, J. N., & Von Zuben, F. J. (1999). *Artificial immune systems: Part I -Basic theory and applications* (Tech. Rep. No. DCA-RT 01/99). Brazil, Campinas: School of Computing and Electrical Engineering, State University of Campinas.

De Mot, J. (2005). *Optimal Agent Cooperation with Local Information*. Unpublished doctoral dissertation, Massachusetts Institute of Technology.

Deb, K., & Goel, T. (2001). Controlled elitist non-dominated sorting genetic algorithm for better convergence. In *Proceedings of the 1st International Conference on Evolutionary Multi-Criterion Optimization*, Zurich, Switzerland (pp. 67-81).

Deb, K., Pratap, A., & Meyarivan, T. (2001). Constrained test problems for multi-objective evolutionary optimization. In *Proceedings of the 1st International Conference on Evolutionary Multi-Criterion Optimization*, Zurich, Switzerland (pp. 284-298).

Deb, K. (1991). Optimal design of a welded beam via genetic algorithms. *AIAA Journal, 29*(11), 2013–2015. doi:10.2514/3.10834

Deb, K. (2001). *Multi-Objective Optimization Using Evolutionary Algorithms*. New York, NY: John Wiley & Sons.

Deb, K., Pratap, A., Agarwal, A., & Meyarivan, T. (2002). A fast and elitist multiobjective genetic algorithm: NSGA-II. *IEEE Transactions on Evolutionary Computation, 6*(2), 182–197. doi:10.1109/4235.996017

Deb, K., Thiele, L., Laumanns, M., & Zitzler, E. (2005). Scalable test problems for evolutionary multi-objective optimization. In Abraham, A., Jain, R., & Goldberg, R. (Eds.), *Evolutionary Multiobjective Optimization: Theoretical Advances and Applications* (pp. 105–145). Berlin, Germany: Springer. doi:10.1007/1-84628-137-7_6

Delande, D., & Zakrzewski, J. (2003). Experimentally attainable example of chaotic tunneling: The hydrogen atom in parallel static electric and magnetic fields. *Physical Review A., 68*(6), 062110. doi:10.1103/PhysRevA.68.062110

Dorigo, M. (1992). *Optimization, learning and natural algorithms*. Unpublished doctoral dissertation, Politecnico di Milano, Milan, Italy.

Dorigo, M., Maniezzo, V., & Colorni, A. (1996). The ant system: Optimization by a colony of cooperating agents. *IEEE Transactions on Systems, Man. Cybernetics B, 26*(2), 29–41. doi:10.1109/3477.484436doi:10.1109/3477.484436

Dorigo, M. (1997). Ant colonies for the travelling salesman problem. *Bio Systems, 43*(2), 73–81. doi:10.1016/S0303-2647(97)01708-5

Dorigo, M., Di Caro, G., & Gambardella, L. (1998). *Ant algorithms for discrete optimization*. Brussels, Belgium: Université Libre de Bruxelles.

Dorigo, M., & Stützle, T. (2004). *Ant colony optimization*. Scituate, MA: Bradford Company.

Dorne, R., & Hao, J.-K. (1998). Tabu search for graph coloring, t-colorings and set t-colorings. *Meta-heuristics Theory and Applications, 98*, 33–47.

Dorronsoro, B., & Bouvry, P. (2011). Improving classical and decentralized differential evolution with new mutation operator and population topologies. *IEEE Transactions on Evolutionary Computation, 15*(1), 67–98. doi:10.1109/TEVC.2010.2081369

Drezner, Z. (2003). A new genetic algorithm for the quadratic assignment problem. *INFORMS Journal on Computing, 15*(3), 320–330. doi:10.1287/ijoc.15.3.320.16076

Drezner, Z. (2005). The extended concentric tabu for the quadratic assignment problem. *European Journal of Operational Research, 160*, 416–422. doi:10.1016/S0377-2217(03)00438-7

Dror, M., Efrat, A., Lubiw, A., & Mitchell, J. S. B. (2003). Touring a sequence of polygons. In *Proceedings of the 35th Annual ACM Symposium on Theory Computing* (pp. 473-482).

Duarte, A., Marti, R., & Glover, F. (2007). *Adaptive memory programming for global optimization*. Valencia, Spain: University of Valencia.

Duarte, A., Marti, R., & Glover, F. (2011). Hybrid scatter-tabu search for unconstrained global optimization. *Annals of Operations Research, 183*, 95–123. doi:10.1007/s10479-009-0596-2

Duarte, A., Marti, R., & Glover, F. (2011). Path relinking for large scale global optimization. *Soft Computing, 15*.

Ducard, G., & Geering, H. (2008). Efficient nonlinear actuator fault detection and isolation system for unmanned aerial vehicles. *Journal of Guidance, Control, and Dynamics, 31*(1), 225–244. doi:10.2514/1.31693

Dudenhoefer, D., & Jones, M. (2000). A formation behavior for large-scale micro-robot force. In *Proceedings of the 32nd Winter Simulation Conference* (pp. 972-982).

Eberhart, E. C., & Shi, Y. (2000). Comparing inertia weights and constriction factors in particle swarm optimization. In *Proceedings of the Congress on Evolutionary Computation* (Vol. 1, pp. 84-88).

Eberhart, R. C., & Shi, Y. (1998). Evolving artificial neural networks. In *Proceedings of the International Conference on Neural Networks and Brain* (pp. 5-13).

Eberhart, R. C., & Shi, Y. (2007). *Computational intelligence, concepts to implementation* (1st ed.). San Francisco, CA: Morgan Kaufmann.

Eberhart, R., & Kennedy, J. (1995). A new optimizer using particle swarm theory. In *Proceedings of the 6th International Symposium on Micro Machine and Human Science* (pp. 39-43).

Eberhart, R., & Shi, Y. (2001). Particle swarm optimization: Developments, applications and resources. In *Proceedings of the 2001 Conference on Evolutionary Computation (CEC2001)* (pp. 81-86).

El-Melegy, M., Zanaty, E. A., Abd-Elhariez, W. M., & Farag, A. (2007). On cluster validity index in fuzzy and hard clustering algorithms for image segmentation. *IEEE International Conference on Image Processing, 6*, 5-8.

Eusuff, M., & Lansey, K. (2006). Shuffled frog-leaping algorithm: A memetic meta-heuristic for discrete optimization. *Engineering Optimization, 38*(2), 129–154. doi:10.1080/03052150500384759doi:10.1080/0305215 0500384759

Felzenszwalb, P. F., & Huttenlocher, D. P. (2004). Efficient graph-based image segmentation. *International Journal of Computer Vision, 59*(2), 167–181. doi:10.1023/B:VISI.0000022288.19776.77

Feng, H. M., Chen, C. Y., & Ye, F. (2007). Evolutionary fuzzy particle swarm optimization vector quantization learning scheme in image compression. *Expert Systems with Applications, 32*, 213–222. doi:10.1016/j.eswa.2005.11.012

Festa, P., Pardalos, P. M., Resende, M. G. C., & Ribeiro, C. C. (2002). Randomized heuristics for the max-cut problem. *Optimization Methods and Software, 7*, 1033–1058. doi:10.1080/1055678021000090033

Fisk, S. (1978). A short proof of Chvatal's watchman theorem. *Journal of Combinatorial Theory Series B, 24*, 374. doi:10.1016/0095-8956(78)90059-X

Fleurent, C., & Ferland, J. A. (1994). Genetic hybrids for the quadratic assignment problem. In Pardalos, P., & Wolkowicz, H. (Eds.), *Quadratic assignment and related problems (DIMACS series in discrete mathematics and theoretical computer science)* (*Vol. 16*, pp. 173–187). Providence, RI: American Mathematical Society.

Fogel, L. J. (1962). Autonomous automata. *Industrial Research, 4*, 14–19.

Fonseca, C. M., & Fleming, P. J. (1998). Multiobjective optimization and multiple constraint handling with evolutionary algorithms, I: a unified formulation. *IEEE Transactions on Systems, Man, and Cybernetics, Part A. Cybernetics, 28*(1), 26–37.

Fredslund, J., & Mataric, M. (2002). A general algorithm for robot formations using local sensing and minimal communication. *IEEE Transactions on Robotics and Automation, 18*(5), 837–846. doi:10.1109/TRA.2002.803458

Füredi, Z., & Kleitman, D. J. (1994). The prison yard problem. *COMBINATORICA, 14*(3), 287–300. doi:10.1007/BF01212977

Gabriely, Y., & Rimon, E. (2001). Spanning-tree based coverage of continuous areas by a mobile robot. *Annals of Mathematics and Artificial Intelligence, 31*(1-4), 77–98. doi:10.1023/A:1016610507833

Galinier, P., Gendreau, M., Soriano, P., & Bisaillon, S. (2005). Solving the frequency assignment problem with polarization by local search and Tabu. *OR, 3*(1), 59–78.

Gandomi, A. H., Yang, X. S., & Alavi, A. H. (in press). Cuckoo search algorithm: a metaheuristic approach to solve structural optimization problems. *Engineering with Computers*.

Gandomi, A. H., Yang, X. S., & Alavi, A. H. (in press). Mixed variable structural optimization using firefly algorithm. *Computers & Structures*.

Garey, M. R., & Johnson, D. S. (1979). *Computers and intractability: A guide to the theory of completeness*. New York, NY: W. H. Freeman and Company.

Geng, H., Zhang, M., Huang, L., & Wang, X. (2006). Infeasible elitists and stochastic ranking selection in constrained evolutionary multi-objective optimization. In *Proceedings of the 6th International Conference on Simulated Evolution and Learning*, Hefei, China (pp. 336-344).

Glover, F. (1989). Tabu search - Part I. *ORSA Journal on Computing, 1*(3) 190-206.

Glover, F. (1998). A template for scatter search and path relinking. In J.-K. Hao, E. Lutton, E. M. A. Ronald, M. Schoenauer, & D. Snyers (Eds.), *Proceedings of the Third European Conference on Artificial Evolution* (LNCS 1363, pp. 3-54).

Glover, F. (1977). Heuristics for integer programming using surrogate constraints. *Decision Sciences, 8*, 156–166. doi:10.1111/j.1540-5915.1977.tb01074.x

Glover, F. (1982). *Ejection chains, reference structures and alternating path methods*. Boulder, CO: University of Colorado.

Glover, F. (1986). Future paths for integer programming and links to artificial intelligence. *Computers & Operations Research, 13*, 533–549. doi:10.1016/0305-0548(86)90048-1

Glover, F. (1994). Tabu search for nonlinear and parametric optimization (with links to genetic algorithms). *Discrete Applied Mathematics, 49*, 231–255. doi:10.1016/0166-218X(94)90211-9

Glover, F. (1996). Ejection chains, reference structures and alternating path methods for traveling salesman problems. *Discrete Applied Mathematics, 65*(1-3), 223–253. doi:10.1016/0166-218X(94)00037-E

Glover, F. (1996). Tabu search and adaptive memory programming - advances, applications and challenges. In Barr, R. S., Helgason, R. V., & Kennington, J. L. (Eds.), *Interfaces in computer science and operations research* (pp. 1–75). Boston, MA: Kluwer Academic.

Glover, F., & Laguna, M. (1993). Tabu search. In Reeves, C. (Ed.), *Modern heuristic techniques for combinatorial problems* (pp. 71–140). Oxford, UK: Blackwell Scientific.

Glover, F., & Laguna, M. (1997). *Tabu search*. Boston, MA: Kluwer Academic.

Glover, F., Laguna, M., & Marti, R. (2000). Fundamentals of scatter search and path relinking. *Control and Cybernetics, 39*, 653–684.

Goemans, M. X., & Williamson, D. (1995). Improved approximation algorithms for maximum cut and satisfiability problems using semidefinite programming. *Journal of the ACM, 42*, 1115–1145. doi:10.1145/227683.227684

Gokce, F., & Sahin, E. (2009). To flock or not to flock: the pros and cons of flocking in long-range migration of mobile robot swarms. In *Proceedings of the 8th International Conference on Autonomous Agents and MultiAgent Systems (AAMAS)* (pp. 65-72).

Goldberg, D. E. (1989). *Genetic Algorithms in Search, Optimization and Machine Learning*. Reading, MA: Addison-Wesley.

Gong, M. G., Jiao, L. C., Bo, L. F., Wang, L., & Zhang, X. G. (2008). Image texture classification using a manifold distance based evolutionary clustering method. *Optical Engineering (Redondo Beach, Calif.), 47*(7), 1–10. doi:10.1117/1.2955785

Guimara, A., & Lapa, C. (2004). Fuzzy inference system for evaluating and improving nuclear power plant operating performance. *Annals of Nuclear Energy, 31*, 311–322. doi:10.1016/S0306-4549(03)00224-X

Guimara, A., & Lapa, C. (2005). *Fuzzy inference to risk assessment on nuclear engineering systems introduction*. Rio de Janeiro, Brazil: Institute de Engenharia Nuclear.

Gupta, S., Ray, A., Sarkar, S., & Yasar, M. (2008). *Fault detection and isolation in aircraft gas turbine engines. Part 1: Underlying concept*. University Park, PA: Department of Mechanical Engineering, The Pennsylvania State University.

Gutowski, M. (2001). *Lévy flights as an underlying mechanism for global optimization algorithms*. Retrieved from http://arxiv.org/abs/math-ph/0106003

Hale, W. K. (1980). Frequency assignment: Theory and applications. *Proceedings of the IEEE, 68*(12), 1497–1514. doi:10.1109/PROC.1980.11899

Harada, K., Sakuma, J., Ono, I., & Kobayashi, S. (2007). Constraint-handling method for multi-objective function optimization: Pareto descent repair operator. In *Proceedings of the 4th International Conference on Evolutionary Multi-Criterion Optimization*, Sendai, Japan (pp. 156-170).

Harper, L. H. (1964). Optimal assignment of numbers to vertices. *SIAM Journal on Applied Mathematics, 12*(1), 131–135. doi:10.1137/0112012

Haupt, R. L., & Haupt, S. E. (2005). *Practical genetic algorithms* (2nd ed.). New York, NY: John Wiley & Sons.

Hedar, A. R., & Fukushima, M. (2006). Derivative-free simulated annealing method for constrained continuous global optimization. *Journal of Global Optimization, 35*(4), 521–649. doi:10.1007/s10898-005-3693-z

Hedar, A., & Fukushima, M. (2006). Tabu search directed by direct search methods for nonlinear global optimization. *European Journal of Operational Research, 170*(2), 329–349. doi:10.1016/j.ejor.2004.05.033

Hellebrandt, M., & Heller, H. (2000). A new heuristic method for frequency assignment. *Number TD, 003*.

Helmberg, C., & Rendl, F. (1999). A spectral bundle method for semidefinite programming. *SIAM Journal on Optimization, 10*(3), 673–696. doi:10.1137/S1052623497328987

He, Q., & Wang, L. (2007). A hybrid particle swarm optimization with a feasibility-based rule for constrained optimization. *Applied Mathematics and Computation, 186*, 1407–1422. doi:10.1016/j.amc.2006.07.134

He, S., Prempain, E., & Wu, Q. H. (2004). An improved particle swarm optimizer for mechanical design optimization problems. *Engineering Optimization, 36*(5), 585–605. doi:10.1080/03052150410001704854

Hijjatoleslami, S. A., & Kitter, J. (1998). Region growing: A new approach. *IEEE Transactions on Image Processing, 7*(7), 1079–1084. doi:10.1109/83.701170

Hingston, P., Barone, L., Huband, S., & While, L. (2006). Multi-level ranking for constrained multi-objective evolutionary optimization. In T. R. Runarsson (Ed.), *Parallel Problem Solving from Nature* (LNCS 4193, pp. 563-572).

Hirsch, M. J., Meneses, C. N., Pardalos, P. M., & Resende, M. G. C. (2007). Global optimization by continuous grasp. *Optimization Letters, 1*(2), 201–212. doi:10.1007/s11590-006-0021-6

Holland, J. H. (1975). *Adaptation in natural and artificial systems*. Ann Arbor, MI: University of Michigan Press.

Ho, S. C., & Gendreau, M. (2006). Path relinking for the vehicle routing problem. *Journal of Heuristics, 12*, 55–72. doi:10.1007/s10732-006-4192-1

Huang, T., & Mohan, A. (2005). A hybrid boundary condition for robust particle swarm optimization. *IEEE Antennas and Wireless Propagation Letters, 4*, 112–117. doi:10.1109/LAWP.2005.846166

Hurley, S., & Smith, D. H. (1997). Bounds for the frequency assignment problem. *Discrete Mathematics*, (167-168): 571–582.

Hurley, S., Smith, D. H., & Thiel, S. U. (1997). A system for discrete channel frequency assignment. *Radio Science, 32*, 1921–1939. doi:10.1029/97RS01866

Hussin, M. S., & Stutzle, T. (2009). Hierarchical iterated local search for the quadratic assignment problem. In *Proceedings of the 6th International Workshop on Hybrid Metaheuristics* (pp. 115-129).

Hvattum, L. M., & Glover, F. (2009). Finding local optima of high-dimensional functions using direct search methods. *European Journal of Operational Research, 195*, 31–45. doi:10.1016/j.ejor.2008.01.039

Idoumghar, L., & Schott, R. (2009). Two distributed algorithms for the frequency assignment problem in the field of radio broadcasting. *IEEE Transactions on Broadcasting, 55*(2), 223–229. doi:10.1109/TBC.2008.2012023

Iordache, S. (2010). Consultant-guided search algorithms for the quadratic assignment problem. In *Proceedings of the 7th International Conference on Hybrid Metaheuristics* (pp. 148-159).

Jain, A. K., Murty, M. N., & Flynn, P. J. (1999). Data clustering: A review. *ACM Computing Surveys, 31*(3), 264–323. doi:10.1145/331499.331504

James, T., Rego, C., & Glover, F. (2005). Sequential and parallel path-relinking algorithms for the quadratic assignment problem. *IEEE Intelligent Systems, 20*(4), 58–65. doi:10.1109/MIS.2005.74

James, T., Rego, C., & Glover, F. (2009). Multistart tabu search and diversification strategies for the quadratic assignment problem. *IEEE Transactions on Systems, Man, and Cybernetics. Part A, Systems and Humans, 39*(3). doi:10.1109/TSMCA.2009.2014556

Janczewski, R., & Kubale, M. (1998). The T-DSATUR algorithm: An interesting generalization of the DSATUR algorithm. In *Proceedings of the International Conference on Advanced Computer Systems* (pp. 288-292).

Janecek, A., & Tan, Y. (2011). Iterative improvement of the multiplicative update NMF algorithm using nature-inspired optimization. In *Proceedings of the 7th International Conference on Natural Computation* (pp. 1668-1672).

Janecek, A., & Tan, Y. (2011). Using population based algorithms for initializing nonnegative matrix factorization. In Y. Tan, Y. Shi, Y. Chai, & G. Wang (Eds.), *Proceedings of the Second International Conference on Advances in Swarm Intelligence* (LNCS 6729, pp. 307-316).

Janecek, A., S. Schulze-Grotthoff, et al. (2011). libNMF - A library for nonnegative matrix factorizatrion. *Computing and Informatic*s, *22*.

Janecek, A. (2010). *Efficient feature reduction and classification methods: Applications in drug discovery and email categorization*. Vienna, Austria: Department of Computer Science, University of Vienna.

Janecek, A., & Gansterer, W. N. (2010). Utilizing nonnegative matrix factorization for e-mail classification problems. In Berry, M. W., & Kogan, J. (Eds.), *Survey of text mining III: Application and theory* (pp. 57–80). New York, NY: John Wiley & Sons.

Janecek, A., Gansterer, W. N., Demel, M., & Ecker, G. (2008). On the relationship between feature selection and classification accuracy. *Journal of Machine Learning Research, 4*, 90–105.

Janssen, J., & Kilakos, K. (1999). An optimal solution to the "Philadelphia" channel assignment problem. *IEEE Transactions on Vehicular Technology, 48*(3), 1012–1014. doi:10.1109/25.765037

Jimenéz, F., Gomez-Skarmeta, A. F., Sanchez, G., & Deb, K. (2002). An evolutionary algorithm for constrained multiobjective optimization. In *Proceedings of the Evolutionary Computation Conference*, Honolulu, HI (pp. 1133-1138).

Jolliffe, I. T. (2002). *Principal component analysis*. New York, NY: Springer.

Juvan, M., & Mohar, B. (1992). Optimal linear labelings and eigenvalues of graphs. *Discrete Applied Mathematics, 36*(2), 153–168. doi:10.1016/0166-218X(92)90229-4

Kahruman, S., Kolotoglu, E., Butenko, S., & Hicks, I. V. (2007). On greedy construction heuristics for the max-cut problem. *International Journal of Computer Science Engineering, 3*(3), 211–218.

Kaminka, G., Schechter, R., & Sadov, V. (2008). Using Sensor Morphology for Multirobot Formations. *IEEE Transactions on Robotics, 24*(2), 271–282. doi:10.1109/TRO.2008.918054

Karp, R. (1972). Reducibility among combinatorial problems. In Miller, R., & Thatcher, J. (Eds.), *Complexity of computer computations* (pp. 85–103). New York, NY: Plenum Press.

Kennedy, J. (1999, July). Small world and mega-minds: Effects of neighbourhood topology on particle swarm performance. In *Proceedings of the Congress on Evolutionary Computation* (pp. 1931-1938).

Kennedy, J. (2007). Some issues and practices for particle swarms. In *Proceedings of the 2007 IEEE Swarm Intelligence Symposium (SIS 2007)* (pp. 162-169).

Kennedy, J., & Eberhart, R. C. (1995). Particle swarm optimization. In *Proceedings of the IEEE International Conference on Neural Networks* (Vol. 4, pp. 1942-1948).

Kennedy, J., Eberhart, R. C., & Shi, Y. (2001). *Swarm intelligence*. San Francisco, CA: Morgan Kaufmann.

Kim, H., & Park, H. (2008). Nonnegative matrix factorization based on alternating nonnegativity constrained least squares and active set method. *SIAM Journal on Matrix Analysis and Applications, 30*, 713–730. doi:10.1137/07069239X

Kirkpatrick, S., Gellat, C. D., & Vecchi, M. P. (1983). Optimization by simulated annealing. *Science, 220*, 670–680. doi:10.1126/science.220.4598.671

Kjellerstrand, H. (2011). *hakanks hemsida*. Retrieved from http://www.hakank.org/weka/

Koenig, S., Szymanski, B., & Liu, Y. (2001). Efficient and Inefficient Ant Coverage Methods. *Annals of Mathematics and Artificial Intelligence, 31*(1-4), 41–76. doi:10.1023/A:1016665115585

Kohler, S., Utermann, R., Hagnni, R., & Dittrich, T. (1998). Coherent and incoherent chaotic tunneling near singlet-doublet crossings. *Physical Review E: Statistical Physics, Plasmas, Fluids, and Related Interdisciplinary Topics, 58*, 7219–7230. doi:10.1103/PhysRevE.58.7219

Kohonen, T., & Honkela, T. (2007). Kohonen network. *Scholarpedia, 2*(1), 1568. doi:10.4249/scholarpedia.1568doi:10.4249/scholarpedia.1568

Koppen, M., Franke, M., & Vicente-Garcia, R. (2006). Tiny GAs for image processing applications. *IEEE Computational Intelligence Magazine, 1*(2), 17–26. doi:10.1109/MCI.2006.1626491

Koza, J. R. (1992). *Genetic programming: On the programming of computers by means of natural selection*. Cambridge, MA: MIT Press.

Kunz, D. (1993). Channel assignment for cellular radio networks. *IEEE Transactions on Vehicular Technology, 42*, 647–656. doi:10.1109/25.260746

Kurpati, A., Azarm, S., & Wu, J. (2002). Constraint handling improvements for multiobjective genetic algorithms. *Structure Multidisciplinary Optimization, 23*, 204–213. doi:10.1007/s00158-002-0178-2

Laguna, M., & Martí, R. (1999). GRASP and path relinking for 2-layer straight line crossing minimization. *INFORMS Journal on Computing, 11*(1), 44–52. doi:10.1287/ijoc.11.1.44

Laguna, M., & Marti, R. (2003). *Scatter search: Methodology and implementation in C.* Boston, MA: Kluwer Academic.

Laguna, M., & Marti, R. (2005). Experimental testing of advanced scatter search designs for global optimization of multimodal functions. *Journal of Global Optimization, 33*, 235–255. doi:10.1007/s10898-004-1936-z

Langville, A. N., Meyer, C. D., & Albright, R. (2006). Initializations for the nonnegative matrix factorization. In *Proceedings of the 12th ACM International Conference on Knowledge Discovery and Data Mining.*

Lee, D. D., & Seung, H. S. (1999). Learning parts of objects by non-negative matrix factorization. *Nature, 401*(6755), 788–791. doi:10.1038/44565

Lee, D. D., & Seung, H. S. (2001). Algorithms for non-negative matrix factorization. *Advances in Neural Information Processing Systems, 13*, 556–562.

Lee, K. S., & Geem, Z. W. (2004). A new meta-heuristic algorithm for continues engineering optimization: harmony search theory and practice. *Computer Methods in Applied Mechanics and Engineering, 194*, 3902–3933. doi:10.1016/j.cma.2004.09.007

Leong, W. F., & Yen, G. G. (2008). PSO-based multiobjective optimization with dynamic population size and adaptive local archives. *IEEE Transactions on Systems, Man, and Cybernetics. Part B, Cybernetics, 38*(5), 1270–1293. doi:10.1109/TSMCB.2008.925757

Lepagnot, J., Nakib, A., Oulhadj, H., & Siarry, P. (2010). A new multiagent algorithm for dynamic continuous optimization. *International Journal of Applied Metaheuristic Computing, 1*(1), 16–38. doi:10.4018/jamc.2010102602

Li, L. D., Li, X., & Yu, X. (2008). A multi-objective constraint-handling method with PSO algorithm for constrained engineering optimization problems. In *Proceedings of the IEEE Conference on Evolutionary Computation*, Hong Kong, China (pp. 1528-1535).

Li, X., & Parker, L. (2007). Sensor analysis for fault detection in tightly-coupled multi-robot team tasks. In *Proceedings of the IEEE International Conference on Robotics and Automation,* Rome, Italy.

Liang, J. J., & Suganthan, P. N. (2006). Dynamic multi-swarm particle swarm optimizer with a novel constraint-handling mechanism. In *Proceedings of the IEEE Conference on Evolutionary Computation*, Vancouver, BC, Canada (pp. 9-16).

Liang, J., Qin, A., Suganthan, P., & Baskar, S. (2006). Comprehensive learning particle swarm optimizer for global optimization of multimodal functions. *IEEE Transactions on Evolutionary Computation, 10*(3), 281–295. doi:10.1109/TEVC.2005.857610

Lin, C.-J. (2007). Projected gradient methods for nonnegative matrix factorization. *Neural Computation, 19*(10), 2756–2779. doi:10.1162/neco.2007.19.10.2756

Liu, Z., Wang, C., & Li, J. (2008). Solving constrained optimization via a modified genetic particle swarm optimization. In *Proceedings of the International Workshop on Knowledge Discovery and Data Mining*, Adelaide, SA, Australia (pp. 217-220).

Liu, J., Zhong, W., & Jiao, L. (2006). A multiagent evolutionary algorithm for constraint satisfaction problems. *IEEE Transactions on Systems, Man, and Cybernetics B, 36*(1), 54–73. doi:10.1109/TSMCB.2005.852980

Liu, J., Zhong, W., & Jiao, L. (2010). A multiagent evolutionary algorithm for combinatorial optimization problems. *IEEE Transactions on Systems, Man, and Cybernetics B, 40*(1), 229–240. doi:10.1109/TSMCB.2009.2025775

Liu, L. P., & Meng, Z. Q. (2004). An initial centrepoints selection method for k-means clustering. *Computer Engineering and Application, 40*(8), 179–180.

Li, Y., Pardalos, P. M., & Resende, M. G. C. (1994). A greedy randomized adaptive search procedure for the quadratic assignment problem. In Pardalos, P. M., & Wolkowicz, H. (Eds.), *Quadratic assignment and related problems (DIMACS series on discrete mathematics and theoretical computer science)* (*Vol. 16*, pp. 237–261). Providence, RI: American Mathematical Society.

Lovbjerg, M., Rasmussen, T. K., & Krink, T. (2001). Hybrid particle swarm optimizer with breeding and subpopulations. In *Proceedings of the Genetic and Evolutionary Computation Conference*.

Lu, Z., Hao, J.-K., & Glover, F. (2010). Neighborhood analysis: A case study on curriculum-based course timetabling. *Journal of Heuristics*.

Luby, M., Sinclair, A., & Zuckerman, D. (1993). Optimal speedup of Las Vegas algorithms. *Information Processing Letters*, *47*(4), 173–180. doi:10.1016/0020-0190(93)90029-9

Lu, H., & Chen, W. (2006). Dynamic-objective particle swarm optimization for constrained optimization problems. *Journal of Combinatorial Optimization*, *2*(4), 409–419. doi:10.1007/s10878-006-9004-x

Luke, S. (2009). *Essentials of metaheuristics*. Retrieved from http://cs.gmu.edu/~sean/book/metaheuristics/

Luo, B., Zheng, J., Xie, J., & Wu, J. (2008). Dynamic crowding distance-a new diversity maintenance strategy for MOEAs. In *Proceedings of the 4th International Conference on Natural Computation*, Jinan, China (pp. 580-585).

MacQueen, J. (1967). Some methods for classification and analysis of multivariate observations. In *Proceedings of the 5th Berkeley Symposium on Mathematical Statistics and Probability* (pp. 281-297).

Maniezzo, V. (1998). *Exact and approximate nondeterministic tree-search procedures for the quadratic assignment problem*. Bologna, Italy: Scienze Dell'informazione, Università Di Bologna.

Mardia, K. V., & Hainsworth, T. J. (1988). A spatial thresholding method for image segmentation. *IEEE Transactions on Pattern Analysis and Machine Intelligence*, *10*(6), 919–927. doi:10.1109/34.9113

Martin, G. (2000). Frequency assignment in mobile phone systems. *Foundations of Software Technology Computer Science*, *1974*, 81–86.

Martí, R. (Ed.). (2006). Feature cluster on scatter search methods for optimization. *European Journal of Operational Research*, *169*(2), 351–698. doi:10.1016/j.ejor.2004.08.003

Marti, R., Duarte, A., & Laguna, M. (2009). Advanced scatter search for the max-cut problem. *INFORMS Journal on Computing*, *21*(1), 26–38. doi:10.1287/ijoc.1080.0275

Martí, R., Laguna, M., Glover, F., & Campos, V. (2001). Reducing the bandwidth of a sparse matrix with tabu search. *European Journal of Operational Research*, *135*(2), 211–220. doi:10.1016/S0377-2217(00)00325-8

Mastellone, S., Stipanovic, D., Graunke, C., Intlekofer, K., & Spong, M. (2008). Formation Control and Collision Avoidance for Multi-agent Non-holonomic Systems: Theory and Experiments. *The International Journal of Robotics Research*, *27*(1), 107–126. doi:10.1177/0278364907084441

Mata, C. S., & Mitchell, J. S. B. (1995). Approximation algorithms for geometric tour and network design problems (extended abstract). In *Proceedings of the Eleventh Annual Symposium on Computational Geometry* (pp. 360-369).

Matsui, S., & Tokoro, K. (2001). Improving the performance of a genetic algorithm for minimum span frequency assignment problem with an adaptive mutation rate and a new initialization method. In *Proceedings of the Conference on Genetic and Evolutionary Computation* (pp. 1359-1366).

Maulik, U. (2009). Medical image segmentation using genetic algorithms. *IEEE Transactions on Information Technology in Biomedicine*, *13*(2), 166–173. doi:10.1109/TITB.2008.2007301

McAllister, A. J. (1999). *A new heuristic algorithm for the linear arrangement problem* (Tech. Rep. No. TR-99-126). New Brunswick, CA: University of New Brunswick.

Melkemi, K. E., Batouche, M., & Foufou, S. (2006). A multiagent system approach for image segmentation using genetic algorithms and extremal optimization heuristics. *Pattern Recognition Letters*, *27*(11), 1230–1238. doi:10.1016/j.patrec.2005.07.021

Mendes, R. (2004). *Population Topologies and Their Influence in Particle Swarm Performance*. Unpublished doctoral dissertation, University of Minho, Portugal.

Mendes, R., Kennedy, J., & Neves, J. (2003). Avoiding the pitfalls of local optima: How topologies can save the day. In *Proceedings of the 12th Conference on Intelligent Systems Application to Power Systems (ISAP 2003)*. Washington, DC: IEEE Computer Society.

Mendes, R., Kennedy, J., & Neves, J. (2004). The fully informed particle swarm: Simpler, maybe better. *IEEE Transactions on Evolutionary Computation, 8*, 204–210. doi:10.1109/TEVC.2004.826074

Merz, P., & Freisleben, B. (2000). Fitness landscape analysis and memetic algorithms for the quadratic assignment problem. *IEEE Transactions on Evolutionary Computation, 4*, 337–352. doi:10.1109/4235.887234

Mezura-Montes, E., & Coello, C. A. (2006). *A survey of constraint-handling techniques based on evolutionary multiobjective optimization* (Tech. Rep. No. EVOC-INV-04-2006). Mexico City, Mexico: Cinvestav-IPN.

Michael, T. S., & Pinciu, V. (2003). Art gallery theorems for guarded guards. *Computational Geometry Theory and Applications, 26*, 247–258.

Michalewicz, Z., & Schoenauer, M. (1996). Evolutionary algorithm for constrained parameter optimization problems. *Evolutionary Computation, 4*(1), 1–32. doi:10.1162/evco.1996.4.1.1

Michel, O. (2004). Webots: Professional Mobile Robot Simulation. *International Journal of Advanced Robotic Systems, 1*(1), 39–42.

Miranda, V., Keko, H., & Jaramillo, A. (2007). EPSO: Evolutionary particle swarms. *Studies in Computational Intelligence, 66*, 139–167. doi:10.1007/978-3-540-72377-6_6

Misevicius, A. (2003). Genetic algorithm hybridized with ruin and recreate procedure: Application to the quadratic assignment problem. *Knowledge-Based Systems, 16*, 261–268. doi:10.1016/S0950-7051(03)00027-3

Misevicius, A. (2004). An improved hybrid genetic algorithm: New results for the quadratic assignment problem. *Knowledge-Based Systems, 17*, 65–73. doi:10.1016/j.knosys.2004.03.001

Misevicius, A. (2005). A tabu search algorithm for the quadratic assignment problem. *Computational Optimization and Applications, 30*(1), 95–111. doi:10.1007/s10589-005-4562-x

Mladenovic, N., & Hansen, P. (1997). Variable neighborhood search. *Computers & Operations Research, 24*, 1097–1100. doi:10.1016/S0305-0548(97)00031-2

Nakano, S., Ishigame, A., & Yasuda, K. (2007). Particle swarm optimization based on the concept of tabu search. In *Proceedings of the IEEE Congress on Evolutionary Computation* (pp. 3258-3263).

Narayanan, S., & Azarm, S. (1999). On improving multiobjective genetic algorithms for design optimization. *Structural Optimization, 18*, 146–155.

Nassef, M. (2005). *Genetic algorithm and its application in control systems.* Unpublished doctoral dissertation, Menoufia University, Eygpt.

Nie, S. D., Zhang, Y. L., & Chen, Z. X. (2008). Improved genetic fuzzy clustering algorithm and its application in segmentation of MR brain images. *Chinese Journal of Biomedical Engineering, 27*(6).

Nikhil, R. P., & Bezdek, J. C. (1995). On cluster validity for the fuzzy c-means model. *IEEE Transactions on Fuzzy Systems, 3*(3), 370–379. doi:10.1109/91.413225

Nilsson, B. J. (1994). *Guarding art galleries – methods for mobile guards*. Lund, Sweden: Lund University.

Nock, R., & Nielsen, F. (2006). On weighting clustering. *IEEE Transactions on Pattern Analysis and Machine Intelligence, 28*(8), 1–13. PubMed doi:10.1109/TPAMI.2006.168doi:10.1109/TPAMI.2006.168

O'Rourke, J. (1987). *Art gallery theorems and algorithms*. Oxford, UK: Oxford University Press.

O'Rourke, J. (1998). *Computational geometry in C (Cambridge tracts in theoretical computer science)* (2nd ed.). Cambridge, UK: Cambridge University Press.

Odgaard, P., Thøgersen, P., & Stoustrup, J. (2010, September). Fault isolation in parallel coupled wind turbine converters. In *Proceedings of the 2010 IEEE Multiconference on Systems and Control*, Yokohama, Japan (pp. 1069-1072).

Olfati Saber, R. (2006). Flocking for Multi-Agent Dynamic Systems: Algorithms and Theory. *IEEE Transactions on Automatic Control, 51*(3), 401–420. doi:10.1109/TAC.2005.864190

Oliva, A. (1998). Sensor fault detection and analytical redundancy satellite launcher flight control system. *SBA Controle & Automação, 9*(3), 156–164.

Oliveira, C. A., Pardalos, P. M., & Resende, M. G. C. (2004). GRASP with path-relinking for the quadratic assignment problem. In C. C. Ribeiro & S. L. Martins (Eds.), *Proceedings of the Third International Conference on Experimental and Efficient Algorithms* (LNCS 3059, pp. 356-368).

Olorunda, O., & Engelbrecht, A. P. (2008) Measuring exploration/exploitation in particle swarms using swarm diversity. In *Proceedings of the 2008 Conference on Evolutionary Computation(CEC 2008)* (pp. 1128-1134).

Osborn, A. F. (1963). *Applied imagination: Principles and procedures of creative problem solving* (3rd ed.). New York, NY: Charles Scribner's Son.

Osyezka, A., & Kundu, S. (1995). A new method to solve generalized multi-criteria optimization problems using the simple genetic algorithm. *Structural Optimization, 10*(2), 94–99. doi:10.1007/BF01743536

Oyama, A., Shimoyama, K., & Fujii, K. (2007). New constraint-handling method for multi-objective and multi-constraint evolutionary optimization. *Transactions of the Japan Society for Aeronautical and Space Sciences, 50*(167), 56–62. doi:10.2322/tjsass.50.56

Paatero, P., & Tapper, U. (1994). Positive matrix factorization: A non-negative factor model with optimal utilization of error estimates of data values. *Environmetrics, 5*(2), 111–126. doi:10.1002/env.3170050203

Packer, E. (2008). Computing multiple watchman routes. In *Proceedings of the 7th International Conference on Experimental Algorithms* (pp. 114-128).

Pal, N. R., & Pal, S. K. (1993). A review on image segmentation techniques. *Pattern Recognition, 26*(9), 1227–1294. doi:10.1016/0031-3203(93)90135-J

Palubeckis, G., & Krivickiene, V. (2004). Application of multistart tabu search to the max-cut problem. *Informaacines Technologijos Ir Valdymas, 2*(31), 29–35.

Pardalos, P. M., Prokopyev, O. A., Shylo, O. V., & Shylo, V. P. (2008). Global equilibrium search applied to the unconstrained binary quadratic optimization problem. *Optimization Methods Software, 23*(1), 129–140. doi:10.1080/10556780701550083

Parsopoulos, K. E., & Vrahatis, M. N. (2002). Particle swarm optimization method for constrained optimization problems. In *Intelligent Technologies: Theory and Applications: New Trends in Intelligent Technologies* (pp. 214-220).

Passino, K. M. (2010). Bacterial foraging optimization. *International Journal of Swarm Intelligence Research, 1*(1), 1–16. doi:10.4018/jsir.2010010101doi:10.4018/jsir.2010010101

Passino, K. M. (2002). Biomimicry of bacterial foraging for distributed optimization and control. *Control Systems Magazine of the Institute of Electrical and Electronics Engineers, 22*(3), 52–67. doi:10.1109/MCS.2002.1004010

Pavlyukevich, I. (2007). Lévy flights, non-local search and simulated annealing. *Journal of Computational Physics, 226*, 1830–1844. doi:10.1016/j.jcp.2007.06.008doi:10.1016/j.jcp.2007.06.008

Pedersen, M. E. H. (2010). *SwarmOps.* Retrieved from http://www.hvass-labs.org/projects/swarmops/cs/files/SwarmOpsCS1_0.pdf

Perona, P., & Malik, J. (1990). Scale-space and edge detection using anisotropic diffusion. *IEEE Transactions on Pattern Analysis and Machine Intelligence, 12*(7), 629–639. doi:10.1109/34.56205

Petit, J. (2003). Experiments on the minimum linear arrangement problem. *ACM Journal of Experimental Algorithmics, 8*.

Petit, J. (2003). Combining spectral sequencing and parallel simulated annealing for the MinLA problem. *Parallel Processing Letters, 13*(1), 71–91. doi:10.1142/S0129626403001161

Piñana, E., Plana, I., Campos, V., & Martí, R. (2004). GRASP and path relinking for the matrix bandwidth minimization. *European Journal of Operational Research, 153*, 200–210. doi:10.1016/S0377-2217(02)00715-4

Podolskiy, V. A., & Narmanov, E. E. (2003). Semiclassical description of chaos-assisted tunneling. *Physical Review Letters, 91*, 263601. doi:10.1103/PhysRevLett.91.263601

Price, K. V., Storn, R. M., & Lampinen, J. A. (2005). *Differential evolution a practical approach to global optimization*. New York, NY: Springer.

Pulido, G. T., & Coello, C. A. (2004). A constraint-handling mechanism for particle swarm optimization. In *Proceedings of the Evolutionary Computation Conference*, Portland, OR (pp. 1396-1403).

Raghavan, V. V., & Wong, S. K. M. (1999). A critical analysis of vector space model for information retrieval. *Journal of the American Society for Information Science American Society for Information Science, 37*(5), 279–287.

Ragsdell, K., & Phillips, D. (1976). Optimal design of a class of welded structures using geometric programming. *Journal of Engineering for Industry, 98*, 1021–1025. doi:10.1115/1.3438995

Ramkumar, A. S., Ponnambalam, S. G., & Jawahar, N. (2009). A new iterated fast local search heuristic for solving QAP formulation in facility layout design. *Robotics and Computer-integrated Manufacturing, 25*(3), 620–629. doi:10.1016/j.rcim.2008.03.022

Ray, T., & Won, K. S. (2005). An evolutionary algorithm for constrained bi-objective optimization using radial slots. In *Proceedings of the 9th International Conference on Knowledge-Based Intelligent Information and Engineering Systems*, Melbourne, VIC, Australia (pp. 49-56).

Rechenberg, I. (1973). *Evolutionsstrategie: Optimierung technischer Systeme nach Prinzipien der biologischen Evolution*. Stuttgart, Germany: Frommann-Holzboog.

Rego, C., & Glover, F. (2009). Ejection chain and filter-and-fan methods in combinatorial optimization. *Annals of Operations Research, 175*(1), 77–105. doi:10.1007/s10479-009-0656-7

Rekleitis, I., New, A., Rankin, E., & Choset, H. (2008). Efficient Boustrophedon Multi-Robot Coverage: an algorithmic approach. *Annals of Mathematics and Artificial Intelligence, 52*(2-4), 109–142. doi:10.1007/s10472-009-9120-2

Resende, M. G. C., & Ribeiro, C. C. (2003). Greedy randomized adaptive search procedures. In Glover, F., & Kochenberger, G. A. (Eds.), *Handbook of metaheuristic* (pp. 219–249). Boston, MA: Kluwer Academic.

Resende, M. G. C., Ribeiro, C. C., Glover, F., & Martí, R. (2010). Scatter search and path-relinking: Fundamentals, advances, and applications. In Gendreau, M., & Potvin, J. Y. (Eds.), *Handbook of metaheuristics* (2nd ed., pp. 87–108). Boston, MA: Kluwer Academic. doi:10.1007/978-1-4419-1665-5_4

Reynolds, A. M., & Rhodes, C. J. (2009). The Lévy flight paradigm: random search patterns and mechanisms. *Ecology, 90*, 877–887. doi:10.1890/08-0153.1

Reynolds, C. (1987). Flocks, herds and schools: A distributed behavioral model. *Computer Graphics, 21*(4), 25–34. doi:10.1145/37402.37406

Riihijärvi, J., Petrova, M., & Mähönen, P. (2005). Frequency allocation for WLANs using graph coloring techniques. In *Proceedings of the Second Annual Conference on Wireless On-demand Network System and Services* (pp. 216-222).

Robotics Trends. (2010). *Stories filed in security and defense*. Retrieved from http://www.roboticstrends.com/topics/security_defense_robotics

Rodriguez-Tello, E., Hao, J., & Torres-Jimenez, J. (2008). An effective two-stage simulated annealing algorithm for the minimum linear arrangement problem. *Computers & Operations Research, 35*(10), 3331–3346. doi:10.1016/j.cor.2007.03.001

Roverso, D. (2000). *Soft computing tools for transient classification*. Oxford, UK: Elsevier Science.

Runarsson, T. P., & Yao, X. (2005). Search biases in constrained evolutionary optimization. *IEEE Transactions on Systems, Man and Cybernetics. Part C, Applications and Reviews, 35*(2), 233–243. doi:10.1109/TSMCC.2004.841906

Rutishauser, S., Correll, N., & Martinoli, A. (2009). Collaborative Coverage using a Swarm of Networked Miniature Robots. *Robotics and Autonomous Systems, 57*(5), 517–525. doi:10.1016/j.robot.2008.10.023

Sahin, T., & Zergeroglu, E. (2008). Mobile Dynamically Reformable Formations for Efficient Flocking Behavior in Complex Environments. In *Proceedings of the IEEE International Conference on Robotics and Automation* (pp. 1910-1915).

Sarkar, S., Yasar, M., Gupta, S., Ray, A., & Mukherjee, K. (2008). *Fault detection and isolation in aircraft gas turbine engines. Part 2: validation on a simulation test bed*. University Park, PA: Department of Mechanical Engineering, The Pennsylvania State University.

Schmidt, M. N., & Laurberg, H. (2008). Non-negative matrix factorization with Gaussian process priors. *Computational Intelligence and Neuroscience*, (1): 1–10. doi:10.1155/2008/361705

Shah-Hosseini, H. (2009). The intelligent water drops algorithm: a nature-inspired swarm-based optimization algorithm. *International Journal of Bio-inspired Computation*, *1*(1-2), 71–79. doi:10.1504/IJBIC.2009.022775doi:10.1504/IJBIC.2009.022775

Shao, Y. C., & Chen, H. N. (2009). Cooperative bacterial foraging optimization. In *Proceedings of the International Conference on Future BioMedical Information Engineering* (pp. 486-488).

Shapiro, L. G., & Stockman, G. C. (2001). *Computer vision* (pp. 279–325). Upper Saddle River, NJ: Prentice Hall.

Shen, Q., Shi, W. M., & Kong, W. (2008). Hybrid particle swarm optimization and tabu search approach for selecting genes for tumor classification using gene expression data. *Computational Biology and Chemistry*, *32*(1), 52–59. doi:10.1016/j.compbiolchem.2007.10.001

Shi, Y. (2011, June 11-15). Brain storm optimization algorithm. In Y. Tan, Y. Shi, Y. Chai, & G. Wang (Eds.), *Proceedings of the Second International Conference on Advances in Swarm Intelligence*, Chongqing, China (LNCS 6728, pp. 303-309).

Shi, Y., & Eberhart, R. (1998). Parameter selection in particle swarm optimization. In *Evolutionary Programming VII* (LNCS 1447, pp. 591-600).

Shi, Y., & Eberhart, R. (1999). Empirical study of particle swarm optimization. In *Proceedings of the 1999 Conference on Evolutionary Computation (CEC 1999)* (pp. 1945-1950).

Shi, Y., & Eberhart, R. (2008). Population diversity of particle swarms. In *Proceedings of the 2008 Congress on Evolutionary Computation (CEC 2008)*. (pp. 1063-1067)

Shi, Y., & Eberhart, R. C. (1998). A modified particle swarm optimizer. In *Proceedings of the IEEE International Conference on Evolutionary Computation* (pp. 69-73).

Shi, Y., & Eberhart, R. C. (2009). Monitoring of particle swarm optimization. *Frontiers of Computer Science in China*, *3*(1), 31–37. doi:10.1007/s11704-009-0008-4doi:10.1007/s11704-009-0008-4

Shigenori, N., Takamu, G., Toshiku, Y., & Yoshikazu, F. (2003). A hybrid particle swarm optimization for distribution state estimation. *IEEE Transactions on Power Systems*, *18*, 60–68. doi:10.1109/TPWRS.2002.807051

Shi, Y., & Eberhart, R. (2009). Monitoring of particle swarm optimization. *Frontiers of Computer Science*, *3*(1), 31–37. doi:10.1007/s11704-009-0008-4

Shudo, A., & Ikeda, K. S. (1998). Chaotic tunneling: a remarkable manifestation of complex classical dynamics in non-integrable quantum phenomena. *Physica D. Nonlinear Phenomena*, *115*, 234–292. doi:10.1016/S0167-2789(97)00239-X

Shudo, A., Ishii, Y., & Ikeda, K. S. (2009). Julia sets and chaotic tunneling: II. *Journal of Physics A. Mathematical and Theoretical*, *42*, 265102. doi:10.1088/1751-8113/42/26/265102

Shylo, O. V., Prokopyev, O. A., & Shylo, V. P. (2008). Solving weighted max-sat via global equilibrium search. *Operations Research Letters*, *36*(4), 434–438. doi:10.1016/j.orl.2007.11.007

Shylo, V. P., & Shylo, O. V. (2010). Solving the maxcut problem by the global equilibrium search. *Cybernetics and Systems Analysis*, *46*, 744–754. doi:10.1007/s10559-010-9256-4

Sierra, M. R., & Coello, C. A. (2005). Improving PSO-based multi-objective optimization using crowding, mutation and ε–dominance. In *Proceedings of the International Conference on Evolutionary Multi-Criteria Optimization*, Guanajuato, Mexico (pp. 505-519).

Smith, R. (2002). *The 7 levels of change* (2nd ed.). Arlington, VA: Tapestry Press.

Smith, B., Egerstedt, M., & Howard, A. (2009). Automatic Generation of Persistent Formations for Multi-Agent Networks Under Range Constraints. *Mobile Networks and Applications Journal, 14*, 322–335. doi:10.1007/s11036-009-0153-x

Snásel, V., Platos, J., & Kromer, P. (2008). Developing genetic algorithms for Boolean matrix factorization. In *Proceedings of the DATESO International Workshop on Current Trends on Databases.*

Sörensen, K., & Glover, F. (2010). Metaheuristics. In Gass, S., & Fu, M. (Eds.), *Encyclopedia of operations research* (3rd ed.). New York, NY: Springer.

Sörensen, K., Sevaux, M., & Schittekat, P. (2008). Multiple neighbourhood search in commercial VRP packages: Evolving towards self-adaptive methods. *Studies in Computational Statistics, 136*, 239–253.

Sowmya, B., & Sheela Rani, B. (2011). Colour image segmentation using fuzzy clustering techniques and competitive neural network. *Applied Soft Computing, 11*(3), 3170–3178. doi:10.1016/j.asoc.2010.12.019

Spears, D., Kerr, W., & Spears, W. (2006). Physics-based Robot Swarms for Coverage Problems. *International Journal of Intelligent Control and Systems, 11*(3), 124–140.

Stachniss, C., Mozos, O., & Burgard, W. (2008). Efficient exploration of unknown indoor environments using a team of mobile robots. *Annals of Mathematics and Artificial Intelligence, 52*(2-4), 205–227. doi:10.1007/s10472-009-9123-z

Stadlthanner, K., Lutter, D., Theis, F. J., Lang, E. W., Tome, A. M., Georgieva, P., & Puntonet, C. G. (2007). Sparse nonnegative matrix factorization with genetic algorithms for microarray analysis. In *Proceedings of the International Joint Conference on Neural Networks* (pp. 294-299).

Staroswiecki, M. (2005). *Fault tolerant control: The pseudo-inverse method revisited.* Lille, France: Ecole Polytechnique Universitaire de Lille.

Stützle, T., & Hoos, H. (1996). *Improving the ant system: A detailed report on the max-min ant system.* Darmstadt, Germany: Technical University of Darmstadt.

Stuzlee, T. (2006). Iterated local search for the quadratic assignment problem. *European Journal of Operational Research, 174*, 1519–1539. doi:10.1016/j.ejor.2005.01.066

Stuzle, T., & Dorigo, M. (1999). ACO algorithms for the quadratic assignment problem. In Corne, D., Dorigo, M., & Glover, F. (Eds.), *New ideas for optimization* (pp. 33–50). New York, NY: McGraw-Hill.

Subramaniam, M., Rajakumar, A., & Chidambaram, M. (1995). Nonlinear control of nuclear reactors. *Control Theory and Advanced Technology, 10*(4), 1531–1540.

Sung, C. W., & Wong, W. S. (1997). Sequential packing algorithm for channel assignment under cochannel and adjacent channel interference constraint. *IEEE Transactions on Vehicular Technology, 46*, 676–685. doi:10.1109/25.618193

Tache, F., Fischer, W., Caprari, G., Siegwart, R., Moser, R., & Mondada, F. (2009). Magnebike: A magnetic wheeled robot with high mobility for inspecting complex-shaped structures. *Journal of Field Robotics, 26*(5), 431–452. doi:10.1002/rob.20296

Taillard, E. (1991). Robust taboo search for the quadratic assignment problem. *Parallel Computing, 17*, 443–455. doi:10.1016/S0167-8191(05)80147-4

Takahama, T., & Sakai, S. (2006). Constrained optimization by the ε constrained differential evolution with gradient-based mutation and feasible elites. In *Proceedings of the IEEE Conference on Evolutionary Computation*, Vancouver, BC, Canada (pp. 1-8).

Talbi, E.-G. (2009). *Metaheuristics: From design to implementation.* New York, NY: John Wiley & Sons.

Tan, Y., & Zhu, Y. (2010). Fireworks algorithm for optimization. In Y. Tan, Y. Shi, & K. C. Tan (Eds.), *Proceeding of the International Conference on Advances in Swarm Intelligence* (LNCS 6145, pp. 355-364).

Tanaka, M. (1995). GA-based decision support system for multi-criteria optimization. In *Proceedings of the International Conference on Evolutionary Multi-Criteria Optimization*, Guanajuato, Mexico (pp. 1556-1561).

Tan, P.-N., Steinbach, M., & Kumar, V. (2005). *Introduction to data mining.* Reading, MA: Addison-Wesley.

Tan, X. (2004). Approximation algorithms for the watchman route and zookeeper's problems. *Discrete Applied Mathematics*, *136*(2-3), 363–376. doi:10.1016/S0166-218X(03)00451-7

Tan, X., & Hirata, T. (2003). Finding shortest safari routes in simple polygons. *Information Processing Letters*, *87*(4), 179–186. doi:10.1016/S0020-0190(03)00284-9

Tan, X., Hirata, T., & Inagaki, Y. (1998). Corrigendum to an incremental algorithm for constructing shortest watchman route. *International Journal of Computational Geometry & Applications*, *9*, 319–323. doi:10.1142/S0218195999000212

Tessema, B., & Yen, G. G. (2009). An adaptive penalty formulation for constrained evolutionary optimization. *IEEE Transactions on Systems, Man, and Cybernetics. Part A, Systems and Humans*, *39*(3), 565–578. doi:10.1109/TSMCA.2009.2013333

Theodoridis, S., & Koutroumbas, K. (2006). *Pattern recognition* (3rd ed.). New York, NY: Academic Press.

Tian, X. L., Jiao, L. C., & Gou, S. P. (2008). SAR image segmentation based on spatially constrained FCM optimized by particle swarm optimization. *Acta Electronica Sinica*, *36*(3), 453–457.

Tomsovic, S. (1994). Chao-assisted tunneling. *Physical Review E: Statistical Physics, Plasmas, Fluids, and Related Interdisciplinary Topics*, *50*, 145–162. doi:10.1103/PhysRevE.50.145

Tovey, C. (2004). The honey bee algorithm: A biological inspired approach to internet server optimization. *Engineering Enterprise, the Alumni Magazine for ISyE at Georgia Institute of Technology*, 13-15.

Tseng, L., & Liang, S. (2006). A hybrid metaheuristic for the quadratic assignment problem. *Computational Optimization and Applications*, *34*, 85–113. doi:10.1007/s10589-005-3069-9

Turgut, A., Celikkanat, H., Gokce, F., & Sahin, E. (2008). Self-organized flocking with a mobile robot swarm. In *Proceedings of the International Conference on Autonomous Agents and MultiAgent Systems* (pp. 39-46).

Tzanov, V. (2006). *Distributed Area Search with a Team of Robots*. Unpublished master's thesis, Massachusetts Institute of Technology.

Valenzuela, C., Hurley, S., & Smith, D. H. (1998). A permutation based genetic algorithm for minimum span frequency assignment. In A. E. Eiben, T. Bäck, M. Schoenauer, & H.-P. Schwefel (Eds.), *Proceedings of the 5th International Conference on Parallel Problem Solving from Nature* (LNCS 1498, pp. 907-916).

Vaz, A. I. F., & Vicente, L. N. (2007). A particle swarm pattern search method for bound constrained global optimization. *Journal of Global Optimization*, *39*, 197–219. doi:10.1007/s10898-007-9133-5

Veenman, C. J., Reinders, M. J. T., & Backer, E. (2003). A cellular coevolutionary algorithm for image segmentation. *IEEE Transactions on Image Processing*, *12*(3), 304–313. doi:10.1109/TIP.2002.806256

Venkatraman, S., & Yen, G. G. (2005). A generic framework for constrained optimization using genetic algorithms. *IEEE Transactions on Evolutionary Computation*, *9*(4), 424–435. doi:10.1109/TEVC.2005.846817

Wagner, I., Altshuler, Y., Yanovski, V., & Bruckstein, A. (2008). Cooperative Cleaners: A Study in Ant Robotics. *The International Journal of Robotics Research*, *27*, 127–151. doi:10.1177/0278364907085789

Wang, L., & Hirsbrunner, B. (2003, December 8-12). An evolutionary algorithm with population immunity and its application on autonomous robot control. In *Proceedings of the IEEE Conference on Evolutionary Computation*, Canberra, Australia (pp. 1-8).

Wang, P. (1989). Navigation Strategies for Multiple Autonomous Mobile Robots. In *Proceedings of the IEEE/RSJ International Workshop on Intelligent Robots & Systems* (pp. 486-493).

Wang, Y. X., Zhao, Z. D., & Ren, R. (2007). Hybrid particle swarm optimizer with tabu strategy for global numerical optimization. In *Proceedings of the IEEE Congress on Evolutionary Computation* (pp. 2310-2316).

Wang, Y., Cai, Z., Guo, G., & Zhou, Y. (2007). Multiobjective optimization and hybrid evolutionary algorithm to solve constrained optimization problems. *IEEE Transactions on System, Man, and Cybernetics, Part B. Cybernetics*, *37*(3), 560–575.

Wang, Y., Cai, Z., Zhou, Y., & Zeng, W. (2008). An adaptive trade-off model for constrained evolutionary optimization. *IEEE Transactions on Evolutionary Computation, 12*(1), 80–92. doi:10.1109/TEVC.2007.902851

Wei, J., & Wang, Y. (2006). A novel multi-objective PSO algorithm for constrained optimization problems. In T. D. Wang *et al.* (Eds.), *Simulated Evolution and Learning* (LNCS 4247, pp. 174-180).

Wild, S. M., Curry, J. H., & Dougherty, A. (2004). Improving non-negative matrix factorizations through structured initialization. *Pattern Recognition, 37*(11), 2217–2232. doi:10.1016/j.patcog.2004.02.013

Witten, I. H., & Frank, E. (2005). *Data mining: Practical machine learning tools and techniques*. San Francisco, CA: Morgan Kaufmann.

Wolberg, W. H., & Mangasarian, O. L. (1990). Multisurface method of pattern separation for medical diagnosis applied to breast cytology. *Proceedings of the National Academy of Sciences of the United States of America, 87*(23), 9193–9196. doi:10.1073/pnas.87.23.9193

Woldesenbet, Y. G., Tessema, B. G., & Yen, G. G. (2009). Constraint handling in multiobjective evolutionary optimization. *IEEE Transactions on Evolutionary Computation, 13*(2), 1–12.

Wolpert, D., & Macready, W. (1997). No free lunch theorems for optimization. *IEEE Transactions on Evolutionary Computation, 1*(1), 67–82. doi:10.1109/4235.585893

Won-Young, S., Soo, Y. C., Jaewwook, L., & Chi-Hyuck, J. (2006). Frequency insertion strategy for channel assignment problem. *Wireless Networks, 12*(1), 45–52. doi:10.1007/s11276-006-6149-6

Wu, K. L., & Yang, M. S. (2002). Alternative c-means clustering algorithms. *Pattern Recognition, 35*(10), 2267–2278. doi:10.1016/S0031-3203(01)00197-2

Wurm, K., Stachniss, C., & Burgard, W. (2008). Coordinated multi-robot exploration using a segmentation of the environment. In *Proceedings of the IEEE/RSJ International Conference on Intelligent Robots and Systems* (pp. 1160-1165).

Xu, R., & Wunsch, D., II. (2005). Survey of clustering algorithms. *IEEE Transactions on Neural Networks, 16*(3), 645–678. PubMed doi:10.1109/TNN.2005.845141doi:10.1109/TNN.2005.845141

Xue, Y., Tong, C. S., Chen, Y., & Chen, W. (2008). Clustering-based initialization for non-negative matrix factorization. *Applied Mathematics and Computation, 205*(2), 525–536. doi:10.1016/j.amc.2008.05.106

Xu, S., & Rahmat-Samii, Y. (2007). Boundary conditions in particle swarm optimization revisited. *IEEE Transactions on Antennas and Propagation, 55*(3), 760–765. doi:10.1109/TAP.2007.891562

Yang, B., Chen, Y., Zhao, Z., & Han, Q. (2006). A master-slave particle swarm optimization algorithm for solving constrained optimization problems. In *Proceedings of the 6th World Conference on Intelligent Control and Automation*, Dalian, China (pp. 3208-3212).

Yang, X. (2008). *Nature-inspired metaheuristic algorithms*. Beckington, UK: Luniver Press.

Yang, L. C., Zhao, L. N., & Wu, X. Q. (2007). Medical image segmentation of fuzzy C-means clustering based on the ant colony algorithm. *Journal of ShanDong University, 37*(3).

Yang, L. J., & Chen, T. L. (2002). Applications of chaos in genetic algorithms. *Communications in Theoretical Physics, 38*, 168–192.

Yang, X. C., Zhao, W. D., Chen, Y. F., & Fang, X. (2008). Image segmentation with a fuzzy clustering algorithm based on ant-tree. *Signal Processing, 88*(10), 2453–2462. doi:10.1016/j.sigpro.2008.04.005

Yang, X. S. (2008). *Nature-inspired metaheuristic algorithms*. Beckington, UK: Luniver Press.

Yang, X. S. (2010). *Engineering optimization: An introduction with metaheuristic applications*. New York, NY: John Wiley & Sons. doi:10.1002/9780470640425

Yang, X. S. (2010). Firefly algorithm, stochastic test functions and design optimisation. *International Journal of Bio-Inspired Computation, 2*, 78–84. doi:10.1504/IJBIC.2010.032124

Yang, X. S., & Deb, S. (2010). Engineering optimization by cuckoo search. *International Journal of Mathematical Modelling & Numerical Optimization, 1*, 330–343. doi:10.1504/IJMMNO.2010.035430

Yao, X., Liu, Y., & Lin, G. (1997). Evolutionary programming made faster. *IEEE Transactions on Evolutionary Computation, 3*, 82–102.

Yen, G. G., & Leong, W. F. (2009). Dynamic multiple swarms in multiobjective particle swarm optimization. *IEEE Transactions on Systems, Man, and Cybernetics. Part A, Systems and Humans, 39*(4), 890–911. doi:10.1109/TSMCA.2009.2013915

Ying, C., Shao, Z. B., Mi, H., & Wu, Q. H. (2008). An application of bacterial foraging algorithm in image compression. *Journal of ShenZhen University, 25*(2).

Yin, P. Y., Glover, F., Laguna, M., & Zhu, J. X. (2010). Cyber swarm algorithms – improving particle swarm optimization using adaptive memory strategies. *European Journal of Operational Research, 201*(2), 377–389. doi:10.1016/j.ejor.2009.03.035

Yoshida, H., Kawata, K., Fukuyama, Y., & Nakanishi, Y. (1999). A particle swarm optimization for reactive power and voltage control considering voltage stability. In *Proceedings of the International Conference on Intelligent System Application to Power Systems* (pp. 117-121).

Yue, X. D., Miao, D. Q., & Zhong, C. M. (2010). Roughness measure approach to color image segmentation. *Acta Automatica Sinica, 36*(6), 807–816. doi:10.3724/SP.J.1004.2010.00807

Zeng, L., Wang, M. L., & Chen, H. F. (2008). Genetic fuzzy c-means clustering algorithm for magnetic resonance images segmentation. *Journal of University of Electronic Science and Technology of China, 37*(4), 627–629.

Zhang, M., Geng, H., Luo, W., Huang, L., & Wang, X. (2006). A hybrid of differential evolution and genetic algorithm for constrained multiobjective optimization problems. In *Simulated Evolution and Learning* (LNC 4247, pp. 318-327).

Zhang, Q., & Berry, M. W., Lamb, B. T., & Samuel, T. (2009). A parallel nonnegative tensor factorization algorithm for mining global climate data. In G. Allen, J. Nabrzyski, E. Seidel, G. Dick van Albada, J. Dongarra, & P. M. A. Sloot (Eds.), *Proceedings of the 9th International Conference on Computational Science* (LNCS 5545, pp. 405-415).

Zhang, Q., Campillo, F., Cerou, F., & Legland, F. (2005, December 12-15). Nonlinear system fault detection and isolation based on bootstrap particle filters. In *Proceedings of the 44th IEEE Conference on Decision and Control and the European Control Conference,* Seville, Spain (pp. 3821-3826).

Zhang, W., Xie, X. F., & Bi, D. C. (2004). Handling boundary constraints for numerical optimization by particle swarm flying in periodic search space. In *Proceedings of the 2004 Conference on Evolutionary Computation (CEC 2004)* (pp. 2307-2311).

Zhang, M., Luo, W., & Wang, X. (2008). Differential evolution with dynamic stochastic selection for constrained optimization. *Information Science, 178*(15), 3043–3074. doi:10.1016/j.ins.2008.02.014

Zhang, Y., & Jiang, J. (2003). Fault tolerant control system design with explicit consideration of performance degradation. *IEEE Transactions on Aerospace and Electronic Systems, 39*(3), 838–848. doi:10.1109/TAES.2003.1238740

Zhong, W., Liu, J., Xue, M., & Jiao, L. (2004). A multi-agent genetic algorithm for global numerical optimization. *IEEE Transactions on Systems. Man and Cybernetics B, 34*(2), 1128–1141. doi:10.1109/TSMCB.2003.821456

Zielinski, K., & Laur, R. (2006). Constrained single-objective optimization using particle swarm optimization. In *Proceedings of the IEEE Conference on Evolutionary Computation*, Vancouver, BC, Canada (pp. 443-450).

Zielinski, K., Weitkemper, P., Laur, R., & Kammeyer, K. D. (2009). Optimization of power allocation for interference cancellation with particle swarm optimization. *IEEE Transactions on Evolutionary Computation, 13*(1), 128–150. doi:10.1109/TEVC.2008.920672

Zitzler, E. (1999). *Evolutionary Algorithms for Multiobjective Optimization: Methods and Applications.* Unpublished doctoral dissertation, Swiss Federal Institute of Technology, Zurich, Switzerland.

Zitzler, E., Thiele, L., Laumanns, M., Fonseca, C. M., & da Fonseca, V. G. (2003). Performance assessment of multiobjective optimizers: an analysis and review. *IEEE Transactions on Evolutionary Computation, 7*(2), 117–132. doi:10.1109/TEVC.2003.810758

Zoellner, J. A., & Beall, C. L. (1977). A breakthrough in spectrum conserving frequency assignment technology. *IEEE Transactions on Electromagnetic Compatibility, 19*(3), 313–319. doi:10.1109/TEMC.1977.303601

Żyliński, P. (2006). Orthogonal art galleries with holes: A coloring proof of Aggarwal's theorem. *Electronic Journal of Combinatorics, 13*(1).

Żyliński, P. (2002). *Some results on cooperative guards.* Gdańsk, Poland: Gdańsk University.

About the Contributors

Yuhui Shi received a PhD degree in electronic engineering from Southeast University, Nanjing, China, in 1992. He is a professor in the department of electrical and electronic engineering, Xi'an Jiaotong-Liverpool University, Suzhou, China. Before joining Xi'an Jiaotong-Liverpool University, he was with Electronic Data Systems Corporation, Indianapolis, IN. His main research interests include the areas of computational intelligence techniques (including swarm intelligence) and their applications. Dr. Shi is the Editor-in-Chief of the International Journal of Swarm Intelligence Research, and an Associate Editor of the IEEE Transactions on Evolutionary Computation. He is the Chair of the IEEE Task Force on Swarm Intelligence.

* * *

Vicente Campos is Professor in the Statistics and Operations Research department at the University of Valencia in Spain. His teaching is devoted to the introduction of Statistics in Biological Sciences, Medicine and Mathematics and also Probability Theory, Integer and Linear Programming and Graph Theory in Mathematics. His research interest mainly focuses on the development of metaheuristics for hard combinatorial problems. Specifically, he has worked on routing problems (arcs and nodes), orienteering, linear ordering and linear arrangement problems and minimum bandwith of a matrix.

Ke Cheng is a Ph.D. candidate in the Computer Science Department at the University of Nebraska, Omaha. His research interests are in the area of multi-agent and multi-robot systems focusing on algorithms for distributed area coverage and swarming. He has published over 10 papers in his area of research. He has received awards including the graduate dissertation scholarship at the University of Nebraska, Omaha in 2010.

Shi Cheng received a bachelor's degree in mechanical and electrical engineering from Xiamen university, Xiamen, and a master's degree in software engineering from Beihang University (BUAA), Beijing, China, in 2005 and 2008, respectively. Currently, he is working toward the PhD degree from the department of electrical engineering and electronic, University of Liverpool, Liverpool, UK and Department of Electrical & Electronic Engineering, Xi'an Jiaotong-Liverpool University, Suzhou, China. His current research interests include swarm intelligence, multiobjective optimization, and data mining techniques and their applications.

Prithviraj (Raj) Dasgupta is an associate professor in the Computer Science Department at the University of Nebraska, Omaha and is the director of the C-MANTIC research group. He received his Master's and Ph.D. degrees from the University of California, Santa Barbara in 1998 and 2001 respectively. His research interests are in the area of multi-agent and multi-robot systems, game theory, computational economics and swarm robotics. He leads a highly successful research program that has been funded by federal agencies including the U. S. Office of Naval Research, U.S. Department of Defense – NavAir and NASA. He has published over 60 papers in premier journals and conferences in the area of his research.

Abraham Duarte is an Associate Professor in the Computer Science Department of the University of Rey Juan Carlos (Madrid, Spain). He received a doctoral degree in Computer Sciences from the University Rey Juan Carlos. His research is devoted to the development of models and solution methods based on metaheuristics for combinatorial optimization and decision problems under uncertainty. He has published more than 30 papers in prestigious scientific journals and conference proceedings such us European Journal of Operational Research, INFORMS Journal on Computing, Computational Optimization and Applications or Computers & Operations Research. Dr Duarte is reviewer of the Journal of Heuristic, Journal of Mathematical Modeling and Algorithms, INFORMS Journal on Computing, Applied Soft Computing, European Journal of Operational Research and Soft Computing. He is also member of the program committee of the conferences MAEB, HIS, ISDA or MHIPL.

Gomaa Zaki El-Far received his B. SC. and M. SC. degrees in Engineering from Menoufia University, Menouf, Egypt. He received his PhD. from Menoufia University. He has been an Assistant Professor. Dr. in Faculty of Electronic Eng. (Menouf) since 1993. His current research interests are the design of control approaches based on neural networks, fuzzy logic control, particle swarm optimization, and immune genetic algorithms. Also, he is interested in designing of robust control approaches for failure detection and isolation of faults.

Fred Glover is the Chief Technology Officer in charge of algorithmic design and strategic planning initiatives for OptTek Systems, Inc., and holds the title of Distinguished Professor at the University of Colorado, Boulder, affiliated with the Leeds School of Business and the Department of Electrical and Computer Engineering. He has authored or co-authored more than 400 published articles and eight books in the fields of mathematical optimization, computer science and artificial intelligence, and is the originator of Tabu Search (Adaptive Memory Programming), an optimization search methodology of which more than 200,000 Web pages are returned by a Google search. Fred Glover is the recipient of the highest honor of the Institute of Operations Research and Management Science, the von Neumann Theory Prize, and is an elected member of the U. S. National Academy of Engineering. He has also received numerous other awards and honorary fellowships, including those from the American Association for the Advancement of Science (AAAS), the NATO Division of Scientific Affairs, the Institute of Operations Research and Management Science (INFORMS), the Decision Sciences Institute (DSI), the U.S. Defense Communications Agency (DCA), the Energy Research Institute (ERI), the American Assembly of Collegiate Schools of Business (AACSB), Alpha Iota Delta, the Institute of Cybernetics of the Ukrainian Academy of Science, and the Miller Institute for Basic Research in Science.

Tabitha James received a Ph.D. degree in business administration from the University of Mississippi, Oxford. She is currently an Associate Professor with the Department of Business Information Technology, Pamplin College of Business, Virginia Polytechnic Institute (Virginia Tech), Blacksburg. Her research interests include combinatorial optimization, heuristics, and parallel computing.

Andreas Janecek is a post-doctoral researcher at the School of Electronic Engineering and Computer Science, Peking University, China. He received his PhD degree in Computer Science in 2010, and his MS degree in Business Informatics in 2005, both from the University of Vienna, Austria. Besides computational intelligence such as swarm optimization and evolutionary computing, his research activities include data mining and machine learning algorithms, with a focus on high performance and distributed computing aspects of these techniques.

Manuel Laguna is the Media One Professor of Management Science and Senior Associate Dean of the Leeds School of Business of the University of Colorado at Boulder. He started his career at the University of Colorado in 1990, after receiving master's (1987) and doctoral (1990) degrees in Operations Research and Industrial Engineering from the University of Texas at Austin. He has done extensive research in the interface between computer science, artificial intelligence and operations research to develop solution methods for practical problems in operations-management areas such as logistics and supply chains, telecommunications, decision-making under uncertainty and optimization of simulated systems. Dr. Laguna has more than one hundred publications, including more than sixty articles in academic journals and four books. He is editor-in-chief of the *Journal of Heuristics*, is in the international advisory board of the *Journal of the Operational Research Society* and has been guest editor of the *Annals of Operations Research* and the *European Journal of Operational Research*. Dr. Laguna has received research funding from government agencies such as the National Science Foundation, Office of Naval Research and the Environmental Protection Agency. He is member of the Institute for Operations Research and the Management Science and was the general chair of the Institute's national meeting in 2004. He is also member of Beta Gamma Sigma and the International Honor Society Omega Rho. Dr. Laguna is co-founder of OptTek Systems, a Boulder-based software and consulting company that provides optimization solutions.

Wen Fung Leong received BS, MS and Ph.D. degrees all in electrical engineering from Oklahoma State University in 2000, 2002 and 2008, respectively. She is currently working at the Boston University. Her research interest includes feature extraction, neural networks, and evolutionary computation.

Jinshu Li is a master student in the Institute of Intelligent Information Processing of Xidian University, Xi'an, China. Her research interests include evolutionary computation and multiagent systems.

Jing Liu received the BS degree in computer science and technology from Xidian University, Xi'an, China, in 2000, and received the PhD degree in circuits and systems from the Institute of Intelligent Information Processing of Xidian University in 2004. Now she is a full professor in Xidian University. Her research interests include evolutionary computation, multiagent systems, and data mining.

Ruochen Liu is currently an associate professor with the Key Laboratory of Intelligent Perception and Image Understanding of Ministry of Education of China at Xidian University, Xi'an, China. She received her Ph.D degree from Xidian University in 2005. Her research interests are broadly in the area of computational intelligence. Her areas of special interest include artificial immune systems, evolutionary computation, data mining, and optimization.

Rafael Martí is Professor in the Statistics and Operations Research department at the University of Valencia, Spain. He received a doctoral degree in Mathematics from the University of Valencia. His teaching is devoted to the introduction of Statistics in Social Sciences, Integer and Linear Programming in Mathematics and Heuristics in postgraduate studies (master and doctoral). His research interest focuses on the development of metaheuristics for hard optimization problems. He is co-author of the Scatter Search (Kluwer 2003) and The Linear Ordering Problem (Springer 2011) monographs. Prof. Martí is currently Area Editor in the Journal of Heuristics and Associate Editor in the Mathematical Programming Computation Journal and the International Journal of Metaheuristics. He has published more than 50 JCR-indexed journal papers on Optimization.

Hongwei Mo, born in 1973, Doctor of engineering, professor of automation College of Harbin Engineering University. He is a visiting scholar of UCDavis, CA, USA from 2003, 10-2004,10. His main research interests include nature-inspired computing (NIC), artificial immune system (AIS), data mining, intelligent system, artificial intelligence. He had published 30 papers and 4 books on AIS and NIC. He is member of program committee of many international conferences, including 2006ICNC-FSKD, 2006ECLC, ISEAL2006, 2007FSKD, 2007ICNC-FSKD, 2008WCCI, 2008BICTA, GECS2009, ICSI2010, ICSI2011. He is the guest editor of special issue on nature inspired computing and applications of Journal of Information Technology Research.

Pawel Paduch is a lecturer in the department of computer science at Kielce University of Technology. His research interests include distributed and parallel computing, cluster systems and natural computing. He received a Master of Engineering from Kielce University of Technology in 2002. He is a Dr. ing. (PhD) candidate.

Juan-José Pantrigo is currently Associate Professor at Universidad Rey Juan Carlos. He received his MS degree in Fundamental Physics at Universidad de Extremadura in 1998 and Ph.D. at Universidad Rey Juan Carlos in 2005. From 1998 to 2002 he was working in the Biomechanics & Ergonomics Group at Universidad de Extremadura. His research interests involve visual tracking and computer vision problems, knowledge modeling for computer vision and combinatorial and dynamic optimization problems using metaheuristics and hybrid approaches.

Quande Qin received PhD. degree in management science and engineering from school of business administration, South China University of Technology, Guangzhou, China. Currently, he is a lecture in the college of management, Shenzhen University, Shenzhen, China. His current research interests include swarm intelligence, evolutionary optimization and their applications in management and economics.

Cesar Rego received a Ph.D. degree in computer science from the University of Versailles, France. He is currently a Professor with the School of Business, University of Mississippi, Oxford. His research focuses on mathematical optimization, computer science, and artificial intelligence. His recent innovations in the field of optimization include the Relaxation Adaptive Memory Programming (RAMP) methodology for solving complex and practical problems.

Krzysztof Sapiecha is a professor in the department of computer science at Kielce University of Technology and a professor in the department of computer engineering at Cracow University of Technology. His research interests include distributed systems, rapid system prototyping and natural computing. He received a Dr. ing. and Dr. hab. in computer science from Warsaw University of Technology. He is a member of the ACM.

Oleg V. Shylo is a Research Associate in the Department of Industrial Engineering at the University of Pittsburgh. He received a B.S. in Applied Mathematics from the National Technical University of Ukraine in Kiev in 2004, and a PhD in Industrial Engineering from the University of Florida in 2009. His research interests include discrete optimization, parallel computing and optimization in health care.

Volodymyr P. Shylo is a Leading Researcher at the Glushkov's Institute of Cybernetics. He received a M.S. from the Moscow Institute of Physics and Technology. In 2003, he received a Doctor of Physical and Mathematical Sciences from the National Academy of Science of Ukraine. In 2005, he received the Ukrainian State Prize for his scientific accomplishments. His research interests include probabilistic and local search methods for discrete optimization. algorithms and software design for complex optimization problems.

Ying Tan received the BS in 1985, the MS in 1988, and the PhD in signal and information processing from Southeast University in 1997, respectively. Since then, he became a postdoctoral fellow then an associate professor at University of Science and Technology of China. He worked with the Chinese University of Hong Kong in 1999 and in 2004-2005. Now, he is a professor at the Key Laboratory of Machine Perception (MOE), Peking University, and department of Machine Intelligence, EECS, Peking University. He is also the director of Computational Intelligence Laboratory (CIL) of Peking University. He has published more than 200 academic papers in refereed journals and conferences and several books and chapters in book and holds 4 invention patents. His current research interests include computational intelligence, artificial immune system, swarm intelligence, data mining, pattern recognition, and their applications. He was the general chair of International Conference on Swarm Intelligence (ICSI 2010, ICSI 2011) and honored the Second-class Prize of National Natural Science Award of China in 2009.

Taylor Whipple is an undergraduate student in the Computer Science and Computer Engineering Departments at the University of Nebraska Omaha. His primary research interests are in multi-agent and multi-robot task allocation and distributed area coverage. His research earned him the Outstanding Undergraduate Award from the Computer Science Department at the University of Nebraska, Omaha in 2010.

Xin-She Yang received his DPhil in Applied Mathematics from Oxford University, and he has been the recipient of Garside Senior Scholar Award in Mathematics of Oxford University. He worked at Cambridge University for 5 years and is now a Senior Research Scientist at National Physical Laboratory. He has written 7 books and published more than 110 papers. He is the Editor-in-Chief of *Int. J. Mathematical Modelling and Numerical Optimisation*. He is also a Guest Professor of Harbin Engineering University, China. He is the vice chair of IEEE CIS task force on business intelligence and knowledge management. He is the inventor of a few metaheuristic algorithms, including bat algorithm, eagle strategy, firefly algorithm, cuckoo search and virtual bee algorithm.

Gary G. Yen received the Ph.D. degree in electrical and computer engineering from the University of Notre Dame in 1992. He is currently a Professor in the School of Electrical and Computer Engineering, Oklahoma State University. Before joined OSU in 1997, he was with the Structure Control Division, U.S. Air Force Research Laboratory. His research is supported by the DoD, DoE, EPA, NASA, NSF, and Process Industry. His research interest includes intelligent control, computational intelligence, conditional health monitoring, signal processing and their industrial/defense applications. He is an IEEE Fellow. Dr. Yen was an associate editor of the *IEEE Control Systems Magazine, IEEE Transactions on Control Systems Technology, Automatica, Mechantronics, IEEE Transactions on Systems, Man and Cybernetics, Part A and Part B* and *IEEE Transactions on Neural Networks*. He is currently serving as an associate editor for the *IEEE Transactions on Evolutionary Computation* and *International Journal of Swarm Intelligence Research*. He served as the General Chair for the *2003 IEEE International Symposium on Intelligent Control* held in Houston, TX and *2006 IEEE World Congress on Computational Intelligence* held in Vancouver, Canada. Dr. Yen served as Vice President for the Technical Activities in 2005-2006 and is currently serving as President of the IEEE Computational intelligence Society in 2010-2011. He is the founding editor-in-chief of the *IEEE Computational Intelligence Magazine*.

Peng-Yeng Yin is a Professor of the Department of Information Management, National Chi Nan University, Taiwan, and he is currently the Dean of the Office of Research and Development. From 1993 to 1994, he was a visiting scholar at the Department of Electrical Engineering, University of Maryland, College Park. In 2000, he was a visiting Professor at the Department of Electrical Engineering, University of California, Riverside. From 2006 to 2007, he was a visiting Professor at Leeds School of Business, University of Colorado. Dr. Yin is a member of the Phi Tau Phi Scholastic Honor Society and listed in *Who's Who in the World, Who's Who in Science and Engineering*, and *Who's Who in Asia*. He is the Editor-in-Chief of the *International Journal of Applied Metaheuristic Computing* and is on the Editorial Board of *International Journal of Advanced Robotic Systems, Journal of Education, Informatics and Cybernetics, The Open Artificial Intelligence Journal, The Open Signal Processing Journal* and served as a program committee member in many international conferences. He has also edited two books in the pattern recognition area. His current research interests include artificial intelligence, evolutionary computation, metaheuristics, pattern recognition, machine learning, and operations research.

Yujing Yin was born in 1988 and he received his bachelor degree of engineering in biomedical engineering from Harbin Engineering University in 2010. He is currently a master student in research institute of pattern recognition and intelligent system in Automation college, Harbin Engineering University. His research interests mainly include machine vision on mobile robot.

Li Zhang received the BS degree in 1997 and the PhD degree in 2002 in electronic engineering from Xidian University, Xi'an, China. From 2003 to 2005, she was a postdoctor at the Institute of Automation of Shanghai Jiao Tong University, Shanghai, China. From 2005 to 2010, she worked at Xidian University. Now she is an associate professor of Soochow University in Suzhou, China. Her research interests have been in the areas of machine learning, pattern recognition, neural networks and intelligent information processing.

Weicai Zhong received the BS degree in computer science and technology from Xidian University, Xi'an, China in 2000, and received the PhD degree in pattern recognition and intelligent information system from the Institute of Intelligent Information Processing of Xidian University in 2004. Now he is a full professor in Northwest A&F University. His research interests include evolutionary computation, data mining, and statistical learning.

Jia-Xian Zhu received his B.S. degree in Information Management at National Formosa University, Yunlin, Taiwan in 2006 and the M.B.A. degree in Information Management at National Chi Nan University, Nantou, Taiwan in 2008. He has published an article in *European Journal of Operational Research*. His research interests include metaheuristics, machine learning, software engineering, and operations research.

Index